# EATING, SLEEPING, AND SEXUALITY
## Treatment of Disorders in Basic Life Functions

# AMERICAN COLLEGE OF PSYCHIATRISTS

# Eating, Sleeping, and Sexuality
## Treatment of Disorders in Basic Life Functions

*Edited by*
MICHAEL R. ZALES, M.D.

*Associate Clinical Professor of Psychiatry,*
*Yale University*

BRUNNER/MAZEL, *Publishers* • New York

**Library of Congress Cataloging in Publication Data**

Main entry under title:

Eating, sleeping, and sexuality.

Papers presented at the 1981 annual meeting
of the American College of Psychiatrists held
in Tucson, Ariz.
Includes bibliographical references and
index.
1. Sexual disorders — Congresses.    2. Sleep
disorders — Congresses.    3. Obesity — Congresses.
4. Anorexia nervosa — Congresses.    I. Zales,
Michael R., 1937–          II. American College
of Psychiatrists.
RC556.E18        616.89      81-17015
ISBN 0-87630-288-6              AACR2

*Published by*
BRUNNER/MAZEL, INC.
19 Union Square
New York, New York 10003

# Contributors

KENNETH Z. ALTSHULER, M.D.

Professor and Chairman of the Department of Psychiatry, University of Texas Southwestern Medical School, Dallas, Texas

CENGIZ ASLAN, M.D.

Postdoctoral Research Fellow, Baylor College of Medicine, Houston, Texas

JULIUS AXELROD, Ph.D.

Chief, Section on Pharmacology, Laboratory of Clinical Sciences, National Institute of Mental Health, Bethesda, Maryland

PIETRO CASTELNUOVO-TEDESCO, M.D.

James G. Blakemore Professor of Psychiatry, Vanderbilt University School of Medicine, Nashville, Tennessee

DONALD V. COSCINA, Ph.D.

Associate Professor, Department of Psychiatry, University of Toronto; Head, Biopsychology Section, Clarke Institute of Psychiatry, Toronto, Canada

SABRI DERMAN, M.D., M.Sc.D.

Associate Director, Sleep Disorders and Research Center, Baylor College of Medicine, Houston, Texas

PAUL E. GARFINKEL, M.D.

Associate Professor, Department of Psychiatry, University of Toronto; Psychiatrist-in-Charge, Psychosomatic Medicine Unit, Clarke Institute of Psychiatry, Toronto, Canada

JOSHUA GOLDEN, M.D.

Professor of Psychiatry, UCLA School of Medicine, Los Angeles, California

KATHERINE A. HALMI, M.D.

Associate Professor of Psychiatry, Cornell University Medical College, New York City, New York

ISMET KARACAN, M.D., D.Sc. (Med.)

Professor of Psychiatry and Director of Sleep Disorders and Research Center, Baylor College of Medicine; Associate Chief of Staff for Research, VA Medical Center, Houston, Texas

SEYMOUR LEVINE, Ph.D.

Professor of Psychology in Psychiatry, Stanford University Medical School, Palo Alto, California

JUDD MARMOR, M.D.

Franz Alexander Professor of Psychiatry, Emeritus, University of Southern California College of Medicine, Los Angeles, California

WILLIAM C. ORR, Ph.D.

Director, Sleep Disorders Center, Presbyterian Hospital; Adjunct Associate Professor of Psychiatry and Behavioral Sciences, University of Oklahoma Health Sciences Center, Oklahoma City, Oklahoma

HOWARD P. ROFFWARG, M.D.

Professor of Psychiatry and Director of the Sleep Study Unit, University of Texas Southwestern Medical School, Dallas, Texas

ROBERT J. STOLLER, M.D.

Professor of Psychiatry, UCLA School of Medicine, Los Angeles, California

ALBERT STUNKARD, M.D.

Professor of Psychiatry, University of Pennsylvania, Philadelphia, Pennsylvania

ROBERT L. WILLIAMS, M.D.

D. C. and Irene Ellwood Professor and Chairman of Psychiatry, Baylor College of Medicine, Houston, Texas

# Contents

## PART III

### SEXUALITY

## PART IV

### THE STANLEY R. DEAN AWARD LECTURE

# Preface

Since one of the goals of the American College of Psychiatrists is to further the continuing professional growth of its members, the subject of the 1981 Annual Meeting—Disorders of Basic Life Functions—was imaginatively chosen, with an unwavering eye toward recency. As we are all aware, there has been in the past years a slow but abiding movement toward our primary identification as physicians, a fact our Program Committee recognized in a most constructive way.

As a result, the exchange of ideas, the unexcelled scientific information, and the highly critical intelligence of the speakers blended together in the 1981 meeting to create a structure of knowledge about a significant part of our education.

The American College of Psychiatrists possesses certain sui generis qualities, all of which are reflected in the high standards of its membership and in the excellence of its publications. The current volume adds to this distinguished list since it is an especially coherent summary of the broad, impeccable scholarship of the 1981 faculty.

SHERVERT H. FRAZIER, M.D.
*President, 1980–81*
*American College of Psychiatrists*

# Introduction

Since its inception, the American College of Psychiatrists has sought to provide through its annual meeting a forum for the discussion of new and synthesized material, leading to the best application and utilization of psychiatric knowledge, principles, and therapy. This volume is the product of the annual scientific meeting held in 1981 in Tucson, Arizona. The theme was "Disorders of Basic Life Functions." Credit for developing the program and assembling the outstanding experts in the three fields selected is due the Program Committee, whose very able Chairperson was Allan Beigel.

The twelve previously published College volumes dealt with markedly diverse topics: psychoanalysis in present-day psychiatry; the interface between psychiatry and anthropology; perspectives on violence; sleep research and clinical practice (I shall return to this later); psychiatric education and image; an overview of the psychotherapies; schizophrenia; depression; psychiatric medicine; aging; the family; and, finally, law and ethics in the practice of psychiatry.

It is appropriate, then, that the Program Committee decided — following the trend of educators internationally — to "return to basics." For many of us, of course, our medical/psychiatric training included only the rudiments of the basic life functions — eating, sleeping, and sexuality. If one chooses just one major psychiatric text published first in 1967 (1), one notices three pages devoted to obesity, one to anorexia nervosa, eleven to sleep *and* dreams, less than seven to normal psychosexual functioning (although 30 to sexual deviations), and four to sexual potency disorders.

In turning to a recent edition of that same textbook (2), one begins to appreciate, through the veritable mushrooming of the literature on basic functions, how far research and clinical application have brought us in such a short period of time. The College publication of 1973 on sleep research (3) was an excellent reflection of the state of that "art" at that time, and yet we have only now, as this year's contributors repeatedly remind us, scratched the surface in our knowledge. It is thus the timely significance of the essays that comprises the substance of this work.

The chapters in this book fall rather naturally into an order of presentation. Part I is devoted to eating disorders. Garfinkel and Coscina's chapter provides an up-to-date review of the physiology of hunger and satiety. They clearly delineate neuroanatomical and neurochemical considerations, explain the glucostatic, lipostatic, thermostatic, and aminostatic theories, and explicate gastrointestinal/endocrine factors. In addition, they clarify the psychosocial characteristics which are so relevant in our understanding of ingestion regulation. The 235 references provide the reader with an extraordinary opportunity for further study.

Halmi's thoughtful chapter on anorexia nervosa (and bulimia), modeled around the DSM-III (4) classification, is a clear and straightforward presentation of anorexia nervosa as a disorder, not a specific disease. After covering demographic and epidemiological features, Halmi then concentrates on treatment, both medical and psychiatric. In the latter she includes pharmacological, behavioral, family, and individual therapies. The appendix is comprised of two case studies illustrating the many facets of the disorder.

The balance of Part I deals with the mildly and moderately obese patient, and, finally, with superobesity. Stunkard, who has contributed so much to psychiatry's understanding of obesity in the past, presents new, exciting, and illuminating information regarding the effectiveness of psychoanalysis and behavior modification techniques in the treatment of the mildly-to-moderate obese patient. Castelnuovo-Tedesco describes in detail the various surgical treatments — intestinal bypass, gastric bypass, and jaw-wiring — employed in more radical cases (the superobese). He concerns himself with the indications and complications of such surgery, the results thereof, and, importantly, the adaptive reactions and personal adjustments of the patients in the often markedly prolonged postoperative period.

Orr's chapter introduces Part II. Although involved in basic research, he is ever-vigilant to the practitioner's needs and directs his attention to the many recently understood clinical applications of sleep physiology. He concentrates on three major areas — sleep and thermoregulation, respiration, and gastrointestinal function.

Roffwarg and Altshuler's illustrative chapter, after examining the growth of the field of sleep disorders medicine, outlines in great detail the four major categories included in the recent major nosological contribution, the *Diagnostic Classifications of Sleep and Arousal Disorders* (5). They focus on two of the four categories: DIMS — Disorders of Initiating and Maintaining Sleep (The Insomnias); and Disorders of the Sleep-Wake Schedule.

It is thus left to Williams, Derman, and Karacan to concentrate on the remaining two: DOES — Disorder of Excessive Somnolence; and Dysfunctions associated with Sleep, Sleep Stages and Partial Arousals (Parasomnias). In their rich and complete consideration of this topic, they truly press the generalist to enhance his* diagnostic and therapeutic acumen through careful history, examination, and appropriate referral — a theme which is carried throughout each of the essays in this sleep section. Too often, the reader is reminded, the psychiatrist has paid attention only to his patient's symptom of insomnia, and too often his response has been only the prescription pad.

Finally, these last three authors, along with Aslan, bridge the gap between sleep and sexuality through their comprehensive presentation regarding impotence and nocturnal penile tumescence. Here one finds a complete review of past and present research as well as concern for the future work necessary for a fuller understanding of what previously has been the wastebasket diagnosis of "impotence."

Part III consists of four chapters. In the first Levine examines the hormonal regulation of sexual behavior in both male and female mammals. He also illustrates how certain aspects of the sexual behaviors themselves influence the regulation of the neuroendocrine systems controlling the pituitary-gonadal axis. Although Levine avoids any attempt to equate other mammalian with human activity, his discussion of the social determinants of testosterone secretion and the environmental determinants of estrogen and progesterone secretion encourages the reader to consider the possible human applications of his research.

Marmor traces sex therapy from an historical perspective and focuses on the psychoanalytic theory and therapy of sexual dysfunction, examining the newer psychodynamic approaches in treatment. Described once as "a pragmatist, willing to give up earlier concepts when they are no longer tenable in the light of newer experiences or studies" (6), Marmor here once again personifies the true eclectic.

Golden's chapter deals with the prevalence of sexual disorders and then provides the reader with Golden's exciting and brilliant behavioral treatment of these disorders. This treatment reflects a specific appreciation of the etiol-

---

*Throughout this volume the generic "he" shall be used unless otherwise indicated.

ogical factor(s) involved and is always tailored to the unique needs of the patient/client.

Closing Part III is Stoller's most current evaluation of, as he calls them, "sex change" treatments. Looking at the practical issues involved in the decision-making process, including morality, ethics, preoperative evaluations, and indications, as well as the many theoretic issues, Stoller reaches his own strong conclusions.

Part IV consists of one essay. Although it is unrelated to the basic theme of the volume, it is the written form of the Stanley R. Dean Award Lecture, given this year by Nobel Laureate Julius Axelrod. The Dean Award is presented for especially meritorious research pertinent to schizophrenia. After an initial historical survey, Axelrod addresses the fate of noradrenaline in sympathetic nerves; the effect of psychoactive drugs; the biosynthesis of catecholamines and their regulation; their role in stress, as well as the clinical implications of catecholamines; sympathetic nerves, the pineal gland, the circadian rhythms; and, last, lipids and the transmission of catecholamine neurotransmitter signals.

It is the hope of the College that this volume, through the topical and sometimes provocative contributions contained herein, will provide the reader with material useful in clinical practice.

Finally, I would like to express my personal appreciation to Shervert H. Frazier, President of the College, and to Evelyn Stone for their support and encouragement, and to those members of the Publications Committee – H. Keith H. Brodie, Chairperson, and Jerry M. Lewis, Joe Yamamoto, and Ransom J. Arthur – for their diligent efforts.

MICHAEL R. ZALES, M.D.
*Greenwich, Connecticut*

## REFERENCES

1. FREEDMAN, A.M. and KAPLAN, H. I. (Eds.): *Comprehensive Textbook of Psychiatry.* Baltimore: Williams & Wilkins, 1967.
2. KAPLAN, H. I., FREEDMAN, A. M., and SADOCK, B. J. (Eds): *Comprehensive Textbook of Psychiatry/III.* Baltimore: Williams & Wilkins, 1980.
3. USDIN, G. (Ed.): *Sleep Research and Clinical Practice.* New York: Brunner/Mazel, 1973.
4. *Diagnostic and Statistical Manual of Mental Disorders, Third Edition.* Washington, DC: American Psychiatric Association, 1980.
5. Association of Sleep Disorders Centers: *Diagnostic Classifications of Sleep and Arousal Disorders,* Ed.1, prepared by the Sleep Disorders Classification Committee, Roffwarg, H. P. (Chairman). *Sleep,* 2, 1–137, 1979.
6. USDIN, G. (Ed.): *Psychiatry: Education and Image.* New York: Brunner/Mazel, 1973.

# EATING, SLEEPING, AND SEXUALITY
Treatment of Disorders in Basic Life Functions

# Part I

# EATING

# 1

# The Physiology and Psychology
# of Hunger and Satiety

*Paul E. Garfinkel, M.D. and*
*Donald V. Coscina, Ph.D.*

"Hunger" can be thought of as a complex of sensations individuals feel when deprived of food; these result in behavior that is relieved by the ingestion of food. In its more pleasant and mild form, these sensations can be termed "appetite," that is, appetite can refer to those sensations by which an individual is aware of a desire for food (1). Bruch (2) has distinguished between the use of the term "hunger" in this sense — of perceptual and conceptual awareness — from the purely physiological state of nutrition deprivation and from a general symbolic expression of any need. Conversely, "satiety" can be said to refer to the active suppression of interest in food and of feeding behavior; it can be more than just the absence of hunger. The purpose of this paper is to review some current knowledge of the mechanisms involved in the regulation of hunger and satiety and to document areas of disturbance in those regulatory systems which may play a role in disorders of clinical relevance — obesity and anorexia nervosa.

The problem can be stated simply: What tells us when we want to eat, and what tells us when we've had enough? This may be similar to, but is not necessarily identical with, the observed behavior — when we actually begin and stop eating and the types and quantities of foods that are chosen. While the question of what makes us want to start and stop eating may be phrased quite simply, a complete understanding of the various mechanisms regulating hunger and satiety is just not possible at the present time. Before reviewing

5

what is known about these mechanisms, a few general points may be useful:

1) There appears to be rigid regulatory control over body weight level and, by inference, eating behaviors. This is evidenced by the following example from Bray and Campfield (3). They have estimated that a normal adult male ingests more than one million calories per year. If 99 percent of this energy is expended, the person will retain about 10,000 calories and gain over 1 kg. If this persisted over several years, there would be a steady weight gain. Therefore, under normal circumstances, energy intake seems to be much more finely linked to energy expenditure: well over 99 percent of the calories ingested would have to be utilized if that person is to remain at a constant adult weight.

2) Much evidence to date suggests that both body weight level and eating behavior are governed by not one but rather a series of factors. This should not be surprising — any system as important and as basic to an organism's existence as its primary source of energy regulation may require multiple, perhaps redundant, subsystems to ensure that renewed needs for food are met despite diverse environmental conditions. However, as Booth, Toates, and Platt (4) have indicated, there is a danger in accepting *prima facie* such multifactorial theories as they may become so trivial as to assert that eating behavior can be affected by almost anything.

3) While it is likely that many factors may influence hunger and satiety perception, it is important to differentiate those which are physiologically relevant from those which do not seemingly contribute to the control of bioenergetic needs. The physiological significance of many purported hunger and satiety signals is not known (5).

4) While little is known about the normal physiology of hunger and satiety, even less is known about specific abnormalities that may relate to the pathophysiologies of weight disorders such as obesity and anorexia nervosa.

5) While much of the literature indicates important roles of brain and peripheral mechanisms in governing the eating behaviors of animals, sociocultural, interpersonal and intrapsychic factors may readily override these controls for humans (6, 7).

A number of theories have purported to explain hunger and satiety mechanisms over the past 25 years. These include the traditional neuroanatomical (e.g., hypothalamic) considerations, Mayer's glucostatic, Brobeck's thermostatic, and Kennedy's lipostatic theories. These will be reviewed first. More recently postulated mechanisms, which include the renewed interest in the potential role of the gastrointestinal tract as well as the involvement of gut hormones and amino acid metabolism, will then be considered.

### NEUROANATOMY

The brain has long been known to play an integrative role in processing sensory, motor, and humoral information concerned with eating. In 1901, Frohlich (8) described an obese patient with a pituitary tumor, suggesting that the two were associated. Camus and Roussy (9) implicated the hypothalamus in obesity after postmortem study of patients with Frohlich's syndrome. Smith (10) later reported that lesions of the hypothalamus alone could result in obesity. This was followed by great interest in hypothalamic controls over eating, culminating in Hetherington and Ranson's (11) demonstration of hyperphagia and obesity following localized lesions of a specific hypothalamic area, the ventromedial nucleus (VMN). Eleven years later, Anand and Brobeck (12) showed that bilateral lesions in the lateral hypothalamic (LH) area resulted in aphagia and adipsia in animals. Based on this type of evidence, Stellar (13) suggested a hypothalamic theory of appetitive motivation which has had considerable impact on investigations of the past 25 years. Peripheral stimuli that occurred during feeding or starving were considered to result in stimulation of cells in the LH or VMH, and relative changes in the activity of these cells would be followed by the initiation or cessation, respectively, of eating. This dual center theory of appetite regulation proposed that these two brain centers mediated eating behaviors by reciprocally inhibiting each other with the LH having predominant control (see Lytle [6] for more complete discussion).

The LH has traditionally been considered to be the "feeding center" of the brain. Lesions in this area produce aphagia and adipsia, whereas electrical stimulation elicits ingestive behaviors (see Grossman, 14). LH-lesioned animals initially exhibit a severe aphagia that results in starving to death unless the animals are fed by gastric tube. If the animal is kept alive, there is slow recovery through a period of "finickiness" (i.e., eating only palatable wet foods), then to eating all palatable foods, and finally to eating a normal diet, but maintaining a lowered body weight (15). Even when these animals have recovered, they do not respond normally to situations that alter water intake. For example, they do not increase water intake after an injection of hypertonic saline (15). Similarly, these animals fail to respond normally to situations that alter eating behaviors. They do not eat adequate amounts of food in short-term tests of insulin-induced hypoglycemia (16), nor do they suppress feeding sufficiently after amphetamine injection (17). Their behavioral changes are not confined to eating. They also display a disinclination to seek warmth in the cold and an inability to learn new tasks (15, 18, 19, 20).

A fascinating feature of LH-lesioned animals is that they display a permanent lowering of body weight in spite of returning to normal food intake (but see Balagura and Harrell [21] for conflicting data). Since this reduced body weight is maintained long after the period of aphagia has passed, a hypothesis has been advanced suggesting that LH-lesioned animals possess an altered level or "set point" for body weight regulation (22). In spite of a variety of challenges, this reduced body weight level will be defended by the animals (23). For example, if the animals are presented with a highly palatable liquid diet which can be varied in caloric density by progressive dilutions with water, LH-lesioned animals increase their daily intake in order to defend their lower weight in the same way as do normals. Similar results are obtained when quinine is added to the diet.

A further test of this hypothesis involves manipulations of the animal's weight after lesioning. If LH-lesioned animals are either starved to further lower their weight or force-fed to increase it, they will, like normal animals, later adjust their intake to defend their lower post-lesion body weight. Keesey, Boyle, Kemmitz, et al. (23) feel that the primary effect of LH damage is to lower the set point for body weight. Since these animals adjust food intake normally to such challenges, it has been suggested that this mechanism for weight regulation may be important only for emergency circumstances, rather than one upon which the animal normally relies to control its food intake and regulate body weight (24).

In contrast to the LH "feeding center," the VMH has traditionally been considered the "satiety center." Hetherington and Ranson (11) were first to report that bilateral, symmetrical lesions in this nucleus produce hyperphagia and obesity in rats. VMH-lesioned animals display marked overeating immediately following recovery from anesthesia, which continues for several months. During this "dynamic" phase, rats generally double their weights (25). As they become heavier, they become less active and display reduced basal metabolic rates (26). After several months this "dynamic" phase of hyperphagia is followed by a "static" period. During this time, animals gradually reduce their food intake to preoperative levels, eat fewer meals per day, and maintain a relatively constant but elevated body weight (27). The overeating of VMH-lesioned animals during the "dynamic" period is characterized by larger individual meals (27, 28, 29). In large part, this has been the basis for suggesting that these animals possess defective satiety mechanisms determining when to end a meal. While it is clear that these animals eat more during any given meal, it is not known if this is because they are initially "hungrier" or because an active satiety process is not inhibiting feeding. While it is generally assumed to be the latter, this is not supported by more recent work. In both monkeys (30) and rats (29, 31) hypothalamic hyperphagic animals ate more than controls, but, like controls, were able to reduce similarly their intakes in response to increasing nutritive densities of preloads. If this response were due to active satiety processes, VMH-lesioned animals would not be expected to reduce intakes in this situation.

While it seems that VMH-lesioned animals display a temporary impairment of short-term eating regulation, once they attain the "static" phase they display reasonably normal feeding in response to a variety of traditional stimuli (32, 33, 34). This fact, together with the persistence of their obesity, suggests that the primary effects of VMH lesions are to alter long-term body weight regulation and energy utilization. That is, these lesions may produce chronic biochemical and endocrinological abnormalities which promote fat storage rather than its utilization. The mechanisms for this are far from being well understood. However, it is known that VMH animals show both hyper-insulinemia and a normal or increased sensitivity to insulin, unlike rats who become obese through force-feeding. This may relate to a direct effect of the brain lesion on the pancreas (35) since it occurs even when lesioned animals are not allowed to be hyperphagic (36).

Other endocrine changes occur in VMH-lesioned animals which may contribute to their permanent obesity. In particular, they display decreased growth hormone levels which may produce reduced lipolysis (35; Coscina and Brown, unpublished observations). Gonadal sex hormones may also be involved since female animals generally show more hyperphagia and weight gain than do males (37). At least some of the weight gain and maintenance in VMH-lesioned animals results from decreased energy expenditure as "static" phase animals are both hypoactive and have lowered metabolic rates (26, 38). Therefore, the results to date suggest that VMH-lesioned animals have short-term "hunger" defects and long-term changes in energy balance and weight regulation.

There are a number of behavioral similarities between VMH-lesioned animals and obese humans. These have recently been reviewed by Schachter and Rodin (39). In addition to the excess weight in both, they display similar eating behaviors. In particular, both tend to be "finicky" eaters. That is, if presented with good-tasting foods, they will eat more than normals, but, if presented with unpalatable foods, they will actually eat less than normals. Both chronic obese humans and VMH-lesioned rats have been observed to eat fewer meals per day, eat somewhat more per meal, and eat more rapidly than do normal controls. Like the VMH-lesioned rat, the obese person is also less active. Both groups, while interested in food, will paradoxically not work to obtain food when the food stimulus is remote. As such, these similarities continue to reinforce interest in the VMH-lesioned animal model as providing helpful clues to the etiology and eventual treatment of human obesity.

## NEUROCHEMISTRY

While it has traditionally been thought that the LH and VMH are two discrete nuclei which reciprocally inhibit each other, more recent evidence shows that the CNS control of feeding is not quite this simple. Both areas contain a variety of cell types, with the LH in particular not being a single, well-defined site (40, 41). Both areas are involved in the reception and transmission of information to and from a variety of brain locations, serving as "way stations" (see [6]). The earlier notion of discrete centers governing food intake has been modified to include the fact that other tracts and areas may be important (42). In particular, recent observations have suggested that both hunger and satiety are substantially influenced by the functional states of neurochemically different brain amine systems which are not exclusively located in the ventromedial or lateral hypothalamus (43, 44, 45). So, for example, many of the behavioral features traditionally labelled the "LH syndrome" can be ascribed to disruption of dopamine (DA) neurons which traverse the nigrostriatal pathway via the lateral hypothalamic area (46, 47). At the same time, damage to specific components of brain norepinephrine (NE) and/or serotonin (5HT) systems may account for portions of the VMH syndrome (43, 48, 49).

The administration of catecholamines, their precursors or inhibitors, has marked effects on food intake. Food-deprived animals will respond to a peripheral injection of NE with anorexia (50); since NE does not substantially cross the blood brain barrier, it is likely that this effect is not centrally elicited. However, Grossman (51) had earlier observed that NE, when injected directly into the brain of a rat in an area just lateral to the VMH, produced increased food intake. Acetylcholine in the same area increased drinking. With chronic administration, such animals would gain significant amounts of weight.

Catecholamines such as NE or DA, when injected into different brain regions, appear to produce different effects on eating; the evidence to date suggests that they are involved in both hunger and satiety. Leibowitz (52, 53, 54) has presented evidence to demonstrate the involvement of $\alpha$-noradrenergic receptors in the medial hypothalamus in hunger regulation, while $\beta$-noradrenergic receptors in the lateral hypothalamus seem involved in satiety regulation. Her evidence is largely indirect, based on the application of various drugs that affect these systems in short-term feeding tests. For example, phentolamine, an $\alpha$-blocker, reliably suppresses food intake of hungry rats after bilateral injection into the medial hypothalamus, but not after injection into the lateral hypothalamus.

Leibowitz has also reported that catecholamines in the lateral hypothalamus may mediate satiety; $\beta$-receptors appear important here since injections of isoproterenol, NE, or amphetamine will suppress the feeding of hungry animals. This suppression of feeding can be prevented completely by β-receptor blockers, such as propanolol, while it is somewhat potentiated by the α-receptor blocker, phentolamine. Chlorpromazine (CPZ) is a further interesting example, since its clinical use is so frequently associated with weight gain. CPZ produces a marked increase in eating in previously satiated as well as hungry rats. Leibowitz (54) has shown that CPZ-induced feeding is abolished by centrally administered phentolamine and is somewhat potentiated by propanolol. Desipramine, which blocks NE re-uptake at the synapse, increases feeding of both satiated and hungry rats (55). This type of evidence (56), in addition to other data, suggests a role for NE in satiety and possibly also in hunger.

The effects of DA using these local injection techniques are quite confusing and inconsistent (6, 56). However, by local use of a neurotoxin, 6-hydroxy-dopamine (6-OHDA), which selectively enters and destroys catecholamine neurones, Ungerstedt (46) was able to show that lesions of the nigrostriatal DA system produced an aphagia adipsia syndrome which resembles that of the LH-lesioned rat. Moreover, Oltmans and Harvey (57) found that the weight loss that occurs after bilateral LH lesions is strongly correlated with decreased striatal DA concentrations but not those of other neurotransmitters (see also Grossman [44]).

6-OHDA may also be used to deplete NE. When administered directly into the ventral noradrenergic pathway, it has been reported to produce hyperphagia and long-lasting weight gain in rats (but see Lorden et al. [58] for evidence questioning the specificity of this effect). This effect appears directly related to the drug's capacity to damage NE neurons since prior administration of desipramine, which blocks 6-OHDA uptake into NE-containing cells, prevents the overeating and weight gain (59). A noradrenergic basis for this hyperphagia has been supported by neurochemical assays and histochemistry (45). Thus, at least some of the symptoms of VMH-lesioned animals may occur after particular disruption of hypothalamic NE-containing neurons.

Further evidence for NE involvement in the VMH syndrome is the finding of significant (15-20 percent) decline in brain NE from obese mice or rats with VMH lesions (48, 60, 61, 62). However, the syndrome produced by destroying ventral noradrenergic cells with 6-OHDA is not identical with that produced by VMH lesions. For example, the hyperphagia and weight gain are never as great as after VMH lesions (see Coscina [43]). Also animals with 6-OHDA injection in the ventral NE pathway as well as VMH lesions display greater hyperphagia and weight gain than animals with either treatment alone (63). Indeed, it has been observed that prior NE and DA depletion in brain by intracisternal 6-OHDA does not substantially alter the ability of VMH lesions to induce hyperphagia and obesity (61). Furthermore, while VMH lesions either enhance or do not change amphetamine-induced anorexia, NE depletion tends to attenuate amphetamine anorexia. This documents a likely mechanism of amphetamine on NE neurons to produce anorexia (45). These data suggest NE-containing neurons may play an important role in hunger regulation, but they certainly do not appear to be the only factor.

Another putative neurotransmitter system implicated in overeating is 5-HT. Peripheral injection of 5-HT decreases food intake in rats eating ad lib; however, the mechanism for this is unclear as 5-HT does not easily cross the blood brain barrier (64). Direct injection of 5-HT into the hypothalamus or ventricles produces less dramatic effects on eating than do the catecholamines. Some studies have reported no effect (65), while others have reported a decrease in food intake (66) which could be counteracted by the 5-HT precursor, 5-HTP. However, very large doses of 5-HT are required for this effect. There is general agreement that 5-HTP injected peripherally will reduce food intake in both satiated and food-deprived rats (67, 68). This is suggestive of a 5-HT role in regulating hunger (see Blundell [69]). However, it must be emphasized that 5-HTP may not be a useful tool since the decarboxylase enzyme which converts it to 5-HT is located in many brain sites where 5-HTP may be taken up and decarboxylated in non-5-HT loci (70). In this respect, tryptophan appears to offer some advantages over 5-HTP in assessing 5-HT systems. This is because the rate-limiting enzyme for 5-HT production, tryptophan hydroxylase, is specific for its substrate L-tryptophan and seems to be found only in 5-HT neurons (71). Peripheral injections of tryptophan have been reported to produce a dose-dependent decrease in food consumption (72). When an MAOI pretreated rat is given tryptophan, more exaggerated decreases in feeding become apparent (73). However, a more recent study by Weinberger, Knapp and Mandell (74) failed to induce changes in eating with systemic tryptophan in doses sufficient to alter brain 5-HT metabolism.

Dietary tryptophan has been suggested to play an important role in regulating eating. Although tryptophan hydroxylase is rate-limiting for 5-HT production, because of the kinetics of the enzyme (75), the overall production of 5-HT depends in large part on the amount of tryptophan available. Since tryptophan hydroxylase is not normally saturated with its substrate, brain 5-HT levels can be influenced by plasma and brain tryptophan levels, and since tryptophan is an essential amino acid, the amount of dietary tryptophan available can be an important regulating factor in brain 5-HT synthesis (76). However, the relationship between dietary tryptophan and brain 5-HT is not a simple one, but depends also on circulating levels of insulin (77), free fatty acids (78), and the ratio of tryptophan to other plasma neutral amino acids with which it competes for uptake into brain (72, 79). This will be discussed further in the section on dietary amino acids.

Fenfluramine is an anorexic agent which produces little direct effect on catecholamines but causes an acute release of 5-HT from presynaptic neurons (80). In platelets it produces a release of 5-HT and blocks its re-uptake. It produces long-term increased 5-HT turnover (81). Fenfluramine's anorexic effects have been markedly reduced by electrolytic lesions of the median raphe nuclei rich in 5-HT cell bodies (82). This suggests that the anorexic effects of this drug operate via 5-HT mechanisms. Also, amphetamine and fenfluramine, while both causing reduced food intake, appear to act by very different means. Amphetamine appears to delay the onset of feeding, while fenfluramine speeds the termination of eating (83). Factors which alter amphetamine-induced anorexia have little effect on fenfluramine anorexia and vice versa (67).

Cyproheptadine is another drug which alters 5-HT metabolism; it is believed to block 5-HT receptors and has been reported to increase feeding and weight gain (84). It has also been reported anecdotally to produce weight gain in anorexia nervosa (85). However, in controlled studies to assess its efficacy in this regard it was not found to be superior to placebo treatment (86).

Of particular interest is the widely-used antidepressant, amitriptyline. One proposed mechanism of action for this compound is to reduce pre-synaptic re-uptake of 5-HT leading to feedback inhibition and ultimate reduction of 5-HT synthesis and turnover (87). At the same time, clinical studies have reported that amitriptyline treatment leads to increased food cravings and bodyweight gain (88, 89) which is dissociable from mood shifts (89). However, chronic administration of this drug to rats produces weight loss rather than gain (90). Consequently, the significance of this clinical weight change and its specificity to 5-HT systems remains uncertain.

While equivocal, the evidence above suggests that brain 5-HT inhibits feeding. If this is so, then depletion of brain 5-HT would be expected to produce hyperphagia. Parachlorophenylalanine (PCPA) inhibits tryptophan hydroxylase and substantially depletes brain 5-HT (91). When injected peripherally, PCPA typically lowers brain 5-HT by about 80 percent and causes much smaller decrements in other amines (91). But peripheral injections of PCPA generally do not produce hyperphagia, possibly because the animals become ill (92). However, when PCPA has been injected directly into the lateral or third cerebral ventricles of rats, hyperphagia and obesity have been observed in association with reduced brain 5-HT (93). More recent work by Coscina, Daniel and Warsh (94), as well as MacKenzie et al. (95), suggests that this PCPA effect is unrelated to forebrain 5-HT depletions. A final problem with the potential importance of 5-HT systems in feeding control is that 5-HT-depleting raphe lesions do not induce overeating (4).

The data reviewed do not provide evidence for distinct, unitary neurotransmitter control over feeding. However, they do implicate multiple neurochemical mechanisms in this control. While DA-containing neurons along the nigrostriatal axis seem important in the LH "feeding center" effects, different aspects of hunger and satiety may be controlled by NE- and 5-HT-containing neurons, perhaps through interactions with each other and/or with other aminergic and peptidergic systems which are only now coming under investigation. One thing seems clear. The brain must serve an important integrative role in assessing and organizing both environmental and somatic sensory information concerned with eating. The multivariate way in which this role is accomplished requires continued scrutiny.

### GLUCOSTATIC THEORY

It has been over 25 years since Mayer (96) postulated that receptors in the VMH are sensitive to circulating glucose levels and that these were in large part responsible for satiety. This concept was based on several lines of reasoning: 1) The central nervous system is dependent on the availability of glucose for its functioning; 2) carbohydrates are preferentially utilized and are not appreciably stored; and 3) there is a greater change in carbohydrate than of fat and protein reserves between meals (1, 97).

Stunkard and colleagues (97a) demonstrated that a slow intravenous glucose infusion in hungry subjects eliminates both the subjective feeling of hunger and gastric contractions. However, changes in the level of blood sugar are not always correlated with hunger or satiety awareness and subsequent eating in, for example, diabetes mellitus (98). It has therefore been suggested that glucose availability to cells and its utilization are the actual signal rather than the absolute sugar level (99). This may be indirectly measured by arteriovenous differences ($\Delta$-glucose) in plasma glucose (that is, peripheral utilization of glucose might be an index of brain utilization in the VMH). There is some correlation between $\Delta$-glucose and subjective hunger, but this is far from perfect (97).

Glucose metabolism is not only regulated by a complex series of endocrine relationships but is also a regulator of fat synthesis and oxidation as well as protein synthesis and mobilization. Glucose in the blood stimulates insulin release from pancreatic cells. This, in turn, stimulates the uptake of glucose as well as free fatty acids (FFA) and amino acids into peripheral tissues. The carbohydrates are used for energy or stored as glycogen; the FFA are converted to triglycerides and stored in adipose tissue; and amino acids are incorporated into protein. When the blood glucose level falls, epinephrine and glucagon are released from the adrenal gland and pancreas, respectively, producing increased blood glucose levels by inhibition of cellular uptake.

There is considerable evidence suggesting the existence of glucoreceptors in the hypothalamus which control feeding. This has recently been reviewed by Lytle (6). Electrical activity in the VMH area increases after eating (hyperglycemia) and decreases during starvation (hypoglycemia) while the opposite is true for the LH area (100, 101). Systemic glucose infusion increases electrical activity of VMH cells and causes satiety; injection of insulin decreases VMH activity and induces eating (100, 102). On the other hand, systemic glucose infusion decreases electrical activity of LH cells; and injection of insulin increases LH electrical activity (103). While these findings of reciprocal changes in the electrical activity of cells in the VMH and LH relating to changes in glucose utilization and feeding are interesting, they do not rule out the possibility that other regions might sense changes in glucose utilization and relay this information to these hypothalamic areas.

VMH cells also accumulate relatively large amounts of radioactive $^{14}$C following intragastric injection of $^{14}$C-glucose; this accumulation of radioactivity can be increased by pretreatment with insulin (104). The rate of glucose turnover is high in the VMH regions of hungry animals (103). Gold thioglucose (GTG) has also been utilized to support the glucostatic theory, but the evidence derived from it has been subject to serious criticism. Systemic injection of GTG produces hyperphagia and obesity in mice (105). This glucose analogue was presumed to operate by uptake into glucoreceptors of the VMH and destroying them. However, more recent work suggests that such action is due to loss of VMH blood circulation via capillary injury, leading to nonspecific ischemia in this part of the brain (106).

A glucose antimetabolite, 2-deoxy-D-glucose (2-DG), has also been used to support the glucostatic theory. 2-DG causes an increase in circulating plasma glucose together with a decrease in cellular glucose utilization (107). It also stimulates epinephrine release, resulting in increased glycogenolysis (107). In animals, 2-DG generally results in increased food intake. In humans, its administration is associated with increased subjective hunger ratings and a greater sense of pleasantness of tasted sucrose solutions (108). The increased eating after 2-DG in animals can also be blocked by vagotomy but not by adrenalectomy (109, 110). Since insulin-induced hyperphagia can be blocked by adrenalectomy but not by vagotomy, it has been suggested that the hyperphagia that occurs with insulin is mediated via a different mechanism (110).

Chronic administration of long-acting forms of insulin produces hyperphagia and obesity (111). Glucagon has been shown by Stunkard, Van Itallie and Reiss (112) regularly to eliminate gastric contractions and hunger sensations in human subjects. Glucagon produces increased satiety sensations in humans and similarly decreased food consumption in animals (113). Finally, administration of glucose directly into the brain may reduce food intake, but this finding has not always been reproduced intravenously and may be quite delayed (104, 114).

While these data implicate a role for glucoreceptors in the brain, their discrete localization vis-à-vis feeding has not been clearly delineated. In addition, there appear to be glucoreceptors in the periphery. These may detect changes in glucose utilization and relay this information to the brain. Russek (115, 116) first suggested that there were glucoreceptors in the liver, based on the fact that reductions in hepatic glucose concentrations were associated with eating, and that increases were associated with cessation of eating. These findings have been replicated by some (117) but not others (118). Novin, Vander Weele and Rezek (119) and Mogenson (5) have provided further evidence for hepatic glucoreceptors by showing that 2-DG infusion into the portal system increased feeding in rabbits and rats.

There is also evidence suggesting the presence of glucoreceptors in the gastrointestinal tract. Several investigators have reported that infusion of glucose into the stomach (42, 110) or the duodenum (120, 121) reduces food intake in animals who have free access to food. These glucostatic receptors in the liver and duodenum depend on the vagus nerve: vagotomy abolishes the eating responses to hepatic 2-DG and the satiety responses to hepatic and duodenal glucose (121). Novin has suggested that there are differences between the hepatic and duodenal glucoreceptors. The former are responsive to glucose infusions in the hepatic-portal circulation only when the animal is starved; duodenal infusion of glucose, on the other hand, may alter food intake only when animals have not been starved but are feeding freely (121). These results suggest that there are at least two peripheral areas mediating hunger and satiety following carbohydrate loads—the liver and the gut. They may be responsive to carbohydrate under differing conditions, but both are involved in the short-term regulation of food intake via the vagus. These glucoreceptors are unlikely to play a role in long-term regulation of intake.

### Lipostatic Theory

In contrast to carbohydrates which play a role in short-term energy regulation, Kennedy (34) suggested that long-term food intake may be regulated by fat stores being maintained as a constant proportion of total body weight.

According to this hypothesis, when fat stores are low, feeding will increase to regulate body weight.

While we do not yet understand the mechanisms involved, there do appear to be significant long-term regulatory controls of body weight via fat stores. Evidence for this comes from several sources, including animals with "physiological anorexias," chronic overfeeding studies, and studies of chronic insulin administration. Animals that become obese through force-feeding or chronic insulin administration later decrease food intake until they return to their pretreatment weights (111, 122). Physiological fasting in the animal world appears important to the animal's well-being in several instances. In particular, these are when the animal is engaged in other important activities, such as incubation of eggs or defending one's territory and during hibernation, the latter permitting the animal to survive seasons of reduced availability of foods (123). Studies involving ground squirrels have shown that even when food is readily available, the animal eats little during the hibernation period. The amount of food eaten increases, however, as energy expenditure increases. For example, when the animal is kept in a warm room or is frequently handled, deep hibernation is prevented and the animal will eat more (124). A few animals in cold rooms will not hibernate and they, too, will eat more than normal for this period. What is important is that whether energy expenditure is high or low, these animals lose weight at similar rates. This suggests that hibernators eat only as much food as is necessary to achieve these decreasing bodyweight values. These animals, therefore, appear to have a programmed regulation of body weight, or "set point," that is seasonally adjusted. For example, if ground squirrels are totally deprived of food for parts of the winter, they will lose more weight. When they can again eat, they return not to their predeprivation weight but to a weight that is appropriate for them for that time of year (124). Since changes in body fat are most responsible for weight changes in hibernators, Mrosovsky and Sherry (123) have suggested this is more appropriately described as a changing set point for body fat.

The set point for long-term body weight regulation may be mediated via hypothalamic mechanisms (23). As noted earlier, LH-lesioned animals will defend their new weights in response to a variety of challenges. The same is true for VMH-lesioned animals. For example, if a VMH-lesioned animal is made even more obese by force-feeding or by repeated insulin injections, it will later reduce its intake when either treatment ceases and return more closely to its original postoperative level of obesity. The opposite occurs if a VMH-lesioned rat is starved to artificially reduce its body weight (125, 126).

While these results suggest both a role for body fat stores in the long-term regulation of weight and a role for hypothalamic mediation of this defence, the precise mechanisms by which this occurs are unknown. It is quite unlikely that there are brain liporeceptors similar to postulated glucoreceptors since the brain itself is believed to be incapable of rapidly utilizing fat for energy. Circulating levels of fats may be one regulator since plasma levels of FFA and glycerol increase during fasting and their release is proportional to the size of the adipose tissue mass (127, 128, 129).

Woods and Porte (130) have postulated that insulin levels, especially in the CSF, may influence the set point for body fat. They suggest that the brain via the VMH region may somehow recognize basal insulin levels as an index of the amount of fat in the body. It has been observed that insulin levels are highly related to body weight in man and other animals: the higher the weight, the greater the circulating insulin. Rats with VMH lesions also have high insulin levels. Since abnormally high insulin levels can exist even if hyperphagia is prevented, a certain degree of hyperinsulinemia seems to be a primary effect of this lesion (130). It has been suggested that the brain may have a direct effect on the pancreas via the vagus to produce this increased insulin since vagotomy or pancreatectomy will eliminate the VMH-induced obesity (131, 132). Woods and Porte (130) have shown that CSF insulin responds slowly to changes in plasma insulin over long rather than brief periods of time. They therefore postulate that CSF insulin levels may serve as an analog signal to the brain of body-fat status. It has also been suggested that growth hormone (GH) may be a similar mediator since high GH levels increase lipolysis and, conversely, high levels of plasma FFA decrease GH secretion (35).

The hypothesis that body fat is actively regulated for long periods of time suggests that both animals and humans vary their food intake as a function of their fat stores. However, a major problem with this concept exists given evidence that body fat and amount eaten can be dissociated from one another. For example, rats deprived of food to lose weight and never given adequate amounts of nutrient to compensate for this loss can nevertheless regain weight to control levels (133). Conversely, some strains of rats permitted access to highly palatable diets have been shown to consume many more calories than controls on standard laboratory chow, yet not gain substantial amounts of weight (134). This finding parallels past observations on human subjects who experienced difficulty in gaining large amounts of weight despite deliberate, protracted overeating (135). All of these data suggest that long-term weight regulation is controlled by metabolic factors in addition to those simply due to food intake.

## THERMOSTATIC CONTROLS

Brobeck (136) proposed that animals will eat more in order to keep warm and stop eating when their body temperature has risen. While homeothermic mammals may eat more in cold settings (137), this theory has not been widely accepted and has been subject to serious criticism (6). For example, eating and fasting are not associated with consistent changes in body temperature. In fact, core body temperature fluctuates slowly through the day. While there are measurable changes in metabolic rate over the day, these do not correlate with eating (136). Although thermostatic control mechanisms must inevitably contribute to food intake, there are at present no good data to indicate that changes in overall body temperature play a major role in the control of eating.DeLuise, Blackburn and Flier (137) have recently found a reduced activity in the red-cell sodium-potassium pump in human obesity and this has been speculated (138) to be related to continued overeating in the obese on the basis of alterations in hypothalamic temperature.

## THE ROLE OF AMINO ACIDS

In recent years a great deal of investigation has been devoted to examining the role of amino acids and proteins in regulating food intake. This very exciting field, which has evolved quickly over the past 10 years, has so far revealed that: 1) protein intake can be closely regulated; 2) regulation of protein intake can be separated from that of energy intake; 3) dietary amino acids may play an important role via their effects on brain neurotransmitters; and 4) these amino acids can exert control over not only protein intake but also over caloric intake.

There is considerable evidence that protein intake is finely regulated. This has recently been reviewed by Anderson (139). Animals will eat far less if they are fed single diets in which the protein content is very low or very high or in which the amino acids pattern is grossly distorted from usual. For example, both adult and weanling rats are capable of adjusting the amount of food they ingest to keep their protein intake constant when their diets are diluted with noncaloric materials such as water or methylcellulose (140, 141). When rats are offered a choice between a diet with no protein or one with 20 percent protein, they will feed almost entirely from the diet with protein (142). There is some indirect evidence that protein is also closely regulated in humans. People fed diets of less than 13 percent protein generally feel hungry, while diets proportionately low in carbohydrate or fat but high in protein are satiating (143). In addition, while humans have a wide variety of foods to choose

from, a remarkably constant 11–13 percent of dietary calories have been derived from protein over the last 40 years in Canada. This latter observation is
quite striking since there have been marked shifts in eating habits over this
time, with a proportionately greater portion of dietary calories being derived
from fat at the expense of carbohydrate (139).

The second important finding to have emerged in this field is that protein
regulation is separable from calorie regulation. Protein intake appears to be
largely dependent on the amino acid content of the diet. Factors which alter
energy intake do not necessarily affect protein intake. For example, hyperphagia and obesity can occur in certain genetically predisposed rats or after
VMH lesions in otherwise normal rats by selective increases in nonprotein
energy consumption while maintaining normal protein intake (144).

Rats fed high protein diets or imbalanced amino acid diets reduce food intake due to signals from dietary/plasma amino acid ratios (139, 145). Two
important ratios have been demonstrated: 1) There is an inverse relationship
between the ratio of plasma tryptophan (Tryp) to other large neutral amino
acids (NAA) (i.e., valine, leucine, isoleucine, tyrosine and phenylalanine)
and protein consumption (146; and 2) there is also a direct relationship between the plasma tyrosine/phenylalanine (and somewhat to NAA) ratio and
the amount of calories consumed (147). These relationships are distinct, that
is, there is no correlation between Tryp/NAA and calories, nor is tyrosine/
phenylalanine correlated with protein intake.

The uptake of these amino acids by brain is based on a general transport
mechanism for large NAAs (148). This mechanism depends in part on the actual plasma concentration of each NAA as well as the competition between
these NAAs for the transport sites. When tyrosine (Tyr) or Tryp concentrations in plasma are high, they are also high in the brain. This is of some significance since Tryp is the precursor of 5-HT, and Tyr is the NE and DA precursor. As noted earlier, the amount of brain Tryp available is generally an
important factor which governs brain 5-HT synthesis. The same is true to a
lesser degree for brain Tyr vis-à-vis brain NE synthesis. Since brain amino
acid levels are dependent on plasma amino acid levels, and since the plasma
levels are dependent on dietary intake, dietary factors that alter the amino
acid patterns help to regulate brain neurotransmitter synthesis.

Ashley and Anderson (146) have suggested that brain 5-HT may be involved in the control of protein intake. This is based on the previously noted
inverse relationship between Tryp/NAAs and protein intake and on the
observed correlation between the plasma Tryp/NAA ratio and brain 5-HT
(72). Recently Woodger, Sirek and Anderson (149) observed that by increasing dietary Tryp they could reduce protein intake that was associated with an

elevated plasma Tryp/NAA ratio, brain 5-HT, and brain 5-HIAA levels. Of significance is the fact that caloric intake was not affected.

The other significant effect of plasma amino acids is to help control energy balance. A direct relationship between the Tyr/Phe ratio and caloric intake has been demonstrated (147). Tyrosine ingestion as part of a high protein meal increases brain Tyr which then increases CNS catecholamine formation and turnover (150). This suggests that along with increased brain Tyr levels and catecholamine turnover there might also be a long-term increase in energy intake. Anderson (139) has hypothesized that by integrating these indoleamine and catecholamine mechanisms, animals can select foods that are able to "control both quantitative (energy) as well as qualitative (protein) aspects of their diet" (p. 1052).

Of additional importance is the fact that this system is not solely under dietary control. It is also affected significantly by hormones. In particular, plasma amino acid concentrations are affected substantially by changes in circulating insulin, GH, and glucagon. For example, after a high-carbohydrate meal which releases insulin, or directly after an injection of exogenous insulin, there is a decrease in plasma NAA and an increase or no change in plasma Tryp (151). The net effect is to increase the Tryp/NAA ratio, to increase brain 5-HT, and to decrease protein intake. Compatible with these changes are data showing that diabetic rats possess low plasma Tryp/NAA ratios and display protein hyperphagia (149).

### The Role of the Gastrointestinal Tract

Gastrointestinal variables involved in hunger and satiety may be divided arbitrarily into local and humoral factors. The former include oropharyngeal sensations, gastric contractions, vagal effects, and distension of the gut. Oropharyngeal sensations that are normally associated with eating may not be of much significance in regulating intake since animals which perform operant responses to obtain food directly via a gastric tube maintain a constant body weight and eat normal quantities of food (152, 153).

Cannon and Washburn (154) first implicated the stomach as a focus of feeding which was controlled by neural signals associated with gastric contractions. They observed that strong gastric contractions preceded subjective hunger reports. Carlson (155) reported that the frequency and intensity of these contractions became more pronounced during starvation. Also, injection of insulin, which increases hunger sensations, was found to increase the rate of gastric contractions; conversely, injection of glucagon, which was associated with satiety, eliminated these contractions (156, 157). However, subsequent research has questioned the generality of gastric mechanisms in control of feeding. For example, humans after gastrectomy or after denervation of the stomach continue to perceive hunger normally except that they do not localize the sensations to the epigastric area (158, 159). Gastric contractions also continue in anorectic LH-lesioned rats as well as in humans despite stomach fullness or emptiness (158) except immediately following a large meal (97). Irrigation of the duodenum with glucose will inhibit these gastric contractions even when the stomach is denervated, suggesting that there is a humoral component to their regulation (97).

An interesting series of findings relates to the effects of vagotomy on hunger and weight loss. Grossman and Stein (160) noted that generalized feelings of hunger continue in patients following vagotomy but this hunger is not well localized. Of importance, as noted previously, VMH-lesioned rats can display hyperinsulinemia with an increased sensitivity to insulin, even when not allowed to be hyperphagic. It has been suggested, therefore, that the brain may have a direct effect on the pancreas via the vagus to produce this increased insulin since vagotomy or pancreatectomy will eliminate the VMH-induced obesity (131, 132). However, this is confusing since vagotomy performed 70 days prior to VMH lesions does not block obesity development (161), and vagotomy performed after VMH lesions does not always reverse the obesity (162). Postvagotomy ulcer patients may or may not lose weight, but Kral (163) has recently demonstrated that bilateral subdiaphragmatic vagotomy produces reasonable weight loss with few side effects in the obese. His subjects ate less but maintained a general awareness of hunger. Circulating insulin levels were significantly reduced, perhaps being the mechanism for the weight loss (as in the vagotomized VMH-lesioned rat). An alternative explanation is that delayed gastric motility affected gut hormones to bring about this weight reduction.

It is well known that food intake ceases before a substantial portion of a meal has been absorbed intestinally. If intake continued until sufficient food had been absorbed to correct the energy deficit, the system would regularly overshoot its mark by the amount eaten but not yet absorbed. Clearly there must be preabsorptive mechanisms which determine adequate meal sizes. In addition to palatability of the food and conditioning and cognitive factors, meal size is determined in part by bulk of food in the gastrointestinal tract (164). An increased osmotic pressure in the gut by the presence of mannitol, for example, will decrease food intake. Total intake in such studies is inversely proportional to the amount of mannitol in the test solution (164). There is some evidence that gastric distension plays a role in signaling satiety. Animals with esophageal fistulas, which prevent food from entering the stomach, eat larger than normal meals (114, 165) which can be decreased by inflating an intragastric balloon (166). Sugar and Gates (167) have studied two infants less than 12 hours old using a gastric balloon. They were able to demonstrate that by so distending the gastric walls the "hunger reflex" was eliminated.

While this information suggests the stomach may play some role in preabsorptive satiety, Gibbs and his colleagues (168) have shown that the first part of the duodenum is of critical importance. They studied monkeys fitted with gastric fistulas so that oral intake could occur but stomach distension could be prevented. When the fistula was open, these animals would generally overeat compared to when the fistulas were closed. This effect could be rapidly abolished by placing small amounts of liquid food directly into the first portion of the duodenum. This intestinal preabsorptive mechanism was found to be very potent as it required only 10 percent of a normal meal volume to elicit satiety. In addition, this mechanism appeared to operate independent of gastric distension. An important question which arises from this work is what mediates this preabsorptive satiety from the small intestine. Recent work suggests that hormones secreted by the gut, especially cholecystokinin (CCK), may be important.

The concept of the gastrointestinal endocrine system and the gut-brain axis has developed greatly in the last few years due to advances in protein chemistry which have permitted the necessary isolation, purification and characterization of a large number of polypeptide hormones. This field has recently been reviewed by Track (169). Two important issues have emerged: 1) The GI tract is very much more active in secreting hormones than had previously been known. The functions of many of these hormones are currently incompletely or poorly understood. They are important in the regulation of carbohydrate metabolism, gastric acid secretion, pancreatic exocrine, and gallbladder function plus gastrointestinal motility and blood flow; and 2) a number of these hormones are located both in the gut and in the brain. This has given rise to the concept of the gut-brain axis. Hormones shared by brain and gut include CCK, somatostatin, thyrotropin-releasing hormone, and adrenocorticotropin.

Gastroenteropancreatic hormones appear to be one of the means of regulating digestion at various levels. It is likely that they are controlled via gastroduodenal-releasing hormones and ingestion of various foods. Fat ingestion causes motilin release from the upper intestinal mucosa. This hormone causes an increased motor activity of the stomach (170). Somatostatin is generated primarily in the hypothalamus as well as in the gastrointestinal mucosa and pancreas. It is involved in the fine-tuning of insulin and glucagon secretion, inhibiting the release of both (169). It also inhibits gastrin release, gastric acid secretion, and delays gastric emptying (171). Vasoactive intestinal polypeptide (VIP) is found in both the mucosa of the gut and the brain. It is a potent vasodilator, stimulates release of insulin, as well as inhibits gastric acid secretion, glycogenolysis, and pancreatic secretion of water and bicarbonate. While it is located in nerve cells (172), there is uncertainty as to whether it functions itself as a neurotransmitter or mediates the action of other neurotransmitters. Gastric inhibitory peptide (GIP) is primarily derived from the mucosa of the duodenum. Both carbohydrate and fat stimulate GIP release. It inhibits gastric emptying and acid secretion (171, 173).

The major source of gastrin is the antral mucosa; the stimulus for its release is an elevated gastric pH. It both stimulates acid release from the stomach and promotes growth of the gastrointestinal mucosa. It has a variety of other functions — for example, enhancing gastric motor activity, exocrine secretion by the pancreas, and insulin secretion from the islet cells. Secretin is responsible for pancreatic bicarbonate flow and is secreted in response to a falling pH value of the fluid in the upper intestinal mucosa. Chymodenin stimulates chymotrypsinogen release (174). Pancreatic polypeptide inhibits pancreatic exocrine function (175). There has been some preliminary work suggesting that pancreatic polypeptide may be lowered in genetically obese mice (176) and may be lowered in obese humans in response to a meal (177).

Of the GI hormones identified to date, CCK is most closely implicated in satiety regulation. A major stimulus for CCK release is the presence of fat in the lumen of the gut. CCK has a variety of functions, including contraction of the gallbladder, pancreatic enzyme secretion, gastric secretion of pepsin, and inhibition of gastric emptying (178). Gibbs, Young and Smith (179) have shown that when CCK is injected intraperitoneally, it inhibits the sham feeding of rats with open gastric fistulas. The same was found for a slow intravenous infusion in monkeys (168). In intact animals, CCK has been shown to elicit satiety in a variety of species (165). There is also indirect evidence demonstrating that endogenous CCK plays a role in eliciting short-term satiety. Mayer and Grossman (180) showed that the L-isomer of phenylalanine was a potent releaser of endogenous CCK in the dog; Smith and Gibbs (181) confirmed that this isomer, but not the D form, was a potent inhibitor of feeding. However, CCK has been reported to have mixed effects in humans: not to alter satiety (182, 183); both to stimulate and inhibit food intake (184); or to decrease subjective hunger ratings in response to food smells (185). We do not yet know how satiety signals from the gut interact with the brain. Circulating CCK may sensitize peripheral receptors which then relay the information to the brain. In this respect there are reports of stress-induced feeding in rats to be more readily blocked by peripheral rather than brain CCK injection

(186). Or CCK may have a direct effect on the brain via vagal afferents. Morley (187) has suggested that CCK may mediate 5-HT-induced satiety. While CCK is unlikely to cross the blood brain barrier, large amounts of it are found in the brain (188, 189). Interestingly, genetically obese ob/ob mice have been found to possess 66 percent less cerebral cortical CCK than lean littermate controls (190). Moreover, intraventricular CCK injection has been reported to reduce food intake in rats (191) and sheep (192). Clearly the relationship between CCK and other gut hormones to hunger and satiety requires further investigation.

## Psychosocial Factors Involved in Hunger and Satiety and the Regulation of Food Intake

In addition to the physiological processes that have been described, a number of psychosocial factors help regulate when, what, and how often we eat. For humans, a number of these are so powerful that they may override the physiological factors. These psychosocial factors include conditioning, learned differentiation of inner states, sensitivity to external stimuli, cognition and education, as well as cultural factors regarding food intake and body size.

Stunkard (193) and Booth (194) have recently reviewed evidence which favors a classical conditioning model of preabsorptive satiety. A similar proposal had been made earlier by Le Magnen (195). In essence, these theories point out that a vast array of stimuli can become associated with the cessation of hunger (e.g., the smell, taste, texture, and appearance of food; the oropharyngeal and gastrointestinal sensations which follow ingestion; the environmental sights, sounds, and even feelings relating to places where eating occurs). The repeated pairing of such stimuli (conditional or CS) with postabsorptive factors which normally produce satiety (unconditional or UCS) may eventually result in the former stimuli alone eliciting premature satiety. The main argument against this hypothesis—that of the lengthy time lag between CS and UCS—has been dealt with (193) by considering earlier work (196) which showed that conditioned aversions to foods may be produced in rats when the CS-UCS interval is several hours in length. Similarly, strong conditioned food preferences can be demonstrated; for example, rats with thiamine deficiency develop a strong preference for the taste of saccharin alone if they had earlier exposure to this taste in diets containing thiamine (197). Again a delay in the CS-UCS interval is demonstrable in these learned taste preferences. What seems most germane about these conditioned responses is that they can be learned quite rapidly (e.g., a very few pairings) and that they are extremely resistant to extinction (193).

Bruch (2, 198) has focused on a different aspect of learning hunger and satiety awareness, that is, the early differentiation of these inner states from other inner tensions or needs. She has emphasized that awareness of hunger and other biological needs are not "innate biological knowledge but that learning is necessary for them to become organized into recognizable patterns" (198, p. 93). She has suggested that children with juvenile onset obesity and anorexia nervosa never properly develop the ability to differentiate hunger and satiety from other internal tensions and never have a sense of mastery or control over their bodies. Consistent with this line of reasoning is the commonly observed finding that some obese people misuse the eating function by eating in response to a variety of psychological states including boredom, anxiety, and depression (199).

Garner, Garfinkel and Moldofsky (200) have recently reviewed the experimental evidence supporting Bruch's assertions. There is some indirect evidence for the presence of these disturbances in interoception in many but not all anorexic and obese patients. The pathogenesis of these disturbances is not understood. Coddington and Bruch (201) found that both anorexic and obese patients were less accurate than normals in perceiving the amount of food (Metrecal) that was directly introduced into their stomachs. Similarly, it has been shown that obese individuals cannot accurately rely on internal sensations to determine the nutritive quality of food eaten. More recently, Campbell, Hashim and Van Itallie (202) reported that juvenile onset obese subjects were unable to adjust appropriately the volume of food necessary to correct for variations in caloric density. Lean subjects, on the other hand, regulated their intake to adapt to the various caloric concentrations delivered and so were able to maintain their weight. But faulty satiety perception alone is not the sole governor of disturbance in dietary intake. Several investigators have shown that obese individuals seem to be hyper-responsive to the taste of food (203, 204) and will rapidly lose weight when put on a bland liquid diet (205). Therefore, it is unclear whether obese subjects are unable to distinguish "internal" satiety cues associated with caloric needs and, therefore, cannot adjust their caloric intake accordingly, or whether they are simply not motivated to ingest less palatable liquid food.

The work of Cabanac and Duclaux (206) also suggests that obese people may not experience some aspects of satiety in the same manner as do the nonobese. They found that obese subjects did not experience any difference in a "pleasantness" rating of sucrose before and after they ingested various amounts of glucose. Normal subjects, in contrast, experienced "satiety" or an aversion to sucrose after glucose preloading. On the basis of these results, they concluded that obese subjects are less responsive than nonobese subjects to internal cues related to energy needs. Grinker (207) and Stellar (208), however, have both reported an instability of this procedure in that subjects' hedonic ratings of sweet stimuli were not consistently related to caloric intake in repeated trials. Stellar (208) concluded that the phenomenon exists but is not robust. Underwood, Belton and Hulme's (209) results support the hypothesis that obesity is associated with an absence of "satiety aversion" because of insensitivity to internal signals. In addition to this, a potentially important but unexpected finding emerged from this study. One of the "normal" subjects, who displayed a typically "obese" absence of aversion to sucrose, was later found to have anorexia nervosa!

In a recent study of a larger group of anorectic patients using a modified version of this procedure, Garfinkel, Moldofsky, Garner, et al. (210) found that anorectics failed to develop an aversion to sucrose tastes compared to normal controls. Moreover the failure to develop a "satiety" aversion was closely related to body image disturbance. On follow-up examination one year later, these same patients demonstrated similar responses, showing the stability of this effect under these conditions. Moreover, in those patients who had attained a reasonable weight, there was still no change in their satiety responses (211).

A contrasting series of studies has challenged the theory that the obese are relatively insensitive to internal stimuli. S. Wooley (212) found that the actual number of calories consumed in a preload had no effect on the subsequent intake of a test meal in both obese and nonobese subjects. Similarly, O. Wooley (213) reported that both obese and nonobese subjects were unable to adjust their intake of an all-liquid diet when caloric content was altered. Both obese and nonobese subjects were later found to be unable to perceive actual changes in the caloric content of their food; rather they reported hunger in accordance with their "belief" about the caloric value of a meal (214). A subsequent study (215) challenged Cabanac and Duclaux's finding by demonstrating that glucose and cyclamate were equally effective in producing sucrose aversion in both obese and normal weight persons. It was concluded that physiological sensations (or their absence) are not important in obesity, but that the differential effects of sensory or cognitive cues (taste) differentiate obese from nonobese individuals. This viewpoint was modified in a more recent study in which Wooley (216) demonstrated that caloric preload affects "appetite" (as measured by salivary responses) but not subjective feelings of hunger. The appetite of obese subjects was less inhibited by a high calorie preload than that of nonobese subjects. Thus, both cognitive and physiological behaviors appear to differentiate obese from nonobese in their responses to food.

In a series of related experiments, Schachter and his colleagues have demonstrated that the eating behavior of obese subjects may be greatly influenced by external circumstances (217). The evidence for this has recently been summarized by Schachter and Rodin (39). While these studies do not address the question of the ability of obese people to perceive their internal state, they indicate that another set of variables may significantly influence their eating behavior. With the hypothesis that external cues may differentially affect eating behavior, Schachter and Gross (218) designed an experiment to determine the effect of "dinner time" on obese and normal subjects. Using "doctored clocks" the experimenters found that obese subjects ate when the clocks indicated that it was dinner time regardless of actual time. On the other hand, the eating of normal weight subjects was less influenced by the apparent time and was presumably more responsive to internal sensations of hunger.

In another study, Nisbett (219) reported that the palatability of food had substantial influence on the eating tendencies of obese subjects. He demonstrated that, regardless of their state of deprivation, the obese ate more good-tasting and less bad-tasting ice cream than did normals who appeared less responsive to taste and more responsive to their deprivation state. These results again support the view that the eating behavior of the obese is governed in part by prevailing external cues related to food. Additional work by Nisbett in which the availability of food (203) and food attractiveness (220) have been manipulated lend further support to this conclusion. It is not clear whether this responsivity is a cause of obesity, a result of it, or due to some third phenomenon, such as chronic dieting. On the one hand, external responsiveness is not well correlated with degree of overweight (221) and therefore may not play a major role in determining the level at which long-term weight regulation occurs. However, in nonobese children at a summer camp, those who were judged to be most externally responsive gained the most weight when food was freely available over the summer (222). Also, an individual's level of responsiveness to external stimuli does not change with marked weight loss through dieting or jejunoileostomy (221). After both procedures individuals who are highly responsive remain vulnerable to the influence of external food cues. However, bypass surgery but not dieting may reduce taste preferences for sweets and increase feelings of satiety, thereby reducing food intake (221). The latter may be related to increased awareness of gastrointestinal filling or altered hormone secretion. For example, Bray and his colleagues (223) have shown insulin levels to decrease significantly, while enteroglucagon, pancreatic polypeptide, and gastrin increased after surgery but not dieting.

A recent series of experiments by Herman, Polivy and associates have shown that normal weight dieters or "restrained" eaters display the same external responsiveness as previously observed in obese subjects (224, 225, 226). They feel that restraint, not obesity, is responsible for increased cognitive responsiveness to external cues. Moreover, it has been demonstrated that the dieting behavior of restrained eaters is disinhibited when they lose the external cues on which they depend for dietary control. For example, Polivy (227) has found that dieters will overeat when they believe that they have already overeaten irrespective of the actual calories consumed. Subsequent studies have shown that anxiety (225) and depression (228) can have disinhibitory effects upon the eating of dieters when compared to nondieters. Finally, alcohol, together with a disinhibitory cognitive set, has been shown to influence the breakdown of dieting in restrained but not unrestrained eaters (229). These studies suggest that the eating of chronic dieters is highly influenced by cognitive and affective states.

There is other evidence that cognitive factors are important in determining what and when we eat. We tend to adopt food habits based on rules and education from other members of our society. Recent changes in eating habits based on such ideas as high cholesterol and heart disease or fat content and longevity are examples of these. Social or religious taboos may influence eating patterns wherein new foods are accepted or rejected, at times in spite of resulting malnutrition. This rejection may be due to unfamiliar taste, color, texture, or connotation of the food (230, 231). Further, society's attitudes toward body size and shape may be determinants of what and when we eat. Evidence for the strong cultural component to eating behaviors and accepted or admired body sizes comes both from examining different cultures and from prevalence of weight disorders in our own culture. Obesity is largely a lower social class disorder (193) while anorexia nervosa is highly related to upper and middle classes (232).

Our Western society tends to value leanness and, as Rakoff (233) has noted, the contemporary ideal figure is most typically represented by those actresses who look "like prepubertal girls onto whom the secondary sexual characteristics of mature females have been grafted." Not all cultures share the ideal of this figure. Poor people as well as more primitive groups tend to value and admire obesity; it becomes a threat only in our affluent society. The ideal body form has varied over time; examination of Rubens' vs. Modigliani's work serves to emphasize temporal differences in preferred women's shapes. In her recent book, *Illness as Metaphor*, Sontag (234) presents an interesting historical example of the power of cultural influence to transform physical symptoms into a romanticized ideal. She describes how fashionable it was 100 years ago to exhibit the sickly pallor and cough of tuberculosis. Currently, the idealized body type for females is for a bony thinness as exemplified by the popularity of Twiggy. This contemporary valuation of thinness is evident from both a review of the changing weights of Playboy's centerfold models and from weights of Miss America contestants over the 1970s (235).

In contrast to the idealized preference in North America for thinness, there has been a general increase in average body size in young women as is evident from comparison of 1959 and 1979 actuarial tables (235). The average young woman in her 20s has gained three to five pounds. At the same time, there has been a growing awareness of health consciousness, the deleterious effects of obesity, and a strong societal pressure for thinness. The result of this biosocial conflict is to force women especially to eat more in response to (external) beliefs and attitudes regarding caloric content of foods rather than in response to their (internal) nutritional needs.

In conclusion, it seems fair to say that there has been significant recent progress in sharpening our awareness of the multiple processes which influence hunger, satiety, and food intake. Having identified many nervous, hormonal, behavioral, and cognitive factors that contribute to these states, we now require new information as to how these factors interrelate normally to produce healthy patterns of eating. Once this has been accomplished, we should be better equipped to deal with the aberrations of these interactions which underlie the recalcitrant eating and weight disorders of persisting clinical concern.

## REFERENCES

1. MAYER, J.: Some aspects of the problem of regulating food intake and obesity. *Int. Psychiat. Clin.,* 7:255, 1970.
2. BRUCH, H.: Hunger and instinct. *J. Nerv. Ment. Dis.,* 149:91, 1969.
3. BRAY, G. A. and CAMPFIELD, L. A.: Metabolic factors in the control of energy stores. *Metabolism,* 24:99, 1975.
4. BOOTH, D. A., TOATES, F. M., and PLATT, S. V.: Control system for hunger and its implication in animals and man. In: D. Novin, W. Wyrwicka, and G. A. Bray (Eds.), *Hunger: Basic Mechanisms and Clinical Implications.* New York: Raven Press, 1976, p. 127.
5. MOGENSON, G.: Neural mechanisms of hunger. Current status and future prospects. In: D. Novin, W. Wyrwicka, and G. A. Bray (Eds.), *Hunger: Basic Mechanisms and Clinical Implications.* New York: Raven Press, 1976, p. 473.
6. LYTLE, L. D.: Control of eating behavior. In: R. J. Wurtman and J. J. Wurtman (Eds.), *Nutrition and the Brain.* New York: Raven Press, 1977, p. 1.
7. BELLISLE, F.: Human feeding behavior. *Neurosci. & Biobehav. Rev.,* 3:163, 1979.
8. FROHLICH, A.: Ein fall von tumor der hypophysis cerebri ohne akromegalie. *Wien. Klin. Wochenschr.,* 15:883, 1901.

9. CAMUS, J. and ROUSSY, G.: Hypophysectomie et polyurie experimental. *C. B. Soc. Biol.* (Paris), 75:483, 1913.
10. SMITH, P. E.: Hypophysectomy and a replacement therapy in the rat. *Am. J. Anat.,* 45:205, 1930.
11. HETHERINGTON, A. W. and RANSON, S. W.: Hypothalamic lesions and adiposity in the rat. *Anat. Rec.,* 78:149, 1940.
12. ANAND, B. K. and BROBECK, J. R.: Hypothalamic control of food intake. *Yale J. Biol. Med.,* 24:123, 1951.
13. STELLAR, E.: The physiology of motivation. *Psychol. Rev.,* 61:5, 1954.
14. GROSSMAN, S. P.: Neuroanatomy of food and water intake. In: D. Novin, W. Wyrwicka, and G. A. Bray (Eds.), *Hunger: Basic Mechanisms and Clinical Implications.* New York: Raven Press, 1976, p. 51.
15. TEITELBAUM, P. and EPSTEIN, A. N.: The lateral hypothalamic syndrome: Recovery of feeding and drinking after lateral hypothalamic lesions. *Psychol. Rev.,* 69:74, 1962.
16. SMITH, G. P. and EPSTEIN, A. N.: Increased feeding in response to decreased glucose utilization in rat and monkey. *Am. J. Physiol.,* 217:1083, 1969.
17. CARLISLE, H. J.: Differential effects of amphetamine on food and water intake in rats with lateral hypothalamic lesions. *J. Comp. Physiol. Psychol.,* 58:47, 1964.
18. COSCINA, D. V. and BALAGURA, S.: Avoidance and escape behavior of rats with aphagia produced by basal diencephalic lesions. *Physiol. Behav.,* 5:651, 1970.
19. VAN ZOEREN, J. G. and STRICKER, E. M.: Thermal homeostasis in rats after intrahypothalamic injections of 6-hydroxydopamine. *Am. J. Physiol.,* 230:932, 1976.
20. ROTH, S. R., SCHWARTZ, M., and TEITELBAUM, P.: Failure of recovered lateral hypothalamic rats to learn specific food aversion. *J. Comp. Physiol. Psych.,* 83:184, 1973.
21. BALAGURA, S. and HARRELL, L. E.: Lateral hypothalamus syndrome: Its modification by obesity and leanness. *Physiol. Behav.,* 13:345, 1974.
22. POWLEY, T. L. and KEESEY, R. E.: Relationship of body weight to the lateral hypothalamic feeding syndrome. *J. Comp. Physiol. Psychol.,* 70:25, 1970.
23. KEESEY, R. E., BOYLE, P. C., KEMMITZ, J. W., et al.: The role of the lateral hypothalamus in determining the body weight set point. In: D. Novin, W. Wrywicka, and G. A. Bray (Eds.), *Hunger: Basic Mechanisms and Clinical Implications.* New York: Raven Press, 1976, p. 243.
24. SMITH, G. P., GIBBS, J., STROHMAYER, A. J., et al.: Threshold doses of 2-deoxy-D-glucose for hypoglycemia and feeding in rats and monkeys. *Am. J. Physiol.,* 222:77, 1972.
25. BROBECK, J. R., TEPPERMAN, J., and LONG, C. N. H.: Experimental hypothalamic hyperphagia in the albino rat. *Yale. J. Biol. Med.,* 15:831, 1943.
26. BROOKS, C. McC.: The relative importance of changes in activity in the development of experimentally produced obesity in the rat. *Am. J. Physiol.,* 147:708, 1946.
27. TEITELBAUM, P. and CAMPBELL, B. A.: Ingestion patterns in hyperphagic and normal rats. *J. Comp. Physiol. Psychol.,* 51:135, 1958.
28. BALAGURA, S. and DEVENPORT, L. D.: Feeding patterns of normal and ventro-

medial hypothalamic lesioned male and female rats. *J. Comp. Physiol. Psychol.,* 71:357, 1970.

29. THOMAS, D. W. and MAYER, J.: Meal taking and regulation of food intake by normal and hypothalamic hyperphagic rats. *J. Comp. Physiol. Psychol.,* 66:642, 1968.

30. McHUGH, P. R. and MORAN, T. H.: An examination of the concept of satiety in hypothalamic hyperphagia. In: R. Vigersky (Ed.), *Anorexia Nervosa.* New York: Raven Press, 1977, p. 67.

31. PANKSEPP, J.: A re-examination of the role of the ventromedial hypothalamus in feeding behavior. *Physiol. Behav.,* 7:385, 1971.

32. TEITELBAUM, P.: Motivation and control of food intake. In: C. F. Code (Ed.), *Handbook of Physiology.* Sect. 6, Vol. 1. Washington, DC: American Physiological Society, 1967, p. 319.

33. ROGERS, Q. R. and LEUNG, P. M-B.: The influence of amino acids on the neuroregulation of food intake. *Fed. Proc.,* 32:1709, 1973.

34. KENNEDY, G. C.: The role of depot fat in the hypothalamic control of food intake in the rat. *Proc. Roy. Soc. Lond. (Biol),* 140:549, 1953.

35. WOODS, S. C., DECKE, E., and VASSELLI, J. R.: Metabolic hormones and regulation of body weight. *Psychol. Rev.,* 81:26, 1974.

36. TANNENBAUM, G. A., PAXINOS, G., and BINDRA, D.: Metabolic and endocrine aspects of the ventromedial hypothalamic syndrome in the rat. *J. Comp. Physiol. Psychol.,* 86:404, 1974.

37. VALENSTEIN, E. S., COX, V. C., and KAKOLEWSKI, J. W.: Sex differences in hyperphagia and body weight following hypothalamic damage. *Ann. NY Acad. Sci.,* 157:1030, 1969.

38. HAN, P. W.: Energy metabolism of tube-fed hypophysectomized rats bearing hypothalamic lesions. *Am. J. Physiol.,* 215:1343, 1968.

39. SCHACHTER, S., and RODIN, J.: *Obese Humans and Rats.* Potomac, MD: Lawrence Erlbaum Associates, 1974.

40. MILLHOUSE, O. E.: A golgi study of the descending medial forebrain bundle. *Brain Res.,* 15:341, 1969.

41. MILLHOUSE, O. E.: The organization of the ventromedial hypothalamic nucleus. *Brain Res.,* 55:71, 1973.

42. PANKSEPP, J.: Is satiety mediated by the ventromedial hypothalamus? *Physiol. Behav.,* 7:381, 1971.

43. COSCINA, D. V.: Brain amines in hypothalamic obesity. In: R. Vigersky (Ed.), *Anorexia Nervosa.* New York: Raven Press, 1977, p. 97.

44. GROSSMAN, S. P.: Correlative analyses of ingestive behavior and regional amine depletions after surgical transections of neural pathways in the mesencephalon, diencephalong and striatum. In: S. Garattini and R. Samanin (Eds.), *Central Mechanisms of Anorectic Drugs.* New York: Raven Press, 1978, p. 1.

45. HOEBEL, B. G.: Satiety: Hypothalamic stimulation, anorectic drugs and neurochemical substrates. In: D. Novin, W. Wyrwicka, and G. A. Bray (Eds.), *Hunger: Basic Mechanisms and Clinical Implications.* New York: Raven Press, 1976, p. 33.

46. UNGERSTEDT, U.: Adipsia and aphagia after 6-hydroxy-dopamine induced degeneration of the nigro-striatal dopamine system. *Acta. Physiol. Scand.,* 367:95, 1971.

47. STRICKER, E. M. and ZIGMOND, M. J.: Brain catecholamines and the lateral hypothalamic syndrome. In: D. Novin, W. Wyrwicka, and G. A. Bray (Eds.), *Hunger: Basic Mechanisms and Clinical Implications.* New York: Raven Press, 1976, p. 19.
48. COSCINA, D. V. and STANCER, H. C.: Selective blockade of hypothalamic hyperphagia and obesity in rats by serotonin-depleting midbrain lesions. *Science,* 195:416, 1977.
49. GOLD, R. M.: Hypothalamic obesity: The myth of the ventromedial nucleus. *Science,* 182:488, 1973.
50. MILLER, N. E.: Chemical coding of behavior in the brain. *Science,* 148:328, 1965.
51. GROSSMAN, S. P.: Eating or drinking elicited by direct adrenergic or cholinergic stimulation of hypothalamus. *Science,* 132:301–302, 1960.
52. LEIBOWITZ, S. F.: Reciprocal hunger-regulating circuits involving alpha- and beta-adrenergic receptors located respectively in the ventromedial and lateral hypothalamus. *Proc. Natl. Acad. Sci. USA,* 67:1063, 1970.
53. LEIBOWITZ, S. F.: Hypothalamic alpha- and beta-adrenergic systems regulate both thirst and hunger in the rat. *Proc. Natl. Acad. Sci. USA,* 68:332, 1971.
54. LEIBOWITZ, S. F.: Brain catecholaminergic mechanisms for control of hunger. In: D. Novin, W. Wyrwicka, and G. A. Bray (Eds.), *Hunger: Basic Mechanisms and Clinical Implications.* New York: Raven Press, 1976, p. 1.
55. MONTGOMERY, R. G., SINGER, G., PURCELL, A. T., et al.: The effects of intrahypothalamic injections of desmethylimipramine on food and water intake of the rat. *Psychopharmacologia,* 19:81, 1971.
56. REDMOND, D. E., JR., HUANG, Y. H., BAULU, J., et al.: Norepinephrine and satiety in monkeys. In: R. Vigersky (Ed.), *Anorexia Nervosa.* New York: Raven Press, 1977, p. 81.
57. OLTMANS, G. A. and HARVEY, J. A.: LH syndrome and brain catecholamine levels after lesions of the nigrostriatal bundle. *Physiol. Behav.,* 8:69, 1972.
58. LORDEN, J., OLTMANS, G. A., and MARGULES, D. L.: Central noradrenergic neurons: Differential effects on body weight of electrolytic and 6-hydroxydopamine lesions in rats. *J. Comp. Physiol. Psychol.,* 90:144, 1976.
59. AHLSKOG, J. E. and HOEBEL, B. G.: Overeating and obesity from damage to a noradrenergic system in the brain. *Science,* 182:166, 1973.
60. COSCINA, D. V., GODSE, D. D., and STANCER, H. C.: Neurochemical correlates of hypothalamic obesity in rats. *Behav. Biol.,* 16:365, 1976.
61. COSCINA, D. V., ROSENBLUM-BLINICK, C., GODSE, D. D., et al.: Consummatory behaviors of hypothalamic hyperphagic rats after central injection of 6-hydroxydopamine. *Pharmacol. Biochem. Behav.,* 1:629, 1973.
62. GLICK, S. D., GREENSTEIN, S., and WATERS, D. H.: Ventromedial hypothalamic lesions and brain catecholamines. *Pharmacol. Biochem. Behav.,* 1:591, 1973.
63. AHLSKOG, J. E., RANDALL, P. K., and HOEBEL, B. G.: Hypothalamic hyperphagia: Dissociation from hyperphagia following destruction of noradrenergic neurons. *Science,* 197:399, 1975.
64. REZEK, M. and NOVIN, D.: The effects of serotonin on feeding in the rabbit. *Psychopharmacologia,* 43: 255, 1975.
65. SLANGEN, J. L. and MILLER, N. E.: Pharmacological tests for the function of hypothalamic norepinephrine in eating behavior. *Physiol. Behav.,* 4:543, 1969.

66. KRUK, Z. L.: Dopamine and 5-hydroxytryptamine inhibit feeding in rats. *Nature* (New Biol), 246:52, 1973.
67. JOYCE, D. and MROSOVSKY, N.: Eating, drinking and activity in rats following 5-hydroxytryptophan (5-HTP) administration. *Psychopharmacologia,* 5:417, 1964.
68. BLUNDELL, J. E. and LESHEM, M. B.: The effect of 5-hydroxytryptophan on food intake and on the anorexic action of amphetamine and fenfluramine. *J. Pharm. Pharmacol.,* 27:31, 1975.
69. BLUNDELL, J. E.: Is there a role for serotonin (5-hydroxytryptamine) in feeding? *Int. J. Obesity,* 1:15, 1977.
70. COSCINA, D. V., WARSH, J. J., GODSE, D. D., et al.: Non-specificity of 5-hydroxytryptophan in repleting serotonin in rats with MFB lesions. *Res. Comm. Chem. Path. Pharmacol.,* 7:617, 1974.
71. AGHAJANIAN, G. K. and ASHER, I. M.: Histochemical fluorescence of raphe neurons: Selective enhancement of tryptophan. *Science,* 172:1159, 1971.
72. FERNSTROM, J. D. and WURTMAN, R.J.: Brain serotonin content: Physiological regulation by plasma neutral amino acids. *Science,* 178:414, 1972.
73. BARRETT, A. M. and McSHARRY, L.: Inhibition of drug-induced anorexia in rats by methysergide. *J. Pharm. Pharmacol.,* 27:889, 1975.
74. WEINBERGER, S. B., KNAPP, S., and MANDELL, A. J.: Failure of tryptophan load-induced increases in brain serotonin to alter food intake in the rat. *Life Sci.,* 22:1595, 1978.
75. LOVENBERG, W., JEQUIER, E., and SJOERDSMA, A.: Tryptophan hydroxylation in mammalian systems. In: S. Garattini and P. A. Shore (Eds.), *Advances in Pharmacology,* Vol. 6. New York: Academic Press, 1968.
76. BIGGIO, G., FADDA, F., FANNI, P., et al.: Rapid depletion of serum tryptophan, brain tryptophan, serotonin and 5-hydroxyindoleacetic acid by a tryptophan free diet. *Life Sci.,* 14:1321, 1974.
77. FERNSTROM, J. D. and WURTMAN, R. J.: Brain serotonin content: Increase following ingestion of carbohydrate diet. *Science,* 173:1023, 1971.
78. CURZON, G., FRIEDEL, J., and KNOTT, P. J.: The effect of fatty acids on the binding of tryptophan to plasma protein. *Nature,* 242:198, 1973.
79. PEREZ-CRUET, J., CHASE, T. N., and MURPHY, D. L.: Dietary regulation of brain tryptophan metabolism by plasma ratio of free tryptophan and neutral amino acids in humans. *Nature,* 248:693, 1974.
80. LESHEM, M. B. and BLUNDELL, J. E.: Interactive effect of ( ± )-fenfluramine and ( + )-amphetamine on feeding in rats. *J. Pharm. Pharmacol.,* 26:905, 1974.
81. COSTA, E., GROPETTI, A., and REQUELTA, A.: Action of fenfluramine on monoamine stores of rat tissues. *Br. J. Pharmacol.,* 41:57, 1971.
82. SAMANIN, R., GHEZZI, D., VALZELLI, L., et al.: The effects of selective lesioning of brain serotonin or catecholamine containing neurons on the anorectic activity of fenfluramine and amphetamine. *Eur. J. Pharmacol.,* 19:318, 1972.
83. BLUNDELL, J. E., LATHAM, C. J., and LESHEM, M. B.: Differences between the anorexic action of amphetamine and fenfluramine: Possible effects on hunger and satiety. *J. Pharm. Pharmacol.,* 28:471, 1976.
84. GHOSH, M. N. and PARVATHY, S.: The effect of cyproheptadine on water and food intake and on body weight in the fasted adult and weanling rat. *Br. J. Pharmacol.,* 48:328, 1973.

85. BENADY, D. R.: Cyproheptadine hydrochloride (periactin) and anorexia nervosa: A case report. *Brit. J. Psychiatry,* 117:681, 1970.
86. GOLDBERG, S. C., HALMI, K. A., ECKERT, E. D., et al.: Cyproheptadine in anorexia nervosa. *Brit. J. Psychiatry,* 134:67, 1979.
87. CARLSSON, A. and LINDQVIST, M.: Effects of antidepressant agents on the synthesis of brain monoamines. *J. Neural. Transm.,* 43:73, 1978.
88. KUPFER, D. J., COBLE, P. A., and RUBENSTEIN, D.: Changes in weight during treatment for depression. *Psychosom. Med.,* 41:535, 1979.
89. PAYKEL, E. S., MUELLER, P. S., and DE LA VERGNE, P. M.: Amitriptyline, weight gain and carbohydrate craving: A side effect. *Brit. J. Psychiat.,* 123:501, 1973.
90. EGAN, J., EARLEY, C. J., and LEONARD, B. E.: The effect of amitriptyline and mianserine (org.GB94) on food motivated behaviour of rats trained in a runway: Possible correlation with biogenic amine concentration in the limbic system. *Psychopharmacology,* 61:143, 1979.
91. KOE, B. K. and WEISSMAN, A.: p-Chlorophenylalanine: Specific depletor of brain serotonin. *J. Pharmacol. Exp. Ther.,* 154:499, 1966.
92. PANKSEPP, J. and NANCE, D. M.: Effects of para-chlorophenylalanine on food intake in rats. *Physiol. Psychol.,* 2:360, 1974.
93. BREISCH, S. T., ZEMLAN, F. P., and HOEBEL, B. G.: Hyperphagia and obesity following serotonin depletion by intraventricular p-chlorophenylalanine. *Science,* 192:382, 1976.
94. COSCINA, D. V., DANIEL, J., and WARSH, J. J.: Potential non-serotonergic basis of hyperphagia elicited by intraventricular p-chlorophenylalanine. *Pharmacol. Biochem. Behav.,* 9:791, 1978.
95. MACKENZIE, R. G., HOEBEL, B. G., DUCRET, R. P., et al.: Hyperphagia following intraventricular p-chlorophenylanine-, leucine- or tryptophan- methyl esters: lack of correlation with whole brain serotonin levels. *Pharmacol. Biochem. Behav.,* 10:951, 1979.
96. MAYER, J.: Glucostatic mechanisms in regulation of food intake. *N. Engl. J. Med.,* 249:13, 1953.
97. MAYER, J.: The physiology of hunger and satiety. In: R. S. Goodbart and M. E. Shils (Eds.), *Modern Nutrition in Health and Disease.* Philadelphia: Lea and Febiger, 1980, p. 560.
97a. Stunkard, A. J.: From explanation to action in psychosomatic medicine: the case of obesity. Presidential Address, 1974. *Psychosom. Med.,* 37:195, 1975.
98. JANOWITZ, H. D. and IVY, A. C., JR.: Role of blood-sugar levels in spontaneous and insulin-induced hunger in man. *J. Appl. Physiol.,* 1:643, 1949.
99. MAYER, J.: General discussion. *Adv. Psychosom. Med.,* 7:322, 1972.
100. ANAND, B. K., DUA, S., and SINGH, B.: Electrical activity of the hypothalamic "feeding centres" under effect of changes in blood chemistry. *Electroencephalogr. Clin. Neurophysiol.,* 13:54, 1961.
101. HOCHMAN, C. H.: EEG and behavioral effects of food deprivation in the albino rat. *Electroencephalogr. Clin. Neurophysiol.,* 17:420, 1964.
102. OOMURA, Y., ONO, T., OOYAMA, H., et al.: Glucose and osmosensitive neurons of the rat hypothalamus. *Nature* (Lond), 222:282, 1969.
103. ANAND, B. K.: Functional importance of the limbic system of the brain. *Indian J. Med. Res.,* 51:175, 1963.
104. PANKSEPP, J.: Hypothalamic radioactivity after intragastric glucose C$^{14}$ in rats.

*Am. J. Physiol.,* 223:396, 1972.

105. LIEBELT, R. A. and PERRY, J. A.: Action of gold thioglucose on the central nervous system. In: C. F. Code (Ed.), *Handbook of Physiology,* Sect. 6, Vol. 1. Washington, DC: American Physiological Society, 1967, p. 271.

106. DEBONS, A. F., KRIMSKY, I., FROM, A., et al.: Action of gold thioglucose on pericapillary structures in the ventromedial hypothalamus. *J. Pathol.,* 129:73, 1979.

107. REZEK, M. and KROEGER, E. A.: Glucose antimetabolites and hunger. *J. Nutr.,* 106:143, 1976.

108. THOMPSON, D. A. and CAMPBELL, R. G.: Hunger in humans controlled by 2-deoxy-d-glucose glucoprivic control of taste preference and food intake. *Science,* 198:1065, 1977.

109. TONGE, D. A. and OATLEY, K.: Feeding and arteriovenous differences of blood glucose in the rat after injection with 2-deoxy-D-glucose and after food deprivation. *Physiol. Behav.,* 10:497, 1973.

110. BOOTH, D. H.: Modulation of the feeding response to peripheral insulin, 2-deoxy-glucose or 3-0-methyl glucose injection. *Physiol. Behav.,* 8:1069, 1972.

111. HOEBEL, B. G. and TEITELBAUM, P.: Weight regulation in normal and hypothalamic hyperphagic rats. *J. Comp. Physiol. Psychol.,* 61:189, 1966.

112. STUNKARD, A. J., VAN ITALLIE, T. B., and REISS, B. B.: Mechanism of satiety: Effect of glucagon on gastric hunger contractions in man. *Proc. Soc. Exp. Biol. Med.,* 89:258, 1955.

113. SALTER, J. M.: Metabolic effects of glucagon in the Wistar rat. *Am. J. Clin. Nutr.,* 8:535, 1960.

114. JANOWITZ, H. D. and GROSSMAN, M. I.: Some factors affecting the food intake of normal dogs and dogs with esophagostomy and gastric fistula. *Am. J. Physiol.,* 159:143, 1949.

115. RUSSEK, M.: Demonstration of an hepatic glucosensitive mechanism on food intake. *Physiol. Behav.,* 5:1207–1209, 1970.

116. RUSSEK, M.: A conceptual equation of intake control. In: D. Novin, W. Wyrwicka, and G. A. Bray (Eds.), *Hunger: Basic Mechanisms and Clinical Implications.* New York: Raven Press, 1976, p. 327.

117. VANDER WEELE, D. A. and SANDERSON, J. D.: Peripheral glucosensitive satiety in the rabbit and the rat. In: D. Novin, W. Wyrwicka, and G. A. Bray (Eds.), *Hunger: Basic Mechanisms and Clinical Implications.* New York: Raven Press, 1976, p. 383.

118. STEPHENS, D. B. and BALDWIN, B. A.: The lack of effect of intrajugular or intraportal injection of glucose or amino-acids on food intake in pigs. *Physiol. Behav.,* 12:923, 1974.

119. NOVIN, D., VANDER WEELE, D., and REZEK, M.: Infusion of 2-Deoxy-D-glucose into the hepatic-portal system causes eating: Evidence for peripheral glucoreceptors. *Science,* 181:858, 1973.

120. NOVIN, D., SANDERSON, J. D., and VANDER WEELE, D. A.: The effect of isotonic glucose on eating as a function of feeding condition and infusion site. *Physiol. Behav.,* 13:3, 1974.

121. NOVIN, D.: Visceral mechanisms in the control of food intake. In: D. Novin, W. Wyrwicka, and G. A. Bray (Eds.), *Hunger: Basic Mechanisms and Clinical*

*Implications.* New York: Raven Press, 1976, p. 357.

122. COHN, C. and JOSEPH, D.: Influence of body weight and body fat on appetite of "normal," lean and obese rats. *Yale J. Biol. Med.,* 34:598, 1962.
123. MROSOVSKY, N. and SHERRY, D. F.: Animal anorexias. *Science,* 207:837, 1980.
124. MROSOVSKY, N. and FISHER, K. C.: Sliding set points for body weight in ground squirrels during the hibernation season. *Can. J. Zool.,* 48:241, 1970.
125. FLEMING, D. A.: Food intake studies in parabiotic rats. *Ann. N. Y. Acad. Sci.,* 157:985, 1969.
126. BROOKS, C. McC. and LAMBERT, E. F.: A study on the effect of limitations of food intake and the method of feeding on the rate of weight gain during hypothalamic obesity in the albino rat. *Am. J. Physiol.,* 147:695, 1946.
127. YOUNG, V. R. and SCRIMSHAW, N. S.: The physiology of starvation. *Sci. Am.,* 225:14, 1971.
128. CAHILL, G. F., JR.: Obesity and the control of fuel metabolism. In: G. A. Bray and J. E. Bethune (Eds.), *Treatment and Management of Obesity.* Hagerstown, MD: Harper and Row, 1974, p. 3.
129. BJORNTORP, P., BERGMAN, H., VARNAUSKAS, E., et al.: Lipid metabolization in relation to body composition in man. *Metabolism,* 18:820, 1969.
130. WOODS, S. C. and PORTE, D., JR.: Insulin and the set-point regulation of body weight. In: D. Novin, W. Wyrwicka, and G. A. Bray (Eds.), *Hunger: Basic Mechanisms and Clinical Implications.* New York: Raven Press, 1976, p. 273.
131. YORK, D. A. and BRAY, G. A.: Dependence of hypothalamic obesity on insulin the pituitary and the adrenal gland. *Endocrinology,* 90:885, 1972.
132. POWLEY, T. L. and OPSAHL, C. A.: Ventromedial hypothalamic obesity abolished by subdiaphragmatic vagotomy. *Am. J. Physiol.,* 226:25, 1974.
133. LEVITSKY, D. A., FAUST, I., and GLASSMAN, M.: The ingestion of food and the recovery of body weight following fasting in the naive rat. *Physiol. Behav.,* 17: 575, 1976.
134. ROTHWELL, N. J. and STOCK, M. J.: A role of brown adipose tissue in diet-induced thermogenesis. *Nature,* 28L:31, 1979.
135. SIMS, E. A. H., DANFORTH, E., JR., HORTON, E. S. et al.: Endocrine and metabolic effects of experimental obesity in man. *Rec. Prog. Horm. Res.,* 29:457–487, 1973.
136. BROBECK, J. R.: Food and temperature. In: G. Pincus (Ed.), *Recent Progress in Hormone Research.* New York: Academic Press, 1960, p. 439.
137. WINSLOW, C. E. A. and HERRINGTON, L. P.: *Temperature and Human Life Treatment.* Princeton: University Press, 1949.
138. BONDY, P. K.: Metabolic obesity? *N. Engl. J. Med.,* 303:1057, 1980.
139. ANDERSON, G. H.: Control of protein and energy intake: Role of plasma amino acids and brain neurotransmitters. *Can. J. Physiol. Pharmacol.,* 57:1043, 1979.
140. BOOTH, D. A.: Food intake compensation for increase or decrease in the protein content of the diet. *Behav. Biol.,* 12:31, 1974.
141. ROZIN, P.: Are carbohydrate and protein intakes separately regulated? *J. Comp. Physiol. Psychol.,* 65:23, 1968.
142. MUSTEN, B., PEACE, D., and ANDERSON, G. H.: Food intake regulation in the weanling rat: Self-selection of protein and energy, *J. Nutr.,* 104:563, 1974.
143. FRYER, J. H., MOORE, N. S., WILLIAMS, H. H., et al.: A study of the interrela-

tionship of the energy yielding nutrients, blood glucose levels and subjective appetite in man. *J. Lab. Clin. Med.,* 45:684, 1955.

144. ANDERSON, G. H., LEPROHAN, C., CHAMBERS, J. W., et al.: Intact regulation of protein intake during the development of hypothalamic or genetic obesity in rats. *Physiol. Behav.,* 23:751, 1979.

145. HARPER, A. E.: Protein and amino acids in the regulation of food intake. In: D. Novin, W. Wyrwicka, and G. A. Bray (Eds.), *Hunger: Basic Mechanisms and Clinical Implications.* New York: Raven Press, 1976, p. 103.

146. ASHLEY, D. V. M. and ANDERSON, G. H.: Correlation between the plasma tryptophan to neutral amino acid ratio and protein intake in the self-selecting weanling rat. *J. Nutr.,* 105:1412, 1975.

147. ANDERSON, G.H. and ASHLEY, D. V. M.: Correlation of plasma tyrosine to phenylalanine ratio with energy intake in self-selecting weanling rats. *Life Sci.,* 21:1227, 1977.

148. PARDRIDGE, W. M.: Regulation of amino acid availability to the brain. In: R. J. Wurtman and J. J. Wurtman (Eds.), *Nutrition and the Brain,* Vol. I. New York: Raven Press, 1977, p. 141.

149. WOODGER, T. L., SIREK, A., and ANDERSON, G. H.: Diabetes, dietary tryptophan and protein intake regulation in weanling rats. *Am. J. Physiol.,* 236: R307, 1979.

150. GIBSON, C. J. and WURTMAN, R. J.: Physiological control of brain norepinephrine synthesis by brain tyrosine concentration. *Life Sci.,* 22:1399, 1978.

151. FERNSTROM, J. D.: The effect of nutritional factors on brain amino acid levels and monoamine synthesis. *Fed. Proc. Fed. Am. Soc. Exp. Biol.,* 35:1151, 1976.

152. JORDAN, H. A.: Voluntary intragastric feeding: Oral and gastric contributions to food intake and hunger in man. *J. Comp. Physiol. Psychol.,* 68:498, 1969.

153. SNOWDON, C. T.: Motivation, regulation, and the control of meal parameters with oral and intragastric feeding. *J. Comp. Physiol. Psychol.,* 69:91, 1969.

154. CANNON, W. B. and WASHBURN, A. L.: An explanation of hunger. *Am. J. Physiol.,* 29:441, 1912.

155. CARLSON, A. J.: *The Control of Hunger in Health and Disease.* Chicago: University of Chicago Press, 1916.

156. LORBER, S. and SHAY, H.: The effect of insulin and glucose on gastric motor activity of dogs. *Gastroenterology,* 43:564, 1965.

157. SUDSANEH, S. and MAYER, J.: Relation of metabolic events to gastric contractions in the rat. *Am. J. Physiol.,* 197:269, 1959.

158. JANOWITZ, H. D.: Role of the gastrointestinal tract in regulation of food intake. In: C. F. Code (Ed.), *Handbook of Physiology,* Sect. 6, Vol. 1. Washington, DC: American Physiological Society, 1967, p. 219.

159. INGLEFINGER, F. J.: The late effects of total and subtotal gastrectomy. *N. Engl. J. Med.,* 231:321, 1944.

160. GROSSMAN, M. I. and STEIN, I. F., JR.: Vagotomy and the hunger producing action of insulin in man. *J. Appl. Physiol.,* 1:263, 1948.

161. KING, B. M., CARPENTER, R. G., STAMOUTOS, B. A., et al.: Hyperphagia and obesity following ventromedial hypothalamic lesions in rats with subdiaphragmatic vagotomy. *Physiol. Behav.,* 20:643, 1978.

162. WAMPLER, R. S. and SNOWDON, C. T.: Development of VMH obesity in vagot-

omized rats. *Physiol. Behav.,* 22:85, 1979.
163. KRAL, J. G.: Effects of truncal vagotomy on body weight and hyperinsulinemia in morbid obesity. *Am. J. Clin. Nutr.,* 33:416, 1980.
164. DAVIS, J. D. and COLLINS, B. J.: Distention of the small intestine, satiety, and the control of food intake. *Am. J. Clin. Nutr.,* 31s:255, 1978.
165. GIBBS, J. and SMITH, G. P.: The gut and preabsorptive satiety. *Acta-Hepato. Gastroenterol.,* 25:413, 1978.
166. SHARE, I., MARTYNIUK, E., and GROSSMAN, M. I.: Effect of prolonged intragastric feeding on oral food intake in dogs. *Am. J. Physiol.,* 169:229, 1952.
167. SUGAR, M. and GATES, G.: Artificial gastric distension and neonatal feeding and hunger reflexes. *Child. Psychiat. Hum. Dev.,* 9:206, 1979.
168. GIBBS, J., FALASCO, J. D., MADDISON, S., et al.: The role of the intestine in satiety examined in sham feeding rhesus monkeys. *6th International Conference on the Physiology of Food and Fluid Intake,* 1977(abst).
169. TRACK, N.: The gastrointestinal endocrine system. *Can. Med. Assoc. J.,* 122: 287, 1980.
170. RAYFORD, P. L., MILLER, T. A., and THOMPSON, J. C.: Secretin, cholecystokinin and newer gastrointestinal hormones. N. Engl. J. Med., 294:1093, 1976.
171. SERNKA, T. and JACOBSON, E.: *Gastrointestinal Physiology.* Baltimore: Williams and Wilkins, 1979.
172. BRYANT, M. G., POLAK, J. M., MODLIN, I., et al.: Possible dual role for vasoactive intestinal peptide as gastrointestinal hormone and neurotransmitter substance. *Lancet,* 1:991, 1976.
173. CATALAND, S., CROCKETT, S. E., BROWN, J. C., et al.: Gastric inhibitory polypeptide (GIP) stimulation by oral glucose in man. *J. Clin. Endocr. Metab.,* 39: 223, 1974.
174. ADELSON, J. W. and ROTHMAN, S. S.: Candidate hormones of the gut 11. *Gastroenterology,* 67:731, 1974.
175. GREENBERG, G. R., McCLOY, R. F., ADRIAN, T. E., et al.: Inhibition of pancreas and gallbladder by pancreatic polypeptide. *Lancet,* 2:1280, 1978.
176. GATES, R. J. and LAZARUS, N. R.: The ability of pancreatic polypeptide (APP and BPP) to return to normal the hyperglycaemia hyperinsulinemia and weight of New Zealand obese mice. *Horm. Res.,* 8:189, 1977.
177. MARCO, J., ZULUETA, M. A., CORREAS, I., et al.: Reduced pancreatic polypeptide secretion in obese subjects. *J. Clin. Endocr. Metab.,* 50:744, 1980.
178. BENNETT, H. P. J. and McMARTIN, C.: Peptide hormones and their analogues: Distribution, clearance from the circulation and inactivation in vivo. *Am. Soc. Pharmacol. Exptl. Ther.,* 30:247, 1979.
179. GIBBS, J., YOUNG, R. C., and SMITH, G. P.: Cholecystokinin elicits satiety in rats with open gastric fistula. *Nature,* 245:323, 1973.
180. MAYER, J. H. and GROSSMAN, M. I.: Comparison of D- and L-phenylalanine as pancreatic stimulants. *Am. J. Physiol.,* 22:1058, 1972.
181. SMITH, G. P. and GIBBS, J.: Cholecystakinin and satiety: Theoretic and therapeutic implications in hunger. In: D. Novin, W. Wyrwicka, and G. A. Bray (Eds.), *Hunger: Basic Mechanisms and Clinical Implications.* New York: Raven Press, 1976, p. 349.
182. GREENWAY, F. L. and BRAY, G. A.: Cholecystokinin and satiety. *Life Sci.,* 21: 769, 1977.

183. STURDEVANT, R. and GOETZ, M.: Effect of cholecystokinin on food intake in man. *Clin. Res.,* 98A, 1976.
184. STURDEVANT, R. A. L. and GOETZ, H.: Cholecystokinin both stimulates and in-inhibits human food intake. *Nature,* 261:713, 1977.
185. STACHER, G., BAUER, H., and STEINRINGER, H.: Cholecystokinin decreases appetite and activation evoked by stimuli arising from the preparation of a meal in man. *Physiol. Behav.,* 23:325, 1979.
186. NEMEROFF, C. B., OSBAHAR, A. J., III, BISSETTE, G., et al.: Cholecystokinin inhibits tail-pinch-induced eating in rats. *Science,* 200:793, 1978.
187. MORLEY, J. E.: The neuroendocrine control of appetite. *Life Sci.,* 27:355, 1980.
188. DOCKRAY, G. J.: Immunochemical evidence of cholecystokinin-like peptides in brain. *Nature,* 264:568, 1976.
189. MULLER, J. E., STRAUS, E., and YALOW, R. S.: Cholecystokinin and its COOH-terminal octapeptide in the pig brain. *Proc. Nat. Acad. Sci.,* 74:3035, 1977.
190. STRAUS, E. and YALOW, R. S.: Cholecystokinin in the brains of obese and non-obese mice. *Science,* 203:68, 1979.
191. MADDISON, S.: Intraperitoneal and intracranial cholecystokinin depress operant responding for food. *Physiol. Behav.,* 19:819, 1978.
192. DELLA-FERA, M. A. and BAILE, C. A.: Cholecystokinin octapeptide: Continuous picomole injections into the cerebral ventricles of sheep suppress feeding. *Science,* 206:471, 1979.
193. STUNKARD, A. J.: From explanation to action in psychosomatic medicine: The case of obesity. Presidential Address—1974. *Psychosom. Med.,* 37:195, 1975.
194. BOOTH, D.A.: Satiety and appetite are conditioned reactions. *Psychosom. Med.,* 39:76, 1977.
195. LE MAGNEN, J.: Sur le mecanisme d'établissement des appétits caloriques. *Comp. Rend. Acad. Sci.,* 240:2436, 1955.
196. GARCIA, J., KIMELDORF, D. J., and KOELLING, R. A.: Conditioned aversion to saccharin resulting from gamma radiation. *Science,* 122:157, 1955.
197. ROGERS, W. L. and ROZIN, P.: Novel food preferences in thiamine-deficient rats. *Comp. Physiol. Psychol.,* 61:1, 1966.
198. BRUCH, H.: *Eating Disorders.* New York: Basic Books, 1973.
199. GLUCKSMAN, M. L., RAND, C. S. W., and STUNKARD, A. J.: Psychodynamics of obesity. *J. Am. Acad. Psychoanal.,* 6:103, 1978.
200. GARNER, D. M., GARFINKEL, P. E., and MOLDOFSKY, H.: Perceptual experiencies in anorexia nervosa and obesity. *Can. J. Psychiatry,* 23:249, 1978.
201. CODDINGTON, R. D. and BRUCH, H.: Gastric perceptivity in normal, obese and schizophrenic subjects. *Psychosomatics,* 11:571, 1970.
202. CAMPBELL, R. G., HASHIM, S. A., and VAN ITALLIE, T. B.: Studies of food intake regulation in man: Responses to variations in nutritive density in lean and obese subjects. *N. Engl. J. Med.,* 285:1402, 1971.
203. NISBETT, R. E.: Determinants of food intake in obesity. *Science,* 159:1254, 1968.
204. NISBETT, R. E.: Eating behavior and obesity in men and animals. *Adv. Psychosom. Med.,* 7:173, 1972.
205. HASHIM, S. A. and VAN ITALLIE, T. B.: Studies in normal and obese subjects with a monitored food dispensing device. *Ann. N.Y. Acad. Sci.,* 131:654, 1965.
206. CABANAC, M. and DUCLAUX, R.: Obesity: Absence of satiety aversion to sucrose. *Science,* 168:496, 1970.

207. GRINKER, J. A.: Effects of metabolic state on taste parameters and intake: Comparisons of human and animal obesity. In: J. M. Weiffenbach (Ed.), *Taste and Development.* DHEW Publication No. (NIH) 76-1068, 1977, p. 309.
208. STELLAR, E.: Sweet preference and hedonic experience. In: J. M. Weiffenbach (Ed.), *Taste and Development.* DHEW Publication No. (NIH) 76-1068, Public Health Service, National Institutes of Health, 1977, p. 363.
209. UNDERWOOD, P. J., BELTON, E., and HULME, P.: Aversion to sucrose in obesity. *Proc. Nutr. Soc.,* 32:94, 1973 (abst).
210. GARFINKEL, P. E., MOLDOFSKY, H., GARNER, D. M., et al.: Body awareness in anorexia nervosa: Disturbances in "Body Image" and "Satiety." *Psychosom. Med.,* 40:487, 1978.
211. GARFINKEL, P. E., MOLDOFSKY, H., and GARNER, D. M.: The stability of perceptual disturbances in anorexia nervosa. *Psychol. Med.,* 9:703, 1979.
212. WOOLEY, S. C.: Physiologic versus cognitive factors in short term food regulation in the obese and nonobese. *Psychosom. Med.,* 34:62, 1972.
213. WOOLEY, O. W.: Long term food regulation in the obese and nonobese. *Psychosom. Med.,* 33:436, 1971.
214. WOOLEY, O. W., WOOLEY, S. C., and DUNHAM, R. B.: Can calories be perceived and do they affect hunger in obese and nonobese humans? *J. Comp. Physiol. Psychol.,* 80:250, 1972.
215. WOOLEY, O. W., WOOLEY, S. C., and DUNHAM, R. B.: Calories and sweet taste: Effects on sucrose preference in the obese and nonobese. *Physiol. Behav.,* 9: 765, 1972.
216. WOOLEY, O. W., WOOLEY, S. C., and WOODS, W. A.: Effect of calories on appetite for palatable food in obese and nonobese humans. *J. Comp. Physiol. Psychol.,* 89:619, 1975.
217. SCHACHTER, S.: *Emotion, Obesity and Crime.* New York: Academic Press, 1971.
218. SCHACHTER, S. and GROSS, L. P.: Manipulated time and eating behavior. *J. Pers. Soc. Psychol.,* 10:98, 1968.
219. NISBETT, R. E.: Taste deprivation and weight determinants of eating behavior. *J. Pers. Soc. Psychol.,* 10:107, 1968.
220. NISBETT, R. E. and KANOUSE, D. E.: Obesity, food deprivation, and supermarket shopping behavior. *J. Pers. Soc. Psychol.,* 12:289, 1969.
221. RODIN, J.: Changes in perceptual responsiveness following jejunoileostomy: Their potential role in reducing food intake. *Am. J. Clin. Nutr.,* 33:457, 1980.
222. RODIN, J. and SLOCHOWER, J.: Externality in the nonobese: The effects of environmental responsiveness on weight. *J. Pers. Soc. Psychol.,* 29:557, 1976.
223. BRAY, G. A., DAHMS, W. T., ATKINSON, R. L., et al.: Factors controlling food intake: A comparison of dieting and intestinal bypass. *Am. J. Clin. Nutr.,* 33: 376, 1980.
224. HERMAN, C. P. and MACK, D.: Restrained and unrestrained eating. *J. Pers.,* 43: 647, 1975.
225. HERMAN, C. P. and POLIVY, J.: Anxiety, restraint and eating behavior. *J. Pers.,* 84:666, 1975.
226. POLIVY, J. and HERMAN, C. P.: Effects of a model on eating behavior: The induction of a restrained eating style. *J. Pers.,* 47:100, 1979.
227. POLIVY, J.: Caloric perception and regulation of intake in restrained and unre-

strained subjects. *Addict. Behav.,* 1:237, 1976.
228. POLIVY, J. and HERMAN, C. P.: Clinical depression and weight change: A complex relation. *J. Abnorm. Psychol.,* 85:338, 1976.
229. POLIVY, J. and HERMAN, C. P.: The effects of alcohol on eating behavior: Disinhibition or sedation? *Addict. Behav.,* 1:121, 1976.
230. DE GARINE, I.: The socio-cultural aspects of nutrition. *Ecol. Food Nutr.,* 1:143, 1972.
231. ROBSON, J. R. K.: Commentary: Changing food habits in developing countries. *Ecol. Food Nutr.,* 4:251, 1976.
232. CRISP, A. H., PALMER, R. L., and KALUCY, R. S.: How common is anorexia nervosa? A prevalence study. *Br. J. Psychiatry,* 128:549, 1976.
233. RAKOFF, V.: The psychiatric aspects of obesity. *Mod. Treat.,* 4:1111, 1967.
234. SONTAG, S.: *Illness as Metaphor.* New York: Farrar, Strauss and Giroux, 1978.
235. GARNER, D. M., GARFINKEL, P. E., SCHWARTZ, D., et al.: The cultural expectation of thinness in women. *Psychol. Reports,* 47:483, 1980.

# 2

# The Diagnosis and Treatment of Anorexia Nervosa

*Katherine A. Halmi, M. D.*

Although anorexia nervosa is regarded as a relatively recent illness, it did, in fact, exist as early as the 13th century. The first well documented case of anorexia nervosa is that of Princess Margaret of Hungary. After the Tarter invasion, King Bela IV of Hungary promised that if the Mongols left, he would dedicate his next child to God. For this baby daughter, born in 1245, he had cloisters built, and she was then raised by nuns. The details of Margaret's life are well documented in Vatican records, because shortly after her death, canonization proceedings were initiated. She was declared a saint in the 20th century.

Margaret had the typical premorbid personality and course of anorexia nervosa. As a child, she excelled in her studies and in all the chores of the monastery. Later, when the fortunes of Hungary had improved, her father changed his mind and wanted to marry her to a proper suitor. At this time she became upset and vowed to make herself as unattractive as possible. She began to practice the austerities of fasting, deprivation of sleep, exhausting menial work, and other bodily penance to an utterly heroic degree. She was always there when there was work to be done. When her family came to visit her, she would have been expected, according to custom, to take meals with them in the parlor, but she would never do this. Often she would sit at the table with the rest of the community and would allow all the food to pass her by un-tasted. When she would eat, she would do so sparingly. Sometimes it happened that the prioress wished to exempt her of duties because of Margaret's obvious frailty. The prioress would send for Margaret to tell her not to fast for a time. On such occasions, Margaret would stand in silence and weep until the prioress, conquered by her tears, let her free to fast as she pleased.

Often Margaret served in the refectory. While the sisters were eating, she would slip away to pray before the crucifix in the church. She made a special practice of cleaning fish and scouring the pots and pans in the kitchen every day. She would also clean and joint the meat, and prepare it on the spit. She was described as never being idle and always most obedient. Her mind was clear and alert. She died in 1271 at the age of 26, a few days after she developed a violent fever. Her body was described as a poor, wasted one (1).

One can never be certain that St. Margaret actually had anorexia nervosa. However, there are some features in the description of her life that allow one to make a cogent argument for the diagnosis. She obviously refused to maintain her weight in a normal range. She fasted continuously and not in relation to religious observances. The combination of overactivity and an abundance of energy associated with an emaciated state is seldom seen in persons fasting for religious reasons. The large amount of time she spent around food in the kitchen and preparing food for her sisters is characteristic anorectic behavior, and, finally, she would certainly have to be considered as from the upper socioeconomic class.

The diagnostic criteria of anorexia nervosa in the Diagnostic and Statistical Manual of Mental Disorders (DSM-III) are descriptive and support the concept of anorexia nervosa as being a disorder and not a specific disease. The DSM-III criteria for anorexia nervosa are presented in Table I. Due to an error in editing the final criteria for anorexia nervosa, amenorrhea was omitted. Patients with DSM-III criteria for anorexia nervosa may, on occasion, also meet DSM-III criteria for depression and schizophrenia. The latter diagnosis will be rare, but can probably be made in two to three percent of the anorectic population (2). The new multi-axial and descriptive approach to diagnosis in the

TABLE 1
Diagnostic Material for Anorexia Nervosa

1) Intense fear of becoming obese, which does not diminish as weight loss progresses.
2) Disturbance of body image, e.g., claiming to "feel fat" even when emaciated.
3) Weight loss of at least 25% of original body weight or, if under 18 years of age, weight loss from original body weight plus projected weight gain expected from growth charts may be combined to make the 25%.
4) Refusal to maintain body weight over a minimal normal weight for age and height.
5) No known physical illness that would account for weight loss.

DSM-III allows the possibility of making several diagnoses on Axis I in addition to making the diagnosis of a personality disorder on Axis II. On those rare occasions when the diagnosis of schizophrenia can be made, it will usually occur after the patient has had anorexia nervosa for a long duration (3).

Often anorexia nervosa patients will have an Axis II diagnosis of a personality disorder. It is not unusual for anorexia nervosa patients to meet criteria for borderline personality disorder, compulsive personality disorder, histrionic personality disorder, schizoid personality, or atypical personality disorder. Recognition of the fact that a variety of personality disorders can exist within the diagnosis of anorexia nervosa was made as far back as 20 years ago by Dally (4). He categorized his anorexia nervosa patients into: 1) hysterical personality type; 2) compulsive personality type; and 3) mixed personality type. Obviously, the existence of a specific personality disorder will affect the prognosis of anorexia nervosa in that patient. Treatment strategies must take into account the underlying personality disorder. Reliable diagnoses of personality disorders are, however, difficult to make. The DSM-III at least provides a descriptive structure on which personality diagnoses can be made and thus a modality for systematic studies of personality disorders among different investigators. The great variety of outcome in various follow-up studies of anorexia nervosa patients could well be explained by a biased sampling of personality disorders within the population's study (see Appendix — Case Study 1).

The diagnostic criteria for anorexia nervosa seem obvious. However, the diagnosis is frequently not easy to make. One of the major reasons for this is that anorectic patients are not motivated for treatment and deny many of the characteristic symptoms of the disorder. Because anorexia nervosa is so well popularized, most patients know the criteria that constitute a diagnosis of anorexia nervosa. Often, it is necessary to obtain information from family or friends who have observed the patient's behavior. At times, not even family can provide sufficient information, and it is necessary to hospitalize the patient for diagnostic observation.

Anorectic patients lose weight through a drastic reduction in total food intake, with a disproportionate decrease in high carbohydrate and fat-containing foods. Unfortunately, the term "anorexia" is a misnomer. The loss of appetite in anorexia nervosa is rare until the patient is emaciated. Anorectic patients are constantly thinking about food. Although they may deny this, one can assume they are thinking about food when it is reported that they are preoccupied with collecting recipes and preparing elaborate meals for others but refusing to eat themselves. Anorectic patients will hoard food and hide it.

Body image distortion in anorexia nervosa is a perplexing phenomenon.

The amount of body image distortion has been measured by various investigators using a visual size estimation apparatus. All studies found emaciated anorectic patients to overestimate the widths of their various body parts. However, there were no significant differences in body perception indices between anorectic patients and normal age-matched controls (5, 6, 7). Large individual differences between patients in the estimation of their body size occurred. In one study it was found that the degree of body image disturbance was related to the severity of the illness (5). Those patients with the greatest overestimation of body parts were also those who were most malnourished and who had experienced the most failures to respond to treatment in previous hospitalizations. They had also gained less weight during treatment. Patients who vomited overestimated their size more than those who did not.

All anorectic patients have an intense fear of gaining weight and becoming obese. This fear exists even in the face of increasing cachexia. Delayed psychosocial sexual development is often seen in adolescents with anorexia nervosa. With the onset of the disorder in adults, there is an associated marked decrease in interest in sex.

Anorectic patients often come to medical attention because of the amenorrhea which appears in one-third of the cases before noticeable weight loss has occurred. In the emaciated state, anorectic patients have a regressed pattern of luteinizing hormone (LH) secretion found in prepubertal and pubertal girls. This regressed pattern of LH secretion changes to a more mature one with weight gain. Although restoration of a normal body weight is a prerequisite to the resumption of menstruation, factors other than nutritional state—most likely psychological in nature—contribute to the prolonged amenorrhea (8). One study has shown that the return of normal menstruation was directly associated with a good psychological state and social adjustment (3).

There is indirect evidence that the incidence of anorexia nervosa has been increasing in the past 10 years. Most of the evidence comes from reports that more patients with anorexia nervosa are being diagnosed and treated in various clinics and hospitals. The best estimate of the occurrence of the disorder is from the following prevalence study. It was estimated that there was one severe case of anorexia nervosa in every 200 girls over the age of 12 in England (9).

Anorexia nervosa occurs predominantly in females. The percentage of males in an anorectic population varies between four and six percent (10, 11). Only indirect evidence is available for familial occurrence of the disorder. One study found that the morbidity risk for a sister of an anorectic patient is about 6.6 percent, and greatly exceeds normal expectation (2). In a study of 56 families with anorexia nervosa, Kalucy et al. (12) found that 16 percent of the mothers and 23 percent of the fathers had a history of significant low adolescent weight or weight phobia. They were not able to make a specific diagnosis of anorexia nervosa in the parents.

Most cases of anorexia nervosa occur or have their onset between the ages of 10 and 30. In a recent study, a bimodal distribution of age onset was found with peaks at 14½ and 18 years (13). These ages coincide with the time when a young woman is attempting to become more independent from her family. At age 14½ most young women are about to enter high school, and, at age 18, they are preparing to leave home for a job or to attend college. Most young women are concerned about their appearance at this time because an attractive appearance is equated by them with better acceptance from the outside world. Almost all young women diet in order to improve their appearance as a result of the great emphasis placed on the association of beauty and thinness in our present culture.

Bulimia (rapid consumption of large amounts of food in a short period of time) is a behavior that is present in about half of anorexia nervosa patients (14, 15, 16). Two recent studies (15, 16) systematically assessed anorectic patients with bulimia and compared them with anorectic patients who only fasted. Both studies provided substantial evidence that those with bulimia form a distinct subgroup among patients with anorexia nervosa. Self-induced vomiting, laxative abuse, and diuretic abuse were behaviors far more prevalent in the bulimic anorectic patients than in the fasting ones. The bulimic group displayed impulsive behavior such as alcohol and street drug abuse, stealing, suicide attempts, and self-mutilation. Bulimic patients were more extroverted and had less denial of their illness and less denial of a strong appetite. They showed greater anxiety, depression, guilt, interpersonal sensitivity, and had more somatic complaints.

Bulimic patients present a special problem with regard to medical care. The self-induced vomiting can cause hypokalemia (low serum potassium level), which can lead to cardiac arrhythmias and, in some cases, sudden death. Chronic hypokalemia is also associated with the development of kidney tubule vacuoles and polyuria. It is advisable to obtain serum electrolyte levels on all anorectic patients with bulimia since there is a possibility of hypokalemia in all of these patients, and the treatment of hypokalemia requires immediate medical attention.

The presence of bulimia in anorexia nervosa has been associated with poor outcome in several studies (16, 17). Bulimia was found to be associated with a longer duration of illness, repeated hospitalizations, and poor social adjustment in comparison to fasting patients. Some bulimic patients describe a relief from stress and tension when they binge eat. It is likely that increased blood sugar levels from the enormous quantity of food eaten produce a relaxation and sleepiness. This type of relief from stress and tension is similar to that induced by alcohol and drugs and, hence, it is not surprising that there is a high association of alcohol and drug abuse in the bulimic anorectic patients (see Appendix—Case Study 2).

Bulimia also occurs in normal weight persons. The DSM-III criteria for bulimia are listed in Table 2. Results of a recent survey of a normal college population showed that 13 percent of the students experienced all of the major symptoms of bulimia as defined in the DSM-III criteria. Bulimia was more prevalent in females than males. Bulimia was also more prevalent in mildly overweight students or students in the upper limits of a normal weight range (18).

Bulimia is differentiated from anorexia nervosa by the fact that bulimic patients maintain their weights within a normal range. In bulimic patients, large fluctuations of weight, as much as 40 pounds, can occur, but still be within a normal range. Virtually no systematic outcome studies have been conducted on bulimic patients who maintain a normal weight.

Anorexia nervosa must also be differentiated from depressive disorders.

TABLE 2

Diagnostic Criteria for Bulimia

1) Recurrent episodes of binge eating (rapid consumption of a large amount of food in a discrete period of time, usually less than two hours).

2) At least three of the following:

    a) Consumption of high caloric, easily ingested food during a binge.

    b) Inconspicuous eating during a binge.

    c) Termination of such eating episodes by abdominal pain, sleep, social interruption, or self-induced vomiting.

    d) Repeated attempts to lose weight by severely restrictive diets, self-induced vomiting, or use of cathartics or diuretics.

    e) Frequent weight fluctuations greater than 10 pounds due to alternating binges and fasts.

3) Awareness that the eating pattern is abnormal and fear of not being able to stop eating voluntarily.

4) Depressed mood and self-deprecating thoughts following eating binges.

5) Bulimic episodes are not due to anorexia nervosa or any known physical disorder.

Generally, patients with depressive disorders complain of decreased appetite. They are not denying the existence of a normal appetite. Depressed patients are not preoccupied with the caloric content of food, nor do they collect recipes and spend an inordinate amount of time cooking and preparing foods. In contrast to depression, the overactivity of anorectic patients is directed towards losing weight, a factor which is constantly on their minds.

Weight loss and vomiting can occur in somatization disorder, but, generally, the weight loss is not as severe as in anorexia nervosa, nor is the patient as preoccupied with losing weight as is the anorectic patient. Amenorrhea is seldom a persistent finding in somatization disorder. However, on rare occasions, both the criteria of somatization disorder and anorexia nervosa can be met and, in this case, both diagnoses should be made.

Schizophrenic patients usually have delusions about the food they are eating but are seldom concerned with the caloric content of the food. Also, schizophrenic patients are rarely preoccupied with the fear of becoming obese and do not have the hyperactivity that is present in the anorectic patient.

The treatment of anorexia nervosa must be a multifaceted endeavor. It involves medical management, and personal, behavioral, and family therapies. All truly effective treatment programs consider and use all of these modalities of treatment. The consideration of effective treatment programs here is based on follow-up studies, since there are few controlled treatment studies of anorexia nervosa. There are two controlled studies comparing behavior therapy to a ward milieu program and one controlled study assessing the efficacy of the drug cyproheptadine (20, 21).

There are some general considerations that must be made when analyzing the efficacy of any treatment program for anorectic patients. There is a great variation in the outcome of the disorder. The course varies from spontaneous recovery without treatment, to recovery after one episode with treatment, fluctuating weight gains followed by relapses, to a gradually deteriorating course resulting in death. It is necessary to consider a sampling effect on the patient populations that are studied from hospitalized treatment programs. The crucial study captures all patients — those who refuse medical treatment, those who see only their family doctors, those who are sidetracked to internists or gynecologists, those who are treated by psychiatrists in general hospitals, and those who are admitted to conventional psychiatric hospitals from a given area.

The outcome of anorexia nervosa is related to certain prognostic factors that override the effect of treatment. Across all follow-up studies, the best indicator of good outcome is early age onset of the illness. The most consistent indicator of poor outcome is late age onset and the number of previous hospitalizations. Such factors as childhood neuroticism, parental conflicts, bulimia, vomiting, laxative abuse, and various behavioral manifestations such as obsessive-compulsive, hysterical, depressive, psychosomatic, neurotic, and the denying of symptoms have all been related to poor outcome in some studies and have not been thought to be significant in others. It is likely that the frequency of vomiting and laxative abuse is consistently related to poor outcome, but this has not been assessed in most studies (2, 3, 17).

The following study is an example of many of the problems listed above. This study evaluated the effects of drugs and behavior modification in 105 anorexia nervosa patients who were randomly assigned to drug or placebo and to behavior modification or its absence in each of three participating hospitals (22). Although the patients were randomly assigned to the drug and behavior modification variables, they were not randomly assigned to the three hospitals. The hospital was included as a "block" variable, so that any variability among hospitals would not be contained in the error mean square and would accordingly allow a more sensitive test of treatment variables. In this study large and significant differences were found among the hospitals in terms of weight gain. The greatest mean weight gain occurred with the greater degree of experience of the therapist. The greatest degree of weight gain also correlated with the degree of "structure" in the environmental milieu. However, when all the patient characteristics that interacted with weight gain were controlled for in statistical analyses, the hospital differences in weight gain were eliminated.

There are some general problems in the treatment of anorectic patients. Since most of these patients are disinterested in and even resistant to treatment, they are brought to a doctor's office unwillingly by agonizing relatives or friends. It is important to convince the patient that she will obtain relief from some unpleasant symptoms such as insomnia or depression. The relatives' support is essential in order for an effective treatment program to be conducted.

The immediate aim of treatment should be to restore the patient's nutritional state to normal. Considerable improvement in the patient's psychological state occurs with nutritional restoration (3). The psychological effect associated with emaciation can cause irritability, depression, preoccupation with food, and sleep disturbance. It is exceedingly difficult to accomplish a behavioral change with psychotherapy in an emaciated patient. Admitting the patient to a structured environment in a hospital allows for an efficient nutritional rehabilitation and a more rapid recovery. The more severely ill patients may cause an extremely difficult medical management problem. They may require daily monitoring of weight, fluid and caloric intake, and urine output. In a patient who is vomiting, frequent assessment of serum electrolytes is necessary. Since these patients are frequently fearful of various types of food, it is easier and more efficient to give all their nutrition in the form of a formula such as Sustacal which contains adequate amounts of vitamins, minerals, proteins, fatty acids, and carbohydrates, all conveniently blended so that the patient cannot selectively discard any item. Complications such as edema and distention of the stomach may occur if the patient is refed too rapidly. To avoid this, the patient should be given a daily caloric intake to maintain her present weight, plus 50 percent for activity. If the formula is given in size-equal feedings throughout the day, the patient will not have to ingest a large amount at any one time.

Hospitalization of anorectic patients has another advantage. It isolates them from a potentially noxious environment. This was recognized over 100 years ago by Sir William Gull when he recommended "the patient should be fed at regular intervals, and surrounded by persons who would have more influence over them, relatives and friends being generally the worst attendants" (23). Nursing treatment programs were developed from this principle. The patient is put to bed and must remain in bed until she achieves a normal weight for her age and height. At that time she is allowed more activity as she continues to cooperate and improve psychologically. Obviously, this nursing treatment program, which is used by both Crisp (24) and Russell (25) in England, is putting behavioral contingencies to work.

Recently, with the careful study of numerous investigators, the use of behavioral contingencies has become more sophisticated. Agras et al. (26), using the technique of systematic analysis, were able to demonstrate in five single case experiments the strong effect of regular feedback of weight and caloric intake information on weight gain. Other investigators have shown the effectiveness of various operant conditioning paradigms (27, 28). Most of these programs have positive reinforcements consisting of increased physical activity, visiting privileges, and social activities contingent on weight gain. Others have included powerful negative reinforcements, such as bedrest, isolation, and tube feeding. The most effective behavior therapy programs are individualized, that is, a behavior therapy program is set up only after a behavioral analysis of the patient is completed. Behavior therapy is most effective in the medical management and nutritional rehabilitation of the patient, although there are times when other target behaviors can be changed with behavior therapy.

Drugs can often be useful adjuncts in the treatment of anorexia nervosa.

The first drug used in treating anorectic patients was chlorpromazine (29). This medication is especially effective in the severely obsessive-compulsive anorectic patients. Phenothiazines are often associated with weight gain although no controlled studies have been conducted to prove this.

Another category of drugs frequently used in the treatment of anorexia nervosa is the antidepressant. Anorectic patients have some features in common with depressed patients — sleep disturbance, admission to feeling depressed, and obsessive concern over items other than food. Amitriptyline has been shown to be effective in inducing weight gain, and several uncontrolled studies (21, 30) suggest amitriptyline may be effective in the treatment of anorexia nervosa. Another drug that has been used is cyproheptadine. This drug is especially attractive because of its relatively benign side effects. In one controlled study, cyproheptadine was found to be effective in inducing weight gain in a subgroup of anorexia nervosa patients who were more emaciated, had a history of prior treatment failures, as well as a history of birth delivery complications (21). Single case reports of the use of other drugs in treating anorectic patients have appeared in the literature. However, there is no large series of open trial studies or controlled studies with any of these drugs. Lithium is definitely contraindicated in a patient who vomits or abuses laxatives or diuretics because of the possibility of rapid lithium toxicity.

Counseling family members is a necessary component to an effective treatment program for the anorectic patient. There is no evidence that family therapy as the sole form of treatment is effective. Other than case reports, there has been no systematic assessment of anorectic families reported in the literature. The same formula for family therapy should not be used for each anorectic family. Rather, each family should be carefully analyzed for problems unique to that family, and therapy with the family should correspond to the needs of that family. In some, it is often wise to do marital therapy with the parents and have only a few family therapy sessions. In others, it is effective to have separate sessions with mother and daughter or siblings and patient. Considerable variation of maladaptive interactional patterns exists within anorexia nervosa families, and, because of this, a treatment strategy for each individual family should be created.

The effectiveness of classical psychodynamically oriented therapy in the treatment of anorexia nervosa has been questioned by experienced psychoanalysts (32, 33). Most effective individual psychotherapy should focus on making the patient aware of her behavior and the effect it has on maintaining her illness. Attention is directed to the anorectic patient's fear of failure, fear of becoming independent from her family, and fear of accepting the responsibilities of an adult woman. There are other common themes dealt with in individual psychotherapy (34). The patient is repeatedly reminded of the fact that she is now dealing with new people whom she cannot incorporate into her previous maladaptive living pattern. She needs to control her environment, and her illness gives her a false sense of confidence and independence. A therapist must also deal with the tremendous amount of denial present. The patient's anxiety and preoccupation with her weight do not disappear after she regains her weight. Most need continuing individual therapy for varying periods of time depending on the severity of their illness and the existence and/or severity of an underlying personality disorder.

APPENDIX

*Case Study 1*

This 15-year-old Caucasian high school student lived with her parents and was referred for hospitalization because of having lost 20 pounds over the past 18 months.

Approximately 18 months prior to admission the patient reached her highest weight of 102 pounds. She was 4'10" tall. Her family, girlfriends, and boyfriends teased her about her large breasts, and she decided to diet in order to lose weight. She lost rapidly down to 81 pounds over a four-month period. She had her last menstrual period at the time she began dieting. The patient became so pleased with her weight loss that she decided her new goal would be to weigh 50 pounds.

After she began dieting, the patient developed a severe appetite. She was unable to control this appetite and developed a pattern of binge eating between midnight and 3 A.M., followed by self-induced vomiting or enemas. A few months later the patient began to take laxatives and diuretics regularly in order to maintain her weight. She exercised daily until a few months before hospitalization when she no longer had the strength to continue. The patient admitted to feeling depressed and having crying spells. She also described a sleep disturbance, both initial and intermittent. The patient's school performance deteriorated after the onset of anorexia nervosa.

The patient was a product of a normal pregnancy. She was bottle-fed and had a problem with colic for the first two months of her life. She was toilet trained at age two-and-a-half years. Throughout her childhood she always had a problem with eczema and later with hayfever in the spring. She obtained above-average grades in grade school. During the third and fourth grades she saw a psychologist because of problems at home—temper outbursts and fights with her parents. In seventh grade she again had problems with her parents and on several occasions ran away from home. She was suspended from school a number of times in seventh and eighth grades for disobeying rules and inciting classmates to act up. She was described as always talking and being disruptive in class.

At age 13 the patient developed a severe drinking problem. For about a seven-month period she drank beer or whiskey every day with her friends. Later she took LSD, mescaline, "speed," and "downers."

Before the onset of the dieting behavior, the patient made two dramatic and ineffective suicide attempts. On one occasion when she broke up with her boyfriend, she attempted to slit her wrists. On another, after fighting with some of her girlfriends, she took 10–15 diazepam tablets and was taken to a hospital emergency room to have her stomach pumped.

The patient's father is a 50-year-old psychologist in private practice. He was in psychotherapy for several years with the diagnosis of "anxiety neurosis." He is overweight. The patient's mother is 54 and works part-time as a family therapist with a degree in social work. She was also in psychotherapy for several years with a diagnosis of obsessive-compulsive neurosis. She is also mildly overweight. The patient has one younger brother aged 13 who is of normal weight and is good in sports and receives average grades in school. He had demonstrated no particular behavior problem.

On admission the patient was extremely quiet and spoke with a very high, childlike voice. She responded with great hesitation to questions; however, she did give a fairly accurate history. There was no evidence of a formal thought disorder. The patient stated she felt depressed and had recent crying spells. She acted and sounded like a frightened child.

Diagnosis—Axis I: Anorexia nervosa; Axis II: Personality disorder, borderline; Axis III: None; Axis IV: Psychosocial stresses: 4—moderate; Axis V: Highest level of adaptive functioning in past year: 3—good.

During her hospitalization, the patient was placed on a behavior therapy program. She reached her target weight in about six weeks. After this she was placed on enough calories to maintain that target weight and was given her food on trays. In the final stage of treatment she was able to eat at the "family" table with the other patients and to maintain her target weight.

The patient received individual psychotherapy twice weekly during her three-month hospitalization. In the initial phase of treatment, emphasis was placed on reducing her anxiety, alleviating her depressive symptoms, and helping her to feel less a passive victim of others' abuse and more a responsible person in control of her life. This was explored in several areas: the issue of hospitalization, which she blamed on her parents; the choice of target weight, which she blamed on the unit chief; and the issue of sexual teasing.

The patient had great difficulty acknowledging that the way others treated her, particularly boys her own age, had something to do with the way she presented herself. Her childlike manner and the effect of being coy and flirtatious to her adolescent peers were provocative. The patient had great difficulty in accepting feedback from the therapist but eventually began to dress differently and move differently, so that people began treating her with more respect, and she did have less difficulty keeping boys from "bothering" her. In the second phase of treatment, the patient developed a few moderately close girlfriends and began to explore some of the issues of her relationship with her family members.

The patient received weekly family therapy sessions with her parents and brother. She accused her family of criticizing her verbally and of physically hurting her. It became quite apparent that the parents were particularly insecure and sensitive and very critical of the patient's appearance — her clothes, weight, and manner. Despite attempts at intervening, the parents, particularly the mother, had great difficulty in refraining from criticizing the daughter. A second issue in family therapy was the basic disagreement between the parents in child-rearing rules. Both the mother's and father's backgrounds were explored to show how they had developed their particular attitudes in this case.

In addition to family treatment, the patient participated in group therapy on the ward twice weekly and in an anorectic patient group therapy once a week.

At the time of discharge the patient was much improved. She was eating normally and had maintained her target weight. She had changed many of her maladaptive behaviors. Discharge planning included outpatient individual psychotherapy and family therapy.

### Case Study Two

This 27-year-old single woman who lives with her parents was referred for hospitalization because her binge eating and vomiting had interfered with her ability to hold a job and have an acceptable social life.

The patient became very conscious of her weight when she was a senior in high school. At that time she was staying up late to study, and she developed the habit of eating large quantities of food at night. Her weight gradually rose from 115 to approximately 125 pounds. (She is 5'6" tall. A normal weight range for her would be between 115 and 145 pounds.) The patient stated at admission that she would like to weigh around 110 pounds but realized that 115 was a reasonable request for her. She also admitted that she would prefer to announce her height as 5'5" so that she could have a lower target weight.

After her senior year in high school, the patient began binge eating. This became much worse during her first year at college. She finished two years of college with a B+ average but was fairly isolated because of her persistent binge eating. She then transferred to another school, started dieting more vigorously, and had fluctuations of weight loss and gain within a normal range. She maintained an A− average, but during her last year of college started to gain and reached 135 pounds. At this time she began the habit of self-induced vomiting and using laxatives. After college the patient went through a series of jobs ranging from working at a ski resort to public information service. Her persistent binge eating and vomiting interfered with her work. The patient denied ever abusing alcohol or drugs.

The patient had normal developmental milestones and had no particular behavioral problems until her last year in high school.

The father is in his 60s and owns a very successful business. He is an immigrant from an eastern European country. He is in good mental and physical health. The mother is aged 59. She was born in Germany and came to this country just before World War II. The patient has one older sister who is single and lives alone but works for her parents. She is of normal weight and has had no particular problems.

On admission the patient was 20 pounds below the normal weight for her age and height. She was amenorrheic and preoccupied with fears of gaining weight. She was neatly dressed and had no evidence of thought disorder.

Diagnosis — Axis I: Anorexia nervosa; Axis II: None; Axis III: None; Axis IV: Psychosocial stressors: 4 — moderate. The patient's illness developed during her first year of college when she had to leave the protection of her family home; Axis V: poor. The patient has not been able to keep a job for any length of time because of her illness.

The patient was hospitalized for a three-month period during which she was placed on a behavioral therapy program for weight gain. The patient stopped her binge eating and vomiting immediately upon entering the hospital but proceeded to gain weight very slowly although steadily. She had individual psychotherapy several times weekly. The main themes dealt with were: the patient's conflict over wanting to be dependent and cared for and yet also wanting to establish herself as being capable and independent of others; the patient's need to protect her vulnerable self-esteem by attempting to maintain tight control over her own feelings and actions, as well as those of others; and the patient's relationships with others which were usually centered around subtle power struggles.

The patient was discharged to a day hospital program with long-term plans involving vocational rehabilitation.

## REFERENCES

1. KONRADYNE, G. M.: *Margitsziget.* Budapest: Kossuth Nyomda, 1973.
2. THEANDER, S.: Anorexia nervosa. *Acta. Psychiatr. Scand. Suppl.,* 214:29–31, 1970.
3. MORGAN, H. G. and RUSSELL, G. F. M.: Value of family background in clinical features as predictors of long term outcome in anorexia nervosa: Four-year follow-up study of 41 patients. *Psychol. Med.,* 5:355–371, 1975.
4. DALLY, P. J.: *Anorexia Nervosa.* New York: Grune and Statton, 1969.
5. CASPER, R. C., HALMI, K. A., GOLDBERG, S. C., ECKERT, E. D., and DAVIS, J. M.: Disturbances in body image estimation as related to other characteristics and outcome in anorexia nervosa. *Brit. J. Psychiat.,* 134:60–66, 1979.
6. CRISP, A. H. and KALUCY, R. S.: Aspects of the perceptual disorder in anorexia nervosa. *Br. J. Med. Psychol.,* 47:349–361, 1974.
7. BUTTON, E. J., FRANSELLA, F., and SLADE, P. D.: A reappraisal of body perception disturbance in anorexia nervosa. *Psychol. Med.,* 7:235–243, 1977.
8. HALMI, K. A.: Anorexia nervosa: Recent investigations. *Ann. Rev. Med.,* 29:137–148, 1978.
9. CRISP, A. H., PALMER, R. L., and KALUCY, R. S.: How common is anorexia nervosa? A prevalence study. *Brit. J. Psychiat.,* 128:549–554, 1976.
10. HALMI, K. A.: Anorexia nervosa: Demographic and clinical features in 94 cases. *Psychosom. Med.,* 36:18–26, 1974.
11. DALLY, P. J., GOMEZ, J., and ISSACS, A. J.: *Anorexia Nervosa.* London: William Heinemann Medical Books, 1979.
12. KALUCY, R. S., CRISP, A. H., and HARDING, B.: A study of 56 families with anorexia nervosa. *Brit. J. Med. Psychol.,* 50:455–500, 1977.
13. HALMI, K. A., CASPER, R. C., ECKERT, E. D., GOLDBERG, S. C., and DAVIS, J. M.: Unique features associated with age onset of anorexia nervosa. *Psychiat. Res.,* 209–215, 1979.
14. HSU, L. K. G., CRISP, A. H., and HARDING, B.: Outcome of anorexia nervosa. *Lancet,* 1:65, 1979.
15. CASPER, R. C., ECKERT, E. D., HALMI, K. A., GOLDBERG, S. C., and DAVIS, J. M.: The incidence and clinical significance of bulimia in patients with anorexia nervosa. *Arch. Gen. Psychiat.,* 37:1030–1035, 1980.
16. GARFINKEL, P. E., MOLDOFSKY, H., and GARNER, D. M.: The heterogeneity of anorexia nervosa. *Arch. Gen. Psychiat.,* 37:1036–1046, 1980.
17. HALMI, K. A., BRODLAND, G., and LONEY, J.: Prognosis in anorexia nervosa. *Ann. Intern. Med.,* 78:907–909, 1973.
18. HALMI, K. A., FALK, J., and SCHWARTZ, E.: Binge eating and vomiting: A survey of a college population. Submitted for publication, 1981.
19. HALMI, K. A., POWERS, P., and CUNNINGHAM, S.: Treatment of anorexia nervosa with behavior modification. *Arch. Gen. Psychiat.,* 32:93–96, 1975.
20. WULLIEMIER, F., ROSSEL, F., and SINCLAIR, K.: La thérapie comportementale de l'anorexie nerveuse. *J. Psychosom. Res.,* 19:267–272, 1975.
21. GOLDBERG, S. C., HALMI, K. A., ECKERT, E. D., CASPER, R. C., and DAVIS, J. M.: Cyproheptadine in anorexia nervosa. *Brit. J. Psychiat.,* 134:67–70, 1979.

22. HALMI, K. A., GOLDBERG, S. C., ECKERT, E. D., and DAVIS, J. M.: Pretreatment predictors of outcome in anorexia nervosa. *Brit. J. Psychiat.,* 134:71–78, 1979.
23. GULL, W.: Anorexia nervosa (apepsia hysterica, anorexia hysterica). *Trans. Clin., Soc. Lond.,* 7:22–28, 1874.
24. CRISP, A. H.: Clinical and therapeutic aspects of anorexia nervosa: A study of 30 cases. *J. Psychosom. Res.,* 9:67–78, 1965.
25. RUSSELL, G. F. M.: The management of anorexia nervosa. In: *Symposium— Anorexia Nervosa and Obesity.* Royal College of Physicians of Edinburgh. Publication No. 42:44. Edinburgh: N.A. Constable, 1973.
26. AGRAS, S., BARLOW, D. H., CHAPIN, H. N., ABEL, G., and LEITENBERG, H.: Behavior modification of anorexia nervosa. *Arch. Gen. Psychiat.,* 30:279–286, 1974.
27. BRADY, J. P. and RIEGER, W.: Behavior treatment of anorexia nervosa. In *Proceedings of the International Symposium on Behavior Modification.* New York: Appleton-Century-Crofts, 1972.
28. ECKERT, E. D., CASPER, R., GOLDBERG, S. C., HALMI, K. A., and DAVIS, J. M.: Behavior therapy in anorexia nervosa. *Brit. J. Psychiat.,* 134:55–59, 1979.
29. DALLY, P. J. and SARGANT, W.: A new treatment of anorexia nervosa. *Br. Med. J.,* 1:1770–1773, 1960.
30. NEEDLEMAN, H. L. and WABER, D.: The use of amitriptyline in anorexia nervosa. In: R. Vigersky (Ed.), *Proceedings of the International Anorexia Nervosa Conference, 1976,* New York: Raven Press, 1977, pp. 357–362.
31. MILLS, I. H.: Amitriptyline therapy in anorexia nervosa. *Lancet,* 2:687–690, 1976.
32. BRUCH, H.: Psychotherapy in primary anorexia nervosa. *J. Nerv. Ment. Dis.,* 150: 51–66, 1970.
33. ROLLINS, N. and BLACKWELL, A.: The treatment of anorexia nervosa in children and adolescents: Stage I. *J. Child Psychol. Psychiat.,* 9:81–91, 1968.
34. CRISP, A. H.: A treatment regimen for anorexia nervosa. *Brit. J. Psychiat.,* 112: 505–512, 1965.

# 3

# Two Psychological Treatments for Obesity: Psychoanalysis and Behavior Therapy

## Albert Stunkard, M.D.

Psychological factors have long been accorded an important place in the treatment of obesity. The treatment of obesity depends upon the establishment of a negative caloric balance, a balance achieved largely through the use of reducing diets (1). Psychological factors in the form of adherence are the key to the success of a reducing diet: If patients stick to their diets, they lose weight; if they break their diets, they do not. For many years physicians have paid attention to psychological factors in the treatment of their obese patients. But these efforts have generally been unsystematic, and psychological damage from scare tactics may have occurred as often as psychological benefit from more constructive approaches.

More systematic psychological approaches to the treatment of obesity and obese persons were introduced by Bruch (2), and both she and I (3) have described the long-term intensive psychotherapy of obese persons; but it is difficult to generalize from the experience of two specialized psychotherapists. Accordingly, we are fortunate that information has recently become available about the effect of clearly specified psychotherapeutic techniques applied by large numbers of therapists in a systematic manner to the treatment

Supported in part by Grant MH 31050 and a Research Scientist Award from the National Institute of Mental Health.

59

of obesity. This chapter will describe the results of two of these techniques—
psychoanalysis and behavior therapy. The goal of the chapter is to provide
readers with an idea of what to expect if they refer an obese patient for psychoanalysis or behavior therapy, or if they undertake such treatment themselves. These results are more favorable than has generally been realized.

PSYCHOANALYSIS

Even the suggestion that psychoanalysis might be useful in the treatment
of obese persons is apt to be met with skepticism, not the least on the part of
psychoanalysts themselves. The exuberant early days of psychoanalysis had
not included obesity among the many disorders for which cures had been
claimed, and even psychoanalysts themselves have doubted the value of
psychoanalysis for the treatment of obesity. Some of these doubts have
clearly resulted from the bias in the selection of obese patients for psychoanalysis and psychotherapy. Information about reducing diets is so widely
available that only people who have already failed to lose weight through
their own efforts become candidates for medical treatment. And only the
failures of medical treatment are referred to the psychotherapist. This sequence makes it easy to understand why the experience of psychotherapists
has led them to believe that obese people are difficult to treat and that their
obesity is unusually resistant to change.

Skepticism as to the usefulness of psychoanalysis in the treatment of
obesity is not based solely on the problem of selection bias. Just as serious a
problem has been the general lack of information. Until very recently there
has been no attempt to assess the outcome of psychoanalysis of obese patients. This lack has now been remedied and the results of a large-scale
assessment of obese patients in psychoanalysis are now available (4, 5).
These results include not only considerable improvement in psychological
status but also, and more surprisingly, considerable loss in weight. Accordingly, they will be reported in some detail, since they are sufficiently encouraging to warrant cautious optimism regarding the value of psychotherapy
and psychoanalysis in the treatment of obesity.

*Description of the Study*

The study to be reported was conducted by 72 psychoanalysts on 84
obese and 63 matched nonobese patients over a period of four years (4, 5). It
was carried out under the auspices of the Research Committee of the American Academy of Psychoanalysis which invited all 572 Fellows of the Academy to participate. Fifty-five percent responded to the invitation, of whom

only one-third (104) reported that they had at least one obese patient in treatment. Detailed questionnaires for each of their obese patients and for matched control patients of normal weight were then mailed to each of these analysts. Seventy-two responded, returning a total of 147 questionnaires. Eighteen months later 70 of the analysts responded to a second inquiry, providing follow-up data on a surprising 98 percent (144) of the patients. Slightly over half of both the obese and nonobese patients were still in treatment at that time. A third follow-up, four years after the first questionnaire, has been completed, and the data have been partially analyzed.

Patients had been in treatment for a median period of 31 months at the time of the first survey; the median period had risen to 42 months at the time of the second survey. (The 11-month difference in duration of treatment in this survey, conducted at an interval of 18 months, is explained by the fact that some patients terminated treatment before the second survey.) The results of the second survey thus combined two different groups — patients still in treatment and those who had terminated.

The demographic characteristics of the patients were quite similar to those of patients in the two previous large-scale surveys of psychoanalysis (6, 7) and were thus quite different from those of obese persons as a group. Most were between the ages of 18 and 50. Over 80 percent were of middle socioeconomic status and over 60 percent were college graduates. More than half were Jewish. The 84 obese patients were statistically comparable to the 63 nonobese patients on every demographic variable except marital status: Far more obese patients were single (48 percent compared to 29 percent); and fewer were married (33 percent compared with 46 percent [p < .05]). Of the 84 obese patients, 64 were women and 20 men; of the 63 control patients, 46 were women and 17 men. Obese women averaged 47 percent overweight; obese men averaged 42 percent overweight.

With the exception of the weight, there was no difference between men and women on any of the relevant variables. Accordingly, data for men and women were collapsed and the results reported as obese-nonobese comparisons.

The first notable finding was the very limited number of obese people who were in psychoanalytic therapy — only one-third of the responding analysts had even one obese patient in treatment. Furthermore, the obese patients had not sought psychoanalysis primarily because of their obesity; obesity was a chief complaint of only six percent! Most patients (60 percent), obese and nonobese alike, had sought treatment because of depression or anxiety, or both.

These findings were surprising and deserve consideration. They may reflect the low prevalence of obesity among the middle and upper middle class persons who seek psychoanalysis (8). But it seems equally probable that they reflect also a general skepticism as to the value of psychoanalysis in the treatment of obesity, a skepticism which extends beyond referring physicians to psychoanalysts themselves.

### Weight Loss

Obese patients lost surprisingly large amounts of weight and maintained this weight loss well following termination of treatment. The three surveys demonstrate this effect at three points in time. The first assessed weight losses at a time when all patients were still in treatment, for a mean duration of 31 months; the second when 30 of the 84 patients had terminated treatment and when the mean duration of treatment was 42 months; the third four years after the first, when most patients had terminated treatment, many for more than one year.

Mean weight loss at the time of the first survey was 4.5 ± 10.8 kg; by the second survey it was 9.5 ± 14.1 kg. The rate of weight loss was thus only 0.15 kg per month during the 31 months before the first survey; it rose to 0.45 kg per month during the subsequent 11 months.

Figure 1 presents a profile of the cumulative weight losses of the obese patients at the time of the first and second surveys, as well as those reported in a literature review of obese patients treated for obesity in general medical practice. At the time of the first survey, 53 percent of the psychoanalytic patients had lost more than 4.5 kg (10 lb). Twenty-six percent had lost more than 9.1 kg (20 lb), and 8 percent had lost more than 18.2 kg (40 lb). These figures compare favorably with the weight losses of obese patients seen in general medical practice (9). At the time of the second survey, the psychoanalytic patients had lost much additional weight: 64 percent had lost more than 4.5 kg, 47 percent had lost more than 9.1 kg, and 19 percent had lost more than 18.2 kg. These figures compare favorably with the best weight losses reported in behavior therapy programs (10). They compare even more favorably with reports of the *maintenance* of weight loss in behavior therapy (11). The still only partially analyzed data of the four-year follow-up provide added support for the efficacy of long-term maintenance of weight loss. They show no apparent regaining of weight lost during treatment.

These remarkably favorable results raise the question of how they were achieved. Since weight losses of this magnitude had been quite unexpected when the study was designed, no provision had been made for inquiring into possible mechanisms. One clue may be the pattern of weight loss — slow

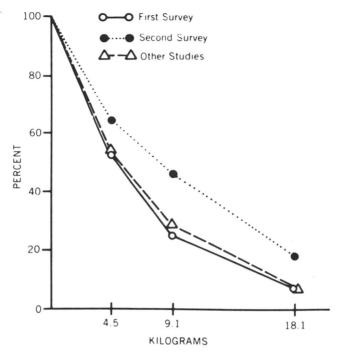

FIGURE 1. Cumulative weight losses for patients in psychoanlaytic therapy. (From Rand, C. S. W. and Stunkard, A. J., *Amer. J. Psychiat.* 135:547–551, 1978, by permission.)

(0.15 kg per month) at first and more rapid later (0.45 kg per month). This pattern is probably unique in the literature on obesity. Thousands of reports agree that weight loss is most rapid at the beginning of treatment and then slows progressively. Why was the sequence reversed in the present study? One possibility is that it was a result of the study itself. It is clear that the participating analysts were quite interested in the study and that it whetted their interest in obesity in general and in the obesity of their patients in particular. It seems quite possible that this interest communicated itself to the patients and induced them to try harder to lose weight. This interest did not take the form of direct encouragement to lose weight, and how the patients achieved their losses is unclear. They may simply have gone on reducing diets or attended Weight Watchers classes.

The apparently excellent maintenance of weight loss, however, argues that something more than a transmission of interest on the part of the analyst may have been involved. It is not clear what this something extra may have been. It is tempting to speculate that improving their personal functioning helped patients to better control their eating, or that those who had eaten in response to feelings of anxiety or depression learned to tolerate or avoid these feelings without overeating. We do not know, and this important topic clearly deserves further attention.

### Body Image Disparagement

Improvement in body image disparagement was as gratifying, if not as surprising, as the loss in weight. Body image disparagement is a disorder characterized by feelings that one's body is grotesque and loathsome and that others can view it only with hostility and contempt (3, 12). The feeling is closely connected with extreme self-consciousness and impaired social functioning. Although it might seem that all obese persons would have such derogatory feelings about their bodies, such is not the case. Emotionally healthy obese persons experience no body image disparagement and, in fact, only a minority of neurotic obese persons suffer from it. The disorder is confined to those who have been obese since childhood, and even among these persons with juvenile onset obesity, less than half suffer from it. The disorder thus occurs only in neurotic persons who have been obese since childhood, a group which contains those persons in whom neurosis is closely linked to obesity.

Body image disparagement is a chronic, intractable disorder, strongly resistant to change, little affected by weight reduction and even by the usual psychotherapeutic intervention. The intensity of the disorder fluctuates with positive and negative moods. Negative affects substantially increase the intensity of body image disparagement, while positive affects decrease it, but such changes are only temporary. Isolated reports of decrease in the intensity of body image disparagement in the course of long-term psychotherapy had given rise to the hope that this study might show such improvement to be a frequent result of psychoanalytic therapy. This hope was realized.

Body image disparagement was particularly common among the obese patients in the present study: 40 percent reported it in severe and 48 percent in mild form at the beginning of treatment. Forty-one percent reported one particularly poignant aspect of the disorder — avoidance of looking at themselves in mirrors (4, 13).

Table 1 shows the marked reduction in numbers of obese patients with severe body image disparagement from the beginning of treatment until the second survey. The table shows the number of patients with no, mild or severe body image disparagement at the beginning of treatment and the

TABLE 1
Change in Body Image Disparagement of Obese Patients
in Psychoanalysis

| Rating of Disparagement Before Treatment | Rating of Disparagement at Time of Second Survey | | |
|---|---|---|---|
| | None (N = 13) | Mild (N = 50) | Severe (N = 10) |
| None (N = 9) | 3 | 6 | 0 |
| Mild (N = 35) | 6 | 25 | 4 |
| Severe (N = 29) | 4 | 19 | 6 |

number of patients with no, mild, or severe body image disparagement at the time of the second survey. The most striking finding is the reduction in the percentage of patients with severe body image disparagement, from 40 percent to 14 percent.

Weight reduction had not previously brought about reduction in the intensity of body image disparagement, and there was no reason to believe that it had exerted such an effect in the present study. Nevertheless, the large number of patients provided an opportunity to exclude this possibility. When weight loss and body image disparagement were examined together, no relationship between the two was found. Some of the greatest weight losses occurred in patients with no change in body image disparagement; conversely, some of the greatest decreases in body image disparagement occurred among patients with little or no weight loss. The two phenomena were separate and distinct.

*Problems in Treatment*

Problems in treatment were clearly more troublesome among obese than among nonobese patients. Table 2, for example, shows that progress in psychological aspects of treatment was significantly poorer for obese than for nonobese patients. Thus, the only four patients whose condition was judged to have worsened during the course of treatment were all obese. Furthermore, only 23 percent of obese patients were judged as "much improved," compared to the 50 percent of nonobese patients who received this rating (p < .01).

Another measure of problems in treatment is premature termination. Obese patients were far more likely to terminate treatment prematurely (62 percent) than were nonobese patients (36 percent, p < .05). Furthermore,

TABLE 2
Relationship* Between Obesity and Progress in Treatment
at Time of Second Survey

| Patients in Psychoanalysis (N = 135) | Progress in Treatment | | | |
|---|---|---|---|---|
| | Much Improved | Improved | Same | Worse |
| Obese (N = 77) | 18 | 46 | 9 | 4 |
| Nonobese (N = 58) | 29 | 26 | 3 | 0 |

*$\chi^2$ = 12.708, 3 d.f., $p < .01$.

premature termination was associated with poorer outcome of treatment for obesity as well as poorer outcome of treatment for psychological issues. Thus, only nine patients failed to lose weight; eight of these terminated treatment prematurely.

### Hope for the Future

These results provide hope for the future. Clearly there is room for improvement in the psychoanalytic treatment of obese persons. As more is learned about this treatment, its effectiveness should be correspondingly enhanced, and we should be able to expect greater and more enduring weight losses and more widespread decrease in body image disparagement.

The surprisingly good results of psychoanalytic treatment raise the question of how accurate they are. Both weight losses and estimates of body image disparagement were, after all, self-reports by patients, as reported by their analysts. Both patients and analysts could well have felt under pressure to put a favorable face on their performance. These double pressures could theoretically have at least doubled the error in their reports. A recent study suggests, however, that the error may have been minimal (14).

Even at the time of the second survey, little was known about the accuracy of self-reported weights. It was generally believed that accuracy was low and that obese patients, in particular, seriously underestimated their body weights. Since then, a careful study of the accuracy of self-reported weights has shown that obese persons report their weights as accurately as do nonobese persons and, furthermore, that both groups are remarkably accurate (14). This study provides some assurance that the results reported here are valid.

Until further research expands our knowledge of the psychoanalytic treatment of obesity, we must be cautious in the interpretation of the results of this study. Its results are so encouraging, however, that such research must surely be forthcoming. There is every reason to believe that psychoanalysis will return to the repertoire of treatments for obesity and its psychological complications. The time and expense of such treatment will prevent it from assuming a major role in the control of obesity, but for some selected obese persons psychoanalysis may be a reasonable option.

## BEHAVIOR THERAPY

In 1967 a small paper on *Behavioral Control of Overeating* signaled the beginning of an explosion of interest in the behavior therapy of obesity (15). Reports of more than 100 clinical trials have made obesity the single most thoroughly researched topic in behavior therapy and perhaps even in all of psychotherapy research (8). Reports of this research have appeared largely in the psychological literature, and psychiatrists are still not well acquainted with these new and important developments. Accordingly, I will give a brief overview of the major results of this vast amount of work, discuss in some detail a new study that has revealed unexpected strengths of behavior therapy, and close with some details of behavior therapy of obesity.

### An Overview of the Results of Behavior Therapy of Obesity

A large number of studies have shown that behavior therapy is more effective than a variety of alternate treatments for mild and moderate obesity (8). But this demonstration, although well established, tells us little about the effectiveness of behavior therapy as a practical measure for the control of obesity. Furthermore, several factors make it difficult to obtain a clear picture of the clinical impact of behavior therapy of obesity. Studies of treatment have been conducted largely by inexperienced therapists in departments of psychology and over short periods of time. Most of the subjects have been mildly overweight college students rather than clinically obese patients, and far too many of the studies have been content with ascertaining the relative effectiveness of small differences in technique.

Despite these problems in assessment, definitive findings have emerged, and a review of 21 recent reports provides a basis for judging the overall efficacy of behavioral treatment for obesity (16). Eight findings have emerged.

1) The first important finding is that great progress has been made in decreasing dropouts from treatment. Whereas dropouts from traditional outpatient treatment were as high as 25 to 75 percent (8), most behavioral programs report rates of 15 percent or less (10). A well-controlled clinical trial

has confirmed the widespread clinical impression that contingency contracting, or the earning back of deposits made by the patient at the beginning of treatment, is very effective in decreasing dropouts (17).

2) The second major advance has been in reducing untoward side effects of weight reduction regimens, a problem that has plagued routine medical office treatment of obesity. As many as half of all obese patients undergoing this treatment may suffer from such symptoms as anxiety, irritability, and depression (18). By contrast, untoward reactions to behavioral programs are uncommon and half the patients feel better.

3) The single most important measure of treatment efficacy is weight loss. The new study described in detail below indicates that clinically significant weight losses can be achieved by behavior therapy. However, until this study, most reports had not been encouraging. Table 3 reviews 21 recent reports which provided sufficient detail to permit assessment of weight losses. These studies met such basic criteria as a) the results were based upon all patients starting treatment; b) reports included weight losses in kilograms rather than solely in percentages of excess weight; and c) drop-outs were excluded. Table 3 shows that the weight losses of no more than half the programs exceeded 4.5 kg and weight losses of only 20 percent exceeded 6.8 kg. There are many reasons for these limitations — most of the programs were short-term, many involved patients who were only mildly overweight, and a large number were carried out by inexperienced therapists. The fact remains that the results are modest and, from the perspective of clinical utility, disappointing.

4) There is great variability in weight changes during treatment and even greater variability following treatment. Wilson notes that this variability suggests that either the critical variables governing weight loss have not been identified, or that current behavioral methods are appropriate only for persons with some still undetermined characteristics (10).

5) Prediction of the outcome of behavioral treatments for obesity has not been very successful and only a few relatively weak predictors have been discovered. This failing is particularly troubling in view of the marked variability in outcome of treatment. For, if one could predict outcome more accurately, one could make more effective use of scarce treatment resources and would spare many patients the time, effort, and discouragement of still another experience of failure.

6) Patients with onset of obesity early in life lose as much weight as those with onset in adult life (16). This finding appears somewhat at variance with predictions based upon expected fat cell size and number.

7) Despite the fact that behavioral techniques can be adapted for use by

TABLE 3

Results of Behavioral Treatments for Obesity

| Study | n | Initial weight (kg) | Mean weight loss* (kg) | Treatment length (weeks) |
|---|---|---|---|---|
| Abrahms & Allen (1974) | 23 | 83.0 | 5.4 | 9 |
| Hagen (1974) | 18 | 69.5 | 6.8 | 10 |
| Hall (1972) | 10 | 78.6 | 1.5 | 4 |
| Hall, et al. (1974) | 40 | — | 5.0 | 10 |
| Hall, et al. (1975) | 25 | 89.8 | 6.8** | 12 |
| Hanson, et al. (1976) | 32 | 96.4 | 5.9** | 10 |
| Harris (1969) | 7 | 77.8 | 3.1 | 10 |
| Harris & Bruner (1971) | 11 | 74.9 | 3.4 | 12 |
| Harris & Bruner (1971) | 6 | 65.3 | .8 | 16 |
| Harris & Hallbauer (1973) | 27 | 75.2 | 3.6 | 12 |
| Jeffrey (1974) | 34 | 83.5 | 2.7 | 7 |
| Levitz & Stunkard (1974) | 73 | 82.2 | 1.9 | 12 |
| Mahoney (1974) | 9 | — | 3.4 | 8 |
| McReynolds & Lutz (1976) | 41 | 81.1 | 7.9 | 15 |
| Penick, et al. (1971) | 15 | 114.1 | 10.1 | 12 |
| Romanczyk (1974) | 17 | 79.9 | 4.8 | 6 |
| Romanczyk, et al. (1973) | 18 | 81.3 | 3.2 | 4 |
| Romanczyk, et al. (1973) | 18 | 78.6 | 3.6 | 4 |
| Stuart (1967) | 8 | 83.4 | 17.2 | 52 |
| Stuart (1971) | 6 | — | 6.4 | 15 |
| Wollersheim (1970) | 18 | 70.0 | 4.7 | 12 |

*Data describe the most effective treatment combination only. Results from control groups and partial treatments are not included.
**Extrapolated from weight-reduction indices.

STUDIES CITED IN TABLE 3

ABRAHMS, J. L. and ALLEN, G. J.: Comparative effectiveness of situational programming, financial pay-offs and group pressure in weight reduction. *Behavior Therapy,* 5:391–400, 1974.
HAGEN, R.: Group therapy versus bibliotherapy in weight reduction. *Behavior Therapy,* 5:222–234, 1974.
HALL, S. M.: Self-control and therapist control in the behavioral treatment of overweight women. *Behaviour Research and Therapy,* 10:59–68, 1972.
HALL, S., HALL, R., HANSON, R., et al.: Permanence of two self-managed treatments of over-

STUDIES CITED IN TABLE 3 *(continued)*

weight in university and community populations. *J. Consult. Clin. Psychol.*, 42:781–786, 1974.

HALL, S. M., HALL, R. G., BORDEN, B. L., et al.: Follow-up strategies in the behavioral treatment of overweight. *Behav. Res. Ther.*, 13:167–172, 1975.

HANSON, R. W., BORDEN, B. L., HALL, S. M., et al.: Use of programmed instruction in teaching self-management skills to overweight adults. *Behav. Ther.*, 7:366–373, 1976.

HARRIS, M. B.: Self-directed program for weight control: A pilot study. *Journal of Abnormal Psychology*, 74:263–270, 1969.

HARRIS, M. B. and BRUNER, C. G. A.: A comparison of self-control and a contract procedure for weight control. *Behav. Res. and Ther.*, 9:347–354, 1971.

HARRIS, M. B. and HALLBAUER, E. S.: Self-directed weight control through eating and exercise. *Behav. Res. Ther.*, 11:523–529, 1973.

JEFFREY, D. B.: A comparison of the effects of external control and self-control on the maintenance of weights. *J. Abnorm. Psychol.*, 83:404–410, 1974.

LEVITZ, L. and STUNKARD, A. J.: A therapeutic coalition for obesity: Behavioral modification and patient self-help. *Am. J. Psychiat.*, 131:423–427, 1974.

MAHONEY, M. J.: Self-reward and self-monitoring techniques for weight control. *Behav. Ther.*, 5:48–57, 1974.

MCREYNOLDS, W. T. and LUTZ, R. N.: Weight loss resulting from two behavior modification procedures with nutritionists as therapists. *Behavior Therapy*, 7:283–289, 1976.

PENICK, S. B., FILION, R., FOX, S., and STUNKARD, A. J.: Behavior modification in the treatment of obesity. *Psychosom. Med.*, 33:49–55, 1971.

ROMANCZYK, R. G.: Self-monitoring in the treatment of obesity. *Behavior Therapy*, 5:531–540, 1974.

ROMANCZYK, R. G., TRACEY, D. A., WILSON, G. T. and THORPE, G. C.: Behavior techniques in the treatment of obesity: A comparative analysis. *Behaviour Research and Therapy*, 11:629–640, 1973.

STUART, R. B.: Behavioral control of overeating. *Behav. Res. Ther.*, 5:357–365, 1967.

STUART, R. B.: A three-dimensional program for the treatment of obesity. *Behav. Res. and Ther.*, 9:177–186, 1971.

WOLLERSHEIM, J. P.: Effectiveness of group therapy based upon learning principles in the treatment of overweight women. *J. Abnorm. Psychol.*, 76:462–474, 1970.

less skilled therapists, the skill of the therapist appears to have a modest effect upon outcome of therapy. Two studies have shown that therapist experience was positively related to weight loss (16, 19).

8) Clinically significant weight losses achieved by behavioral treatment have generally not been well maintained for more than a year. A recent review by Stunkard and Penick contains the first five-year follow-up of behavioral treatment for obesity plus an analysis of nine other follow-up studies of at least one year in duration (11). The five-year follow-up was carried out on 28 of the 29 survivors of a study by Penick et al. (20). For one year following treatment, most patients continued to lose weight; during the next four years, they began to regain it. The continuing weight loss at one year applied equally to the behavioral (eight of 13) and traditional (nine of 15) treatment groups.

Similarly, the weight gain four years later was also characteristic of both groups.

The results of this follow-up study were paralleled by those of nine other one-year follow-up studies of patients who had lost smaller amounts of weight (11).

### The Encouraging Results of a Recent Study

As I have noted, most reports of behavior therapy of obesity have been characterized by only modest weight losses. Accordingly, the results of a recent study deserve attention (21). They suggest that behavior therapy can produce clinically significant weight losses and that these weight losses are better maintained than those produced by pharmacotherapy.

This large-scale controlled clinical trial was undertaken to assess the relative efficacy of behavior therapy, pharmacotherapy, and their combination (21). For this purpose 120 obese (63 percent overweight) women were treated for six months and assessed again at a one-year follow-up. There were two control groups. One was a standard waiting list control group. The other was a "doctor's office medication group" designed to approximate traditional office treatment for obesity.

### Procedures

*Behavior therapy* was presented in a highly structured program that utilized Ferguson's manual (22) and modifications of the Mahoneys' book (23). It included standard behavioral techniques of self-monitoring, stimulus control, slowing of eating, self-reinforcement, cognitive restructuring, contingency contracting, and exercise management.

*Pharmacotherapy* consisted of fenfluramine in doses up to 120 mg/day, as tolerated, with tapering of dosage during the last month of treatment (24). Resident physicians met with each patient twice during the first month of treatment and then monthly as needed. In addition, patients received supportive group counseling designed to reproduce the nonspecific elements of the behavior therapy condition.

*Combined treatment* included both behavior therapy as described for the first condition and fenfluramine as prescribed by resident physicians in the second condition.

The *doctor's office medication control group* was composed of patients of resident physicians who provided traditional medical treatment including medication (fenfluramine), a reducing diet, instructions for exercise, and advice and encouragement. After an initial history and physical examination, they were seen individually for 20 minutes twice during the first month and then once a month for the remaining five months. At this time they were given additional treatment in groups and so were not included in the follow-up.

The *waiting list control group* patients were assessed, placed on a waiting list, weighed at four and six months, and then provided treatment. They were also not included in the follow-up.

Patients in the three major treatment conditions met weekly in groups of 10 for one-and-a-half hours. Patients paid $3.00 for each session and, in addition, deposited $25.00 that was refunded for attendance (not weight loss) at the end of the program. Two female therapists, one a doctoral and one a master's level clinical psychologist, each led two 10-person groups in each of the three major treatment conditions — a total of 12 groups. Resident physicians were responsible for administration of the fenfluramine.

*Patients*

Patients consisted of 120 obese women recruited by public service announcements in Williamsport, Pennsylvania, a town of 35,000. Their median percentage overweight was 63 with a range of 21 to 156. Median age was 47 with a range from 23 to 66. Most were of middle socioeconomic status; over half were housewives.

Of the 120 patients, 18 were assigned to the two control conditions: 10 to the waiting list control, and eight to the doctor's office medication condition. Of the 102 women assigned to the three major treatment conditions, 11 dropped out, leaving 91 who completed treatment, a drop-out rate of 11 percent. Of the 91 who completed treatment, 11 patients in the pharmacotherapy and combined treatment conditions did not take their medication. The analyses were thus carried out on 80 women in the three major treatment conditions: behavior therapy, 32; pharmacotherapy, 25; and combined treatment, 23.

*Weight Changes*

Patients in all treatment groups lost significantly more weight than those in the waiting list control group, who actually gained 1.3 kg ($p < 0.001$). (See Figure 2 and Table 4.) Weight losses of pharmacotherapy (14.5 kg) and combined treatment patients (15.3 kg) did not differ significantly, both being significantly greater than those of behavior therapy patients (10.9 kg, $p < 0.05$). For the first three months the rate of weight loss in the two major drug treatment conditions was constant. The rate decreased slightly during the second three months, in part because some patients were approaching their target weight. Similar changes occurred in the behavior therapy condition.

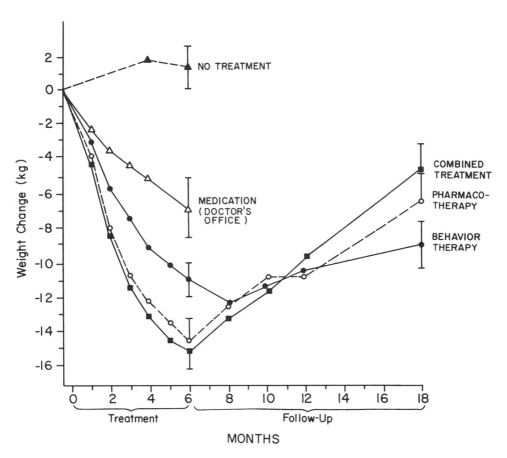

FIGURE 2. Weight changes during six months of treatment and 12 months of follow-up. The three major treatment groups lost large amounts of weight during treatment: behavior therapy (solid circles) 10.9 kg, pharmacotherapy (open circles) 14.5 kg, and combined treatment (solid squares) 15.3 kg. Behavior therapy patients continued to lose for two months and then slowly regained it, in contrast to rapid regain of weight by pharmacotherapy and combined treatment groups. Among the control groups, the no-treatment (waiting list) control group gained weight, while the doctor's office medication group lost 6.0 kg. Patients in these two groups received additional treatment at six months and so were not available for follow-up. Vertical lines represent one standard error of the mean. (From Stunkard, A. J., Craighead, L. W., and O'Brien, R., *Lancet,* Nov. 15, 1980, pp. 1045–1047, by permission.)

TABLE 4
Unadjusted Means and Standard Error of Weight and Weight Changes (kg)

| | | Weight Loss | |
| --- | --- | --- | --- |
| | Initial Weight | After Treatment | One-Year Follow-Up |
| Behavior Therapy | 91.6 ± 2.2 | 10.9 ± 1.0 | 9.0 ± 1.3 |
| Pharmacotherapy | 95.6 ± 3.1 | 14.5 ± 1.1 | 6.3 ± 1.5 |
| Combined Treatment | 98.1 ± 3.6 | 15.3 ± 1.2 | 4.6 ± 1.6 |
| Doctor's Office Medication | 82.2 ± 6.1 | 6.0 ± 1.7 | − |
| Waiting List Control | 93.5 ± 6.0 | + 1.3 ± 1.3 | − |

Patients in the doctor's office medication condition lost only 6.0 kg, compared to the 14.5 kg lost by pharmacotherapy patients ($p < 0.05$). Drug dosage of the two groups was the same; only the circumstances of its administration differed.

A striking reversal of the treatment results was found at a one-year follow-up, a finding whose significance is enhanced by the fact that this follow-up included every living patient who finished treatment (one patient had died.) Behavior therapy patients regained far less weight (1.9 kg) than pharmacotherapy (8.2 kg) and combined treatment (10.7 kg) patients. The result was a net weight loss from the beginning of treatment to one-year follow-up of 9.0 kg for behavior therapy patients, which was somewhat greater ($p < 0.07$) than the net loss of 6.3 kg for pharmacotherapy patients and 4.6 kg for combined treatment patients.

*Discussion of the Results*

Although fenfluramine, administered in a group setting, produced significantly greater weight loss than did behavior therapy, this benefit was short-lived. Patients who had received fenfluramine regained weight far more rapidly following treatment than did those who received only behavior therapy. This poor maintenance of weight loss soon erased any advantage of pharmacotherapy. One year after treatment, patients who had received only behavior therapy showed a net weight loss greater than those who had received medication. Furthermore, adding fenfluramine to behavior modification not only did not improve the long-term results, but compromised them. The long-term results were actually poorer among behavior therapy patients who had also received fenfluramine than among those who had not.

The study showed in a dramatic manner how the circumstances of its administration may influence the effects of a medication. Administered in a traditional doctor's office format, fenfluramine produced a weight loss of 6.0 kg, a little more than is customary in routine clinical practice. Slightly altering the circumstances of its administration (group meeting with the use of a deposit to encourage attendance) more than doubled this loss, from 6.0 kg to 14.5 kg. Furthermore, this altered format showed a highly favorable cost/effectiveness ratio. Far less professional time was spent with each patient than in the traditional one-to-one format.

The strengths of this study add to the confidence with which its results can be regarded. First, the dropout rate of no more than 11 percent resulted in little bias in the patients who remained in treatment. Second, the weight loss of 10.9 kg by behavior therapy patients is one of the largest ever achieved in a controlled trial of behavior therapy of obesity. Finally, confining the basic analyses to women, by increasing the homogeneity of the sample over one that included both sexes, added to the already high level of statistical significance of the results.

Fourteen men were included in the study. A separate analysis of their results indicated that the results with women can be generalized to men.

## Some Details of Behavior Therapy of Obesity

Behavior therapy of obesity has often been equated with tricks or gimmicks, such as laying down one's fork between bites, pausing during the course of a meal, or using distinctive table settings. As such, it appears to fill a need for something new and different for those people who are constantly preoccupied with their weight and how to control it. As useful as some of these tricks or gimmicks may be, this view of behavior therapy does a serious disservice to attempts to understand this field. It confuses specific tactics with a system of therapy and, perhaps more important, a distinctive way of looking at human behavior. Behavior therapy, or its equivalent, behavior modification, is derived from a set of assumptions that extends directly back to the radical behaviorism of John B. Watson and, less directly, to the nominalist schoolmen of the Middle Ages. Although it developed out of the systematic application of experimentally derived principles of learning to the modification of problem behaviors, behavior therapy has extended far beyond its origins, so that today there is no generally accepted definition. Nevertheless, a series of core characteristics convey a sense of the boundaries of this new and rapidly developing field.

The first of these core characteristics is the assumption that all behavior, normal and abnormal, is acquired and maintained according to definable principles, many of which are already known. A second characteristic is one that contrasts strongly with those of other psychological systems. It is that people are best described by their behavior—what they think, feel, and do in specific situations—and not by dispositional tendencies such as hostility and insecurity. A third characteristic of behavior therapy is the attempt to specify treatment measures as precisely as possible and to evaluate outcomes by the most objective possible measures. Behavior therapists have been in the forefront of efforts to introduce treatment manuals of ever greater specificity and to evaluate outcomes in the patient's environment. For example, they were the first to assess the efficacy of treatments for phobias by observation of patients in the phobic situation.

A fourth characteristic of behavior therapy is the individualization of treatment. Although this characteristic is not peculiar to behavior therapy, it is important to mention it as a corrective to some popular views which equate behavior therapy with a kind of "Clockwork Orange" disregard of individuality in the single-minded pursuit of behavior change. Similarly, the goals of treatment are set by negotiation between the patient and therapist, and they are renegotiated at periodic intervals. Finally, every effort is made to provide continuing and critical assessment of treatment throughout its course.

Application of behavior therapy to the problem of obesity begins with a consideration of methods of producing a negative caloric balance in order to metabolize excess body fat. There are two basic methods—decreasing caloric intake and increasing caloric expenditure. Several excellent books describe in some detail how these results are achieved, and the interested reader is referred to works of Mahoney and Mahoney (23), Jordan, Levitz and Kimbrell (25), and Stuart (26), and to the manuals of Ferguson (22). Nevertheless, a brief description of some of the specifics of a behavioral weight control program may be useful. Measures to increase physical activity and provide nutritional education are important components, but I will focus here upon five more explicitly behavioral measures designed to control food intake. Four have long been elements of most behavioral programs, the fifth is a relatively new measure: 1) Self-monitoring—description of the behavior to be controlled; 2) control of the stimuli which precede eating; 3) development of techniques to control the act of eating; 4) reinforcement of the prescribed behaviors; and 5) cognitive restructuring.

1) *Self-monitoring—Description of the behavior to be controlled.* Patients are asked to keep careful records of the food they eat. Each time they eat,

they write down precisely what it was, how much, at what time of day, where they were, whom they were with, and how they felt. Figure 3 provides an example of such a record.

The immediate reaction of many patients to this time-consuming and inconvenient procedure is grumbling and complaining. Such reactions occurred far more frequently in the early days of these programs and may well have been due to the therapists' own uncertainty about the techniques. More recently, patients have responded more positively. Many come to the view that record-keeping may be the single most important part of the behavioral program. It vastly increases patients' awareness of their eating behavior. Despite their years of struggling with the problem, once patients begin to keep records, they are surprised at how much they eat and how varied are the circumstances in which they eat.

There is a surprising unanimity on the value of self-monitoring. The more specific the items monitored, the more effective the results. Not only is self-monitoring a key element in the process of behavior change, but it is also the mainstay of the behavioral assessment of obesity.

2) *Control of the stimuli which precede eating.* A behavioral analysis traditionally begins with a study of the events antecedent to the behavior to be controlled. Stimulus control of eating involves many kinds of measures which are traditional in weight-reduction programs. For example, every effort is made to limit the amount of high-calorie food kept in the house and to limit accessibility to food that must be kept in the house. For times when eating cannot be resisted, adequate amounts of low-calorie foods, such as celery and raw carrots, are kept readily available.

In addition, behavioral programs introduced new and distinctive measures. For example, most patients reported that their eating took place in a wide variety of places and at many different times during the day. Some noted that if they ate while watching television, it was not long before watching television made them eat. It is as if the various times and places had become discriminative stimuli for eating. In an effort to decrease the number and potency of discriminative stimuli that control their eating, patients are encouraged to confine all eating, including snacking, to one place. In order not to disrupt domestic routines, this place is very frequently the kitchen.

A parallel effort is made to develop new discriminative stimuli for eating and to increase their power. For example, patients are encouraged to use distinctive table settings, perhaps an unusually colored placemat and napkin, and special silver. No effort is made to decrease the amount of food the patients eat, but they are encouraged to use the distinctive table settings when-

**FOOD DIARY** – Lesson One

Day of Week _____          Name_____

| Time | Minutes Spent Eating | M/S | H | Body Position | Activity While Eating | Location Of Eating | Food Type and Quantity | Eating With Whom | Feeling While Eating |
|---|---|---|---|---|---|---|---|---|---|
| 6:00 | | | | | | | | | |
| 11:00 | | | | | | | | | |
| 4:00 | | | | | | | | | |
| 9:00 | | | | | | | | | |

M/S: Meal or Snack  H: Degree of Hunger (0 = None, 3 = Maximum)
Body Position: 1 = Walking, 2 = Standing, 3 = Sitting, 4 = Lying Down

FIGURE 3. Copy of a page from a food diary early in treatment. Patients are expected to fill in each page in the evening. Abbreviations: M/S: Meal or Snack. H: Degree of hunger (0 = none, 3+ = maximum). Body position: 1 = walking, 2 = standing, 3 = sitting, 4 = lying down.

ever they eat, even for a small between-meals snack. One middle-aged house-wife, convinced of the importance of this measure, went so far as to take her distinctive table setting with her whenever she dined out. She was an early success.

Stimulus control has occupied a central position in most behavioral weight control programs of the past decade, but its independent contribution to the efficacy of these programs is still unknown. However, it appears sufficiently useful to continue as a major element in behavioral programs despite the sparsity of controlled evidence. Its efficacy is likely to be considerably increased if it is used specifically for persons in whom pretreatment behavioral assessment has revealed deficiencies in this area.

3) *Development of techniques to control the act of eating.* Specific techniques are utilized to help patients decrease their speed of eating, to become aware of all the components of the eating process, and to gain control over these components. Exercises include counting each mouthful of food eaten during a meal, or each chew, or each swallow. Patients are encouraged to practice putting down their eating utensils after every third mouthful until that mouthful is chewed and swallowed. Then longer delays are introduced, starting with one minute towards the end of the meal when it is more easily tolerated, and moving to more frequent delays, longer ones, and ones earlier in the meal.

Patients are encouraged to stop pairing their eating with such activities as reading the newspaper and watching television, and to make conscious efforts to make eating a pure experience. They are urged to do whatever they can to make meals a time of comfort and relaxation, particularly to avoid old arguments and new problems at the dinner table. They are encouraged to savor the food as they eat it, to make a conscious effort to become aware of it as they are chewing, and to enjoy the act of swallowing and the warmth and fullness in their stomachs. To the extent that they succeed in this endeavor, they eat less and enjoy it more.

4) *Reinforcement of the prescribed behaviors.* In addition to the informal and incidental rewards which patients receive from the behavioral program, a system of formal rewards is also used. Separating the reward schedules for changes in behavior and for weight loss is useful; rewards for changing behavior may be the more effective.

In order to decrease the time between the exercise of a specific behavior and the attendant reward, patients are awarded a certain number of points for each of the activities that they are learning—record-keeping, counting chews and swallows, pausing during the meal, eating in one place, and so forth. Not only do patients receive a certain number of points for each activity, but they can also earn extras, such as double the number of points, when they devise an alternative to eating in the face of strong temptation.

These points, which serve to provide immediate reinforcement of a behavior, are cumulated and converted into more tangible rewards, often in concert with the spouse. Popular rewards include a trip to the movies or relief from housekeeping chores. A more impersonal reward is conversion of points into money which patients bring to the next meeting and donate to the group. Surprisingly altruistic courses may be chosen. In an early program one group donated its savings to the Salvation Army, another to a needy friend of one of the members.

Promptness of the reinforcement seems a key to success. One middle-aged housewife said, "My husband was always offering to buy me a car if I lost 50 pounds. I used to work away at it and knock myself out and lost 30 pounds, which was a lot of weight, but what did it get me? I didn't get half a car. I got nothing. I've only lost eight pounds in this program so far, and he's done all sorts of good things for me" (3).

5) *Cognitive restructuring.* In the recent past, behavior therapy has been enriched by an interest in cognitions and by the whole new field of cognitive-behavior modification. Concern with cognitions has received less attention in the treatment of obesity than have more traditional operant concerns, and there has been as yet only limited experimental evidence for the efficacy of cognitive strategies in the treatment of obesity. Nevertheless, these strategies have been attracting increasing attention and several clinicians believe that they can make a useful contribution to an overall program of treatment for obesity.

A feature that has made cognitions palatable to the more behavioristic therapists is recognition that the internal monologues that occupy so much of our time are readily accessible. Furthermore, they can be quantified and treated very much as any traditional operant in terms of reinforcement, extinction, and so forth. Mahoney and Mahoney (23) have directed attention to the critical role that cognitions and private monologues may play in the maintenance and control of obesity. The first step in applying cognitive strategies to weight control is to help patients discover their most common negative monologues, or self-statements, and to estimate their frequency. Then, in the manner described by Beck (27) and by Meichenbaum (28), patients are taught arguments against these monologues. Since negative monologues tend to be stereotyped and limited in number, it is usually not difficult to construct arguments against them. The patient is then helped to learn — and overlearn — these more appropriate self-statements so that they can use them almost automatically in response to the negative statements. Training in this kind of arguing with oneself seems to produce benefits in terms of improved morale, as has been shown quite convincingly in the case of depression, and probably also in more effective weight-reducing behaviors. Simply repeating the counterarguments over a period of time may help, even if the person does not completely believe them at the onset.

Five kinds of negative self-statements are common. Examples of such self-statements, together with counterarguments are:

*Weight loss.* "It's taking so long to lose weight." A counterargument is, "But I am losing it. And this time I'm going to learn how to keep it off."

*Ability to lose weight.* "I've never done it before. Why should I succeed this time?" A counterargument is, "There always has to be a first time. And this time I've got a good new program going for me."

*Goals.* "I've got to stop snacking." A counterargument is, "That is an unrealistic goal. Just keep on trying to cut down the number of snacks."

*Food thoughts.* "I keep finding myself thinking how good chocolate tastes." A useful response is, "Stop that! It's just frustrating you. Think of lying on the beach in the sun" (or whatever activity the patient finds particularly enjoyable).

*Excuses.* "Everyone in my family has a weight problem. It's in my genes." A counterargument is, "That just makes it harder, not impossible. If I stick with this program I will succeed."

### SUMMARY AND CONCLUSIONS

The importance of psychological factors in the treatment of obesity has long been recognized. Only recently, however, has the systematic application of psychological treatment to obesity been studied. A large-scale collaborative study by 72 psychoanalysts has assessed the efficacy of psychoanalysis in the treatment of obesity. Although it has been more difficult to treat obese than nonobese people, obese people have achieved significant psychological benefits from psychoanalysis, including marked alleviation of the usually intractable problem of body image disparagement. In addition, to the surprise of many, including psychoanalysts, obese persons have achieved significant weight losses and maintained these weight losses as effectively as have persons treated by other methods.

Behavior therapy has been the second form of psychological treatment to be applied to obesity in recent years. A vast amount of research on behavioral treatments of obesity has been conducted, and we now have a relatively clear picture of the strengths and limitations of this form of treatment. The low drop-out rates from treatment, the favorable psychological changes, and the availability of care from less highly trained therapists has made this modality the treatment of choice for mild obesity, even though weight losses have tended to be modest. A recent study (21), described in some detail, indicates that it is possible to achieve larger weight losses than have occurred in the past, and that these weight losses are better maintained than those achieved by effective pharmacotherapy.

## REFERENCES

1. STUNKARD, A. J. (Ed.): *Obesity*. Philadelphia: W. B. Saunders Co., 1980.
2. BRUCH, H.: *Eating Disorders: Obesity, Anorexia Nervosa and the Person Within*. New York: Basic Books, 1973.
3. STUNKARD, A. J.: *The Pain of Obesity*. Palo Alto: Bull Publishing Co., 1975.
4. RAND, C. S. W. and STUNKARD, A. J.: Psychoanalysis and obesity. *J. Am. Acad. Psychol.*, 5:459–497, 1977.
5. RAND, C. S. W. and STUNKARD, A. J.: Obesity and psychoanalysis. *Am. J. Psychiat.*, 135:547–551, 1978.
6. HAMBURG, D. A., BIBRING, G. L., FISHER, C., et al.: Report of the ad hoc committee on central fact-gathering data of the American Psychoanalytic Association. *J. Am. Psychoanal. Assoc.*, 15:841–861, 1967.
7. WEBER, J. J., ELINSON, J., and MOSS, L. M.: Psychoanalysis and change: A study of psychoanalytic clinic records using electronic data processing techniques. *Arch. Gen. Psychiat.*, 17:687–709, 1967.
8. STUNKARD, A. J.: From explanation to action in psychosomatic medicine: The case of obesity. *Psychosom. Med.*, 37:195–236, 1975.
9. STUNKARD, A. J. and McLAREN-HUME, M.: The results of treatment of obesity. A review of the literature and report of a series. *Arch. Int. Med.*, 103:79–85, 1959.
10. WILSON, G. T.: Behavioral modification and the treatment of obesity. In: A. J. Stunkard (Ed.), *Obesity*. Philadelphia: W. B. Saunders Co., 1980, pp. 325–344.
11. STUNKARD, A. J. and PENICK, S. B.: Behavior modification in the treatment of obesity: The problem of maintaining weight loss. *Arch. Gen. Psychiat.*, 36:801–806, 1979.
12. STUNKARD, A. J. and MENDELSON, M.: Obesity and the body image. *Am. J. Psychiat.*, 123:1443–1447, 1967.
13. HORAN, J. J.: Negative covariant probability: An analogue study. *Behav. Res. Ther.*, 12:263–266, 1974.
14. STUNKARD, A. J. and ALBAUM, J. M.: The accuracy of self-reported weights. *Am. J. Clin. Nutr.*, 34:1593–1599, 1981.
15. STUART, R. B.: Behavioral control of overeating. *Behav. Res. Ther.*, 5:357–365, 1967.
16. JEFFERY, R. W., WING, R. R., and STUNKARD, A. J.: Behavioral treatment of obesity: The state of the art in 1976. *Behav. Ther.*, 9:189–199, 1978.

17. HAGEN, R. L., FOREYT, J. P., and DURHAM, T. W.: The dropout problem: Reducing attrition in obesity research. *Behav. Ther.,* 7:463–471, 1976.
18. STUNKARD, A. J. and RUSH, J.: Dieting and depression reexamined: A critical review of reports of untoward responses during weight reduction for obesity. *Ann. Intern. Med.,* 81:526–533, 1974.
19. LEVITZ, L. and STUNKARD, A. J.: A therapeutic coalition for obesity: Behavioral modification and patient self-help. *Am. J. Psychiat.,* 131:423–427, 1974.
20. PENICK, S. B., FILION, R., FOX, S., and STUNKARD, A. J.: Behavior modification in the treatment of obesity. *Psychosom. Med.,* 33:49–55, 1971.
21. STUNKARD, A. J., CRAIGHEAD, L. W., and O'BRIEN, R.: Controlled trial of behavior therapy, pharmacotherapy and their combination in the treatment of obesity. *Lancet,* November 15, 1980, pp. 1045–1047.
22. FERGUSON, J. M.: *Learning to Eat.* Leaders Manual and Patients Manual. Palo Alto: Bull Publishing Co., 1975.
23. MAHONEY, M. J. and MAHONEY, K. *Permanent Weight Control.* New York: Norton, 1976.
24. GOODMAN, L. A. and GILMAN, A.: *The Pharmacological Basis of Therapeutics.* New York: Macmillan, 1975.
25. JORDAN, H. A., LEVITZ, L. S., and KIMBRELL, G. M.: *Eating is Okay.* New York: New American Library, 1978.
26. STUART, R. B.: *Act Thin, Stay Thin.* New York: Norton, 1978.
27. BECK, A. T.: *Cognitive Therapy and the Emotional Disorders.* New York: International Universities Press, 1976.
28. MEICHENBAUM, D.: *Cognitive Behavior Modification.* New York: Plenum Press, 1977.

# 4

# Surgical Treatment of Obesity: Psychiatric Aspects

## *Pietro Castelnuovo-Tedesco, M.D.*

### INTRODUCTION

Obesity is a condition of complex etiology for which we do not have a really satisfactory treatment. This is true especially of its more severe forms. For this reason, a variety of methods have been tried. Therapies based on diet, anorectic agents, psychotherapy, or membership in weight reduction groups have limited effectiveness. They have no more than a 13 percent success rate when measured by the percentage of patients who lose 40 pounds or more after entering treatment (1). Because a 40-pound weight loss clearly is inconclusive for the patient who is superobese, conservative methods have proven a failure in most cases.

This experience and the finding that mortality among the grossly obese is approximately three times that of a comparable group of normal weight have prompted experimentation with more radical approaches, prominently starvation and surgical treatment (1).

In the 1960s, treatment based on starvation was tried, but this also proved unsatisfactory because it requires prolonged hospitalization which is costly and disrupts the patient's life. Moreover, its benefits are short-lived; patients begin regaining weight soon after their discharge from the hospital (2, 3). Although starvation methods have little to offer most superobese, this approach still has merit for some with serious medical problems which preclude surgical therapy.

84

## SURGICAL TREATMENT: RATIONALE

The surgical treatment of superobesity was first developed approximately 20 years ago using intestinal bypass operations (4). Since that time these procedures have been very widely performed. A gastric bypass operation was introduced over 10 years ago, but it has achieved popularity only in the past five years (5). It is now being employed with increasing frequency because it does not have most of the metabolic complications that can occur after jejunoileal bypass.

The rationale for the surgical treatment of obesity has been to reduce either the intake or the absorption of food (6). Most procedures involve a combination of these two factors. Prominent in the first group of operations (reduction of food intake) is gastric bypass. Several modifications of the latter exist; these include gastric partition and gastroplasty ("stapling operation"). Jaw-wiring, a relatively simple procedure, also reduces food intake. In the second group (reduction of food absorption) is the jejunoileal bypass, which also has several modifications to be described more fully later.

Two additional procedures, bilio-pancreatic bypass and bilio-intestinal bypass, have been tried recently in Europe (6, 7). While they show promise, experience with them so far has been limited. The first is a modification of gastric bypass, the second of jejunoileal bypass. Their common feature is that they preserve the enterohepatic circulation of bile acids; this helps to prevent otherwise frequent diarrhea.

This description of surgical treatment will emphasize intestinal bypass and gastric bypass operations, at present the most representative and widely employed procedures, but will also include some discussion of jaw-wiring.

## SURGICAL TREATMENT: PROCEDURES, INDICATIONS, COMPLICATIONS

Intestinal bypass surgery was introduced clinically in the late 1950s by Payne and Dewind (4). Their first operation was a jejunocolic anastomosis; soon, however, they discarded it because of serious side effects (diarrhea and electrolyte disturbances) in favor of a jejunoileal anastomosis, which has remained through the years the basic intestinal bypass operation. Several variants of jejunoileal bypass have been tried. Typical are Payne and Dewind's original "14 + 4" (i.e., 14 inches of jejunum anastomosed end-to-side to four inches of ileum) and Scott's "12 + 8" or "12 + 6" (i.e., 12 inches of jejunum anastomosed to eight or six inches of ileum, end-to-end) (4, 8, 9). Both the Payne and the Scott operations are in common use and no clear preference has been established for one over the other. There is, however, general agreement that the length of the jejunum is particularly important in the production of weight loss and that accurate intraoperative measurement of intestinal length is essential (10).

Gastric bypass consists of several alternative procedures that reduce the functional gastric cavity to an antral pouch of about 50 cc capacity with an exit stoma approximately 12 mm in diameter. The basic feature is the creation of the very small gastric pouch which markedly limits food intake. This may be achieved by gastric partition or by gastroplasty ("stapling") (11, 12). This operation also may be combined with a gastroenteric anastomosis, produced by connecting the small stomach pouch with a loop of jejunum. The latter variant is the gastric bypass proper. Reduction of gastric capacity by wrapping the stomach with polypropylene mesh ("gastric wrapping") or by folding the stomach ("gastric plication") have also been tried; these are experimental procedures (13, 14).

An assessment of these procedures must first take into account that, although different in some important respects, both intestinal and gastric bypasses are major surgical interventions with significant risks of morbidity and mortality. For jejunoileal bypass, the mortality at major medical centers is in the range of three to four percent, although in some reports it has been over 10 percent (1, 15). Morbidity includes somatic complications that may follow any major abdominal procedure (e.g., wound infections, dehiscence, and thrombophlebitis) as well as others that are characteristic of intestinal bypass surgery (1, 9, 15). These commonly include diarrhea, electrolyte disturbances (manifested by weakness, nausea and vomiting, or tetany) and hypoproteinemia with hair loss. Other complications are cholelithiasis, liver disturbances (which rarely may progress to liver failure), bacterial overgrowth in the defunctionalized bowel (with symptoms of colonic obstruction, distention, fever, toxicity, and occasionally arthralgias and arthropathy). Over 50 percent of patients suffer some adverse sequelae of the operation (1). The most serious metabolic complications occur during the first one to three years, after which there is a tendency for the physical status of the patient to stabilize. Diarrhea may continue for years. Some major complications, mainly arthropathy and uropathy, can occur later, well after the first three years (9, 15).

The complications of gastric bypass are different from those of jejunoileal bypass. Mortality appears to be less than for jejunoileal bypass (approximately, 0.5 to 3 percent) (11, 12, 16, 17). The principal complications of gastric bypass are seen early in the postoperative period and include repeated vomiting, rupture of the suture line, or stretching of the gastric pouch. The last two make the operation ineffective so that reoperation is necessary. Leakage of the gastroenteric anastomosis with resulting peritonitis may also occur. Stomal ulceration or dumping syndrome may develop. On the other hand, gastric bypass does not have any of the serious metabolic complications (electrolyte, liver, kidney or gallbladder problems, arthritis, abdominal distention, diarrhea) that are seen months or years after jejunoileal bypass. Therefore, once the patient has weathered the early postoperative period, the long-term course is generally uncomplicated and benign. Patients experience a satisfactory weight loss without evidence of chronic ill health.

The indications for bypass surgery, whether intestinal or gastric, are essentially the same and are readily summarized. Either procedure may be considered when obesity is very severe and when the patient has made repeated but unsuccessful attempts at weight reduction (1, 18). The patient is considered a candidate for bypass surgery if he weighs at least twice his ideal body weight or over 250 to 300 pounds. Most candidates are young adults (in Scott's [9] series of 200 patients, ages ranged between 16 and 63, the average being 36 years). Although there is a satisfactory weight loss after gastric bypass, patients with jejunoileal bypass generally lose somewhat more weight than patients with gastric bypass (19).

As noted above, gastric bypass not only is being used increasingly as the "first operation," but also is employed when jejunoileal bypass has failed (11, 16). In cases where jejunoileal bypass has been reversed because of complications and converted into a gastric bypass, the results usually have been very satisfactory. On the other hand, jejunoileal bypass has the capacity to lower permanently cholesterol and serum triglycerides, which gastric bypass does not. For this reason, Scott prefers the jejunoileal bypass in those cases with sustained hyperlipidemia (19). The major physical contraindications to all forms of bypass surgery are renal insufficiency, progressive myocardial disease, inflammatory bowel disease, pulmonary embolization, progressive liver disease, and alcoholism (1). Because alcoholism has serious implications for the success of jejunoileal bypass, initial history-taking must specifically exclude heavy use of alcohol, past as well as present. Inasmuch as this may not be an obvious feature of the history, it must be watched for carefully.

The psychiatric contraindications to bypass surgery have not been clearly established. Although psychiatric screening is generally part of the preoperative work-up and is considered important, definite psychiatric criteria for assessment have not yet been evolved. In earlier years, psychiatric participation was limited to the "post hoc" assessment of patients who had already been selected by medical criteria. More recently there has been a tendency to include psychiatric assessment in the initial selection process.

From the experience to date, several key points have emerged. First, most superobese patients, although handicapped by excessive size, are surprisingly free of major psychopathology. Often they show some character problems of passive dependency or passive aggressiveness, particularly the latter (20, 21). These are usually quite compatible with satisfactory everyday functioning. Serious emotional disturbances (psychosis or incapacitating neurosis, including severe depression) are rare (20–26). These clinical findings have also been confirmed by psychological testing (20, 21, 23). Most patients appear sufficiently stable to withstand the stress of surgery and to make the necessary adaptations of the postoperative period (20–24). Currently, the principal goal of the psychiatric assessment is to identify the very rare patient who has a chronic psychosis and the occasional patient with a history of recurrent depression, alcoholism, emotional instability, marked impulsivity, or hypochondriasis. Emotional instability and impulsivity are generally associated with poor capacity to cooperate with follow-up. Alcoholism has similar implications, in addition to the likelihood of complicating liver disease.

A very important function of the psychiatric evaluation is to help assess the patient's motivation for surgery. One wishes to recognize those who are seriously ambivalent (21) or who have grossly unrealistic expectations (27, 28). Ambivalence and impulsivity are often associated. The request for surgery may be prompted largely by the search for a magical solution. It is essential, therefore, to establish a basis for true informed consent. To this end, one wishes to review with the patient carefully, in detail, and on more than one occasion, what the surgery actually entails. The patient should be informed about risk, outcome, and possible major complications. This should be done not only for the sake of "informed consent" about the procedure itself, but also to advise the patient about its probable impact on his life, about the possibility of complications both early and late, and about the importance of adequate postoperative follow-up. An effective way of dealing with the patient's ambivalence is to arrange for a long period of evaluation. We recommend that at least one month elapse between the first contact with the treatment team and the time of surgery (21). Given enough time, those who are significantly ambivalent drop out on their own and generally do not have to be excluded. The staff should avoid urging the procedure on the prospective candidate. In fact, it is best not to persuade, however indirectly, those who seem reluctant. The prospective candidate, in short, should both be well informed and essentially positive about the forthcoming procedure.

The patient's family plays an important role and should be involved in the preliminary discussions and in the final decision for or against surgery.

Some, in fact, believe that surgery should not be performed unless there is full concurrence by a key member of the family (27, 28). It is also desirable that the prospective candidate, to be informed adequately, talk with someone who already has had the operation (27, 28).

Psychological testing, principally the Minnesota Multiphasic Personality Inventory (MMPI), is generally included in the initial psychiatric evaluation (8, 9, 21–24, 28–30). Formal psychotherapy, however, is usually not indicated and, even if it is offered, superobese patients seldom avail themselves of it (20, 21, 25). Of 12 superobese women who after jejunoileal bypass were offered regular once-per-week psychotherapy without fee, none availed herself of the offer. All, however, maintained monthly follow-up appointments and seven spontaneously asked for additional visits during especially stressful periods (20, 21). In short, these patients are inclined to try to handle their own affairs, although they may turn to the physician for help if a crisis arises.

The indications for jaw-wiring are substantially different from those for the bypass procedures. The principal characteristic of jaw-wiring is that it does not involve a major surgical procedure and carries no particular risk. Therefore, it may be employed to treat mild as well as severe cases of obesity. It is appropriate for patients who are 30–50 pounds overweight as well as for those who weigh over 300 pounds (31, 32).

Jaw-wiring has been available for some time, but it has been performed mainly by dentists and has not yet received extensive study. Jaw-wiring or temporomandibular fixation involves placing small buttons on the premolars and then wiring these buttons together to keep the jaws shut. The patient is given an 800-calorie liquid diet and, if he adheres to it, weight loss occurs very satisfactorily (31, 32).

The problem with jaw-wiring is that compliance is generally poor (31). Although the wires are not painful and do not interfere with speech, many patients find them confining and unpleasant over long periods. The patient at first loses weight without experiencing hunger or weakness, is able to function effectively in his usual activities, and is pleased with the overall result. After the initial outburst of enthusiasm, however, he is likely to feel restricted by the wires and then begins to resent them. The wires appear to mobilize the patients' not inconsiderable passive-aggressiveness. The result is that most patients "cheat" on their diet (31). Therefore, they stop losing weight or actually regain the weight they have just lost and then become discouraged and frustrated. A number of them experience the restriction imposed by the procedure so keenly that they find a variety of excuses for clipping their wires. Jaw-wiring initially appeals to both patients and physicians because it seems to demand very little from the patient. Actually, this is not the case. The patient needs to collaborate actively with the program and inability to do so results in failure of the treatment. Not surprisingly, the patients who respond best to jaw-wiring are those who are psychologically fairly well integrated and motivated. Because of these psychological limitations, jaw-wiring does not appear particularly effective in the routine treatment of unselected patients with minor degrees of obesity (31). It may have value in the treatment of superobese patients who, because of coexisting major medical problems, are not candidates for bypass treatment. It has not, however, been adequately tested with this population.

## RESULTS OF JEJUNOILEAL AND GASTRIC BYPASS SURGERY

In this section the postoperative course and related problems of psychological adjustment, following both intestinal and gastric bypass, will be considered.

### Weight Loss

After jejunoileal bypass, the significant weight loss occurs during the first postoperative year. Most patients lose approximately eight to 15 pounds per month. The weight loss then slows down and the weight generally stabilizes in two or three years between 150 and 200 pounds — in other words, well above the patient's "ideal" weight (1, 21). Most patients lose between 100 and 150 pounds. A modest weight gain may occur after two years, as the intestine stretches and the absorbing mucosa hypertrophies (8). Although the period of active weight loss may be associated, as has been described above, with a variety of physical symptoms and may therefore be stressful, patients usually are very pleased by the weight loss itself. They experience it as a major personal achievement and seem quite willing to accept the physical discomforts that may accompany it. There is often an atmosphere of pleasurable excitement and patients often say that they "can't wait" to get down to a normal weight. According to some reports (22, 30, 33) very rapid weight loss may be associated with greater psychological distress than if it occurs more slowly. This is not well established. However, those who do *not* lose an adequate amount of weight typically show much unhappiness and disappointment. Often this leads them to seek reoperation for revision of the bypass (21, 25).

After gastric bypass, weight loss proceeds rapidly, as after jejunoileal bypass, and most weight loss similarly occurs during the first postoperative year. The average weight loss after gastric bypass, however, is approximately 75 pounds, i.e., less than the average after jejunoileal bypass (16, 19).

*Appetite and Food Intake*

After jejunoileal bypass, weight loss occurs not only because food absorption has been curtailed surgically but also because food intake now is less (1, 21). During the first postoperative year, patients report that they eat significantly less and less often than they had before surgery. Occasionally, they may eat only one or two meals a day; sometimes they even "forget" to eat for an entire day. Snacking between meals and binge eating decrease markedly. The reasons for this are not altogether clear, but an important factor is the effect of food intake which promptly results in diarrhea, abdominal cramping, and flatus. In other words, the operation creates a spontaneous aversive conditioning which serves to monitor and regulate food intake. Postoperatively, patients also become aware of the passage of food through the intestine ("like it is falling down a chute"); this sensation also contributes to the phenomenon of aversive conditioning. I have been struck that superobese persons seem endowed with "superior" gastrointestinal tracts. With a detailed history one can ascertain that prior to bypass surgery these patients usually were remarkably free of common digestive complaints. By contrast, after bypass surgery they become aware, for the first time, of a variety of sensations coming from the gastrointestinal tract.

Another interesting postoperative finding is the change in the taste preference for sweets. The subjective preference for a 40 percent sucrose solution was significantly lower after surgery than before, although preference for 2.5, 5, or 10 percent solutions was not affected (1, 34). Patients also learned to moderate the intake of roughage and of fried or spicy food because they are irritating to the bowel and cause diarrhea. Some patients report cravings for other foods, especially fruits and vegetables, that generally were not an important part of their preoperative diet. After the first postoperative year, when gastrointestinal symptoms have significantly subsided, food intake gradually increases again so that beyond the second or third year it approximates once more, both in amount and in kind, the preoperative pattern (21). However, detailed studies of the late postoperative eating habits are lacking.

After gastric bypass, an immediate change in eating habits is required (11, 16). The patient must learn to reduce markedly his food intake at any one meal in order to adapt to the now much smaller size of the functional stomach. To this end, some surgeons give the patient special instruction, both preoperatively and immediately postoperatively, on the importance of accommodating to the new gastric capacity. Most patients manage this without too much difficulty, and appropriate weight loss follows. On the other hand, if the patient persists in eating large portions, vomiting may result or tearing of the suture lines and stretching of the gastric pouch. This, in fact, should be suspected if the patient fails to show steady weight loss. Gastric bypass, in other words, is not "foolproof." If the patient is not able to cooperate, he can "override" the procedure, either by eating large portions (and stretching the gastric pouch), or by eating frequent portions and managing thereby to sustain a high caloric intake (16, 17). Again, a true change in the patient's eating habits must take place for a successful outcome of, and adaptation to, the operation. Because the basis of the procedure is a restriction of food intake, no special change in food preferences has been noted (35). There is also no postoperative diarrhea.

### Adaptive Reactions and Personal Adjustment in the Postoperative Period

According to most studies, patients' response to intestinal bypass surgery is generally positive (1, 8, 9, 21, 22, 24, 28, 33, 36–42). Approximately 66–90 percent of patients are pleased or very pleased with the result (1, 9, 22). Some reports (22, 25, 28, 33, 43) are more tentative and mention the occurrence of some psychiatric complications during the postoperative period. In the main, however, there is substantial agreement that patients generally derive significant psychological benefits.

Patients' emotional responses to gastric bypass have not yet received extensive study, but the evidence available to date indicates that the usual reaction is positive and that the results closely parallel those of jejunoileal bypass (12, 16, 19, 42). The principal difference is that after gastric bypass serious metabolic complications generally do not occur and that the psychiatric complications of protracted ill health are therefore not seen.

The following description of postoperative adaptation is drawn largely from the literature on jejunoileal bypass, but most of the findings to be described appear applicable to gastric bypass as well (with the exception, as already noted, of the absence of psychiatric complications due to chronic metabolic derangements).

Very soon after surgery, patients become aware that they are losing weight at a steady rate. Inasmuch as they have battled obesity unsuccessfully for years, patients typically respond to the experience of seeing their fat disappear week by week with great satisfaction, a sense of achievement, and even with mild euphoria (21, 24, 36). They see their lives as finally taking a positive turn and have a sense of becoming free from the restrictions and limitations that for years their obesity had imposed on them (21, 24). They rediscover the pleasure of greater activity. This, first, is physical activity, especially walking without becoming fatigued or short of breath. Soon patients also report that they are more active socially, that they have taken steps toward finding employment (33), that they are losing their shyness and self-consciousness, and that they are mingling with people more freely. They also report that they are dating, perhaps for the first time in years, and that they are becoming sexually active. These changes are reflected in increased self-confidence, in a lighter and more optimistic mood, in greater assertiveness, and in a reappraisal of their body size.

The main complications at this time are frequent diarrhea, nausea, and abdominal distress after eating. There may be weakness and vomiting; at times, these have been looked upon as "psychogenic" in origin, but usually they are manifestations of electrolyte imbalance or hepatic disturbance (21, 44). During this period patients are so pleased by their weight loss that they are not inclined to dwell on the complications and seek to deemphasize their significance. Thus, at early follow-up, patients may need to be carefully questioned to establish whether they are experiencing physical difficulties.

After six months, patients report other changes which they regard as major milestones. They rediscover the capacity to cross their legs, to sit comfortably in an ordinary arm chair so that they can attend the movies or the theater and pass through turnstiles at the supermarket. These events are new, for the first time in years, and are experienced as great accomplishments (21). Being able to move through a crowd without eliciting the attention and comments of passersby further helps to increase self-confidence and evokes in some patients a sense akin to "being reborn."

Patients also derive a new sense of pride and self-enhancement from their experience with clothes (21). They discover that they require progressively smaller sizes and are able once more to find ready-made clothes. Women tend to choose dresses that are more shapely and colorful than those that they had worn before surgery. They also begin to pay attention to their grooming, to use lipstick and other beauty aids, so that generally they look more attractive. They receive compliments about their appearance from friends and family, and almost every patient reports the experience, which is exciting as well as troublesome, of not being recognized by acquaintances during a casual encounter. These experiences confirm and consolidate the patient's sense of a "new self." Sometimes patients find themselves the object of envy, a not altogether unpleasant experience; one of our patients, for example, learned that her mother had decided to undergo bypass surgery herself. Also, often there is reluctance to mingle with fat people (21). This attitude is noticeable approximately six months after surgery and becomes more firmly established thereafter. Patients typically explain that they do not wish to be reminded of when they were fat—associating with fat people hinders them in developing "a normal identity."

Improvement in patients' self-esteem is frequently accompanied by reports that they have become more outspoken, less concerned about pleasing others, and generally more assertive (21, 22, 24, 36). They are pleased with these changes, which further contribute to their positive view of the surgery.

Patients, however, also encounter stress during the postoperative period (21, 22, 25, 28). Although generally they have gained in self-esteem, most patients also become aware of greater emotionality and fluctuations of anxiety, depression, and hostility. It is not unusual for patients to mention spontaneously that they "have developed quite a temper." This, in turn, may increase the tension in patients' close interpersonal relations, particularly with parents and spouses. Some patients' marriages, which prior to surgery had been quiescent, become more strained and end in divorce (28, 45). Patients who are single or recently divorced experience stress when they begin dating actively and particularly when new relationships finally bring requirements of closeness and permanence (21, 40, 45). I have seen several women patients do well as long as they could view a new relationship as a temporary "affair"; they became upset when the men they were dating "became serious" and proposed marriage.

The changes in body image are an important aspect of the postoperative adaptation and for this reason deserve special comment. We need to remind ourselves that the alteration in body size is extreme and that patients lose approximately half of their preoperative body weight in the course of one year. Despite this, the alteration in body size is for the most part psychologically uncomplicated and, in fact, eagerly sought. Immediately after the operation, patients report feeling slimmer, even before there has been time for significant weight loss to occur. This may be regarded as "a placebo effect" of the operation and is, again, an expression of the patients' strong wish to lose weight (21, 40, 46). During the ensuing months, as weight is lost, patients are able to assess with reasonable accuracy the progressive changes in body size. In other words, the perceptual-cognitive component of the body image is fundamentally realistic and seems to adapt quite promptly to the marked weight loss. If asked to make figure drawings depicting their own size, patients have little difficulty in monitoring their level of weight loss at any particular time (46). The affective component of the body image, however, changes much more slowly and appears much more independent of external influences. Although pleased that they have lost weight, one to three years after surgery patients still retain dysphoric feelings about their bodies which they still do not consider attractive (46). In a late follow-up study, we found that these feelings are significantly retained six or more years after surgery (47). These findings are in agreement with an observation by Stunkard and Mendelson (48), made prior to the advent of bypass surgery, that the affective distortions of the body image "may persist long after successful weight reduction." I want to note in passing that not all the literature is in agreement on this point. Kalucy and Crisp (28, 33) observed a lag in the response of the body image to the progressive reduction in body size. These apparently discrepant findings are likely due to the fact that these authors did not separate the perceptual-cognitive from the affective component of the body image in their study.

We still lack clarity on the matter of postoperative psychiatric complications. Some authors have given the impression that fairly serious reactions, mainly depressions, are not uncommon (25, 28, 33, 43). Unfortunately, detailed descriptions of these depressions or of the circumstances surrounding them are not usually given. Little is said about the difficulties of the patients and the impression is conveyed that these were "psychogenic" disturbances in response to the weight loss. Espmark (43), for example, noted that 40 of his 65 patients needed postoperative psychotherapy "due to anxiety and depression," that three had "serious psychogenic vomiting," that four made "serious suicidal attempts," and that 17 "reported thoughts of suicide or weariness of life." Still others experienced what Espmark termed "crises of self assertion" and "body image crises." Other psychiatric authors give the impression that the main physical problem that patients encounter postoperatively is diarrhea (22, 25, 33) and hardly mention the other complications — much more serious, yet not uncommon — that caused protracted ill health. In my experience, serious depressions are very infrequent although, as noted above, rapid weight loss may be somewhat stressful and accompanied by mood fluctuations (21, 40). More specifically, I have not seen major postoperative psychiatric complications or decompensations occur spontaneously or de novo in bypass patients. In every instance of serious emotional disturbance that I have observed, they occurred in the context and as a consequence of prolonged physical complications.

It is not difficult to understand that patients who experience painful or debilitating physical symptoms for prolonged periods — for weeks, months, and occasionally for years — often *do* become very depressed and discouraged; they may even feel suicidal. Various factors contribute to these feelings. Patients realize that the treatment of some of the major complications of intestinal bypass surgery (e.g., bypass enteritis, liver involvement) is not yet fully established and that physicians, despite their best efforts, at times have difficulty controlling them (40). Patients who live far from the medical center where the operation was performed may discover that their hometown physician is unfamiliar with the complications themselves and uncertain about how to treat them. For instance, a patient who had recurrent episodes of shaking chills and high fever (probably due to bacterial overgrowth in the intestine) had been advised repeatedly not to worry and that "it was nothing, just the flu." She had reacted to this advice with discouragement and perplexity until finally she had returned to the medical center where her symptoms were diagnosed as complications of the jejunoileal bypass and treated appropriately. In patients with repeated vomiting, electrolyte disturbance or bypass enteritis sometimes goes unrecognized, and the vomiting may be considered "psychogenic" (44). Thus, a patient whose anxiety and increasing discouragement were associated with deteriorating health and progressive renal insufficiency had been referred in his hometown for intensive psychotherapy, while his worsening physical status had gone unnoticed.

The emotional disturbances that occur in these instances typically manifest themselves as profound misery, discouragement, agitation, and crying spells; these occur when major physical symptoms remain unrelieved for long periods. Many bypass patients are particularly frightened and upset by prolonged ill health because, prior to their operation, they generally had felt well and strong despite the handicaps of obesity. Most had had no experience with chronic illness or with major surgery.

If serious physical symptoms continue, the patient may require reoperation. Reversal of the bypass (with reestablishment of normal intestinal continuity) or revision of the bypass (with exteriorization of the end of the jejunal loop) may be called for. Reversal of the bypass can be life-saving, and it becomes necessary in eight to 25 percent of cases (19, 49). It is important to note that the emotional as well as the physical symptoms usually subside promptly following reversal of the bypass (25, 50). Problems, however, do not end here; after reversal, patients tend to regain their original weight and this becomes, once more, a source of great frustration and discouragement. When serious metabolic problems arise, rather than simply reverse the intestinal bypass, the tendency has recently been to convert it to a gastric bypass (11). This combined procedure usually seems to have good results.

Bypass patients generally maintain a positive view of the surgery, even when they are struggling with serious complications (1, 21, 40, 47). Although they may be having major difficulties, they try to maintain a positive outlook and are still willing to endorse the operation and recommend it to others. I can recall only very few patients who, as a result of their own unsatisfactory experience, had clearly negative views about the procedure and had become outspoken against it. Thus, one often has the impression that denial is prominently at work. For example, a physician who had undergone bypass surgery and who was in poor health because of electrolyte and kidney problems referred one of his own patients for bypass surgery; the latter, parenthetically, did much better than the physician. Another patient spoke positively about the operation even though she had been in poor health for several years because of electrolyte problems and recurrent thrombophlebitis. After a young acquaintance to whom she had recommended bypass surgery died during the procedure, our patient no longer endorsed the operation but, when asked about it, assumed a neutral stance, telling each inquirer to make up his own mind.

It is striking that patients are usually willing to endure ill health from bypass complications for long periods, months, or even years, before they will agree to a reversal of the bypass (40, 47). When they do, generally it is with great reluctance. The reasons for this attitude are not difficult to understand. They are hesitant to conclude that their original decision had been "a mistake" and that they must submit to further surgery. However, they are also very grateful for their weight loss, even though it may have been purchased at the cost of new health problems. They are fearful — realistically — that after reversal of the bypass they will gain weight once more to their preoperative level (as noted above, this can now be avoided by converting the intestinal to a gastric bypass). It is important to keep these attitudes in mind because most assessments of the success of bypass surgery are based in part on patients' satisfaction with the results. Such assessments do not reflect adequately the patients' tendency to understate negative experiences and tend to be artificially skewed toward the positive.

## CONCLUSIONS

It is not the purpose of this paper to provide an assessment of bypass surgery; yet a few summarizing comments — particularly about the psychiatric aspects of these procedures — are in order.

As was pointed out at the outset, extreme obesity is a condition which usually does not respond to conservative measures. Therefore, the merits of surgical therapy must be viewed in this context, keeping in mind the risks and disability of untreated obesity.

Both procedures, jejunoileal and gastric bypass, have been tried extensively and have emerged from the experimental stage, although controversy regarding their appropriateness remains and strongly dissenting voices continue to be heard (51–54). At this time, gastric bypass seems to be increasingly favored as the operation of choice because it is free of most of the long-term metabolic complications of jejunoileal bypass.

It is well to keep in mind, however, that both operations have risks consistent with major surgical procedures. These have been discussed. Inasmuch as these procedures are elective, a decision to intervene surgically should be made only most deliberately and after informing the patient fully of its implications.

Most superobese patients, especially those gravely limited by their obesity, benefit from these operations (40, 42). Psychiatrically, both operations appear benign, although this has not yet been studied adequately in the case of gastric bypass, the newer operation. "Psychogenic" complications are rare. Most emotional complications reflect the patient's physical status. In a few cases, though, negative reactions are simply a continuation of preexisting emotional difficulties which had not been adequately recognized prior to surgery. Generally, patients who do well surgically and metabolically do well psychiatrically also. Typically, those whose response is positive find their lives greatly enhanced and are very pleased. Conversely, negative psychological reactions usually occur as complications of prolonged ill health.

The role of psychiatric factors in determining outcome has not been established. As noted earlier, serious psychopathology is rare in those seeking bypass surgery. In the case of jejunoileal bypass, a key unanswered question is why most patients do very well while a few do so poorly (47). It is unclear to what the differences in outcome are due and therefore what can be done to prevent complications. In the case of gastric bypass, psychological factors play a more obvious role in that difficulty accepting a limited food intake postoperatively can result in failure of the operation. These instances, however, have not been sufficiently studied to date.

In summary, both jejunoileal and gastric bypass operations, while not without risk or serious limitations, offer the most effective currently available treatment for a condition that otherwise brings grave, progressive, life-long handicap.

## REFERENCES

1. BRAY, G. A. and BENFIELD, J. R.: Intestinal bypass for obesity: A summary and perspective. *Am. J. Clin. Nutr.,* 30:121–127, 1977.
2. DRENICK, E. G.: Weight reduction by prolonged fasting. In: G. A. Bray, *Obesity in Perspective.* Fogarty Int. Center Series on Preventive Medicine, sect. 6, vol. 2, chapt. 44, pp. 341–360. Washington, DC: US Government Printing Office, DHEW No. NIH 75-705, 1976.
3. KOLLAR, E. G., ATKINSON, R. M., and ALBIN, D. L.: The effectiveness of fasting in the treatment of superobesity. *Psychosomatics,* 10: 125–135, 1969.
4. PAYNE, J. H., DEWIND, L. T., and COMMONS, R. R.: Metabolic observations in patients with jejunocolic shunts. *Am. J. Surg.,* 106:273–289, 1963.

5. MASON, E. E. and ITO, C.: Gastric bypass. *Ann. Surg.,* 170:329–339, 1969.
6. HALLBERG, D.: A survey of surgical techniques for treatment of obesity and a remark on the bilio-intestinal bypass method. *Am. J. Clin. Nutr.,* 33:499–501, 1980.
7. SCOPINARO, N., GIANETTA, E., CIVALLERI, D., et al.: Two years of clinical experience with bilio-pancreatic bypass for obesity. *Am. J. Clin. Nutr.,* 33:506–514, 1980.
8. DEWIND, L. T. and PAYNE, J. H.: Intestinal bypass surgery for morbid obesity. Long term results. *J. Am. Med. Ass.,* 236:2298–2301, 1976.
9. SCOTT, H. W., JR., DEAN, R. H., SHULL, H. J., et al.: Results of jejunoileal bypass in two hundred patients with morbid obesity. *Surg. Gynec. Obstet.,* 145:661–673, 1977.
10. GASPAR, M. R., MOVIUS, H. J., ROSENTAL, J. J., et al.: Comparison of Payne and Scott operations for morbid obesity. *Ann. Surg.,* 184:507–515, 1976.
11. MASON, E. E., PRINTEN, K. J., BLOMMERS, T. J., et al.: Gastric bypass in morbid obesity. *Am. J. Clin. Nutr.,* 33:395–405, 1980.
12. GOMEZ, C. A.: Gastroplasty in the surgical treatment of morbid obesity. *Am. J. Clin. Nutr.,* 33:406–415, 1980.
13. WILKINSON, L. H.: Reduction of gastric reservoir capacity. *Am. J. Clin. Nutr.,* 33:515–517, 1980.
14. TRETBAR, L. L., TAYLOR, T. L., and SIFERS, E. C.: Weight reduction. Gastric plication in morbid obesity. *J. Kans. Med. Soc.,* 77:488–490, 1976.
15. PI-SUNYER, F. X.: Jejunoileal bypass surgery for obesity. *Am. J. Clin. Nutr.,* 29:409–416, 1976.
16. MASON, E. E., PRINTEN, K. J., BLOMMERS, T. J., et al.: Gastric bypass for obesity after ten years experience. *Int. J. Obes.,* 2:197–206, 1978.
17. BUCHWALD, H.: True informed consent in surgical treatment of morbid obesity: The current case for both jejunoileal and gastric bypass. *Am. J. Clin. Nutr.,* 33:482–494, 1980.
18. FALOON, W. W.: Ileal bypass for obesity: Postoperative perspective. *Hosp. Pract.,* 12:73–82, 1977.
19. SCOTT, H. W., JR.: Jejunoileal bypass versus gastric bypass or gastroplasty in the operative treatment of obesity. *Langenbeck's Archiv. für Chirurgie* (In Press).
20. CASTELNUOVO-TEDESCO, P. and SCHIEBEL, D.: Studies of superobesity. I. Psychological characteristics of superobese patients. *Int. J. Psychiat. in Med.,* 6:465–480, 1975.
21. CASTELNUOVO-TEDESCO, P. and SCHIEBEL, D.: Studies of superobesity. II. Psychiatric appraisal of jejuno-ileal bypass surgery. *Am. J. Psychiat.,* 133:26–31, 1976.
22. ABRAM, H. S., MEIXEL, S. A., WEBB, W. W., et al.: Psychological adaptation to jejuno-ileal bypass for morbid obesity. *J. Nerv. Ment. Dis.,* 162:151–157, 1976.
23. WEBB, W. W., PHARES, R., ABRAM, H. S., et al.: Jejunoileal bypass procedures in morbid obesity; preoperative psychological findings. *J. Clin. Psychol.,* 32:82–85, 1976.
24. SOLOW, C., SILBERFARB, P. M., and SWIFT, K.: Psychosocial effects of intestinal bypass surgery for severe obesity. *New Engl. J. Med.,* 290:300–304, 1974.
25. WISE, T. N.: Adverse psychologic reactions to ileal bypass surgery. *South Med. J.,* 69:1533–1535, 1976.

26. HALMI, K. A., LONG, M., STUNKARD, A. J., and MASON, E.: Psychiatric diagnosis of morbidly obese gastric bypass patients. *Am. J. Psychiat.,* 137(4):470–472, 1980.
27. WEHLAGE, D. F. and BECHTOLD, D. L.: Description of the evaluation process for surgically treated obesity. *J. Indiana St. Med. Ass.,* 69:833–835, 1976.
28. KALUCY, R. S. and CRISP, A. H.: Some psychological and social implications of massive obesity. *J. Psychosom. Res.,* 18:465–473, 1974.
29. LUNDGREN, K. D., SCOTT, G., and GRABSKI, D. A.: The value of psychiatric team screening of candidates for jejunoileal bypass surgery. *Am. J. Surg.,* 133:569–571, 1977.
30. NEILL, J. R. and MARSHALL, J. R.: End-to-end jejunoileal bypass for morbid obesity: The psychosocial outcome. *Wisc. Med. J.,* 76:103–105, 1976.
31. CASTELNUOVO-TEDESCO, P., BUCHANAN, D. C., and HALL, H. D.: Jaw-wiring for obesity. *Gen. Hosp. Psychiat.,* 2:156–159, 1980.
32. KARK, A. E.: Jaw wiring. *Am. J. Clin. Nutr.,* 33:420–424, 1980.
33. CRISP, A. H., KALUCY, R. S., PILKINGTON, T. R. E., et al.: Some psychosocial consequences of ileojejunal bypass surgery. *Am. J. Clin. Nutr.,* 30:109–120, 1977.
34. BRAY, G. A., DAHMS, W. T., ATKINSON, R. L., et al.: Factors controlling food intake: A comparison of dieting and intestinal bypass. *Am. J. Nutr.,* 33:376–382, 1980.
35. HALMI, K. A., MASON, E., FALK, J., et al.: Appetite behavior after gastric bypass for obesity. *Int. J. Obes.,* (In Press).
36. SOLOW, C.: Psychosocial aspects of intestinal bypass for massive obesity: Current status. *Am. J. Clin. Nutr.,* 30:103–108, 1977.
37. ISHIDA, Y.: Sexuality after small bowel bypass. *Curr. Med. Dialog,* 41:659–662, 1974.
38. HARRIS, J. and FRAME, B.: *A Psychiatric Study of Patients Undergoing Intestinal Bypass for Treatment of Intractable Obesity.* 124th Annual Meeting of American Psychiatric Association, 1968.
39. MILLS, M. J. and STUNKARD, A. J.: Behavioral changes following surgery for obesity. *Am. J. Psychiat.,* 133:527–531, 1976.
40. CASTELNUOVO-TEDESCO, P.: Jejuno-ileal bypass for superobesity: A psychiatric assessment. *Adv. Psychosom. Med.,* 10:196–206, 1980.
41. DANÖ, P. and HAHN-PEDERSEN, J.: Improvement in quality of life following jejunoileal bypass surgery for obesity. *Scand. J. Gastroenterol.,* 12:769–774, 1977.
42. HALMI, K. A., STUNKARD, A. J., and MASON, E. E.: Emotional responses to weight reduction by three methods: Gastric bypass, jejunoileal bypass, diet. *Am. J. Clin. Nutr.,* 33:446–451, 1980.
43. ESPMARK, S.: *Psychological Adjustment Before and After Bypass Surgery for Extreme Obesity — A Preliminary Report.* 1st International Congress on Obesity, London, 1974.
44. STARKLOFF, G. B., DONOVAN, J. F., RAMACH, R., et al.: Metabolic intestinal surgery. Its complications and management. *Arch. Surg.,* Chicago, 11:652–657, 1975.
45. MARSHALL, J. R. and NEILL, J.: The removal of a psychosomatic symptom: Effects on the marriage. *Fam. Process,* 16:273–280, 1977.
46. SCHIEBEL, D. and CASTELNUOVO-TEDESCO, P.: Studies of superobesity: III. Body

image changes after jejuno-ileal bypass surgery. *Int. J. Psychiat. in Med.,* 8: 117–123, 1978.

47. CASTELNUOVO-TEDESCO, P., WEINBERG, J., BUCHANAN, D. C., and SCOTT, H. W., JR.: *Am. J. Psychiat.* (In Press)

48. STUNKARD, A. and MENDELSON, M.: Obesity and the body image: I. Characteristics of disturbances in the body image of some obese persons. *Am. J. Psychiat.,* 123:1296–1300, 1967.

49. HALVERSON, J. D., SCHEFF, R. J., GENTRY, K., et al.: Long-term follow-up of jejunoileal bypass patients. *Am. J. Clin. Nutr.,* 33:472–475, 1980.

50. REYNOLDS, T. B.: Medical complications of intestinal bypass surgery. In: Stollerman, G. H. (Ed.), *Advances in Internal Medicine.* Chicago: Year Book Medical Publications, 1978, vol. 23, pp. 47–59.

51. HIRSCH, J.: Jejunoileal shunt for obesity. *New Engl. J. Med.,* 290:962–963, 1974.

52. WOOLEY, S. C., WOOLEY, O. W., and DYRENFORTH, S.: The case against radical interventions. *Am. J. Clin. Nutr.,* 33:465–471, 1980.

53. GARROW, J. S.: Combined medical-surgical approaches to treatment of obesity. *Am. J. Clin. Nutr.,* 33:425–430, 1980.

54. RAVITCH, M. M. and BROLIN, R. E.: The price of weight loss by jejunoileal shunt. *Ann. Surg.,* 190:382–391, 1979.

# Part II

# SLEEPING

# 5

# The Biology of Sleep: Recent Developments and Clinical Applications

## William C. Orr, Ph.D.

During the last quarter of a century a remarkable proliferation of research has occurred concerned with various processes related to sleep. Investigations have ranged from the cognitive aspects of sleep to physiological and biochemical mechanisms. More recent endeavors have continued to document the original findings of unique physiological changes associated with the sleep state. The initial observations of Kleitman, Aserinsky and Dement, documenting the phenomenon of periodic rapid eye movements during sleep and their association with dreaming in humans, created enthusiasm that the study of sleep could make a significant contribution to understanding the pathogenesis of mental illness (1, 2). This enthusiasm was based on the simplistic notion that the waking thought processes of some schizophrenics resembled the rather capricious mental content of a normal dream. Consequently, the great majority of subsequent investigative efforts in sleep have been primarily concerned with psychophysiological phenomena.

As interest has intensified in the basic physiological and biochemical alterations during sleep, a unique physiology of sleep has emerged. It is patently clear that an understanding of basic life processes, and aberrations of basic life functions, cannot be fully understood without consideration of the complementary aspects of sleeping and waking physiology. Increasing awareness of the importance of sleep to basic life processes has markedly altered the focus on the applications of research in sleep physiology. The dec-

105

ade of the 1970s saw a dramatic shift in the emphasis of research on sleep towards the problems of clinical medicine. During the last 10 years, articles concerning pathophysiological processes during sleep have appeared in journals of nearly every subspecialty of medicine (3). Two particularly salient examples are endocrinology and pulmonary medicine. In these two medical subspecialties, sleep studies have become an integral part of the evaluation of many patients since numerous investigations have shown unique alterations in basic endocrine and respiratory functions during sleep (4, 5).

The increasing interest in sleep phenomena in the diagnosis and management of a variety of medical conditions has resulted in the establishment of facilities specifically devoted to the diagnostic assessment of patients during sleep. As these facilities proliferated at numerous major medical centers throughout the United States, a formal organization was formed in order to establish and maintain high quality in the delivery of clinical services in this area. This organization is called the Association of Sleep Disorders Centers. This group currently certifies individual units which provide service in the area of sleep disorders medicine, as well as individual practitioners in this specialty area. Further evidence of the continuing growth and viability of the field of sleep disorders medicine has been the recent publication of a Sleep Disorders Nosology (6). This landmark effort represents tangible evidence that sleep must be considered in concert with waking physiology and pathophysiology in the modern practice of medicine.

Thus, the emergence of sleep physiology as a basic science and clinical medical discipline represents a unique convergence of scientific and clinical endeavors. This is evidenced by the fact that numerous Ph.D. basic scientists have become certified as practitioners in sleep disorders medicine. The continuous and growing cross-fertilization of the basic and clinical aspects of sleep has clearly fostered rapid developments in both areas. Subsequent discussion will focus on recent developments and clinical applications in three areas of sleep physiology — thermoregulation, respiration, and gastrointestinal functioning (specifically sleep-related gastroesophageal reflux and esophageal acid clearance).

## Basic Sleep Physiology

As background for the ensuing discussion, a cursory review of basic sleep physiology is in order. Sleep is composed of two relatively distinct physiological and behavioral states which can be polygraphically distinguished by recording the electroencephalogram (EEG), electro-oculogram (EOG), and electromyogram (EMG). Sleep begins with the successive occurrence of four discriminable stages, collectively referred to as non-rapid eye movement (NREM) sleep. Stage 1 is a transition stage between waking and sleep which is characterized by a decrease in EEG alpha (12-14 Hz) activity and a predominance of theta (4-7 Hz) EEG activity. Stage 2 begins with the occurrence of sleep spindles which are 12 to 14 Hz bursts of EEG activity. Next, the increasing concentration of delta activity in the EEG heralds the appearance of stages 3 and 4 sleep. These are defined by 20-50 percent of the EEG tracing occupied by delta (2-4 Hz) activity. Greater than 50 percent identifies that segment as stage 4 while between 20-50 percent characterizes stage 3 sleep.

The first episode of rapid eye movement (REM) sleep generally occurs approximately 90 minutes after sleep onset, and is identified by three polygraphic characteristics. These are: the occurrence of low voltage mixed frequency activity in the EEG; a precipitous drop in the EMG activity; and conjugate eye movements in the EOG. Behaviorally, REM sleep is generally associated with the familiar thematic dreaming, while non-REM (NREM) sleep, when cognitive activity can be elicited, is generally associated with more primitive mental content. In addition, REM is associated with a characteristic skeletal muscle paralysis which can be demonstrated by the lack of spinal monosynaptic reflexes. In the normal adult sleep pattern, REM sleep occupies approximately 20–25 percent of the sleeping time, stages 1, 2, 3 and 4 approximately 5, 40, 12 and 8 percent, respectively.

Physiologically, NREM sleep is associated with slow and quite regular heart rate and respiratory rate, with systemic blood pressure reaching its lowest level of the sleeping interval. In contrast, REM sleep is associated with considerable autonomic activation. Heart and respiratory rates are slightly elevated and considerably more variable. There are periodic elevations in systemic blood pressure which can be as much as 30 mmHg systolic pressure over those found during NREM sleep. In addition, brain oxygen consumption is increased during REM. As will be pointed out subsequently, the regulation of a variety of vital life functions is altered during REM sleep, i.e., respiration and thermoregulation. (The regular alternation of REM and NREM sleep constitutes a periodicity of approximately 90 minutes, and this oscillation is precisely regulated by brain stem mechanisms.)

### SLEEP AND THERMOREGULATION

The regulation of core body temperature is a vital homeostatic function. This regulatory process maintains the internal ambiance necessary for all life functions. The importance of maintaining and regulating core body temperature manifests itself in daily life in terms of shivering, sweating, and the malaise associated with a febrile state. That behavioral processes interact intimately with the regulation of body temperature has been known for some time. For example, it has been recognized for many years that the homeostatic "setpoint" or core body temperature is lower during sleep than in the waking state. The circadian temperature cycle has been well established and charted in virtually every homeothermic species (Figure 1). The coupling of thermoregulatory processes and behavior can be further documented by an examination of the extensive literature documenting a close correlation between measures of body temperature and performance (7).

Recent research has shown an even closer relationship between the distribution of sleep stages and the course of the temperature cycle. Zulley has demonstrated distinctly different patterns in the distribution of REM sleep throughout the sleep cycle in free running (absence of time cues) and normally entrained (normal light/dark cycle) conditions (8). Under the free running conditions the temperature trough occurs during the first third of the sleep cycle, and during the entrained circadian cycle the temperature trough occurs during the last third. He also demonstrated that under the former condition REM sleep was distributed evenly throughout the sleep cycle, while under entrained conditions REM sleep tended to concentrate itself in the last third of the sleeping interval.

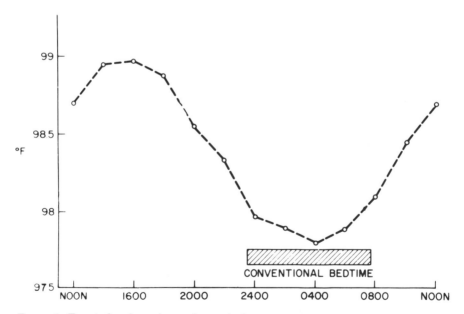

FIGURE 1. Twenty-four hour changes in core body temperature.

Work by Czeisler et al. has shown a tight coupling between the circadian core temperature rhythm and the tendency for REM sleep to occur (9). Their work has shown that REM periods occurring on the rising slope of the temperature cycle have a shorter latency and last longer. In fact, they have described sleep onset REM periods in some individuals during this phase of the temperature cycle. The occurrence of the sleep onset REM periods has previously been thought to be a pathognomonic sign of narcolepsy. Furthermore, alterations in the endogenous body temperature cycle have been linked to sleep disorders associated with both insomnia and hypersomnia (6). Thus, a more precise understanding of the regulatory mechanisms controlling core body temperature and its relationship to REM sleep and other sleep processes has the potential of contributing to our understanding of the pathophysiology of a variety of sleep disorders.

The physiological regulation of core temperature has been shown to be remarkably altered as a function of REM sleep. In a series of brilliant investigations this has been clearly elucidated by Parmeggiani and his collaborators who demonstrated that the regulation of body temperature was quite different during REM sleep when compared with NREM sleep (10). At low ambient temperatures, body temperature tended to show an increase during NREM sleep with a decrease during REM sleep. The opposite occurred under conditions of high ambient temperature. From these data they concluded that NREM sleep is associated with a homeothermic condition, while REM sleep is a poikilothermic state.

Subsequent investigations have verified these initial observations with peripheral skin temperature measurements (11). Peripheral skin temperature measures reflect thermoregulatory vasomotor responses. Increases in ambient temperature during NREM sleep showed an appropriate homeothermic increase in skin temperature reflecting an increase in vasomotor activity. Decreases in ambient temperature again showed decreases in skin temperature and correspondingly a decrease in vasomotor activity. These responses were precisely the opposite during REM sleep. Again, these data confirm the presence of a homeothermic state in NREM sleep and a poikilothermic state in REM sleep. The effects of direct heating of the preoptic hypothalamic area lead these investigators to infer that a depression in the responsiveness of hypothalamic thermo-receptive structures is responsible for the lack of appropriate homeothermic thermoregulatory vasomotor responses during REM sleep.

Behavioral observations have confirmed these physiological findings. For example, high ambient temperatures have been shown to induce panting in cats during NREM sleep but not during REM sleep. In addition, low ambient temperatures will induce shivering during NREM sleep which is suppressed during REM sleep (12). Obviously, the inhibition of postural muscles during REM sleep would clearly preclude an appropriate shivering response to a decrease in ambient temperature. It appears that large alterations in ambient temperature during episodes of REM sleep could result in dire consequences for the organism. In this regard, it is of interest that there appears to be a hypothalamic temperature "gate" for entry into REM sleep (13). This temperature gate is considerably more narrow at zero degrees centigrade than at 20 degrees centigrade. As a survival mechanism, it would be logical that in the poikilothermic state which exists during REM sleep it would be considerably more dangerous to enter into REM sleep at zero degrees centigrade ambient temperature than at higher ambient temperatures. Correspondingly, clinical studies in humans who have been experimentally administered pyrogens show decreases in REM sleep (14). In addition, this study showed appreciably lighter and more fitful sleep with pyrogen administration.

Advances in the understanding of the regulation of core body temperature during sleep, as well as the interrelationships between sleep processes and the circadian temperature cycle, provide a cogent example of how progress in basic physiology can provide important clues to the understanding of basic disease processes. The demonstration of REM sleep as a poikilothermic state provides the rationale for a decrease in REM sleep as an adaptive response to a pathologic rise in core body temperature. Similarly, experimental data confirming the relationship between the circadian temperature cycle and the distribution of sleep stages provides the basic pathophysiologic explanation for the well known clinical observation of the "jet lag" syndrome and its association with sleep disturbances. It is especially encouraging that advances in the understanding of basic sleep regulatory mechanisms have provided immediate application to problems not only in clinical medicine but also in day-to-day behavior.

## SLEEP AND RESPIRATION

Although observations during sleep have provided a unique conceptualization of the basic physiology and pathophysiology of thermoregulatory processes, there is no arena of basic physiology where observations during sleep have had a more profound impact than respiration. At this point in time it is safe to say that observations over the past five years of alteration of basic respiratory functions during sleep have completely revolutionized standard notions of respiratory function and respiratory disease (5, 15). It is becoming increasingly obvious that a comprehensive understanding of the mechanisms of respiratory control as well as a wide variety of respiratory diseases cannot be accomplished without the evaluation of respiratory functions during sleep. The recognition of sleep-related breathing disorders has not only altered the management of common respiratory diseases such as chronic obstructive pulmonary disease (COPD), but has also uncovered a variety of heretofore unrecognized pathologic conditions occurring exclusively during sleep—for example, the sleep apnea syndromes (15).

Observations of sleep-related alterations in breathing in both normals and patients with respiratory diseases occurred coincident with, but apparently independent of, the modern era of sleep laboratory investigations. A case study published by Burwell and his colleagues would have to be considered a major stimulus to future investigative efforts in sleep-related respiratory disorders (16). This paper described what was referred to as the obesity-hypoventilation, or "Pickwickian" syndrome characterized by obesity, alveolar hypoventilation, and hypersomnolence. The authors ascribed the profound hypersomnolence and cardiopulmonary abnormalities to obesity and hypoventilation. It is a tribute to the brilliance of this particular case report that, in spite of a plethora of data to the contrary, this proposed mechanism for the pathologies noted in this patient remains fixed in the minds of most physicians and is still taught in most medical schools today.

Subsequent investigations by Birchfield et al. and Pierce et al. reflected concern on the part of the clinician that sleep processes may indeed have an appreciable and clinically significant effect on breathing (17, 18). Their work documented a mild alveolar hypoventilation associated with sleep onset, and an exacerbation of this effect in patients with COPD. Simultaneous observations published by Gastaut and his colleagues further documented the profound influence of sleep on breathing patterns (19). By monitoring several respiratory parameters during sleep, including airflow and thoracic breathing movements, these investigators documented the occurrence of numerous episodes of upper airway occlusion during sleep in a group of patients with the Pickwickian syndrome. It is difficult to exaggerate the importance and impact of this investigation. First, it documented the existence of a sleep-dependent alteration in respiratory functioning. These respiratory abnormalities could not be predicted by any cardiopulmonary or behavioral evaluation in the waking state. Second, the methodology and results testify to the importance of monitoring both airflow and inspiratory effort during sleep in order to distinguish three types of apneic events: the obstructive apnea characterized by a cessation of airflow with the continuation of inspiratory effort (Figure 2); the central apnea characterized by a simultaneous cessation of inspiratory effort and airflow and a simultaneous resumption of both (Figure 3); and the mixed apnea which is characterized by an initial central apnea followed by an obstructive apnea (Figure 4). Last, the sleep-respiratory investigation, and the documentation of arousals from

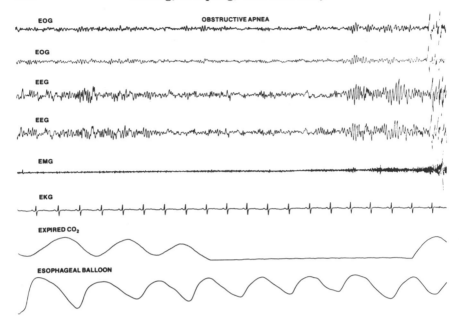

FIGURE 2. Obstructive apnea.

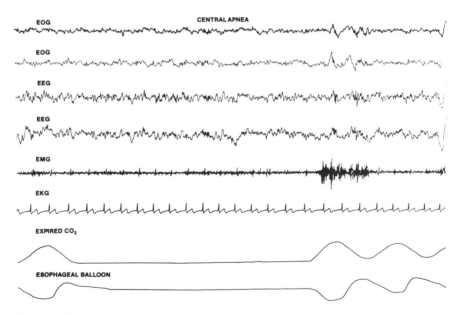

FIGURE 3. Central apnea.

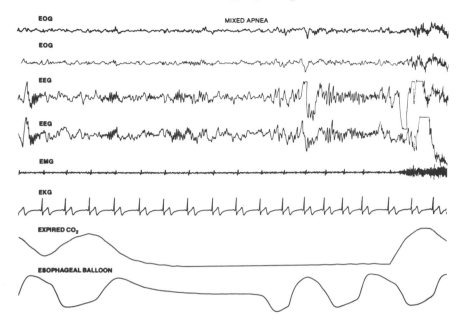

FIGURE 4. Mixed apnea.

sleep associated with the termination of obstructive apneic events, lead the authors to postulate chronic sleep deprivation as the primary cause of these patients' complaints of excessive daytime sleepiness.

There has been a recent proliferation of sleep investigations related to basic respiratory physiology as well as to respiratory diseases. Attempts to understand the pathogenesis of sleep-related respiratory disorders have provided a unique domain of investigation in which basic science and clinical application become nearly indistinguishable. For example, original work by Sauerland and Harper on genioglossal functioning during sleep has contributed substantially to ideas concerning the pathophysiology of obstructive sleep apnea (20). This study clearly documented a phenomenon which has been shown subsequently to exist in other muscles of the upper airway, namely a phasic burst of activity associated with inspiratory effort. In the case of the genioglossus muscle and the control of the tongue, this has clear implications in terms of maintaining upper airway patency. As is the case with other skeletal muscles, this investigation documented the relative inhibition of genioglossal muscle activity during REM sleep.

These studies have also proved heuristic in that they have stimulated a variety of additional observations concerning upper airway functioning during sleep. For example, a number of studies have suggested that a relatively large tongue in a relatively small oropharynx can be considered to be a risk factor for the development of obstructive sleep apnea. In addition, Orr, Males, and Imes have implicated macroglossia in the pathogenesis of obstructive sleep apnea documented in patients with myxedema (21). In this series of three patients, treatment with thyroxin completely resolved the myxedematous condition as well as the obstructive sleep apnea and resulting hypersomnolence. These results are analogous to those which have been obtained by bypassing the upper airway with a tracheostomy.

The increasing recognition of obstructive sleep apnea in association with a wide variety of medical conditions has focused considerable attention on its most obvious clinical manifestation, snoring. In our laboratory we have studied a number of patients who were referred for evaluation of sleep apnea with the sole complaint of snoring. The bed partner consistently reported not only loud sonorous snoring in these patients, but also observations of a cessation of breathing with continued inspiratory effort. None of the other sequelae of obstructive sleep apnea such as systemic hypertension, signs and symptoms of right heart failure, and hypersomnolence were present. When studied in the sleep laboratory, many of these patients were observed to have repeated episodes of obstructive sleep apnea varying from as few as 30–40 episodes per night to well over 300.

Impressed with the apparent existence of benign obstructive sleep apnea, we compared a group of such patients with a group of patients with severe obstructive sleep apnea including hypersomnolence and signs and symptoms compatible with right heart failure (22). The two groups were matched on the basis of the number of obstructive episodes per unit of time. This comparison revealed the symptomatic group to be significantly more hypoxemic than the asymptomatic group, despite the fact that there was no significant difference in the mean duration of the apneic episodes. This indicates that the mere existence of repetitive episodes of upper airway obstruction during sleep is necessary, but not sufficient, to produce the severe cardiopulmonary and behavioral sequelae often associated with this condition. Furthermore, in this study it was demonstrated that there was no difference in any sleep parameter between the symptomatic and asymptomatic groups. Since there was not a significant difference in the number of brief arousals and awake time subsequent to sleep onset in these groups, the argument that the hypersomnolence in patients with obstructive sleep apnea can be accounted for on the basis of chronic sleep deprivation is not supported. This study also documented that episodes of upper airway obstruction during REM sleep were significantly longer than those episodes occurring during NREM sleep in both groups. This has been a consistent finding in our laboratory in patients with obstructive sleep apnea. In fact, in individuals with mild to moderate sleep apnea, the episodes of upper airway obstruction may manifest themselves only during periods of REM sleep.

These data strongly suggest an alteration in respiratory function during REM sleep. The exact mechanisms underlying the lengthening of obstructive apneic events during REM sleep have yet to be elucidated. However, the inhibition of skeletal muscle tone and the consequent production of paradoxical breathing (i.e., paradoxical movements of the abdominal and thoracic components of breathing) clearly contribute to this phenomenon. Observations on infants have further elucidated breathing alterations during REM sleep. Paradoxical breathing during REM has been amply demonstrated in infants, and Henderson-Smart and Read have postulated that both paradoxical breathing and decreases in lung volume are secondary to the intercostal paralysis during REM (23). In fact, respiratory load compensation in infants has been shown to be irregular and weak during REM, when compared to loaded responses during NREM (24).

These observations led our group to a more intensive investigation of respiratory parameters and measures of control of breathing in patients with obstructive sleep apnea. These studies involved more precise measurements of the timing components of ventilation, including pulmonary resistance, air flow, esophageal and gastric pressures before and during upper airway obstructions, as well as the timing of the components of the respiratory cycle (25). Several results from this study pointed to a decrease in central nervous system respiratory drive as a primary feature in the initiation of episodes of obstructive apnea. There is, for example, a discernible decrease in inspiratory effort associated with the onset of the obstructive episode (Figure 5). In addition, intervals between obstructive episodes were associated with an increase in pulmonary resistance and a decrease in ventilation.

The pulmonary resistance during sleep was found to be much higher than would be predicted from the measurement of airway resistance in the waking state. As the pulmonary resistance increased in intervals between obstructive events, inspiratory and expiratory flows were cut in half; however, the esophageal pressure (a reflection of inspiratory effort) did not change. This is compatible with a waning of respiratory drive in that an increase in inspiratory effort would be considered an appropriate response to an increase in pulmonary resistance. Additional support for the finding of a progressive decrease in central respiratory drive is the fact that the ratio of inspiratory to total respiratory cycle time showed a progressive decrease prior to the onset of an obstructive apnea. This ratio is said to reflect central respiratory drive.

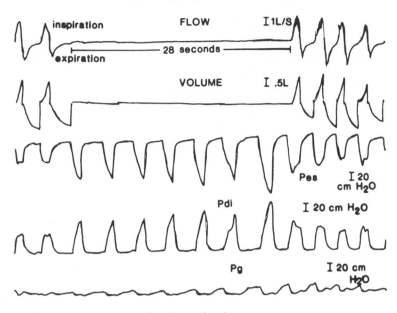

FIGURE 5. Pulmonary measures during obstructive sleep apnea.

In general, during the obstructive apneic event, there is a progressive increase in inspiratory effort (negative esophageal pressure swings) until the obstruction is broken. This is characteristically preceded by a brief arousal. It is of interest that the airway of three normal subjects was occluded during sleep in our laboratory by occluding airflow at end expiration under similar monitoring conditions. This resulted in an arousal from sleep within three breaths. The mean increase in inspiratory effort on the first occluded breath was double that of the patients with sleep apnea. The longer apneic episodes prior to an arousal and termination of the obstructive event and the decrease in the inspiratory effort in response to the occluded airway indicate that patients with obstructive sleep apnea have altered pulmonary reflexes as well as inappropriate responses to an occluded airway. Thus, these data suggest that a defective arousal mechanism may play an important role in sleep-related breathing disorders. Similar observations have been cogently discussed by Phillipson and Sullivan (26).

Other fundamental alterations in respiratory control have been documented during sleep in animal studies. In a series of experiments with dogs, Phillipson and his colleagues have demonstrated that the normal mechanisms of respiratory control are markedly altered during REM sleep (5). For example, in NREM sleep, elevations in arterial $CO_2$ concentration will normally produce an increase in minute ventilation. Experiments in dogs have shown that during REM sleep there is very little compensatory change in minute ventilation with an increase in arterial $CO_2$ (27). These results have been generally replicated in cats by Davies et al. (28). Their results, however, indicated that $CO_2$ responsiveness during REM was dependent upon whether the animal had previous exposure to $CO_2$ during the immediately preceding period of NREM sleep. Although responses during REM were consistently less than during NREM or waking, the discrepancies were decreased with previous exposure during NREM sleep. With regard to the hypoxic drive, Phillipson et al. demonstrated that the hypoxic drive remains intact, but a lower oxygen saturation is required to arouse the organism in REM when compared with NREM sleep (29). Ventilation during the REM state has been shown to be unresponsive to other metabolic inputs which normally have respiratory consequences such as metabolic alkalosis (30). In addition, vagal blockade during NREM sleep severely depresses respiratory rate and minute ventilation, while there appear to be only minimal consequences during REM (30). Thus, respiratory control during REM sleep is not subject to vagal mediation so obvious in waking and NREM sleep.

Collectively, these experiments have demonstrated a rather profound alteration during REM sleep in a system which normally is regulated with exquisite precision. Parmeggiani describes these REM-related changes in terms of an interruption of the integrative properties of the hypothalamus (31). He reports, for example, that during NREM sleep stimulation of the anterior hypothalamus elicits respiratory phase switching or chronotropic effects which are not observed with similar stimulation during REM sleep. These REM-related changes in the regulation of respiration and ventilation are attributed to what Parmeggiani describes as an "open loop" system where homeostatic feedback regulation is suspended (31).

Further documentation of the clinical relevance of sleep-dependent respiratory phenomena comes from a series of investigations on sleep-related respiratory changes in patients with COPD. Initial observations on such patients by Flick and Block showed that sleep was associated with levels of oxygen desaturation as great as 30 to 40 percent (32). Subsequent investigations by Wynne et al. have documented the presence of disordered breathing in association with episodes of oxygen desaturation during sleep (33). These investigations included more sophisticated monitoring of sleep parameters in order to allow the staging of sleep and the correlations of respiratory abnormalities with sleep stages. They described 42 percent of the episodes of oxygen desaturation (greater than four percent) associated with disordered breathing (i.e., apnea or hypopnea). These episodes tended to be somewhat shorter and associated with greater degrees of desaturation. In contrast, the remaining 58 percent of the apneic episodes were spontaneous in that they were not associated with any evidence of disordered respiration. These events tended to be somewhat longer (two to five minutes) and were associated with less severe degrees of desaturation.

REM sleep was consistently found to be associated with the longest episodes of oxygen desaturation. An extension of these observations is provided by work done by Douglas et al., who have shown that there are specific subcategories of COPD patients who tend to show a greater proclivity for oxygen desaturation during sleep (34). They have demonstrated that individuals categorized as "blue bloaters" tend to show spontaneous desaturation during sleep, whereas those categorized as "pink puffers" do not. In general, blue bloaters tend to have significant $CO_2$ retention in the waking state, whereas pink puffers tend to maintain normal waking blood gases.

These studies demonstrate the utility of the sleep evaluation in a complete understanding of the pathogenesis of respiratory disease. It is becoming increasingly clear that a comprehensive evaluation of many patients with respiratory diseases cannot be accomplished without a polysomnographic evaluation. The obvious clinical relevance of sleep-dependent changes in respiratory and upper airway functioning has also stimulated a burgeoning of interest in these areas by neurophysiologists as well as respiratory physiologists. The continued interaction of basic scientists and clinicians promises to bring many exciting new findings in the basic mechanisms of both sleep and respiration.

### ESOPHAGEAL FUNCTION DURING SLEEP

Relatively little work has been done on gastrointestinal functioning during sleep. More than likely this is attributable to the relative inaccessibility of gastrointestinal organs to convenient noninvasive measurement. The majority of investigations pertaining to sleep and gastroenterologic phenomena have been concerned with acid secretion during sleep (35, 36, 37, 38). More recently, however, considerable attention has been focused on the occurrence of sleep-dependent gastroesophageal reflux (GER) and esophageal acid clearance during sleep in the pathogenesis of esophagitis.

Initial observations which focused attention on the occurrence of GER and acid clearance during sleep were published by Johnson and DeMeester (39). In this most important investigation three types of reflux were described in symptomatic individuals with esophagitis. *Upright* reflux was characterized by multiple episodes which were rapidly cleared and occurred exclusively in the upright position; *supine* reflux was characterized by fewer episodes with prolonged clearance occurring primarily during the sleeping interval; and *combined* reflux occurred in individuals who demonstrated both upright and supine reflux. In subsequent investigations, Johnson and colleagues described a relation between the histologically documented severity of esophagitis and the occurrence of supine and combined reflux (40). Since supine reflux occurs predominantly during the sleeping interval, this series of investigations has clearly focused attention on the occurrence of sleep-related GER and prolonged acid clearance in the pathogenesis of esophagitis. In collaboration with Johnson and Malcolm Robinson of our institution, we have undertaken a series of investigations which have concentrated on the specific issue of esophageal acid clearance during sleep (41). A group of normal controls and patients with esophagitis were studied during polygraphically monitored sleep. The normals were studied for two successive nights in the sleep laboratory. Six infusions of sterile water were accomplished during the first night of study, and six infusions of .1 N HCl on the subsequent night. The patients were studied on one night only with six infusions of .1 N HCl. A schematic diagram of a typical infusion and clearance episode is shown in Figure 6. This shows the drop in distal esophageal pH associated with the infusion of acid. The pH is monitored with a small

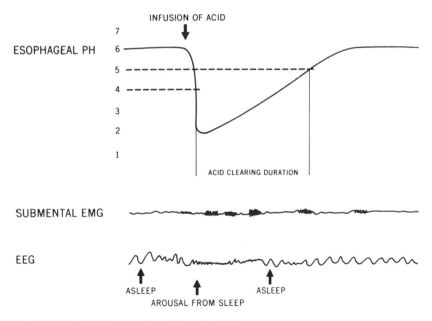

FIGURE 6. Schematic diagram of esophageal acid clearance.

DURATION TO CLEAR/WAKE INFUSIONS VS SLEEP INFUSIONS

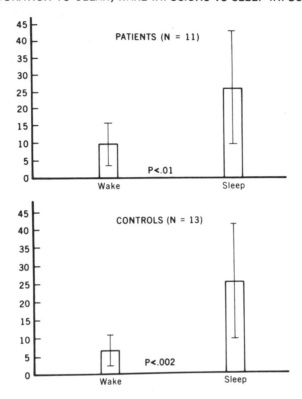

FIGURE 7. Acid-clearing durations during wake and sleep.

pH probe placed 5 cm above the manometrically determined lower esophageal sphincter. Parameters of interest in this investigation are as follows:

1) The acid clearing duration is defined as the interval of time between the drop in pH to below 4 until the reestablishment of an esophageal pH of 5 or above.
2) Swallows during the acid clearing duration are determined in terms of the number per unit time (min).
3) The percent of wakefulness during the acid clearing interval is determined by this formula:

$$\frac{\text{waking time}}{\text{total acid clearing time}} \times 100.$$

Figure 7 shows the comparison of acid clearing with infusions during the waking state compared with infusions during sleep. In both patient and control groups it is apparent that acid clearance is longer with acid infusions during sleep. There was, however, no difference in acid clearance when the patient group was compared to the control group. In analyzing these data in more detail, it became clear that acid clearance during sleep is a complex process involving a number of psychophysiologic responses. For example, whether or not the subject was aroused from sleep by the acid in the distal esophagus was clearly an important factor in determining the acid clearance time—that is, if an arousal occurred shortly after the infusion of the acid

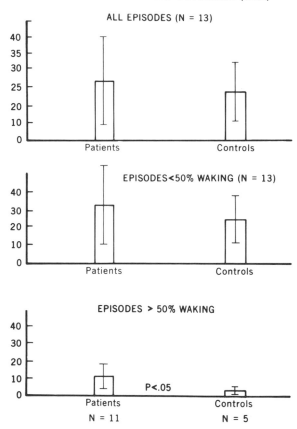

FIGURE 8. Acid-clearing duration with different percentages of waking time.

stimulus, normal subjects would generally swallow several times, clear the acid from the distal esophagus, and then go back to sleep. If, however, there was a delayed arousal or no arousal, acid clearance time was markedly prolonged.

Thus, it was decided to analyze these data in terms of clearance times associated with wakefulness (greater than 50 percent waking in the acid clearing duration), and those associated predominantly with sleep (less than 50 percent waking in the acid clearing duration). These data are presented in Figure 8. The middle panel depicts acid clearance associated predominantly with sleep, and it is clear that the patients and controls are not significantly different.

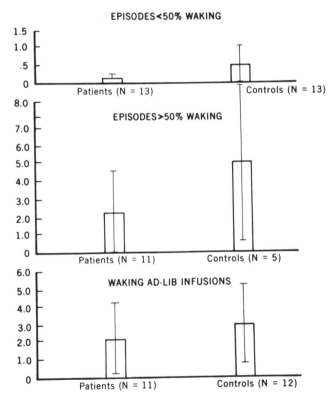

FIGURE 9. Swallowing during acid clearance.

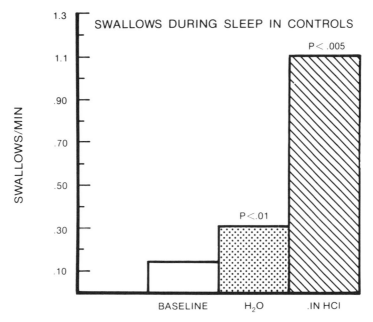

FIGURE 10. Swallowing frequency with acid versus water infusions during sleep.

However, in the bottom panel, where clearance is compared during episodes associated predominantly with wakefulness, the patients show significantly longer acid clearance.

The swallowing data from this study are particularly interesting. The swallowing frequency did not differentiate the patient group from the control group under any of the acid clearing conditions described above (Figure 9). Thus, this particular parameter cannot account for the differences in acid clearing. Although the patients and controls appear not to be differentially sensitive to the provocative acid stimulus in terms of swallowing frequency, the data on control subjects clearly indicate that the acid stimulus does affect swallowing frequency during sleep. These data are shown in Figure 10. It can be seen here that swallowing frequency increases with sterile water infusion, and subsequently with acid infusion. It is of interest that the acid infusions in controls also resulted in greater numbers of arousals in the five-minute interval subsequent to acid infusion (Figure 11). The data in Figure 8 are analogous in that it can be seen that shorter acid clearing durations are associated with greater degrees of wakefulness in both groups.

It seems clear from these data that sleep is associated with prolonged acid

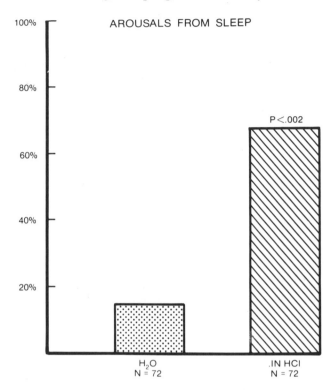

FIGURE 11. Arousals from sleep comparing water versus acid infusions.

clearance; that both patients and controls have episodes of prolonged acid clearance during sleep; and that arousals from sleep, and the subsequent increase in swallowing frequency, constitute the primary mechanism of acid clearance during sleep. Thus, esophageal end-organ sensitivity, as well as central arousal mechanisms, are both necessary to provide appropriate protective functions against the development of more severe forms of esophagitis and pulmonary aspiration.

### AROUSALS FROM SLEEP

There is one element that appears to tie these seemingly diverse bits of data together in terms of the basic physiology of sleep. That is the importance of arousal mechanisms in protecting the organism against untoward events occurring during sleep, i.e., upper airway obstruction, gastroesophageal reflux, and wide variations in ambient temperature (42). Any of these events can lead to a patient complaint of fitful and restless sleep, often resulting in the prescription of a hypnotic drug on the part of the physician. This results in a depression of arousal mechanisms and decreased responsiveness to such interoceptive stimuli. Thus, as has been emphasized in this review, arousals from sleep serve an important function in many circumstances, indicating the appropriate functioning of afferent and efferent stimulus response mechanisms. These clearly can serve a protective function for the organism during the decreased vigilance of sleep.

## CONCLUSIONS

This chapter has attempted to emphasize the unique physiology and pathophysiology of sleep, and the development of these areas into a discipline of sleep disorders medicine. Great strides have been made in the development of this new discipline, and the continuing cross-fertilization of the basic science aspects of sleep and their clinical applications will clearly result in a more comprehensive understanding of a wide variety of medical disorders, and consequently more effective patient care. Sleep has too long been considered a "time-out" period in the care of the patient. Recent developments described herein have resulted in the ability to approach pathophysiology and therapeutics with a far more comprehensive understanding of the organism's functioning throughout the circadian sleep/wake cycle. This has been stated in a very succinct and cogent comment by Eugene Robin:

> The sleeping patient is still a patient. His disease goes on not only while he sleeps but indeed may progress in an entirely different fashion from its progression in the waking state (43).

## REFERENCES

1. ASERINSKY, E. and KLEITMAN, N.: Regularly occurring periods of eye motility, and concomitant phenomena, during sleep. *Science,* 118:273-274, 1953.
2. DEMENT, W. and KLEITMAN, N.: Cyclic variations in EEG during sleep and their relation to eye movements, body motility and dreaming. *Electroencephalogr. Clin. Neruophysiol.,* 9:673-690, 1975.
3. ORR, W. C., STAHL, M. L., DEMENT, W. C., and REDDINGTON, D.: Physician education in sleep disorders. *J. Med. Ed.,* 55:368-369, 1981.
4. RUBIN, R., POLAND, R., ROBIN, L., and GOUIN, P.: The neuroendocrinology of human sleep. *Life Sci.,* 14:1041-1052, 1974.
5. PHILLIPSON, E.: Respiratory adaptations in sleep. *Ann. Rev. Physiol.,* 40:133-156, 1978.
6. Association of Sleep Disorders Centers: *Diagnostic Classification of Sleep and Arousal Disorders,* Ed. 1, prepared by the Sleep Disorders Classification Committee, Roffwarg, H. P. (Chairman). *Sleep,* 2:1-137, 1979.

7. COLQUHOUN, W.: Circadian variations in mental efficiency. In: W. Colquhoun (Ed.), *Biological Rhythms in Human Performance*. New York: Academic Press, 1971, pp. 39–108.
8. ZULLEY, J.: Distribution of REM sleep in entrained 24-hour and free running sleep-wake cycles. *Sleep,* 2:377–389, 1980.
9. CZEISLER, C., ZIMMERMAN, A., RONDA, J., MOORE-EDE, M., and WEITZMAN, E.: Timing of REM sleep is coupled to the circadian rhythm of body temperature in man. *Sleep,* 2:329–346, 1980.
10. PARMEGGIANI, P., FRANZINI, C., LENZI, P., and TULLIA, C.: Inguinal subcutaneous temperature changes in cats sleeping at different environmental temperatures. *Brain Res.,* 33:397–404, 1971.
11. PARMEGGIANI, P., ZAMBONI, G., CIANCI, T., and CALASSO, M.: Absence of thermoregulatory vasomotor responses during fast wave sleep in cats. *Electroencephalogr. Clin. Neurophysiol.,* 42:372–380, 1977.
12. PARMEGGIANI, P. and SABATTINI, L.: Electromyographic aspects of postual respiratory and thermoregulatory mechanisms in sleeping cats. *Electroencephalogr. Clin. Neurophysiol.,* 33:1–13, 1972.
13. PARMEGGIANI, P., AGNATI, L., ZAMBONI, G., and CIANCI, T.: Hypothalamic temperature during the sleep cycle at different ambient temperatures. *Electroencephalogra. Clin. Neurophysiol.,* 38:589–596, 1975.
14. KARACAN, I., WOLFF, S., WILLIAMS, R., HURSCH, C., and WEBB, W.: The effects of fever on sleep and dream patterns. *Psychosom.,* 9:331–339, 1968.
15. GUILLEMINAULT, C., TILKIAN, A., and DEMENT, W.: The sleep apnea syndromes. *Ann. Rev. Med.,* 27:465–484, 1976.
16. BURWELL, C., ROBIN, E., WHALEY, R., and BIKELMAN, A.: Extreme obesity associated with alveolar hypoventilation; a Pickwickian syndrome. *Am. J. Med.,* 21:811–818, 1956.
17. BIRCHFIELD, R., SIEKER, H., and HEYMAN, A.: Alterations in blood gases during natural sleep and narcolepsy: A correlation with electroencephalographic stages of sleep. *Neurology,* 8:107–112, 1958.
18. PIERCE, A., JARRETT, C., WERKLE, G., JR., and MILLER, W.: Respiratory function during sleep in patients with chronic obstructive lung disease. *J. Clin. Invest.,* 45:631–636, 1966.
19. GASTAUT, H., TASSINARI, C., and DURON, B.: Polygraphic study of the episodic and diurnal and nocturnal (hypnic and respiratory) manifestations of the Pickwick syndrome. *Brain Res.,* 2:167–186, 1966.
20. SAUERLAND, E. and HARPER, R.: The human tongue during sleep: Electromyographic activity of the genioglossus muscle. *Experi. Neurol.,* 51:160–170, 1976.
21. ORR, W. C., MALES, J. L., and IMES, N. K.: Myxedema and obstructive sleep apnea. *Am. J. Med.,* 70(5):1061–1066, 1981.
22. ORR, W. C., IMES, N. K., MARTIN, R. J., ROGERS, R. M., and STAHL, M. L.: Hypersomnolent and nonhypersomnolent patients with upper airway obstruction during sleep. *Chest,* 75:418–422, 1979.
23. HENDERSON-SMART, D. and READ, D. J. C.: Depression of intercostal and abdominal muscle activity and vulnerability to asphyxia during active sleep in the newborn. In: C. Guilleminault and W. Dement (Eds.), *Sleep Apnea Syndromes.* New York: Allen R. Liss, 1978, pp. 93–118.

24. KNILL, R., ANDREWS, W., BRYAN, A. C., and BRYAN, H. H.: Respiratory load compensation in infants. *J. Appl. Physiol.,* 40:357–361, 1976.
25. MARTIN, R., PENNOCK, B., ORR, W., SANDERS, M., and ROGERS, R.: Respiratory mechanics and timing during sleep in occlusive sleep apnea. *J. Appl. Physiol.,* 84:432–437, 1980.
26. PHILLIPSON, E. A. and SULLIVAN, C. E.: Arousal: The forgotten response to respiratory stimuli. *Am. Rev. Respir. Dis.,* 118:807–809, 1978.
27. PHILLIPSON, E., KOZAR, L., REBUCK, A., and MURPHY, E.: Ventilatory and waking responses to $CO_2$ in sleeping dogs. *Am. Rev. Respir. Dis.,* 18:807–809, 1978.
28. DAVIES, D. G., LITTLE, D. D., LUST, R., NADER, P. C., and OREM, J.: Effect of previous history on ventilatory sensitivity to $CO_2$ during sleep. *Federation Proceedings,* 38:1033, 1979, (ABST).
29. PHILLIPSON, E., SULLIVAN, C., REED, D., MURPHY, E., and KOZAR, L.: Ventilatory and waking responses to hypoxia in sleeping dogs. *J. Appl. Physiol.,* 44: 512–520, 1978.
30. SULLIVAN, C., KOZAR, L., MURPHY, E., and PHILLIPSON, E.: Primary role of respiratory afferents in sustaining breathing rhythm. *J. Appl. Physiol.,* 45:11–17, 1978.
31. PARMEGGIANI, P.: Integrative aspects of hypothalamic influences on respiratory brain stem mechanisms during wakefulness and sleep. In: C. von Euler and H. Lagercrantz (Eds.), *Central Nervous Control Mechanisms in Breathing.* New York: Pergamon Press, 1979, pp. 53–69.
32. FLICK, M. and BLOCK, A. J.: Continuous in-vivo monitoring of arterial oxygenation in chronic obstructive lung disease. *Ann. Intern. Med.,* 86:725–730, 1977.
33. WYNNE, J., BLOCK, A. J., HEMENWAY, J., HUNT, L., and FLICK, M.: Disordered breathing and oxygen desaturation during sleep in patients with chronic obstructive lung disease (COLD). *Am. J. Med.,* 66:573–579, 1979.
34. DOUGLAS, N., CALVERLEY, P., LEGGETT, R., BRASH, H., FLENLEY, D., and BREZINOVA, V.: Transient hypoxemia during sleep in chronic bronchitis and emphysema. *Lancet,* 1(8106):1–4, 1979.
35. LEVIN, E., KIRSNER, J., PALMER, W., and BUTLER, C.: A comparison of the nocturnal gastric secretion in patients with duodenal ulcer and in normal individuals. *Gastroenterol.,* 10:952–964, 1948.
36. REICHSMAN, F., COHEN, J., COLWILL, J., DAVIS, N., KESSLER, W., SHEPARDSON, C., and ENGEL, G.: Natural and histamine induced gastric secretion during waking and sleeping states. *Psychoso. Med.,* 1:14–23, 1960.
37. ARMSTRONG, R. H., BURNAP, D., JACOBSON, A., KALES, A., WARD, S., and GOLDEN, J.: Dreams and acid secretions in duodenal ulcer patients. *New Physician,* 33:241–243, 1965.
38. ORR, W., HALL, W., STAHL, M., DURKIN, M., and WHITSETT, T.: Sleep patterns in gastric acid secretion in duodenal ulcer disease. *Arch. Intern. Med.,* 136:655–660, 1976.
39. JOHNSON, L. and DEMEESTER, T.: Twenty-four pH monitoring of the distal esophagus, a quantitative measure of gastroesophageal reflux. *Am. J. Gastroenterol.,* 62:325–332, 1974.
40. JOHNSON, L., DEMEESTER, T., and HAGGITT, R.: Esophageal epihelial response

to gastroesophageal reflux, a quantitative study. *Am. J. Dig. Dis.,* 23:498–509, 1978.

41. ORR, W. C., ROBINSON, M. G., and JOHNSON, L. F.: Acid clearing during sleep in the pathogenesis of reflux esophagitis. *Dig. Dis. Sci.,* 1, 26(5):423–427, 1981.

42. ORR, W. C.: Arousals from sleep: Is a good night's sleep really good? *Int. J. Neruosci.,* 11:143–144, 1980.

43. ROBIN, E.: Some interrelations between sleep and disease. *Arch. Intern. Med.,* 102:669–675, 1958.

# 6

# The Diagnosis of Sleep Disorders

*Howard P. Roffwarg, M.D., and*
*Kenneth Z. Altshuler, M.D.*

### INTRODUCTION

Many signs point to the gradual emergence of a specialized and multi-disciplinary branch of medical practice—sleep disorders medicine. In this chapter, we examine the reasons for the growth of this field and some of its attempts to gain greater certainty about the matrix of pathology with which it deals. A significant step in this development was the recent construction of a new Diagnostic Classification System of Sleep and Arousal Disorders (1), which has moved our field a long way in the ordering of a diagnostic approach to the vast array of conditions that affect sleep. In the second portion of the chapter, we will further delineate two of the four major categories—the Disorders of Initiating and Maintaining Sleep (the Insomnias) and the Disorders of the Sleep-Wake Schedule—which comprise the new nosology.

Academic psychiatry has been particularly encouraging and supportive of sleep physiology and psychophysiology research in the last 20 years. A good deal of the active work in this area has been carried out in departments of psychiatry, which are also organizational havens for the sleep disorders centers that are fostering a comprehensive psychophysiologic orientation to sleep disorders.

### CONVENTIONAL MEDICAL APPROACHES TO SLEEP COMPLAINTS

Sleep occupies between one-fifth and one-third of our entire existence and is clearly a physiological process that substantially affects subjective well-being and capacity to discharge daily functions. However, knowledge of the

sleep behavior of an individual has traditionally been viewed as only inciden-
tally pertinent to an evaluation of his medical status. Patients' accounts of the
quantity and integrity of their sleep have rarely been accepted by their physicians as providing more than anecdotal information — perhaps owing to the
earlier absence of objective means of documenting the sleep pattern.

The trivialization of sleep's important and medically relevant physiology
(though many medical symptoms often find a favorite portal of expression
during the dormant hours) is exemplified by the lack of teaching about sleep
dysfunctions in medical school curricula and clinical training. (Less than ten
medical schools in the country offer any formal course work in sleep disorders.) It is not surprising, considering the traditional preparation of doctors for
medical practice, that the sleep symptoms of their patients are minimized.
Without an awareness of the symptoms of sleep disorders, even easily made
clinical differentiations go unrecognized. Not only are the sleep pathologies
per se undiagnosed or underdiagnosed, but much of the value of sleep symptoms in elucidating other medical and psychiatric disorders is also forfeited.

A vicious cycle of medical misunderstanding and mistreatment of sleep
disorders has become the inevitable consequence of a double standard in the
customary medical approach to exploring clinical problems. Whereas the average practitioner takes it as an article of faith that every attempt be made to
elucidate, by means of diagnostic tests, the pathology underlying his patient's
symptoms, he routinely manages sleep complaints — unlike his exquisite attempts to plumb the source of somatic symptoms — either by ignoring them or
by smothering them with drugs. The situation is even more startling considering that the physician, until recently, little questioned his use of sedative
agents, though their chemical actions in the brain are, for the most part, unknown. Until polygraphic sleep recording, even the physiologic effects of
drugs upon sleep were unknown (2).

Treatment cannot be rational in the absence of diagnosis. Without sufficient motivation in the halls of medicine to apply optimal standards of diagnostic identification to sleep symptoms, the practitioner cannot be expected
to gain the ability to diagnose sleep disorders with precision. Consequently,
inappropriate and patently harmful treatments are, at this moment, being offered to patients by otherwise well-meaning physicians.

### EVOLUTION OF SLEEP DISORDERS MEDICINE

Though greater awareness of sleep as a vital function is still required in
medicine, a number of developments have begun to reverse the practitioner's
attitudes about sleep dysfunctions and the use of drugs. For example, though
6,000,000 prescriptions per year for sedative agents are still written, doctors
are taking note of the addicting potential, rapid loss of effect, and sleep dis-

ruptive actions of particularly the barbiturates and similar drugs. Overall, the number of prescriptions for sleeping pills is falling yearly. Prevalence of use has switched to the safer and less sleep-disrupting benzodiazepine agents (3).

Another change is that diagnostic units devoted to investigation of sleep complaints are being developed in every major city. At this time, about 25 centers have received accreditation from the Association of Sleep Disorders Centers, and many more are in the process of applying. This organization also establishes qualified sleep disorders specialists as "certified clinical polysomnographers" when they pass a rigorous examination.

Sleep disorders units take the responsibility of employing a wide range of medical and psychological examinations in identifying the causes of sleep complaints. Most centers operate within general hospitals and are associated with medical schools. Functioning mainly as consultation units, their staffs communicate actively with referring physicians. Whether or not a formal specialty of sleep disorders medicine yet exists, the presence of committed, full-time, sleep disorders specialists, and their assumption of medical responsibility for patients during diagnostic investigation is a fact. These specialists are teaching sleep disorders medicine in numerous settings, and they are also formulating basic courses in sleep disorders to teach to medical students. New as well as established physicians are gaining knowledge regarding the chief signs and symptoms of the sleep disorders. This growing awareness of practitioners to sleep pathology has led to more numerous as well as earlier referrals for special testing to ascertain precise diagnoses.

In certain circumstances the experience of sleep disorders specialists has unexpectedly placed them at the cutting edge of new breakthroughs in medicine. Because of their capacity to discriminate among the disorders of excessive daytime somnolence, they have been in a unique position to recognize when a patient has obstructive sleep apnea, the occult inducer of a serious form of hypertensive cardiovascular disease, which was completely unrecognized until less than ten years ago (4). A good deal of new research into the mechanisms and manifestations of clinical sleep syndromes and the effects of sedative drugs is being carried out in sleep disorders centers. "State of the art" electrophysiological recording and measures of waking performance and alertness characterize this research (5, 6).

### WHAT DEVELOPMENTS LED TO INCREASED RECOGNITION OF THE SLEEP DISORDERS?

*1) The Polysomnogram (PSG)*

Excellent techniques for all-night, electrophysiological (polysomnographic) monitoring of multiple central nervous system (CNS) and somatic functions are now available. This reliable and sensitive system of recording has expanded from the three basic recording variables for identification of sleep stage—the sleep electroencephalogram, electro-oculogram, and submental electromyogram (7)—to include measurements of ventilatory air exchange at the nares and mouth, respiratory effort, electrical heart activity, leg movement (by means of electrodes over the anterior tibialis muscles), and blood oxygen saturation. Simultaneous video recording monitors the sleep behavior of the patient. Specialized transducers are used in particular conditions (e.g., an indwelling gastric pH probe in cases of suspected gastro-esophageal reflux). The availability of a reliable system of physiological assessment, yielding data that can be interpreted in association with information about the patient's behavioral, cognitive, and emotional functioning, has helped make sense of the often multi-system expressions of insomnia and excessive sleepiness syndromes.

It is now well understood that sleep, which is behaviorally defined as an eyes-closed, reversible state of unconsciousness, is actually composed of two qualitatively different, alternating, CNS states. The two distinctive states depend on separate systems of brain activity. All evidence points to the brainstem as the point of initiation of the rapid eye movement (REM) stage. In REM sleep, the metabolic activity of brain is high; autonomic functions are active; and intense hallucinations (dreaming) are continuous, reflecting the effects of the intense phasic activity of brainstem origin, which is transmitted to cortex as well as to many other areas of the CNS during this stage. Non-REM (NREM) sleep, the only sleep known until 25 years ago, is accompanied by more basal and less variable levels of physiological activity.

Some of the pathologies of sleep may be traceable to insufficiencies or relative imbalances in the generating systems underlying REM and NREM sleep. Others may be referable to dissociated manifestations of REM sleep phasic phenomena, or to aberrancies in the bioperiodicity of the two stages of sleep or of the major periods of sleep and waking. A number of the parasomnias appear to be due to abnormal physiological upsurges in activity during one or more of the sleep stages.

Polysomnographic recording is used to verify a history of disturbed nocturnal sleep and to explore its source. The PSG is also used as an objective measure of sleepiness (Multiple Sleep Latency Test). Many covert causes of insomnia remain unsuspected unless PSG recording is carried out.

## 2) The Relation of Sleep Complaints to Physiological Derangements

A leading hope is that the many symptoms and complaints reported by patients will have parallels in physiological measures that are objectively verifiable. Prime examples of such covariance are the association of hypnagogic imagery, or the "quick dream," in narcolepsy with premature triggering of REM sleep at sleep onset, and the appearance of cataplexy with the abrupt diminution of resting muscle tone, recorded in the submental leads (dissociated REM state). Among the insomnias, the numerous awakenings from sleep reported by snoring individuals are coupled to the repeated interruptions of respiratory effort (central sleep apnea). Periodic nocturnal awakenings, with little to explain them in the history, may be diagnosed as sleep-related (nocturnal) myoclonus if periodic episodes of repetitive, leg twitches followed by arousals are recorded. Alternatively, a history of disturbed sleep, characterized by awakenings at approximately 90-minute intervals, productive of dream recall, may be identified as repetitive REM sleep interruption insomnia if the PSG recording verifies that the awakenings take place only in the REM periods of the night.

It must be emphasized, however, that a number of different insomnia conditions (e.g., persistent psychophysiological insomnia, insomnia associated with acute anxiety, chronic alcoholism, and incipient dementia) may show a similar polysomnographic picture. It usually includes increases in the number of awakenings and body movements, higher than normal heart rate, reduced total sleep time and stages delta and REM, and an increase in alpha activity in the EEG. The reverse may also be true; for example, persistent psychophysiological insomnia, alpha-delta sleep and sleep-related (nocturnal) myoclonus, though distinctive in their polysomnographic manifestations, can present with identical symptomatology.

Whereas the PSG does not always reveal the definitive or precise cause of a sleep disturbance, a persistently interrupted yet not pathognomonic PSG tracing is nonetheless an indication that some pathological process, somatic or psychological, is at work. This survey function of a nonspecifically abnormal PSG, one generally showing numerous arousals and reduced REM and deep NREM sleep, is analogous to the medical suspicion raised by a fast erythrocyte sedimentation rate in the absence of manifest disease. By the same token, a normal PSG, like a normal sedimentation rate, suggests a healthy system.

Nevertheless, the standard association of particular complaints with certain physiological findings has led to some important clinical rules of thumb. Common wisdom suggests that disturbed sleep at night leads to excessive "sleepiness" by day. However, this relationship does not hold if sleepiness is strictly defined as the tendency to fall asleep. The insomnia patient may use the term "sleepiness" to refer to his daytime symptoms but, when this allegation is investigated, it turns out that the individual is not "sleepy" so much as suffering the sense of physical fatigue, weakness, or lassitude. This is particularly true of the sleep disturbances associated with excess psychophysiological arousal, anxiety, or depression. It generally pertains in relation to physiological causes of insomnia as well. True sleepiness, in the sense of a virtual inability to stay awake during the day, is, surprisingly, not a mark of disturbed nocturnal sleep. Rather, it is the cardinal complaint in severe disorders of excessive daytime somnolence, such as obstructive sleep apnea and narcolepsy. Patient accounts of persistent sleepiness and sleep attacks in sedentary situations and even in the face of stimulating activities — physical exercise, eating, sexual activity, entertaining and emotional circumstances — constitute strong clinical indication of a major disorder of excessive somnolence. In narcolepsy, nocturnal sleep may be well maintained (though often not), but the characteristic daytime sleepiness and sleep attacks are not alleviated. The only situation involving partial or total sleep loss at night that is productive of the same sort of "big league" daytime sleepiness typically reported with the disorders of excessive somnolence is when normal individuals voluntarily stay awake during usual sleep hours.

### 3) The Chronobiological Approach

There has been a burgeoning of data concerning the influence and constraints imposed by entrained biological periodicities (usually circadian) upon sleep and awake functioning. A distinct 24-hour periodicity governs the functioning of the hypothalamo-adrenal axis as well as the quotidian rises and falls of temperature. The major sleep-wake periods are, of course, also circumscribed by 24-hour periodicity, which is predictably related to the timing of the other circadian rhythms so long as regularity of the 24-hour sleep-wake pattern is maintained.

The insomnias and disorders of excessive sleep, as classes of sleep disorders, are each represented by characteristic, 24-hour assemblages of symptomatology. Sleep and wake functions are intertwined. In sleep disorders medicine, the focus is not simply on sleep. The diagnostician, when presented with a story of disturbed sleep, will think not only of exploring the polysomnographic character of the patient's nocturnal sleep, but also of assessing the awake functioning of the individual in terms of his ability to maintain alertness (in contradistinction to a tendency for sleepiness and napping). Cognitive and motor performance will also be assessed. Similarly, a history of excessive sleepiness in the course of waking hours must be objectively studied in regard to the intrusions of sleep by day and the polysomnographic character of that sleep. To complete the parallel, the quality and quantity of the patient's nocturnal sleep must be measured.

*4) Individual Variation in Terms of Total Sleep Requirements*

For reasons that are not yet understood, individuals differ sharply from each other in terms of the requirement for sleep. Most people can be reasonably accurate in determining the amount of sleep they need if they think in terms of the amount of sleep that allows them to feel wide awake during the whole day. Assessment of the quota of sleep required should be made calculating the same amount of sleep obtained every day without weekday/weekend variations. Some individuals require only one to four hours of sleep each night to function pleasurably and capably by day, whereas others consistently require eight to 12 hours of sleep. Approximately 60 percent of people obtain from six to eight hours of sleep nightly, a range that was formerly regarded as the "golden mean."

If a short-sleeping individual has no daytime symptoms of insomnia such as fatigue, weakness, distractibility, poor concentration, and muscle aches, he should not be considered to have insomnia irrespective of obtaining an unconventionally brief period of sleep at night (without daytime napping). It may be speculated that genetic variation accounts for differences in the neurochemistry-neurophysiology interaction that is responsible for sleep requirements. In certain individuals, shorter or longer periods of sleep may be necessary to allow time for removal of sleep-inducing substances that have accumulated in the brain during waking hours.

*5) Polysomnographic and Daytime Performance Studies in*
*Individuals Taking Sedative-hypnotic Drugs*

Because of their common utilization, it is important to obtain information about the sleep-inducing, sleep-maintenance effects of drugs, and their residual effects during the desired time of awake functioning. Many drugs have been studied by investigators despite the fact that the federal government has not supported a single, long-term drug trial (8). If an ideal sleep medication could be designed, it would be one that elicited no tolerance to its actions and, accordingly, had little addictive potential. It would be absorbed readily so that sleep was induced rapidly. But it would be maintained in the brain long enough to support a full night of sleep without interruption. However, the drug, or its active metabolites, should be cleared by the desired morning awakening time so that arousal is quick and complete, and daytime drowsiness and reduced mental and motor performance are not problems. Finally, the effects of the drug should be immediately reversible even at the peak of its action if arousal and alert-functioning are suddenly demanded during the middle of the sleep period. Clearly, few drugs can fulfill all these requirements.

Sleep research has made important advances in evaluating drugs of different classes (9). Many of the favorite sleep-inducing drugs of the past such as barbiturates and alcohol have been found to lose their potency in as little as two weeks unless the dose is increased. Taken chronically, these agents actually "fragment" and reduce sleep, often more than the original sleep disturbance. Termination of the agent poses the additional jeopardy of a difficult period of withdrawal. Benzodiazepine agents, like flurazepam, appear to maintain their effectiveness at constant doses much longer than barbiturates. They also cause less respiratory depression. However, the presence of long-enduring active metabolites (as in flurazepam) seems to explain the mild degree of daytime sleepiness and poor waking performance that is seen. There is some hope that new "single phase," short-acting benzodiazepines, which are currently being marketed, will support sleep during the major portion of the desired sleep period but be eliminated from the body by the proposed time of arousal. As yet, however, no agent has satisfied these features evenly.

*6) The Sleep History*

As indicated earlier, the gathering of a detailed sleep history is important in all medical patients and is especially critical in the correct identification of sleep pathology. The sleep history that follows covers most areas of concern. Additional questions may be necessary to characterize fully all facets of presentation of a specific sleep disorder.

MEDICAL HISTORY SURVEY FOR THE SLEEP DISORDERS

a) Times of retiring and arising?
   Variations?
b) Amount of daily sleep needed to feel alert and energetic during awake functioning?
   How often is that amount obtained?
c) Amount of total sleep on weekdays, weekends?
   Variations?
   Sleep requirements and bedtimes in childhood and in other periods of life?
d) What is the subjective quality (i.e., soundness, restorativeness) of sleep currently; during earlier periods?
   What is the level of alertness upon waking up in the morning?
e) If difficulty sleeping is reported:
   Is the disorder constant or intermittent?
   Is there a difficulty getting to sleep or awakening too soon from

sleep, or both (i.e., pattern and timing of sleep disturbance during sleep period)?

How much sleep is lost from the ideal amount?

What are the daytime symptoms of the sleep disturbance?

What helps reduce the insomnia?

What makes it worse?

Is there evidence of tension, anxiety, depression?

Have the symptoms progressed over time?

f) What drugs have disturbed sleep?

What drugs have been or are taken to promote sleep?

Has a difficulty ever been encountered in terminating a sleep medication?

g) Is there a difficulty maintaining alertness during waking hours?

Is napping necessary to get through the day?

Is napping habitual?

h) If sleepiness by day is reported:

What time of day is sleepiness maximal?

What is the character of other daytime symptoms?

Are naps irresistible? Are they brief but refreshing and associated with a quick dream, or longer and non-refreshing without associated dreaming?

Is hypersomnia daily or periodic?

Have the symptoms progressed over time?

i) Description of sleep from "bed partner," if available: Specifically does the patient snore, or have respiratory and gagging problems during the night, or experience leg twitching in sleep?

Is there muscle weakness with emotional reactions in the awake state, particularly with laughter (cataplexy)?

Is there hypnagogic imagery, or a brief period of complete inability to move when waking up or falling asleep (sleep paralysis)?

Evidence of automatic behaviors?

j) Additional survey items to explore insomnia and excessive sleep syndromes:

Amount of moving about in sleep.

Preferred sleep position.

Painful conditions.

Symptoms of hypoglycemia during waking hours.

Seizure history: incontinence at night, blood on pillow, sore tongue, stereotyped dream intrusions.

Thyroid functioning.

Shortness of breath during the night.

Morning headaches.

Impotency problems.

Difficulty waking up in the morning, confusion, inappropriate behavior when waking up.

k) If sleep onset is delayed, can the required sleep be obtained by sleeping late? If so, are there any daytime symptoms of true insomnia or inadequate sleep (as in delayed sleep phase syndrome)?

Is the patient unable to stay awake past the early part of the evening and also unable to sleep past the middle of the night (as in advanced sleep phase syndrome)?

Does delay of the sleep period show a tendency for *progressive* delay in the time of falling asleep and waking up each day (as in non-24-hour sleep-wake syndrome)?

l) Symptoms of night terrors, nightmares, sleepwalking, bedwetting, angina pectoris, asthma, headaches, and teeth grinding. Other unusual symptoms during sleep.

### 7) Sleep Hygiene

The concept of a hygiene of sleep-wake behavior is well justified in terms of optimal maximization of both functions. The "sleep hygiene abuser" may seriously dilute the quality and effectiveness of his sleep and wake periods.

Many of the elements in the following discussion of sleep hygiene have been derived from Hauri (10). Regular arousal times and bedtimes are important because of the recruitment of other circadian rhythms to the sleep-wake cycle (temperature, ACTH-cortisol, etc.). Sleep becomes less efficient when moved to habitual waking hours, and alertness and cognitive functioning are severely compromised when wakefulness is forcibly maintained during habitual sleep periods.

An individual should have a reasonably accurate knowledge of his daily sleep needs. The period of time spent in bed is best not substantially greater than the actual sleep requirement. Too much time spent in and around bed leads to the danger of random napping and the threat of an irregular or random sleep-wake cycle, with consequent disruption of the circadian bimodality of sleep-waking and associated flattening and disruption of hormone and temperature curves.

Sleep suffers if there is excessive irregularity in the amount of exercise obtained daily or if there are wide variations in the quantity and types of foods eaten, particularly before bedtime. A steady and (for the particular individual) an appropriate amount of exercise should be maintained on a daily basis. Adequate nutrition promotes sleep by preventing hunger during the night. Overly large intakes of food or difficult-to-digest items eaten late in the evening may cause digestive problems and lead to poor sleep. Though a "nip" of alcohol has been a favorite sleep-promoting agent throughout antiquity, if taken on a daily basis, alcohol will lose its sleep-onset sedative potency. Unfortunately, however, so long as alcohol is ingested regularly, it will maintain its countervailing property of increasing the number of awakenings later in the night.

*8) The New Diagnostic Classification System of Sleep*
*and Arousal Disorders and its Importance*
*in Sleep Disorders Medicine*

The new nosology is rooted at the most fundamental clinical level, patient complaint, because most etiologies and mechanisms of sleep disorders still await discovery. Key to the classification system is the discriminability it provides for the major diagnostic groupings of disorders according to symptom pattern. At present, the overriding aim of the diagnostic classification schema is for greater reliability in the recognition of disorders. We must be able to teach these discriminations so that improved diagnostic capability among practitioners will eventuate in more appropriate and effective treatment efforts.

Few people who are not concerned with the sleep disorders can possibly be as enthusiastic about the first edition of the Diagnostic Classification of Sleep and Arousal Disorders as those of us in the field.* For that reason we will not here describe in detail its presumptions, objectives, advantages, and limitations. Briefly put, we needed a framework that would cover the full spectrum of normal and abnormal sleep, one that was formulated from the shared experience of working experts, with consensus agreements concerning diagnostic criteria, terminology and the most fruitful categorization of disorders. We needed a cornerstone of shared conventions to permit diagnostic standardization, greater homogeneity of research populations (so that cross-center case series could be studied), improved opportunities for teaching and training, and thus an improved base for advances in our knowledge as well as in our diagnostic acumen. The classification that resulted should be viewed not as a fixed system but as a clearer target than available previously for testing new concepts and findings.

Turning to the Classification System, it categorizes four major types of disorders:

*A. DIMS: Disorders of Initiating and Maintaining Sleep (Insomnias).* The

---

*The classification was requested in 1976 by the Association of Sleep Disorders Centers and the Association for the Psychophysiological Study of Sleep (APSS). A joint ASDC-APSS Committee, chaired by one of us (H. P. R.), created the diagnostic system, which was ratified by the two bodies in 1979.

disorders of initiating and maintaining sleep are a heterogenous group of conditions, which are clustered together because they are all responsible for inducing disturbed or diminished sleep. The substitution of the term DIMS for insomnia aims at centering our attention on the multiplicity of conditions as well as on the considerable variation in expression of sleep disturbances. Insomnia has been given a unidimensional interpretation previously. It deserves to be seen as an entity only insofar as it may be a final, common symptom pathway, actuated by a wide variety of arousing influences.

Each condition in the DIMS grouping is marked by one or more distinctive features. This allows one to use a "logic-tree" scheme of differentiation to locate a particular disorder among the group. It is particularly useful to pay close attention to the timing of a sleep difficulty (at the beginning, over the course, or exclusively toward the end of the sleep period?). Whereas anxiety syndromes and situational disturbances frequently inhibit the capacity to cross the threshold into sleep, endogenous depression generally manifests itself in progressive development of awakenings after some hours of sleep have been obtained.

*B. DOES: Disorders of Excessive Somnolence.* The disorders of excessive somnolence are a varied group of functional and organic conditions in which the chief symptoms may include inappropriate and undesirable sleepiness during waking hours, decreased cognitive and motor performance, excessive tendency to sleep, unavoidable napping, increase in total 24-hour sleep, and difficulty in achieving full arousal on awakening.

*C. Disorders of the Sleep-Wake Schedule.* The disorders of the sleep-wake schedule consist of an arbitrary collection of clinical syndromes, some exogenously instigated, and others, like delayed sleep phase, that appear to have an endogenous component. The conditions deserve to be treated as a separate group because of a shared, cardinal feature — every disorder represents one form or another of *initial misalignment* between the behaviors of sleep and waking in an individual and the internal circadian phases with which the behaviors are usually associated. In these conditions, delayed sleep phase and advanced sleep phase, the misalignment is not between the individual's sleep-wake behavior and his internal periodicities (they are aligned), but rather between the individual's phase relationships and those prevailing in the environment. For example, a schoolchild with delayed sleep phase does fine sleeping until 11 A.M.; nevertheless, the principal suggests 8 A.M. for him to be at school.

*D. Dysfunctions Associated with Sleep, Sleep Stages and Partial Arousals (Parasomnias).* The parasomnias are a group of clinical conditions that are not disorders of the processes responsible for the sleep and wake states per se. Rather, they are undesirable physical phenomena, either appearing exclusively in sleep (e.g., somnambulism) or exacerbated by sleep (e.g., asthma). These behaviors (some of which are pathological only in sleep, walking, urinating), are manifestations of CNS activation that is either translated into skeletal muscle activity or expressed in one of the several channels of autonomic nervous system activity.

For purposes of completeness, the individual conditions in each of the four dysfunction rubrics are listed below:

OUTLINE OF DIAGNOSTIC CLASSIFICATION OF SLEEP AND
AROUSAL DISORDERS (1)
(ASSOCIATION OF SLEEP DISORDERS CENTERS, 1979)

A. DIMS: Disorders of Initiating and Maintaining Sleep (Insomnias)
   1. Psychophysiological
      a. Transient and Situational
      b. Persistent
   2. *associated with*
      Psychiatric Disorders
      a. Symptom and Personality Disorders
      b. Affective Disorders
      c. Other Functional Psychoses
   3. *associated with*
      Use of Drugs and Alcohol
      a. Tolerance to or Withdrawal from CNS Depressants
      b. Sustained Use of CNS Stimulants
      c. Sustained Use of or Withdrawal from Other Drugs
      d. Chronic Alcoholism
   4. *associated with*
      Sleep-induced Respiratory Impairment
      a. Sleep Apnea DIMS Syndrome
      b. Alveolar Hypoventilation DIMS Syndrome
   5. *associated with*
      Sleep-related (Nocturnal) Myoclonus and "Restless Legs"
      a. Sleep-related (Nocturnal) Myoclonus DIMS Syndrome
      b. "Restless Legs" DIMS Syndrome
   6. *associated with*
      Other Medical, Toxic, and Environmental Conditions
   7. Childhood-Onset DIMS
   8. *associated with*
      Other DIMS Conditions
      a. Repeated REM Sleep Interruptions

      b. Atypical Polysomnographic Features

      c. Not Otherwise Specified

   9. No DIMS Abnormality

      a. Short Sleeper

      b. Subjective DIMS Complaint without Objective Findings

      c. Not Otherwise Specified

B. DOES: Disorders of Excessive Somnolence

   1. Psychophysiological

      a. Transient and Situational

      b. Persistent

   2. *associated with*

    Psychiatric Disorders

      a. Affective Disorders

      b. Other Functional Disorders

   3. *associated with*

    Use of Drugs and Alcohol

      a. Tolerance to or Withdrawal from CNS Stimulants

      b. Sustained Use of CNS Depressants

   4. *associated with*

    Sleep-induced Respiratory Impairment

      a. Sleep Apnea DOES Syndrome

      b. Alveolar Hypoventilation DOES Syndrome

   5. *associated with*

    Sleep-related (Nocturnal) Myoclonus and "Restless Legs"

      a. Sleep-related (Nocturnal) Myoclonus DOES Syndrome

      b. "Restless Legs" DOES Syndrome

   6. Narcolepsy

   7. Idiopathic CNS Hypersomnolence

   8. *associated with*

    Other Medical, Toxic, and Environmental Conditions

   9. *associated with*

    Other DOES Conditions

      a. Intermittent DOES (Periodic) Syndromes

         i. Kleine-Levin Syndrome

         ii. Menstrual-associated Syndrome

      b. Insufficient Sleep

      c. Sleep Drunkenness

      d. Not Otherwise Specified

  10. No DOES Abnormality

      a. Long Sleeper

      b. Subjective DOES Complaint without Objective Findings

      c. Not Otherwise Specified

C. Disorders of the Sleep-Wake Schedule

    1. Transient

      a. Rapid Time Zone Change ("Jet Lag") Syndrome

      b. "Work Shift" Change in Conventional Sleep-Wake Schedule

    2. Persistent

      a. Frequently Changing Sleep-Wake Schedule

      b. Delayed Sleep Phase Syndrome

      c. Advanced Sleep Phase Syndrome

      d. Non-24-Hour Sleep-Wake Syndrome

      e. Irregular Sleep-Wake Pattern

      f. Not Otherwise Specified

D. Dysfunctions Associated with Sleep, Sleep Stages, or Partial Arousals (Parasomnias)

    1. Sleepwalking (Somnambulism)

    2. Sleep Terror (Pavor Nocturnus, Incubus)

    3. Sleep-related Enuresis

    4. Other Dysfunctions

      a. Dream Anxiety Attacks (Nightmares)

      b. Sleep-related Epileptic Seizures

      c. Sleep-related Bruxism

      d. Sleep-related Headbanging (Jactatio Capitis Nocturnus)

      e. Familial Sleep Paralysis

      f. Impaired Sleep-related Penile Tumescence

      g. Sleep-related Painful Erections

      h. Sleep-related Cluster Headaches and Chronic Paroxysmal Hemicrania

      i. Sleep-related Abnormal Swallowing Syndrome

      j. Sleep-related Asthma

      k. Sleep-related Cardiovascular Symptoms

      l. Sleep-related Gastroesophageal Reflux

      m. Sleep-related Hemolysis (Paroxysmal Nocturnal Hemoglobinuria)

      n. Asymptomatic Polysomnographic Finding

      o. Not Otherwise Specified

### DISORDERS OF INITIATING AND MAINTAINING SLEEP

For the remainder of this chapter, we will focus upon two of the four major categories: Disorders of Initiating and Maintaining Sleep (DIMS); and Disorders of the Sleep-Wake Schedule.

Among the Disorders of Initiating and Maintaining Sleep, psychophysiological and psychiatric disorders account for about 50 percent, drug and alcohol-related 15–20 percent, and the physiologic-organic-medical-neurologic group 30–35 percent of the total.*

*Transient and situational physiological DIMS.* A transitory episode of sleep disruption characterizes this insomnia, which generally occurs in reaction to acute disappointment, loss, or perceived threat. It may also be induced by acute emotional arousal and by unfamiliar sleep environments (the "first night effect").

*Persistent psychophysiological DIMS.* This disorder is distinguished by a sleep onset and intermediary sleep maintenance insomnia associated with high levels of somatized tension-anxiety. Patients with this diagnosis are tense but do not have anxiety attacks. They often have psychosomatic disorders. Their anxiety is usually not approachable in terms of psychological conflict; rather, the patient considers high tension part of his "nature."

Also included under this diagnosis, but frequently separable in terms of causative factors, are DIMS associated with *a conditioned internal factor* and with a *conditioned external factor.* In the former case, the internal factor (which conceptually is a conditioned negative sleep reinforcer) amounts to an apprehension that one will not fall asleep when the desire and need are present. The harder the individual "makes himself" fall asleep, the more he arouses. This internal arousal, which develops when one is trying too hard to sleep, often plays a critical role in the perpetuation of a psychophysiological insomnia due to generalized tension, but, as a secondary factor, it may aggravate an insomnia from *any* cause. Patients who have this problem have a characteristic experience—they are able to fall asleep quickly when not endeavoring or expecting to sleep, implicating, again, the individual's usual overworked attempts to fall asleep coupled with negative anticipation about the possibility of sleep. Recognition of these factors and behavioral deconditioning are necessary to alleviate this insomnia.

The conditioned external factor may enter an insomnia picture after the patient has had several sleepless nights that were induced by some other (perhaps situational) cause of insomnia. The patient may begin unwittingly to associate his usual sleep environment—the bedroom—with *not sleeping* rather than with *sleeping.* Accordingly, the bedroom and its trappings become a negative, external stimulus. These patients frequently sleep better

---

*These proportions are taken from the 1980 ASDC survey of patient diagnoses in ten leading sleep disorders centers, to be published shortly.

away from their bedrooms even if only in another room in the same house. Recognition and deconditioning are required for "cure."

*DIMS with symptom and personality disorders.* This disorder is characterized by a sleep-onset and intermediary sleep maintenance insomnia that is clearly related to the psychological and behavioral symptoms of the clinically well-known and classified, nonaffective, and nonpsychotic psychiatric disorders. Unlike the patients with persistent psychophysiological DIMS, these individuals have DSM III disorders encompassing generalized anxiety, panic and phobic disorders, hypochondriasis, obsessive-compulsive disorder, and various personality disorders.

*DIMS with affective disorders.* In depression, the patient generally maintains the ability to fall asleep but has a sleep maintenance disturbance typical of depression—foreshortened sleep or "early morning" (premature) arousal. A reduced REM sleep latency in endogenous depression has achieved the status of a biological marker. In mania, there is frequently a sleep-onset insomnia and very abbreviated sleep. Nevertheless, the patient awakens feeling bright. In bipolar depression, though the REM sleep latency is short, there is a tendency for longer periods of sleep than in unipolar depression.

*DIMS with other functional psychoses.* Generally, this insomnia is characterized by severe sleep onset difficulties and often sleep discontinuity. The symptoms exacerbate in connection with acute psychotic decompensations. The sleep disturbance is highly associated with the patient's anxiety, suspiciousness, urgency of thought, and obsessive guilt. In chronic psychosis, insomnia tends to remain a problem but is usually less severe than in the acute phase.

*DIMS with tolerance to or withdrawal from CNS depressants.* With sustained use of sleep medication of the CNS depressant variety, pharmacological tolerance increases, the drugs lose their sleep-inducing effects, and the patient frequently decides to increase the dose. During the period of chronic use, the hypnotic agent rapidly loses its effect in the second half of the night's sleep, irrespective of dose. This means that sleep is poor *while* the patient may be on heavy intake. With sudden termination of the hypnotic agent, a full-blown drug withdrawal syndrome is seen marked by nightmarish dreams coupled with a "rebound insomnia." Withdrawal from sleeping pills should be no faster than one therapeutic dose every seven to ten days.

*DIMS with chronic alcoholism.* During drinking episodes, there is progressive disintegration of the sleep architecture. Persistent sleep interruptions lead to low total sleep time, fragmented REM sleep periods, and reduced REM sleep. When the chronic alcoholic withdraws from alcohol, stages 3 and 4 and REM sleep diminish, and REM sleep rebounds until withdrawal is complete. These findings frequently accompany delirium tremens. In several alcoholics, deep NREM and REM sleep may be chronically reduced.

*Sleep Apnea DIMS Syndrome.* In this condition, sleep-related cessation of breathing occurs. Patients with this condition are snorers, and the condition is frequently occult because the patient is not aware of the apnea, which has aroused him. Insomnia is usually the chief symptom. On polysomnographic recording, respiratory effort is not observed, indicating a central termination of breathing. (When upper airway obstruction is the major cause of apnea, respiratory effort persists. The presenting complaint in the latter syndrome is excessive daytime somnolence.) The disorder is worsened by ingestion of CNS depressants and by advancing age. Only a sleep partner may be able to provide a description of the interruptions of breathing.

*Sleep-related (nocturnal) myoclonus.* This is a condition in which insomnia is associated with the occurrence in sleep of periodic episodes of repetitive and highly stereotyped leg muscle jerks. In some individuals, excessive daytime sleepiness rather than insomnia is the chief complaint. This syndrome may be called the "great mimicker." It is the frequent experience of diagnosticians that the patient, who is usually unaware of the leg jerks, appears to have many of the characteristics of a psychological insomnia. A history from the bed partner is also crucial in this condition because an accounting of the excessive leg movement must be provided for diagnosis, particularly if polysomnographic recording is not available.

*Childhood-onset DIMS.* In this disorder, a sleep-onset and sleep-maintenance insomnia, resulting in daytime symptoms of inadequate sleep, is characterized by the distinctive history of unexplained development of sleeplessness *before* puberty, with persistence into adulthood. In adulthood, its clinical features are not differentiable from persistent psychophysiological DIMS.

*Atypical polysomnographic features.* This is a condition in which sleep is experienced as frequently interrupted or "nonrestorative." The sleep stage structure is marked by abnormal physiological features, usually of excessive alpha activity running through most of NREM sleep.

*Short sleeper (not a DIMS abnormality).* Short sleeper is the designation for an individual who consistently sleeps, and only needs to sleep, a short period of time for his age (one to five hours). Though short, sleep is unbroken and electrophysiologically normal. There is an absence of complaints about the quality of sleep. Daytime sleepiness, difficulties with awake mood, motivation, and performance are not observed. Short sleep is at one end of the continuum of normal sleep requirement. A true DIMS does not exist with this condition. However, the individual often attempts to find methods that will help him to sleep longer, and, consequently, usually has been on many drugs provided by many doctors simply because he claims he sleeps only a few hours.

*Subjective DIMS complaint without objective findings.* This pseudoinsomnia is a convincing and honest complaint of insomnia made by an individual lacking apparent psychopathology. It is not coupled with polysomnographic evidence of disturbed or shortened sleep. Although in the laboratory normal sleep is recorded, the patient sticks to the same description of subjectively disturbed sleep as reported at home. The patient is sure that reversal of the "insomnia" will improve his awake functioning. It is not known what is responsible for this curious distortion of a somatic process. Several possibilities have been considered, such as excessive sleep mentation, micro-wakes, and hypochondriasis related to the physiological process of sleep.

Several conditions for which a PSG is necessary to make a diagnosis frequently present with a set of complaints that suggest psychological difficulties. Indeed, psychological problems may also be present, but they are adventitious to the cause of the sleeplessness. The often confused conditions are listed below.

CONDITIONS THAT OFTEN MASQUERADE AS PSYCHOLOGICALLY-RELATED DIMS

Sleep Apnea DIMS Syndrome (Central Apnea)
Sleep-related (Nocturnal) Myoclonus
Atypical Polysomnographic Features (Alpha Sleep)
Subjective DIMS Complaint without Objective Findings (Pseudoinsomnia)

Short Sleeper*
Advanced Sleep Phase*
Delayed Sleep Phase*
Childhood Onset DIMS*
Secondary Depression*
Sustained Use of Stimulant Drugs, Alcohol, or Sleeping Pills*
Sustained Use of Drugs for Medical Conditions*
   (e.g., thyroid, chemotherapeutic agents, antimetabolites, oral contraceptives, propranolol, etc.)
Other Medical and Toxic Conditions*
   (e.g., incipient dementia, endocrine and metabolic diseases, hyperthyroidism, hypoglycemia, nutritional disorders, and food allergies)

---

*These conditions can usually be ruled out by careful sleep-pattern, drug intake, or medical histories.

### Disorders of the Sleep-Wake Schedule

Turning to the Disorders of the Sleep-Wake Schedule, this group contains some situational (exogenous) disorders such as rapid time zone change ("jet lag") and work shift schedule change. In the delayed sleep phase syndrome and the advanced sleep phase syndrome, as well as in the non-24-hour sleep-wake schedule, the causes are at least in part endogenous.

In these disorders, the patients usually present symptoms of insomnia or excessive daytime sleepiness. They experience inability to fall asleep or have broken sleep, daytime sleepiness, and poor performance. However, a careful sleep history reveals no evidence of an abnormality in initiating or maintaining either sleep or wakefulness. The abnormality is in the *rhythm of sleep and waking* with respect to either the phase of the individual's inner milieu or the expected societal sleep/wake phase. Jet lag and work shift syndromes occur because the individual's regular sleep-wake periodicity has become physiologically associated with other bodily functions. When sleep and awake periods are removed to new positions in the 24-hour cycle, the other processes become misaligned with the sleep-wake schedule. The period of symptomatology in these syndromes occurs between misalignment and realignment. An abrupt change in sleep-wake periodicity (jet lag, work shift change) may require six to eight weeks for complete realignment of the sleep-wake cycle with temperature and other functions.

An important endogenous disorder is the delayed sleep phase syndrome. It is marked by stable sleep onset and wake times, though they are intractably later than desired. There is no reported difficulty in maintaining sleep once begun. One notes a curious *inability* to advance the sleep phase through enforcement of conventional sleep and wake times. The syndrome often presents with the major complaint of difficulty in falling asleep at a desired conventional time, giving the picture of a sleep onset insomnia. However, the patient is able to sleep late in the morning and to obtain a completely restitutive night of sleep. Accordingly, delayed sleep phase is not an insomnia so much as a misalignment with customary, societal sleep-wake times. A promising therapy is therapeutic sleep phase delay (chronotherapy) in which, over a sequence of days, the patient goes to bed later and wakes up later (two to three hours each day), thus moving the sleep period around the clock and finally stopping when the patient's sleep onset time is at the desired clock time. This chronotherapy has been amazingly successful.

### REFERENCES

1. Association of Sleep Disorders Centers: *Diagnostic Classification of Sleep and Arousal Disorders,* Ed. 1, prepared by the Sleep Disorders Classification Committee, H. P. Roffwarg (Chairman). *Sleep,* 2:1–137, 1979.

2. KALES, A., MALINSTROM, E. J., SCHARF, M. B. and RUBIN, R. T.: Psychophysiological and biochemical changes following use and withdrawal of hypnotics. In: Kales, A. (Ed.), *Sleep: Physiology and Pathology,* Philadelphia: J. B. Lippincott, 1969, pp. 331–343.
3. Institute of Medicine. Report of a study: Sleeping pills, insomnia, and medical practice. National Academy of Sciences, Washington, D.C., 1979. p. 198.
4. GUILLEMINAULT, C. and DEMENT, W. C.: *Sleep Apnea Syndromes.* New York: Alan R. Liss, 1978.
5. ROTH, T., KRAMER, M. and LUTZ, T.: The effects of hypnotics on sleep, performance, and subjective state. *Drugs Exptl. Clin. Res.,* 1:279–286, 1977.
6. OSWALD, I., ADAM, K., BORROW, S. and IDZIDKOWSKI, C.: The effects of two hypnotics on sleep, subjective feelings and skilled performance. In: Passouant, D. and Oswald, I. (Eds.), *Pharmacology of the States of Alertness.* Oxford and New York: Pergamon Press, 1979, pp. 51–63.
7. RECHTSCHAFFEN, A., and KALES, A. (Eds.), *A Manual of Standardized Terminology, Techniques, and Scoring System for Sleep Stages of Human Subjects.* Brain Information Unit/Brain Research Institute, U.C.L.A., Los Angeles, 1968.
8. KAY, D. C., BLACKBURN, A. B., BUCKINGHAM, J. A. and KARACAN, I.: Human pharmacology of sleep. In: R. L. William and I. Karacan (Eds.), *Pharmacology of Sleep.* New York: John Wiley, 1976, pp. 83–210.
9. KALES, A., BIXLEY, E., TAN, T., SCHARF, M. and KALES, J.: Chronic hypnotic drug use: Ineffectiveness, drug withdrawal insomnia and dependence. *J.A.M.A.,* 227:513–517, 1974.
10. HAURI, P.: *The Sleep Disorders.* Kalamazoo: The Upjohn Company, 1977. pp. 22–27.

# 7

# Disorders of Excessive Sleep and the Parasomnias

*Robert L. Williams, M.D.,*
*Sabri Derman, M.D., M.Sc.D., and*
*Ismet Karacan, M.D., D.Sc. (Med.)*

## DISORDERS OF EXCESSIVE SOMNOLENCE (DOES)

Over the decades, the term "sleep disorder" has become synonymous with insomnia. Patients' complaints of excessive sleepiness have elicited very little attention and understanding from their families and their physicians. Dozing off at inappropriate times is typically attributed to laziness or to a hectic lifestyle. That more than one-third of patients with excessive daytime sleepiness (EDS) delay seeking medical advice until five years after symptom onset and that the reported mean interval between symptom onset and definite diagnosis of narcolepsy—the best-known DOES—is 15.2 years (1) are disturbing statistics for the clinical polysomnographer. Even more tragic is the number of obese, middle-aged "lazy" men who die quietly in their sleep from "natural causes." Yet according to a recent survey (2), 25 percent of all patients evaluated in sleep disorders centers in the United States suffer from sleep-related respiratory disorders. We can only surmise how many "natural" deaths are the unnatural result of undiagnosed nocturnal respiratory failure. Education of physicians and the general public about the disorders of excessive somnolence and their complications is critically needed. Prompt, accurate diagnosis and suitable treatment can improve the quality of life of the victims of such disorders and their families, as well as increase their productivity and capacity to contribute to society.

The disorders of excessive somnolence are a heterogeneous group of syndromes for which increased and continuous sleepiness during the day and/or sudden, irresistible sleep attacks, are the major symptoms. Certain syndromes, sleep apnea and narcolepsy, are diagnosed through routine sleep laboratory evaluation; some, i.e., idiopathic hypersomnolence and hypersomnolence due to psychophysiological disturbances, have more complex clinical pictures. Other disorders, such as the Kleine-Levin syndrome, have relatively unexplored, puzzling features; a better understanding of their etiology must rely on future research findings. Too often, physicians prescribe CNS stimulants to patients who complain of EDS without attempting to identify the underlying pathology. This practice is usually more harmful than beneficial because stimulants not only tend to increase sleep disturbance, but can also lead to a vicious cycle of dependency and withdrawal problems.

## DOES Associated with Psychophysiological Disorders

*Transient and situational.* Some individuals respond with increased somnolence to a serious, identifiable psychological stress such as death in the family, severe illness of a loved one, marital problems, or job changes or difficulties. Excessive daytime sleepiness, fatigue, and exhaustion are often associated with increased total time in bed and frequent pseudo-naps; the patient may not actually sleep although his eyes are closed and he is lying down. Total sleep time either increases or remains unchanged from the premorbid duration. Sleep architecture remains basically normal. Transient and situational DOES disappear within one to three weeks after the source of stress ends. Some patients, however, develop the habit of reacting to stress by seeking shelter in bed. These episodes usually last only a few days and have no regular pattern.

*Persistent.* DOES are considered persistent when the patient complains of having excessive sleepiness for more than three weeks. Some individuals have a chronic disposition to weariness, bed rest, and napping when they encounter tension and stress. Although the amount of time in bed may increase, there is no polysomnographic demonstration of greatly increased total sleep time. The clinical picture of DOES due to persistent, psychophysiological disturbance is usually further complicated by a disturbed sleep-wake schedule leading to nocturnal insomnia, excessive daytime sleepiness, and irregular bedtime schedule. Taking sedatives also exacerbates the condition.

This type of hypersomnolence may be a somatically expressed form of mild depression, although clinically the patient may not seem to be depressed. The clinician must therefore differentiate this rare form of DOES from chronic depression. A sleep laboratory evaluation can help eliminate sleep apnea and nocturnal myoclonus as possible sources of nocturnal sleep disturbance causing chronic sleepiness during the day. The practitioner is cautioned to take a thorough history because drug abusers often malinger, feigning the symptoms of persistent DOES to obtain prescriptions for stimulants.

### DOES Associated with Psychiatric Disorders

*Affective Disorders.* Excessive daytime sleepiness associated with major affective and other depressive syndromes is most pronounced in the early stages of the disorder and especially during the depressed phase of the bipolar affective syndrome. DOES is often the first symptom of impending depression.

There is a direct correlation between the severity of the affective disorder and the degree of sleep disturbance. In most of the cases, polysomnographic evaluation reveals normal or increased total sleep time, decreased slow wave sleep, and decreased latency to the first REM episode. Patients may or may not show early morning awakenings, but usually complain of insufficient sleep, feeling unrefreshed, and grogginess.

Clinical and polysomnographic evaluations are essential in differentiating DOES due to affective disorders from toxic and metabolic diseases and organic brain disease. Other sleep disorders such as narcolepsy, sleep apnea syndrome, nocturnal myoclonus, and idiopathic CNS hypersomnolence should also be excluded as alternative diagnoses.

*Other Functional Disorders.* Functional disorders associated with excessive somnolence include personality disorders, dissociative disorders, hypochondriasis, borderline states, conversion, and schizophrenia. Despite complaints of excessive sleepiness, the patient's total amount of daily sleep is not necessarily increased. Schizophrenic patients suffering from nocturnal sleep onset and maintenance problems typically push their arising time toward late morning and early afternoon and may appear sleepy during the day. Correct diagnosis of the underlying psychiatric disorder is important and the possibility of drug interactions must be considered for patients who are taking psychoactive agents.

Disorders of excessive somnolence and their association with psychiatric disorders are more extensively reviewed elsewhere (3, 4, 5, 6).

### DOES Associated with Use of Drugs and Alcohol

The prolonged use of CNS stimulants and depressants and their withdrawal result in either problems initiating and maintaining sleep or in disorders of excessive hypersomnolence.

The growth of tolerance to and/or withdrawal from CNS stimulan⁺⁻ such as amphetamines and methylphenidate results in irritability, rapid mood changes, automatic behaviors, and seemingly paradoxical hypersomnolence. Self-imposed withdrawal increases daytime sleepiness and napping which, in turn, strengthens psychological habituation to stimulants, creating a vicious cycle that is difficult to break. On the other hand, increasing dosages of CNS stimulants extends their effects into the night hours, causing drug-induced insomnia. The patient typically compensates by taking sleeping pills to get a normal night of sleep.

Frequently overlooked by the patient and physician alike, the excessive use of caffeinated beverages such as coffee strongly affects sleep. Because tolerance to and dependence on the stimulating effects of caffeine progresses gradually, patients experience marked morning drowsiness, excessive daytime sleepiness, and tiredness when they try to reduce their intake of caffeine.

Patients taking CNS depressants (including alcohol) on a regular basis to combat insomnia, or various medications (e.g., antidepressants, tranquilizers, antihistamines, beta adrenergic blockers, muscle relaxants, contraceptive pills, anticonvulsants, and antihypertensive drugs) for prolonged periods at moderate-to-high doses, may also develop drug-induced excessive daytime sleepiness. The sustained use of depressants, like CNS stimulants, results in irritability, episodes of amnesia, paranoid thinking, automatic behavior, depression, restlessness, and hypersomnolence. Polysomnographic evaluation reveals increased total sleep time, decreased REM and slow wave sleep, and increased stages 1 and 2 NREM sleep.

The diagnosis of drug- and alcohol-related DOES is seldom difficult when a careful and dependable medical and social history is obtained. Medically supervised withdrawal from all stimulants and/or depressants is important to evaluate the possibility of any other underlying general or sleep pathology. Clinicians, particularly general practitioners, should be aware of the dangers of prescribing stimulants and/or depressants PRN for patients during and after extended hospitalization; the primary source of introduction to CNS-active drugs is the hospital. Drug dependence can easily become a greater problem than the initial disease. Oswald (7) and Sutherland (8) provide more comprehensive information on drug dependence.

### DOES Associated with Sleep-induced Respiratory Impairment

*Sleep Apnea Syndrome.* Sleep apnea syndrome consists of a group of breathing disturbances occurring in sleep that are characterized by the episodic cessation of respiratory airflow. As described in the Diagnostic Classification of Sleep and Arousal Disorders (9), "Sleep apnea (DOES) syndrome is a potentially lethal condition characterized by multiple obstructive or mixed apneas during sleep associated with repetitive episodes of inordinately loud snoring and excessive daytime sleepiness" (p. 65).

Since minor irregularities of respiratory rate and depth during transitions from wakefulness to sleep and during REM sleep are not uncommon, the recommended criterion for diagnosis of sleep apnea syndrome is the observation of at least 30 apneic episodes lasting at least ten seconds during seven hours of nocturnal sleep. Most apnea patients far exceed these minimum values. The severity of the disorder is most accurately measured by using an "apnea index," i.e., the number of apneas per sleep-hour, as proposed by Guilleminault et al. (10).

Although sleep apnea syndrome is an area of relatively recent clinical and research interest, it is rapidly becoming a significant medical concern due to its proven or hypothesized relationship to cardiac diseases, systemic and pulmonary hypertension, cerebral blood flow insufficiencies, headaches, stroke, sudden infant death, and chronic obstructive lung disease. Furthermore, its obscure, complex pathology has attracted researchers from the basic sciences who are exploring the regulatory mechanisms of respiratory, cardiovascular, and hormonal functions and their interactions with the equally complicated mechanisms of sleep and wakefulness.

A comprehensive review and discussion of the sometimes controversial aspects of sleep apnea syndromes are beyond the scope of this chapter, but are provided by Guilleminault and Dement (11), Derman and Karacan (12), Block (13), and Lugaresi et al. (14). This discussion will be limited to the basic features of the syndrome.

Evaluated by nasal and oral thermistors as well as thoracic and abdominal strain gauges, sleep apnea episodes have been divided into three subgroups reflecting the respiratory motor output of the CNS: central, obstructive, and mixed. In central sleep apnea, the airflow through the nose and the mouth ceases due to a lack of motor output to the respiratory muscles of the chest and diaphragm. In the obstructive type, also known as the upper airways or occlusive type, airflow ceases due to an obstruction of the oropharynx, but respiratory efforts increasingly continue until respiration resumes; the patient often awakens. In the mixed type, the episode of apnea starts as a central one, but continues as an obstructive one. More than one type of apnea is observed in most patients, but usually, one type clearly predominates.

Sleep apnea may be associated with numerous conditions — diseases and trauma to the CNS such as bulbar poliomyelitis, brainstem infarct, bilateral cordotomy, Ondine's curse syndrome (failure of the automatic control of ventilation such that breathing stops during sleep), Shy-Drager syndrome (a rare cerebellar syndrome producing secondary autonomic dysfunction primarily in elderly men), tumors, intoxication from CNS depressants, and abnormalities of the respiratory system such as chronic obstructive lung disease, nasopharyngitis in infants, muscular dystrophy, kyphoscoliosis, Pierre-Robin syndrome (partially cleft palate and unusually large tongue), and conditions such as micrognathia and acromegaly in which the pharynx is bulged by the tongue. Hodgkin's infiltration to the hypopharynx, lymphoma, and polyps of the hypopharynx have also been reported to lead to sleep apnea episodes. Simple tonsillar and/or adenoid hypertrophy can cause severe sleep apnea, at least in children, and 10 percent of narcoleptics have sleep apnea. However, in the majority of the cases, there is no clear causal relationship between a medical condition and nocturnal episodic cessation of ventilation.

Most obstructive-type sleep apnea patients are mildly to massively obese, yet normal or even underweight people have been observed to suffer from obstructive apnea. Sometimes, a short neck and a double chin that is muscular and firmer than the fat double chin associated only with obesity are indicative of possible upper airway obstruction in sleep.

A high percentage of sleep-apnea patients exhibit a rich combination of the following complaints, but none of them are pathognomonic and no patient will exhibit all of these symptoms. The main complaint of central-apnea patients is tiredness during the day. Some patients mistakenly describe their condition as excessive sleepiness. Compared to obstructive and mixed apnea, central apnea shows less obvious signs of excessive sleepiness. However, central-apnea patients, unlike obstructive apnea patients, may also complain of chronic insomnia that is basically a sleep-maintenance rather than a sleep-onset problem. Frequently, they consult their physician with complaints of insomnia "causing" daytime fatigue and receive prescriptions for a sleeping pill; the complaint consequently worsens.

Many sleep apnea patients of both types complain of headaches, especially morning, frontal headaches. They usually disappear after a few hours, but greatly increase the patient's usual misery in the morning and after daytime naps. Although the mechanism of the headache in sleep apnea patients is not fully understood, available data indicate a possible relationship to impaired regional cerebral blood flow changes in sleep (15).

A long history of loud, obnoxious snoring interspersed with episodes of quiet breathing or silent episodes is one of the most important features of obstructive apnea. Some of our patients have stated that their "terrible snoring even wakes them up," but the patient's bed partner and family members are usually better sources of information. Patients and their bed partners may describe a worsening of snoring associated with weight gain, flu injections, and alcohol consumption. Lugaresi et al. (14, 16) report in their series of cases that heavy snoring precedes the full development of the disease by years, often decades. They conclude that 1) snoring is produced by incomplete obstruction of the upper airway; 2) heavy snorers undergo numerous obstructive apneas; and 3) heavy snorers develop alveolar hypoventilation.

Other symptoms accompanying sleep apnea, particularly the obstructive type, include abnormal motor activity in sleep, hypnagogic hallucinations, personality changes, automatic behavior, inability to concentrate, diminished libido, enuresis, and polycythemia.

Cardiovascular symptoms, the most important manifestation of sleep apnea syndrome, are potentially fatal. Although insufficient, data on the cardiac performance and hemodynamic changes of central sleep apnea patients indicate that pulmonary artery pressure rises during apnea episodes and returns to normal limits in the eupneic stage; the systemic arterial pressure remains unaffected. Sinus arrhythmias are reported during continuous ECG recording (1). There are some significant cardiovascular findings for obstructive sleep apnea, despite the paucity of studies (17, 18, 19, 20).

Tilkian et al. (18) studied pulmonary arterial pressure (PAP), cardiac output, systemic arterial blood pressure, arterial blood gases, and pH in a group of 10 sleep apnea patients while awake and sleep. Except for one with borderline elevated PAP and capillary pressure, the patients showed no pathological findings. Nine of the patients developed elevations in systemic arterial pressure (SAP) during sleep. These elevations were generally transient, occurring periodically with each episode of apnea. When apnea episodes were long and frequent enough, SAP did not return to baseline values but showed a stepwise increase. Guilleminault et al. (1) reported similar findings and elevations in PAP during sleep. There was a direct correlation between the severity of the apnea episode and the increase in PAP. Maximum PAP increases occurred at the end of the apneic spell and frequent episodes led to a persistent elevation in PAP.

Unless an unrelated heart disease already exists, the ECG of sleep apnea patients shows little or no irregularity during wakefulness, at least in the early stages of the disorder. Continuous ECG recordings during sleep, however, indicate that cardiac arrhythmias almost always accompany sleep apnea episodes. Typical changes in the heart rate are bradycardia during the apnea episode and tachycardia at the onset of breathing. This cycle of heart-rate acceleration and deceleration usually repeats itself about every 30 to 120 seconds, depending on the frequency of apneas. Although the mean difference between the slowest and fastest heart rate is usually 10 to 40 beats per minute, we have recorded rate changes of up to 80 beats per minute within 30-second episodes in extreme cases. Tilkian et al. (18) reported that extreme sinus arrhythmias were more abundant in patients with obstructive apneas throughout the night. They also noted prolonged asystoles of up to 6.3 seconds and some cases of AV blockage. They concluded that marked sinus arrhythmias are observed essentially with mixed and obstructive apneas while asystoles and AV blockage are noted predominantly with central apneas.

Most of the daytime complaints, as well as polysomnographically demonstrated manifestations of sleep apnea syndrome, can be directly associated with partial or complete cessation of ventilation and the resulting oxygen desaturation. This desaturation causes the patient to spend a great deal of the night in hypoxemia and sometimes in hypercarbia. The etiology of this interruption of normal breathing in sleep remains obscure. In central apnea, the failure is blamed on the respiratory rhythm-generating mechanisms in the brainstem. Both the reticular activating system and the higher levels of the CNS seem to influence respiratory centers during wakefulness and contribute to the maintenance and control of the normal rhythm. When those "governing" influences are withdrawn during sleep, failures of respiratory rhythm generators cause apneic spells.

Current attempts to explain the pathogenesis of obstructive sleep apnea are based primarily on the neuromuscular control deficiencies of the oropharynx. Recent postulates, based predominantly on the works of Remmers et al. (21) and Sauerland and Harper (22, 23), attribute obstructive apnea to the sleep-induced collapse of the oropharynx. Since this portion of the airways is not a rigid passage made of cartilage, only continuous tonus of the surrounding muscles can keep it open. During inspiration, expansion of the thorax creates negative pressure in the extrathoracic airways which is counteracted by the contraction of related muscles. Recordings of simultaneous EMG activity of various muscles, particularly of the genioglossus muscle, as well as pressure measurements from the esophagus (intrathoracic pressure) and from just above the pharynx indicate several important relationships:

1) An increase in pressure in the pharynx, due primarily to a compromise in genioglossal contraction, causes the pharynx to contract.
2) The inspiratory forces of respiratory muscles continuously increase, probably due to increasing input from central and peripheral chemoreceptors, and contribute to the maintenance of the obstruction.

3) Genioglossal EMG activity increases two- to five-fold, most likely because of hypoxic stimuli. A plausible alternative explanation for EMG-activity increase is that extensive recruitment of genioglossal motor neurons leads to contractions of the oropharyngeal muscles sufficient to overcome the pressure differences and reopen the air passage.

Obviously, any existing narrowing of the upper airway related to, for example, obesity, creates a predisposition for this obstructive process. These polysomnographic findings, supported by direct fibre-optic observations during apneic spells (24), locate the site of obstruction in the pharynx, which explains why tracheostomy quickly alleviates all nocturnal and daytime symptoms of sleep apnea.

Cessation of ventilation leads to mild to extreme oxygen desaturation. Using a Hewlett-Packard model 47201A ear oximeter, we have recorded in severe cases saturations as low as the 20 percent range. Although the accuracy of the oximeter is questionable below 50 percent saturation, this instrument can reveal the seriousness of oxygen desaturations in sleep. The possible consequences of nocturnal oxygen desaturation in sleep apnea, as well as in chronic obstructive pulmonary disease, have been discussed in recent publications (25, 26).

Psychiatric evaluation of sleep apnea patients has demonstrated no consistent or prominent pathological feature. Obstructive-apnea patients and their families often report personality changes. Anxiety and depression are the main effects; confusion, marked irritability, and aggression are less common. Patients may also show exaggerated reactions such as diminished patience, sudden emotional changes, and episodes of anger, suspicion, and jealousy. The patient is often aware of a decreased intellectual capacity, inability to concentrate, and the easy onset of tiredness while performing intellectual tasks. In comparisons of narcoleptic and apneic patients, apneic patients have been found to have a greater tendency to be relatively neurotic and body-focused. Hysteric and hypochondriac configurations were much more likely to occur in apnea patients than in normal controls (27).

Sleep apnea DOES syndromes need to be differentiated from narcolepsy, alveolar hypoventilation syndrome, DOES due to nocturnal myoclonus, sleep epilepsy, idiopathic CNS hypersomnolence, and other medical, toxic, and environmental conditions of excessive somnolence. Since sleep apnea occurs in both sexes and in nearly all ages, a careful history and polysomnographic evaluation is necessary to make a correct diagnosis. The routine evaluation includes an ear, nose, and throat exam to identify any local obstruction to breathing as well as cardiovascular and pulmonary examinations. Adequate monitoring is essential to differentiate Pickwickian patients with sleep apnea from COPD patients with partial obstruction and/or decreased ventilation rather than apnea. Cheyne-Stokes respiration is also easily misidentified as sleep apnea.

The present treatment of sleep apnea syndromes leaves much to be desired. Clinicians have already noticed the tremendous variability in individual responses to weight reduction and pharmacological treatment by protriptyline, pemoline, or progesterone in patients with predominantly obstructive sleep apnea.

Weight loss through diet or surgical intervention (gastric stapling) (28) has yielded contradictory findings. Some investigators have reported decreases in excessive daytime sleepiness and in the number and duration of apneic episodes after patients have lost between nine and 20 kg (29–31). Others have reported little or no effect (1).

At the present time, a permanent tracheostomy seems to be the most effective solution to the symptoms and complications of predominantly obstructive sleep apnea. Obviously, this is not a treatment and should not be considered a routine approach to sleep apnea. A permanent tracheostomy requires pre- and postoperative patient management. The patient must be selected carefully for clear evidence of cardiovascular complications and indications that apnea and daytime symptoms interfere with business and social life. Possible short-term complications from tracheostomy are respiratory problems associated with the use of anesthetics and sedatives, soreness, coughing episodes, and infections. The most common long-term complication from permanent tracheostomy is depression (32).

There is no proven pharmacological treatment for central sleep apnea. Further research is needed to clarify the pathogenesis of sleep apneas and specific respiratory stimulants with minimal side effects must be developed. Diaphragm pacing (33, 34) is a promising surgical treatment. However, since this procedure has been performed on few patients, conclusions concerning its efficacy and long-term effects await further development and experience.

*Alveolar Hypoventilation Syndrome.* Alveolar hypoventilation syndrome, diminished ventilation because of decreased respiratory rate or tidal volume, appears only in sleep or significantly worsens during sleep. Several medical conditions have been associated with this syndrome — deformities of the thorax, neuromuscular diseases, ventrolateral cervical spinal cord lesions and other CNS disorders. Some degree of impaired ventilation during sleep often occurs with obesity. Since there are no actual apneas in alveolar hypoventilation syndrome, this disorder must be differentiated from sleep apnea.

Some patients present with both sleep apnea and hypoventilation episodes which need to be diagnosed and treated properly.

### DOES Associated with Sleep-related Myoclonus and "Restless Legs" Syndrome

Nocturnal myoclonus is a disorder consisting of brief, stereotyped, repetitive, nonepileptiform movements or jerks of one or both legs occurring primarily in NREM sleep. "Restless legs" syndrome is marked by a disturbing tightness or jerking in the legs or deep in the calves just before falling asleep. The patient typically moves the legs vigorously to alleviate these disturbing sensations or walks around for awhile until the restlessness subsides.

Nocturnal myoclonus, far more common than the "restless legs" syndrome, is seen predominantly in middle-aged and older individuals of either sex. The contractions always consist of an extension of the big toe with partial flexion of the ankle, knee, and occasionally the hip. The disorder can be easily monitored polysomnographically using an anterior tibialis EMG; myoclonic jerks appear as brief (0.5–5.0 sec) contractions in regular intervals of 20 to 40 seconds. Myoclonic contractions usually come in groups of several repetitive jerks, lasting a few minutes to one hour or more. For correct diagnosis, it is important to notice that the myoclonic contractions precede rather than follow signs of arousal in the EEG; contractions following arousal are a normal, common finding in drowsiness and during stage changes.

Nocturnal myoclonus can disturb normal sleep architecture and decrease sleep efficiency considerably. Depending on the severity of the disorder and personal differences, it may lead to complaints of insomnia or of excessive daytime sleepiness. Physical and emotional stress seem to affect significantly the degree of disturbance. Estimates of its incidence in the insomnia population vary from one to 15 percent. This disorder frequently mimics persistent psychophysiological or drug-related excessive daytime somnolence. However, it is easier to differentiate from jerks associated with epileptic discharges or from the tossing and turning of the restless sleep apneic.

A bed partner's conscientious description of episodic jerks in relatively regular intervals should alert the physician to the possibility of nocturnal myoclonus. However, a sleep laboratory evaluation is required for definitive diagnosis of the condition and its severity, as well as for the objective follow-up of the treatment. We have satisfactorily treated myoclonus by giving clonazepam at bedtime; very few patients have complained of side effects. Other clinicians have reported varied results with a number of drugs such as baclofen, methysergide, 5-hydroxy-tryptophan and other hypnotics and muscle relaxants. Coleman et al. (35, 36) have recently discussed nocturnal myoclonus and its relationship to other sleep disorders.

*Narcolepsy*

One of the better known sleep disorders, narcolepsy is estimated to affect 0.02 to 0.09 percent of the general population. A century ago, Gélineau (37) first used the term "narcolepsie" for a disorder described as "diurnal sleep accompanied by falls," but the narcoleptic tetrad – daytime sleep attacks, cataplexy, sleep paralysis, and hypnagogic hallucinations – was not recognized until the 1940s (33). The 1979 nosology of sleep disorders (9) defines narcolepsy as "a syndrome consisting of excessive daytime sleepiness and abnormal manifestation of REM sleep. The latter includes frequent sleep-onset REM periods, which may be subjectively appreciated as cataplexy and sleep paralysis. The appearance of REM sleep within 10 minutes of sleep onset is considered evidence for narcolepsy" (p. 72).

The sleepiness of narcoleptic patients differs markedly from that of other DOES. In narcolepsy, attacks of sleepiness are unintended, irresistible, and often inappropriate, lasting from 30 seconds to more than 30 minutes and usually superimposed on a day of more-or-less reduced wakefulness. Usually the first symptom to appear, sleep attacks begin in the teenage years or in the '20s. They occur very often whenever the patient is inactive, but are also common while eating, talking, driving, or playing, and during sexual intercourse. Usually, sleepiness disappears and the patient feels refreshed after napping. The frequency of sleep attacks varies from once a week to several dozen times a day in different individuals, but an untreated patient typically experiences two to six sleep attacks daily.

A prominent feature of the typical narcolepsy syndrome, cataplectic attacks consist of a sudden and reversible loss of skeletal muscle tonus lasting from a few seconds to several minutes. The most frequently affected muscles are those of the jaw, neck, and knees, and the severity of the attack ranges from a momentary feeling of weakness to total involvement of voluntary muscles. Since the cataplectic attacks usually spare the extraocular muscles, many patients learn to terminate the attack by vigorously moving their eyes. Patients remain aware of the attack and of their surroundings, but cannot respond until the episode ends. They apparently suffer no lasting ill effects from these episodes. The attacks are most often triggered by strong emotions or heavy physical activity; laughter, anger, and sexual excitement are frequent catalysts. As they become aware of the conditions that trigger cataplectic attacks, many patients try to control their emotions to avoid attacks.

Less common symptoms, sleep paralysis and hypnagogic and/or hypno-pompic hallucinations, are estimated to occur in less than half of narcoleptic patients (39). Sleep paralysis is the inability to move voluntarily upon falling asleep or upon awakening. Although transient and easily terminated by an external stimulus such as touching, calling the person's name, or ringing a bell, sleep paralysis is a frightening experience for the patient. Hypnagogic or hypnopompic hallucinations may or may not accompany sleep paralysis. They are usually of short duration with immediate and full orientation at their termination.

Automatic behavior during the day is occasionally found in narcoleptics. Patients usually describe them as "blackouts" during which they lose track of time and their actions. Typically, there is no later recall of the episode. Repet-itive episodes of "microsleep" have been polysomnographically identified in some patients (40).

Other symptoms reported include ptosis, blurred vision, diplopia, head-aches, decreased libido, and impotence, as well as a common complaint of disturbed sleep with frequent awakenings.

Although its etiology is unknown, narcolepsy is believed to be a neurolog-ical syndrome in which the REM-sleep mechanism is at least partially in-volved, rather than a psychological disturbance. Recent findings on regional cerebral hemodynamics during daytime naps and wakefulness showed that throughout both hemispheres, especially in brainstem-cerebellar areas, nar-coleptic patients had blood flow changes that were entirely opposite to those of sleep apnea patients and normal subjects (41). A comprehensive collection of papers exploring the etiology and phenomenology of narcolepsy is avail-able in a book edited by Guilleminault et al. (42).

The treatment of narcolepsy imposes ongoing responsibilites on both the patient and the physician. Since this is a permanent disorder with no definite cure, management of the narcoleptic patient involves education and behavior modification as well as medical treatment. Patients must acquire a thorough understanding of their disease, the effects of medication, and possible com-plications. Therefore, an extensive and frank discussion of the syndrome is crucial. Although a patient may currently experience only sleep attacks, he must also fully understand cataplexy, sleep paralysis, and hallucinations which may appear later in the disease process. Patients should be reassured that their paralysis will not become permanent and that narcolepsy is not evi-dence of "going crazy." The family must be educated to understand the in-appropriate "sleeps" and "collapses" which may ruin sex life, upset children and friends, and aggravate uninformed bosses.

Like diabetic patients, narcoleptic patients must learn to modify their daily behavioral routines to accommodate their misfortune. This entails assumption of an appropriate lifestyle involving changes in both employment and leisure activities. Neither high pressure, demanding jobs nor inactive, monotonous jobs are recommended for narcoleptic patients. Occupations in which alertness is mandatory for the safety of the worker and other people must be avoided. It may be necessary to refrain from driving alone, drinking alcoholic beverages, or angry outbursts if these activities bring on sleep attacks or cataplexy.

Besides the avoidance of situations and activities which trigger symptoms, a good night's sleep and carefully spaced, brief daytime naps can also help control daytime sleep and cataplexy attacks and enable the usage of minimal, effective doses of pharmacological agents. Methylphenidate hydrochloride is the drug of choice to combat excessive daytime sleepiness. Due to well-known complications, amphetamine use has declined over the years and is reserved for refractory cases. A tricyclic antidepressant, frequently imipramine, can effectively control cataplexy. MAO inhibitors are also effective anticataplectic drugs but serious side effects limit their usage. Patients must be cautioned about the possible side effects, withdrawal symptoms, and abuse potential of such medications. Drug holidays on weekends and vacations and the substitution of naps for medicine whenever possible will keep drug use to a minimum. With careful, constant management and in complete cooperation with their physicians, narcoleptic patients can lead relatively normal and productive lives.

### Idiopathic CNS Hypersomnolence

The excessive daytime sleepiness associated with idiopathic CNS hypersomnolence is recurrent and persistent but does not take the form of irresistible sleep attacks. Patients evaluated in the sleep laboratory show increased or undisturbed nocturnal sleep as well as shortened sleep latencies during daytime multiple sleep latency tests. There is no sleep-onset REM episode, apnea, or periodic muscle activity to disturb sleep. Patients tend to take long, unrefreshing naps which are preceded by long periods of drowsiness and followed by "sleep drunkenness" — grogginess sometimes accompanied by headaches. Depression is common in patients with CNS hypersomnolence.

Idiopathic CNS hypersomnolence is encountered in familial or isolated cases. Fainting attacks and the peripheral vascular symptoms of Raynaud's disease are frequent, related findings, suggesting autonomic nervous system dysfunction.

Also called idiopathic NREM narcolepsy or idiopathic, functional, mixed, or harmonious hypersomnia, this condition is a serious, disabling disease which is difficult to counteract with various CNS stimulants. In some cases, methysergide has alleviated daytime sleepiness. Idiopathic CNS hypersomnolence must be differentiated from narcolepsy, hypersomnolence due to medical, toxic, and environmental causes, and persistent psychophysiological DOES (6, 43).

### DOES Associated with Other Medical, Toxic, and Environmental Conditions

A wide variety of medical conditions — infections, hormone imbalance, CNS trauma and other neurological conditions, food allergies, and intoxication — may cause hypersomnolence. The distinguishing feature of this type of excessive daytime sleepiness is that the hypersomnolence either directly results from the medical, toxic, or environmental condition or is secondary to nocturnal sleep disturbance caused by the condition. Alleviation of the responsible condition should result in immediate or gradual improvement of the daytime sleepiness; usually, no prolonged sleep pathology remains. A thorough medical history is necessary to differentiate this condition from other DOES, especially DOES due to chronic use of or withdrawal from CNS stimulants and persistent use of CNS depressants. Treatment and prognosis of DOES associated with medical, toxic, and environmental conditions depend on its etiology as well as correct diagnosis. Several references (9, 44, 45, 46, 47) provide a comprehensive review of DOES related to such conditions.

### DOES Associated with Other DOES Conditions

This group of sleep disorders includes such rare disorders as Kleine-Levin syndrome as well as very common causes of daytime sleepiness such as insufficient sleep.

Critchley (48) describes the Kleine-Levin syndrome as periodic hypersomnia and megaphagia in adolescent males. The disorder is accompanied by certain behavioral abnormalities such as excessive sexual excitement or disinhibition and excessive eating, preferably of sweets. Some degree of amnesia, depression, and insomnia follow the attack, which usually disappears spontaneously. An intermittent sleep disorder, Kleine-Levin syndrome probably results from an organic dysfunction of limbic and/or hypothalamic structures. Although some observations suggest the importance of psychological factors, the rarity of the disorder and incomplete sleep laboratory evaluations prevent satisfactory explanations of its etiology (49). Differentiation from other infectious, vascular, or neoplastic conditions of the CNS associated with hypersomnolence is necessary. Since patients with Kleine-Levin syndrome exhibit no sleep pathology during intervening remissions, careful psychiatric evaluation is necessary to exclude bipolar affective disorder and other DOES associated with psychophysiological and psychiatric conditions.

Another intermittent type of DOES is the menstrual-associated syndrome, a marked hypersomnolence in a regular, temporal relationship with menstrual periods. Some aspects of this syndrome, such as strange behavior, resemble the Kleine-Levin syndrome in men, but extensive research is needed to uncover its etiology (50).

DOES due to insufficient sleep, although superficially appearing to be simple to recognize and treat, is a serious condition that can continue for extensive periods or create secondary problems such as irritability, difficulty in concentration, reduced vigilance, distractibility, reduced motivation, depression, fatigue, restlessness, incoordination, malaise, loss or increase of appetite, gastrointestinal disturbances, muscle and joint pains, diplopia, and dry mouth. That sleep deprivation is chronic and voluntary (yet often unintentional) is an important diagnostic criterion. Polysomnographic evaluation often reveals normal sleep latency, cycles and stages, increased slow wave sleep, but short total sleep time. When allowed to remain in bed longer, the sleep-deprived individual gets undisturbed normal sleep. Modern lifestyles often encourage the deliberate shortening of sleep time so that this "wasted" time can be used for more work or pleasure. People holding two jobs, students working and studying at the same time, and ambitious, hard-driving workers often neglect to get sufficient sleep (the amount ot sleep an individual requires daily to maintain alert wakefulness—usually, but not necessarily, about seven to eight hours). Unaware of the true nature of their sleep problems, they focus on the secondary symptoms of chronic sleep deprivation because hard work is encouraged whereas sleepiness is unacceptable. This often-overlooked source of sleep disturbance must be differentiated from persistent psychophysiological hypersomnolence and DOES associated with psychiatric illness.

Most DOES patients complain of feeling tired and unrefreshed in the morning. In some individuals, however, the transition from sleep to wakefulness is prolonged and exaggerated with a lack of clear sensorium. They remain in a confused state called "sleep drunkenness" which creates considerable social inconvenience. Sometimes irrational, impulsive, or even violent behavior results. There are few reports on "sleep drunkenness," but available data suggest that it occurs in adult males only (51). Some sleep researchers question whether "sleep drunkenness" should be considered a specific syndrome. Instead, they consider it a symptom associated with other DOES such as sleep apnea or idiopathic CNS hypersomnolence syndromes.

### No DOES Abnormality

Just as some people require significantly less sleep in 24 hours than the majority of the population, others require a longer total sleep time per day. The sleep of these "long sleepers" or healthy, asymptomatic hypersomniacs is otherwise normal. However, they may develop daytime sleepiness when social and job requirements force them to get less sleep than they need. Individuals who require nine to 14 hours of sleep per day but try to assume the "normal" time of up to eight hours consequently develop all the signs and symptoms of patients suffering from chronic insufficient sleep.

### DYSFUNCTIONS ASSOCIATED WITH SLEEP, SLEEP STAGES, OR PARTIAL AROUSALS (PARASOMNIAS)

Parasomnias initially referred to activities considered normal during the waking state but abnormal during sleep (49) — for example, somnambulism, sleep talking, nocturnal enuresis, bruxism, and jactatio capitis. The new diagnostic classification (9) extended this group to include a wide spectrum of clinical conditions that either appear only in sleep or are exacerbated by sleep. Since CNS activation is transmitted to different skeletal muscles and the autonomic nervous system, sleep-related dysfunctions manifest in a wide variety of ways. Some of them appear in certain sleep stages. For example, sleep-related impaired tumescence, sleep-related painful erections, and dream anxiety attacks occur primarily in REM sleep; sleepwalking and sleep terror in slow wave sleep (stages 3 and 4, NREM sleep); and bruxism in stage 2 NREM sleep. Sleep paralysis is a phenomenon of the transition periods between sleep and wakefulness. Other conditions such as sleepwalking, sleep terror, and nocturnal enuresis are disorders of partial arousal.

### Sleepwalking (Somnambulism)

Sleepwalking, an automatism occuring in the first third of nocturnal sleep, ranges from simple, purposeless, stereotyped movements to complex behavioral sequences that continue frequently to the point of sitting up or getting out of bed and walking. Once out of bed, sleepwalkers can open doors, turn on lights and appliances, get dressed, or use the bathroom. They might return to bed, lie down, and continue to sleep or awaken spontaneously. Generally, their eyes are open and vision is intact. Although sleepwalkers maintain a certain degree of CNS coordination, permitting the

## TABLE 1
### Differential Diagnosis and Treatment of DOES

| Disorder | Sleep laboratory evaluation | Further evaluation needed | Critical differential diagnosis | Treatment suggestions |
|---|---|---|---|---|
| **Psychophysiological DOES** | | | | |
| Transient | Detailed history of illness Battery of psychological tests EEG, EOG, EMG (leg and chin) Respiration | | DOES associated with other medical, toxic, environmental conditions DOES associated with use of drugs and alcohol | No treatment necessary due to transient nature of problem |
| Persistent | As above, plus at least two weeks of sleep log and temperature chart | Full psychiatric evaluation | Same as above, plus DOES due to affective and other functional disorders, disorders of sleep-wake schedule | Psychological approach possibly supplemented by controlled short-term use of CNS stimulants |
| DOES associated with psychiatric disorders | | | | |
| Affective disorders | As above | Full psychiatric evaluation | Persistent psychophysiological DOES | Treat psychiatric disorder, e.g., tricyclics for depression, lithium for bipolar disorder |
| Other functional disorders | As above | Full psychiatric evaluation | | Treat psychiatric disorder —neuroleptics, etc. |
| DOES associated with use of drugs and alcohol | As above; Repeat studies after an appropriate drug-free period | | Clarify primary pathological conditions leading to use of drugs and alcohol | Withdrawal under medical supervision Training in sleep hygiene Consider effects on sleep |

TABLE 1 (continued)

| Disorder | Sleep laboratory evaluation | Further evaluation needed | Critical differential diagnosis | Treatment suggestions |
|---|---|---|---|---|
| DOES associated with nocturnal myoclonus and restless legs syndrome | History of illness Psychological evaluation, EEG, EOG, EKG, respiration, EMG (bilateral tibialis anterior muscle activity) | | Seizure disorders and other medical, toxic and environmental conditions Sleep apnea | of drugs given for other medical conditions Clonazepam is highly recommended; also try baclofen, methysergide, 5-hydroxy-tryptophan or other hypnotics, muscle relaxants |
| DOES due to sleep-related respiratory impairment | History of illness EEG, EOG, EMG (chin, leg, intercostal), EKG, respiration (nasal and buccal airflow, thoracic and abdominal strain gauges), respiratory pressure, esophageal pressure, oxygen saturation (ear oximeter), tissue oxygenation (transcutaneous oxygen and carbon dioxide monitor) Psychological tests | Pulmonary function tests ENT consultation Xerography of upper airways Cerebral blood flow Cardiological work-up | Alveolar hypoventilation syndrome Cheyne-Stokes breathing Narcolepsy Nocturnal myoclonus | Obstructive: Tracheostomy Pemoline Protriptyline Weight loss if obese Central: Diaphragm pacing Follow-up evaluations 2 to 4 times a year, especially if there is indication of cardiovascular involvement |
| Alveolar hypoventilation syndrome | Same as above | Same as above | Same as above | No proven treatment Try various respiratory stimulants |
| Kleine-Levin syndrome | Same as above Sleep log over several weeks or months | Detailed psychiatric evaluation | Neoplastic and inflammatory CNS disorders, i.e., limbic system, epilepsy, bipolar disorder, sleep- | No treatment for the disorder is available; focus on symptoms |

| Disorder | Procedures | | Differential Diagnosis | Treatment |
|---|---|---|---|---|
| Menstrual-associated DOES | Same as above | Same as above | wake schedule disorder | Same as above |
| DOES due to insufficient sleep | Same as above | Same as above | Sedative-hypnotics and sleep-wake schedule disorders | Educate patient about sleep and correct sleep hygiene<br>Encourage patient to get more sleep |
| DOES without polysomnographic findings | Same as above | Same as above | Same as above | Same as above |
| Narcolepsy | History of illness<br>EEG, EOG, EMG (chin, leg, intercostal), EKG, respiration (nasal and buccal airflow, thoracic and abdominal strain gauges), respi-trace, esophageal pressure, oxygen saturation (ear oximeter), tissue oxygenation (transcutaneous oxygen and carbon dioxide monitor)<br>Psychological tests | Complete neurological and psychiatric evaluation | Psychophysiological and psychiatric disorders<br>Other DOES, especially sleep apnea | Behavior modification<br>Brief daytime naps<br>Minimal doses of drugs:<br>EDS—methylphenidate<br>Cataplexy—imipramine or other tricyclic antidepressant |
| Idiopathic CNS hypersomnolence | Same as above | Same as above | Narcolepsy<br>DOES associated with medical, toxic, and environmental causes<br>Persistent psychophysiological DOES | Methysergide |
| DOES associated with other medical, toxic, and environmental conditions | Same as above | Depends on the nature of the exacerbating condition (post-surgical, intoxication, etc.) | DOES associated with use of drugs | Alleviate the precipitating condition |

avoidance of objects in their path, they can easily lose their balance and injure themselves. If they are awakened or awaken spontaneously, they experience mild to moderate confusion. Sleepwalking episodes may last from a few minutes to one hour and there is no recall of the episode the next morning.

In some patients, polysomnographic evaluation of sleepwalking reveals markedly high-amplitude EEG activity prior to the incident, replaced by low-amplitude, high-frequency activity just before complex motor activity and behavior begins.

Sleepwalking affects slightly more males than females, and familial trends have been noted in several studies. It is not a rare disorder; incidence studies indicate that some 10–20 percent of the general population have experienced sleepwalking. Episodes can be induced in predisposed or normal children by forcing them to stand up during slow wave sleep.

A wide variety of clinical conditions have been associated with sleepwalking — epilepsy, CNS infection and trauma, genitourinary complaints, nocturnal enuresis, sleep talking, and dream anxiety attacks. For a thorough review of the literature and discussion of the possible etiology, refer to Kales et al. (52, 53), Broughton (54), Orme (55), and Williams et al. (49).

### Sleep Terror (Pavor Nocturnus, Incubus)

Sleep terror is an arousal, with intense anxiety and screaming, from stages 3 and 4 sleep in the first half of the night. Automatism, fast heart and respiration rates, perspiration, and mydriasis accompany the abrupt arousal. Frightened and agitated, the patient does not gain full consciousness for five to 15 minutes. As a rule, there is no vivid recall of frightening dreams, although adults may recall sensations of paralysis, shortness of breath, and palpitations. As in sleepwalking, polysomnographic evaluation may show high-voltage delta waves that rapidly yield to an alpha pattern at the onset of the attack.

The incidence of sleep terror is higher in males than in females and certain families are predisposed to the disorder. It is most frequent at ages three to 13. The incidence in children (pavor nocturnus) is about one to five percent, but a much greater percentage of children probably experience sleep terror at one time or another. Some children with sleep terrors also experience nocturnal enuresis, sleepwalking, and sleep talking. Sleep terror has been associated with psychopathology such as severe anxiety in adults (incubus), but not in children.

A careful history with special emphasis on time of the episode, absence of dream recall, and excessive autonomic and motor activation enables differential diagnosis between sleep terror and dream anxiety attacks (nightmares).

Although sleep-related epileptic seizures and the hypnagogic hallucinations of narcoleptics may present with a similar history, they can be easily excluded by sleep laboratory evaluation.

## Nocturnal Enuresis

Sleep-related enuresis is one of the most prevalent sleep disorders. It is primarily a disorder of childhood, but some adults also suffer from enuresis. Although bedwetting after age three should be considered abnormal, a large percentage of children occasionally experience enuresis. Incidence studies indicate that as few as four percent (56) or as many as 87 percent (57) of children are enuretic, depending on age, sex, and mental development. At age five, incidence is approximately 10–15 percent.

Nocturnal enuresis can occur during any stage of sleep, but it is most frequent in slow wave sleep and in transition periods to lighter sleep stages. Like somnambulism and night terrors, it can be considered a partial arousal phenomenon. A typical pattern of body movements precedes the loss of sphincter control. Although the actual micturition begins after EEG arousal starts, the patient is usually difficult to awaken after an episode and remains disoriented for several minutes after awakening.

There are two basic types of enuresis—primary, when toilet training is never successfully accomplished, and secondary, when enuresis follows the completion of toilet training. Nocturnal enuresis associated with urologic, neurologic, or other medical conditions (symptomatic) requires specific treatment of the underlying pathology. Idiopathic enuresis, on the other hand, is usually benign and most children grow out of the disease. Although observations of nonrandomly selected patients have led to the widespread belief that enuresis is associated with behavioral and psychological abnormalities, some researchers (58) have not found significant emotional problems, typical personality patterns, or psychopathological features in randomly selected idiopathic bedwetters. However, the embarrassment, shame, and feelings of guilt are often serious enough to create problems in the family and to limit social interactions, e.g., travel and overnight visits.

Frequently encountered by polysomnographers and other clinicians, nocturnal enuresis is discussed more thoroughly by several authors (54, 59, 60, 61, 62).

## Dream Anxiety Attacks

Dream anxiety attacks are awakenings from REM sleep with a moderate degree of autonomic arousal and vivid recall of a disturbing, frightening dream. Since REM sleep is prominent in the last third of nocturnal sleep, dream anxiety attacks usually occur toward the morning hours. Both the timing of the episode and the vivid dream recall distinguish dream anxiety attacks from sleep terror. The patient awakens without disorientation and gains full consciousness. A moderate degree of tachycardia accompanies the attacks but, in contrast to sleep terrors, other signs of autonomic arousal are mild.

### Sleep-related Epileptic Seizures

Epileptic phenomena occurring in sleep take the form of either generalized seizures or a partial seizure of complex symptomatology, often the psychomotor type with confusion and automatism. Sleep is probably the most effective activator of seizures, even more so than hyperventilation and stroboscopic stimulation (63). Sleep-related seizures are most prevalent in childhood, but may occur at any age. Twenty to 25 percent of the epileptic seizures are exclusively confined to sleep (sleep epilepsy). Considering the prevalence of epilepsy in the general population (0.5 percent), this is a fairly large patient population.

Sometimes associated with awakenings, seizures usually occur during the first and last few hours of sleep. A common type of sleep epilepsy is the Lennox-Gastaut syndrome in children, in which many brief seizures occur during the night. As such sleep-related epileptic disorders progress, sleep architecture may be disturbed. REM sleep is decreased early in progressive myoclonus epilepsy and becomes indistinguishable from NREM sleep late in the disorder (64, 65). Stages 3 and 4, on the other hand, are decreased in psychomotor epilepsy (46).

Certain types of nocturnal epileptic seizures seem to appear more frequently in certain sleep stages than in others, suggesting that medications which suppress that stage could effectively eliminate seizure activity. For example, Sato (66) found that petit mal seizures in six children were less frequent but longer in REM sleep than in any stage of NREM sleep. Six other children treated with anticonvulsant drugs had no seizures during REM sleep. Most Rolandic-type seizures also occur during NREM stages (67).

A reliable differential diagnosis of sleep-related epileptic seizures from nocturnal myoclonus, "restless legs" syndrome, and the restless sleep of patients suffering from sleep apnea syndrome is crucial. In addition, psychomotor seizures must be carefully distinguished from somnambulism. Polysomnographic evaluation is therefore an invaluable tool in the proper diagnosis and follow-up of epileptic patients, particularly of "sleep epilepsy" patients.

For a comprehensive discussion of sleep epilepsy, refer to Freemon (46).

*Other Sleep-related Disorders*

Sleep-related teeth grinding (nocturnal bruxism), a relatively rare condition, consists of rhythmic masseter muscle activity, accompanied by a loud grating and clicking sound, during sleep. Although it may occur in all sleep stages, it is most frequent in stage 2 sleep. Bruxism is not associated with abnormal EEG discharges or recall of mental content. However, it is usually associated with body movements and a mild increase in heart rate. Systematic research (68) has failed to demonstrate any associated psychopathology, relationship to certain personality types, or any contribution of stress and emotional factors to the disorder. There may be a heredofamilial trend and children and young adults have a higher incidence of bruxism. It is easily identified—usually by the parents or the bed partner—by the irritating grating sounds. There is no pharmacological cure at the present time. In severe cases, however, a special teeth-protecting prosthesis must be fitted to prevent dental damage (68, 69, 70).

*Sleep-related headbanging* (jactatio capitis nocturnus) is characterized by rhythmic activity of the neck muscles during the transition from wakefulness to sleep and in stage 1 sleep, causing shaking movements of the head. Most common in young children, it usually disappears after adolescence (71).

*Familial sleep paralysis* is a sudden inability to move all or a specific part of the body. There is a strong heredofamilial trend; the mother transmits the disorder via a dominant trait bound to the X-chromosome. Although paralysis is one of the symptoms in the narcoleptic tetrad, it is not yet clear whether isolated paralysis has the same neurological mechanism. Several psychological and neurological explanations have been offered, but, since any attempt to investigate the condition systematically results in termination of the episode, neurophysiological data are limited. Often accompanied by hypnagogic hallucinations, sleep paralysis is experienced more often at the onset of sleep, during the first REM episode, than during awakenings or at the end of the sleep period.

Sleep paralysis is a frightening experience for the patient. The physician must fully explain the condition and reassure the patient that the attacks are brief and transient rather than a stroke. Nevertheless, regular follow-up is important to determine whether the paralysis will develop into narcolepsy. Present experience with this dysfunction indicates that treatment with clomipramine, imipramine and desmethylimipramine is very effective. Hishikawa (72) offers a detailed discussion of sleep paralysis.

It is not unusual for people complaining of sleep disturbances to also complain of headaches; for example, morning headaches are a common secondary complaint of sleep apnea patients. *Cluster headaches* and *chronic paroxysmal hemicrania*, on the other hand, are sleep-related severe headaches that may occur in the absence of any other sleep disorder. Cluster headaches, unilateral and marked by an on-off pattern, can occur one to four times a day and last up to five hours each. Although chronic paroxysmal hemicrania is also a very severe, unilateral headache, it occurs much more frequently and lasts only a few minutes. Both types of headaches are most common toward the morning hours and are associated with REM sleep periods (73, 74, 75). These headaches appear to be related to dilation of the cerebral arteries leading to edema, which in turn causes the pain. Since in normal subjects, REM sleep is associated with an up-to-twofold increase in regional cerebral blood flow compared to the preceding slow-wave sleep flow values (76), cerebral hemodynamic regulatory mechanism impairment may be responsible for the vessel dilation leading to the headaches.

*Sleep-related abnormal swallowing syndrome* is a relatively rare condition in which the patient coughs and chokes due to inadequate swallowing of saliva. The patient's sleep is restless, he is aware of his nocturnal problem, and may complain of insomnia. This is in contrast to the findings for the obstructive sleep apnea patient, who is seldom aware of his obstructed breathing and complains of excessive sleepiness (77). Essential differential diagnosis from sleep apnea syndrome, incubus, and gastroesophageal reflux is possible through sleep laboratory evaluation.

Although asthma is known to disturb sleep, systematic sleep laboratory studies of *sleep-related asthma* are limited. It is not clear from available studies of adults (78, 79, 80) whether there is any obvious relationship between asthma attacks and sleep stages and/or time of night. Patients exhibit significantly less stage 4 sleep but normal REM amounts. However, these studies concur in stating that asthma attacks are the rarest in stages 3 and 4 of the first third of the night. Attacks during REM sleep are greater and more often associated with dream recall.

Several explanations for nocturnal asthma attacks have been suggested— cyclic changes of cholinesterase, nocturnal differences in sensitivity to histamine associated with catecholamines and corticosteroids, increased airway resistance, and psychogenic factors causing disturbing dreams. However, a satisfactory explanation of their etiology awaits further study using larger patient populations (44).

Patients with *chronic obstructive pulmonary disease* (COPD) are increasingly gaining the attention of both pulmonary clinicians and sleep researchers (26, 81, 82, 83). Available data suggest that patients with COPD have disturbed sleep, frequent oxygen desaturations, and increased pulmonary artery pressure that is especially pronounced during REM sleep. Nocturnal administration of oxygen has been reported to improve oxygenation and to prolong sleep (84). However, others caution against the possibility of worsening the patient's condition by inducing carbon dioxide retention (85) and the prolongation of concomitant apnea episodes (26).

*Sleep-related cardiovascular symptoms* are particularly important to clinicians because the peak time of cardiac deaths is the early morning hours (4–6 A.M.) of sleep, when REM sleep is most likely to predominate. Nocturnal angina and nocturnal dyspnea are common cardiological problems and strokes occur more often during sleep than during wakefulness. Unfortunately, studies of the association between sleep parameters and nocturnal angina, hypertension, dysrhythmias, and postoperative intensive care are too few and the number of patients and completeness of evaluation too limited. Considering the prevalence of cardiac disease nationwide and worldwide, the establishment of conclusive information as to whether sleep, particularly REM sleep, is a more vulnerable time for cardiac patients and whether pharmacological suppression of REM sleep may have preventive value has both clinical and scientific relevance. At the present time, research on angina episodes and their association with REM sleep is somewhat inconsistent. Nowlin et al. (86) reported in four angina subjects a total of 39 episodes of significant EKG changes, i.e., S-T segment depression, 82 percent of which occurred in REM sleep. Karacan et al. (87) found that in 10 subjects, only 7.6 percent of awakenings were associated with angina pain, although their sleep was significantly disturbed. Stern and Tzivoni (88), on the other hand, studied the EKG, but not the sleep parameters, of 140 patients with chronic ischemic heart disease, 97 of them with persistent abnormal S-T changes while awake. EKG irregularities decreased in the sleep of 40 percent of these patients, remained unchanged in 30 percent, and became more marked in 23 percent.

Systematic studies of the relationship between sleep and hypertension are scarce. Khatri and Freis (89) studied both hemodynamic parameters and polysomnographic parameters in 14 patients with essential systemic hypertension. The results do not confirm the speculation that hypertensive patients have a higher level of centrally induced vasomotor activity. With the exception of a significant increase in total peripheral resistance during REM sleep, hypertensive patients' blood pressure and peripheral resistance changes were basically similar to those reported in normal subjects.

The incidence of dysrhythmias related to sleep and wakefulness has also not been adequately investigated. Ventricular and atrial premature beats seem to decrease somewhat in sleep generally, although ventricular prema-

## TABLE 2
### Differential Diagnosis and Treatment of Parasomnias

| Disorder | Sleep laboratory evaluation | Further evaluation needed | Critical differential diagnosis | Treatment suggestions |
| --- | --- | --- | --- | --- |
| Abnormal swallowing syndrome | History of illness EEG, EOG, EMG, EKG, respiration | Upper GI tract | Sleep apnea syndrome Sleep terror attacks Gastroesophageal reflux Sleep-related asthma | Treat underlying pathology if revealed by upper GI tract |
| Asthma | Same as above, plus breathing sounds | Pulmonary and cardio-vascular studies | Paroxysmal nocturnal dyspnea Sleep apnea syndromes Abnormal swallowing Esophageal reflux | Conventional asthma treat-ment |
| COPD | Same as above | Same as above | Same as above, plus asthma | Nocturnal oxygen admin-istration Consider tracheostomy in severe cases with superim-posed obstructive sleep apnea |
| Cardiovascular symptoms | History of illness EEG, EOG, EMG, EKG, respiration, oxy-gen saturation, arterial blood pressure | Nocturnal hemody-namic studies, i.e., catheterization, pul-monary artery pres-sure | Gastroesophageal reflux Sleep apnea syndromes Asthma Epileptic seizures Sleep terrors | Coronary dilators Anti-arrhythmic agents Nocturnal oxygen admin-istration |
| Paroxysmal nocturnal hemoglobinuria | History of illness EEG, EOG, EMG, EKG, respiration | 24th urine collection in small samples | Acute hematuria and porphyria | No specific treatment is available Blood transfusions as needed Prophylactic treatment |
| Gastroesophageal | Same as above | Bernstein (acid infu- | Infections and tumors | Diet |

| Disorder | Recording procedures | Diagnostic tests/evaluation | Conditions to rule out | Treatment |
|---|---|---|---|---|
| reflux | | sion) test<br>Overnight pH study<br>Acid clearance test during sleep<br>Acid reflux test<br>Upper GI endoscopy | of upper GI tract<br>Cardiovascular symptoms<br>Sleep-related asthma<br>Sleep apnea syndromes<br>Abnormal swallowing syndrome | Elevation of the head of the bed<br>Treatment of infections or tumors of upper GI tract and larynx-pharynx |
| Sleepwalking | History of illness<br>Psychological testing<br>EEG, EOG, EMG, EKG, respiration<br>Infrared video monitoring | Full clinical EEG evaluation as part of thorough neurologic examination | Seizure disorders | Benzodiazepines or other drugs that suppress slow wave sleep |
| Sleep terror | Same as above | Same as above, plus complete psychiatric evaluation | Dream anxiety attacks | Same as above |
| Nocturnal enuresis | Same as above, plus detailed respiration and EEG recordings | Same as above, plus full urological evaluation | Seizure disorders<br>Sleep apnea syndrome | Tricyclics to suppress slow wave sleep |
| Dream anxiety attacks | Same as above | Complete psychiatric and neurological evaluation | Seizure disorders<br>DIMS and DOES due to psychological and psychiatric disorders | Suppress REM sleep |
| Sleep-related epileptic seizures | Same as above | Same as above | Sleep apnea syndrome<br>Nocturnal myoclonus<br>Narcolepsy<br>Sleepwalking<br>Sleep terrors<br>Dream anxiety attacks | Suppress sleep stage in which particular type of seizure occurs<br>Conventional treatment with anticonvulsant drugs such as phenytoin and phenobarbital for grand mal and focal; these drugs or primidone and carbamazepine for psychomotor seizures; clonazepam and |

**TABLE 2** *(continued)*

| Disorder | Sleep laboratory evaluation | Further evaluation needed | Critical differential diagnosis | Treatment suggestions |
|---|---|---|---|---|
| | | | | succinimide for petit mal seizures |
| Cluster headaches and chronic paroxysmal hemicrania | Same as above | Regional cerebral blood flow, CT scan, full neurological evaluation | | Conventional treatment Suppress REM if headaches are REM-sleep related |
| Sleep-related teeth grinding | History of illness EEG, EOG, EMG, EKG, respiration | Complete orthodontal work-up | | Teeth-protecting prosthesis in severe cases |
| Sleep-related headbanging | History of illness Psychological testing EEG, EOG, EMG, EKG, respiration Infrared video monitoring | Complete psychiatric and neurological evaluation | Seizure disorders Sleep apnea syndrome Nocturnal myoclonus Narcolepsy Sleepwalking Sleep terrors Dream anxiety attacks | Anticonvulsant drugs |
| Familial sleep paralysis | History of illness EEG, EOG, EMG (chin, leg, intercostal), EKG, respiration (nasal and buccal airflow, thoracic and abdominal strain gauges), respiratory trace, esophageal pressure, oxygen saturation (ear oximeter), tissue oxygenation (transcutaneous oxygen and carbon dioxide monitor) Psychological tests | Same as above | Narcolepsy Familial periodic (hypokalemic) paralysis | None necessary |

ture beats are more heavily distributed in REM sleep than in other sleep stages. On the other hand, in patients with sleep-related respiratory disorders, cardiovascular abnormalities are significantly pronounced in sleep and seem to be associated with duration and degree of oxygen desaturation.

For a detailed overview of cardiovascular diseases and their relationship to sleep, refer to Williams (44).

Patients with or without daytime symptoms of cardialgia (heartburn), postprandial regurgitation, dysphagia, esophagitis, or laryngopharyngitis may awaken from sleep with a burning sensation and substernal pain, tightness in the chest, and a sour taste in the mouth. Frequent coughing and choking occurring with *gastroesophageal reflux* also severely disturb sleep. Due to potential, significant complications of this disorder (e.g., aspiration, pneumonia, laryngopharyngitis), early diagnosis and treatment are critical (90).

Another rare condition related to sleep is *paroxysmal nocturnal hemoglobinuria.* Intravascular hemolysis and consequent hemoglobinuria can be linked to sleep in either the daytime or the nighttime. Therefore, sleep-related hemolysis is a more accurate name for the disorder. Since there are no systematic studies using complete polysomnographic evaluation and laboratory tests for this disease, its etiology has not been established. This chronic disease, in which anemia, infections, and thromboses are the main causes of death, has a poor prognosis.

## CONCLUSION

Although much progress has been made in classifying DOES and parasomnias and in associating them with organic or psychological pathology, drug use, and certain sleep stages or states of arousal, the fact that so few of them have a clearly established etiology impedes differential diagnosis and treatment. However, the identification of characteristic polysomnographic patterns for many of these disorders is facilitating their differentiation from other sleep disorders and medical conditions, as well as emphasizing the importance of sleep laboratory evaluation. This evaluation routinely includes a history of illness; EEG, EOG, EMG, and EKG recording; and monitoring of respiration. Certain DOES and parasomnias (e.g., narcolepsy, sleep apnea syndromes, sleepwalking, sleep terror, cardiovascular symptoms) may require additional sleep evaluations and medical procedures such as infrared video monitoring, oxygen saturation tests, nocturnal hemodynamic studies, upper-GI endoscopy, or thorough neurologic or psychiatric examinations.

Treatment of DOES and parasomnias may include pharmacologic therapy to suppress the sleep stage in which the disorder typically occurs (e.g., dream anxiety attacks, epileptic seizures), conventional medical treatment of a precipitating disease or condition, adjustment of lifestyle to the symptoms (e.g., narcolepsy), or education about changing habits that may exacerbate the sleep disorder. No treatment may be indicated if impairment is minimal. Until the etiology of these two heterogeneous groups of disorders is better understood, in many cases treatment must remain limited to a trial and error approach, waiting until the patient "grows out of" the disorder or makes a permanent adjustment to a disease with no known cure.

Since a respiratory, cardiovascular, or neurologic problem may appear only in sleep, and any medical condition which impairs daytime functioning will probably disturb sleep as well, physicians from a variety of specialties must be educated to recognize the signs and symptoms of sleep disorders. Paralleling our rapidly growing understanding of this interface between disturbed sleep and other medical pathology is an awareness of the need for more communication and teamwork among all members of the medical community. Health professionals are encouraged to form a "cooperative" in which sleep researchers work closely with other physicians, psychologists, technicians, and computer specialists throughout the evaluation and treatment process.

## REFERENCES

1. GUILLEMINAULT, C. and DEMENT, W.C.: Sleep apnea syndromes and related sleep disorders. In: R. L. Williams, and I. Karacan (Eds.), *Sleep Disorders: Diagnosis and Treatment.* New York: John Wiley & Sons, 1978, pp. 9–28.
2. Association of Sleep Disorders Centers, unpublished data, 1980.
3. GOLDSTEIN, N. P. and GRIFFIN, M. E.: Psychogenic hypersomnia. *Am. J. Psychiatry,* 115:922–928, 1959.
4. KUPFER, D. J. and FOSTER, F. G.: The sleep of psychotic patients: Does it all look alike? In: D. X. Freedman (Ed.): *Biology of the Major Psychoses: A Comparative Analysis.* New York: Raven Press, 1975, pp. 143–164.
5. MURRAY, E. J.: *Sleep, Dreams and Arousal.* New York: Appleton-Century Crofts, 1965, pp. 257–261.
6. ROTH, B.: Narcolepsy and hypersomnia. In: R. L. Williams, and I. Karacan (Eds.), *Sleep Disorders: Diagnosis and Treatment.* New York: John Wiley & Sons, 1978, pp. 29–59.
7. OSWALD, I.: Sleep and dependence on amphetamine and other drugs. In: A. Kales (Ed.): *Sleep: Physiology and Pathology.* Philadelphia: J. B. Lippincott, 1969, pp. 317–330.
8. SUTHERLAND, E. W.: Dependence on barbiturates and other CNS depressants. In: S. N. Pradhan and S. N. Dutta (Eds.): *Drug Abuse: Clinical and Basic Aspects.* St. Louis: C. V. Mosby, 1977, pp. 235–247.
9. Association of Sleep Disorders Centers: *Diagnostic Classification of Sleep and Arousal Disorders,* Ed. 1, prepared by the Sleep Disorders Classification Committee, Roffwarg, H. P. (Chairman). *Sleep,* 2:58–86, 99–121, 1979.
10. GUILLEMINAULT, C., VAN DEN HOED, J., and MITLER, M. M.: Clinical overview of the sleep apnea syndromes. In: C. Guilleminault and W. C. Dement (Eds.),

*Sleep Apnea Syndromes.* New York: Alan R. Liss, Inc., 1978, Kroc Foundation Series, vol. 11, pp. 1-12.

11. GUILLEMINAULT, C. and DEMENT, W. C. (Eds.): *Sleep Apnea Syndromes.* New York: Alan R. Liss, Inc., 1978, Kroc Foundation Series, vol. 11.
12. DERMAN, S. and KARACAN, I.: Sleep-induced respiratory disorders. *Psych. Ann.,* 9:41-62, 1979.
13. BLOCK, A. J.: Respiratory disorders during sleep. Part 1. *Heart Lung,* 9:1011-1024, 1980.
14. LUGARESI, E., COCCAGNA, G., and MANTOVANI, M.: Hypersomnia with periodic apneas. In: E. Weitzman (Ed.), *Advances in Sleep Research,* vol. 4. New York: Spectrum Publications, 1978, pp. 1-131.
15. MEYER, J. S., SAKAI, F., KARACAN, I., DERMAN, S., and YAMAMOTO, M.: Sleep apnea, narcolepsy, and dreaming: Regional cerebral hemodynamics. *Ann. Neurol.,* 7:479-485, 1980.
16. LUGARESI, E.: Snoring and its clinical implications. In: C. Guilleminault and W. C. Dement (Eds.): *Sleep Apnea Syndromes.* New York: Alan R. Liss, Inc., 1978, Kroc Foundation Series, vol. 11, pp. 13-21.
17. TILKIAN, A. G., GUILLEMINAULT, C., SCHROEDER, J. S., LEHRMAN, K. L., SIM-MONS, F. B., and DEMENT, W. C.: Hemodynamics in sleep-induced apnea syndrome: Studies during wakefulness and sleep. *Ann. Intern. Med.,* 85:714-719, 1976.
18. TILKIAN, A., GUILLEMINAULT, C., SCHROEDER, J. S., LEHRMAN, K. L., SIMMONS, F. B., and DEMENT, W. C.: Sleep induced apnea syndrome: Prevalence of cardiac arrhythmias and their reversal after tracheostomy. *Am. J. Med.,* 63: 348-358, 1977.
19. GUILLEMINAULT, C., ELDRIDGE, F. L., SIMMONS, F. B., and DEMENT, W. C.: Sleep apnea syndrome: Can it induce hemodynamic changes. *West. J. Med.,* 123:7-16, 1975.
20. COCCAGNA, G., MANTOVANI, M., BRIGNANI, F., PARCHI, C., and LUGARESI, E.: Continuous recording of the pulmonary and systematic arterial pressure during sleep in syndromes of hypersomnia with periodic breathing. *Bull. Physiopath. Respir.* (Nancy), 8:1159-1172, 1972.
21. REMMERS, J. E., ANCH, A. M., and DEGROOT, W. J.: Respiratory disturbances during sleep. *Clin. Chest Med.,* 1:57-71, 1980.
22. SAUERLAND, E. K. and HARPER, R. M.: The human tongue during sleep: Electro-myographic activity of the genioglossus muscle. *Exp. Neurol.,* 51:160-170, 1976.
23. HARPER, M. R. and SAUERLAND, E. K.: The role of the tongue in sleep apnea. In: C. Guilleminault and W. C. Dement (Eds.), *Sleep Apnea Syndromes.* New York: Alan R. Liss, Inc., Kroc Foundation Series, vol. 11, 1978, pp. 219-234.
24. WEITZMAN, E. D., POLLACK, C. P., BOROWIECKI, B., BURACK, B., SHPRINTZEN, R., and RAKOFF, S.: The hypersomnia-sleep apnea syndrome: Site and mechanism of upper airway obstruction. In: C. Guilleminault and W. C. Dement (Eds.), *Sleep Apnea Syndromes.* New York: Alan R. Liss, Inc., Kroc Foundation Series, vol. 11, 1978, pp. 219-234.
25. WYNNE, J. W., BLOCK, A. J., and BOYSEN, P. G., JR.: Oxygen desaturation in sleep: Sleep apnea and COPD. *Hosp. Pract.,* 77-85, October 1980.
26. GUILLEMINAULT, C., CUMMISKEY, J., and MOTTA, J.: Chronic obstruction airflow disease and sleep studies. *Am. Rev. Respir. Dis.,* 122:397-406, 1980.

27. BEUTLER, L., KARACAN, I., and THORNBY, J.: Distinguishing character and personality traits of sleep apneics and narcoleptics. *Sleep Res.,* 7:181, 1972 (abstract).

28. KARACAN, I., DERMAN, S., and FISHER, P. D.: Gastric stapling in the management of obstructive sleep-apnea syndrome: A case report. Presented at the 20th annual meeting of the APSS, Mexico City, Mexico, March 25-29, 1980.

29. KARACAN, I., WARE, C., MOORE, C. A., DERVENT, B., and WILLIAMS, R. L.: Disturbed sleep as a function of sleep apnea: Too much sleep but not enough. *Tex. Med.,* 73:39-56, 1977.

30. FISHER, J. G., DE LA PENA, A., and DONOVAN, N. W.: Initial treatment of mixed sleep apnea syndrome in obese patient by starvation. *Sleep Res.,* 5:168, 1976.

31. FISHER, J. G., DE LA PENA, A., MAYFIELD, D., and FLICKINGER, R.: Starvation and behavior modification as a treatment in obese patients with sleep apnea–a follow up. *Sleep Res.,* 7:222, 1978 (abstract).

32. HILL, W. M., SIMMONS, F. B., and GUILLEMINAULT, C.: Tracheostomy and sleep apnea. In: C. Guilleminault and W. C. Dement (Eds.), *Sleep Apnea Syndromes.* New York: Alan R. Liss, Inc., Kroc Foundation Series, vol. 11, 1978, pp. 347-355.

33. GLENN, W. L., PHELPS, M., and GERSTEN, L. M.: Diaphragm pacing in the management of central alveolar hypoventilation. In: C. Guilleminault and W. C. Dement (Eds.), *Sleep Apnea Syndromes.* New York: Alan R. Liss, Inc., Kroc Foundation Series, vol. 11, 1978, pp. 333-345.

34. SHAW, R. K., GLENN, W. W. L., HOGAN, J. F., and PHELPS, M. L.: Electrophysiological evaluation of phrenic nerve function in candidates for diaphragm pacing. *J. Neurosurg.,* 53:345-354, 1980.

35. COLEMAN, R. M., POLLAK, C. P., KOKKORIS, C. P., MCGREGOR, P. A., and WEITZMAN, E. D.: Periodic nocturnal myoclonus in patients with sleep-wake disorders: A case series analysis. *Sleep Res.,* 8:175, 1979 (abstract).

36. COLEMAN, R. M., POLLAK, C. P., and WEITZMAN, E. D.: Periodic movements in sleep (nocturnal myoclonus): Relation to sleep disorders. *Ann. Neurol.,* 8:416-421, 1980.

37. GÉLINEAU, J.: De la narcolepsie. *Gaz. d. Hop.* (Paris), 53:626-628; 54:635-637, 1880.

38. PASSOUANT, P.: The history of narcolepsy. In: C. Guilleminault, W. C. Dement, and P. Passouant, *Narcolepsy, Advances in Sleep Research,* vol. 3. New York: Spectrum Publications, 1976, pp. 3-14.

39. ROTH, B.: *Narkolepsie und Hypersomnie vom Standpunkt der Physiologie des Schlafes.* Berlin: V. E. B. Verlag, 1962.

40. GUILLEMINAULT, C., PHILLIPS, R., and DEMENT, W.: A syndrome of hypersomnia with automatic behavior. *Electroencephalogr. Clin. Neurophysiol.,* 38:403-413, 1975.

41. SAKAI, F., MEYER, J. S., KARACAN, I., DERMAN, S., and YAMAMOTO, M.: Normal human sleep: Reginal cerebral hemodynamics. *Ann. Neurol.,* 7:471-478, 1980.

42. GUILLEMINAULT, C., DEMENT, W. C., and PASSOUANT, P. (Eds.): Narcolepsy. In: E. D. Weitzman (Series Ed.), *Advances in Sleep Research,* vol. 3. New York: Spectrum Publications, 1976.

43. ROTH, B.: Functional hypersomnia. In: C. Guilleminault, W. C. Dement, and P. Passouant, *Narcolepsy, Advances in Sleep Research,* vol. 3. New York: Spectrum Publications, 1976.

44. WILLIAMS, R. L.: Sleep disturbances in various medical and surgical conditions. In: R. L. Williams and I. Karacan (Eds.), *Sleep Disorders: Diagnosis and Treatment.* New York: John Wiley & Sons, 1978, pp. 285-301.
45. MENDELSON, W. B., GILLIN, J. C., and WYATT, R. J.: *Human Sleep and Its Disorders.* New York: Plenum Press, 1977.
46. FREEMON, F. R.: Sleep in patients with organic diseases of the nervous system. In: R. L. Williams and I. Karacan (Eds.), *Sleep Disorders: Diagnosis and Treatment.* New York: John Wiley & Sons, 1978, pp. 261-283.
47. KALES, A. and TAN, T.: Sleep alterations associated with medical illnesses. In: A. Kales (Ed.), *Sleep: Physiology and Pathology.* Philadelphia: J. B. Lippincott, 1969, pp. 148-157.
48. CRITCHLEY, M.: Periodic hypersomnia and megaphagia in adolescent males. *Brain,* 85:627-657, 1962.
49. WILLIAMS, R. L., KARACAN, I., and HURSCH, C. J.: Clinical sleep disorders — dyssomnias (Chap. 6). In: *Electroencephalography (EEG) of Human Sleep: Clinical Applications.* New York: John Wiley & Sons, 1974, pp. 119-160.
50. BILLIARD, M., GUILLEMINAULT, C., and DEMENT, W. C.: A menstruation-linked periodic hypersomnia. *Neurology,* 25:436-443, 1975.
51. ROTH, B., NEVSIMALOVA, S., and RECHTSCHAFFEN, A.: Hypersomnia with "sleep drunkenness." *Arch. Gen. Psychiatry,* 26:456-462, 1972.
52. KALES, A., JACOBSON, A., PAULSON, M. J., KALES, J. D., and WALTER, R. D.: Somnambulism: Psychophysiological correlates. I. All night EEG studies. *Arch. Gen. Psychiatry,* 14:586-594, 1966.
53. KALES, A., PAULSON, M. J., JACOBSON, A., and KALES, J. D.: Somnambulism: Psychophysiological correlates. II. Psychiatric interviews, psychological testing, and discussion. *Arch. Gen. Psychiatry,* 14:395-404, 1966.
54. BROUGHTON, R.: Sleep disorders: Disorders of arousal? *Science,* 159:1070-1078, 1968.
55. ORME, J. E.: The incidence of sleepwalking in various groups. *Acta Psychiat. Scand.,* 43:279-281, 1967.
56. KLACKENBERG, G.: Primary enuresis. When is a child dry at night? *Acta Paediatr.,* 44:513-518, 1955.
57. THORNE, F. C.: The incidence of nocturnal enuresis after age five. *Am. J. Psychiatry,* 100:686-689, 1944.
58. WERRY, J. S. and COHRSSEN, J.: Enuresis — an etiologic and therapeutic study. *J. Pediatr.,* 67:423-431, 1965.
59. GASTAUT, H. and BROUGHTON, R.: A clinical and polygraphic study of episodic phenomena during sleep. *Recent Adv. Biol. Psychiatry,* 7:197-221, 1964.
60. WILLIAMS, R. L. and KARACAN, I.: Sleep disorders and disordered sleep. In: M. F. Reiser (Ed.), *American Handbook of Psychiatry, vol. 4, Organic Disorders and Psychosomatic Medicine.* New York: Basic Books, 1975, pp. 880-884.
61. MIKKELSEN, E. J. and RAPOPORT, J. L.: Enuresis: Psychopathology, sleep stage and drug response. *Urol. Clin. North America,* 7:361-379, 1980.
62. MIKKELSEN, E. J., RAPOPORT, J. L., NEE, L., GRUENAU, C., MENDELSON, W., and GILLIN, C. J.: Childhood enuresis. *Arch. Gen. Psychiatry,* 37:1139-1152, 1980.
63. KOOI, K. A.: *Fundamentals of Electroencephalography.* New York: Harper and Row, 1971.
64. GAMBI, D., FERRO, F. M., and MAZZA, S.: Analysis of sleep in progressive my-

oclonus epilepsy. *Europ. Neurol.,* 3:347–364, 1970.

65. HAMBERT, O. and PETERSON, I.: Clinical, electroencephalographical and neuro-pharmacological studies in syndromes of progressive myoclonus epilepsy. *Acta. Neurol. Scandinav.,* 46:149–186, 1970.

66. SATO, S., DREIFUSS, F. E., and PENRY, J. K.: The effect of sleep on spike-wave discharges in absence seizures. *Neurology,* 23:1335–1345, 1973.

67. BERNARDINA, B. D. and TASSINARI, C. A.: EEG of a nocturnal seizure in a patient with benign epilepsy of childhood with Rolandic spikes. *Epilepsia,* 16:497–501, 1975.

68. REDING, G., SEPELIN, H., ROBINSON, J. E., JR., ZIMMERMAN, S. O., and SMITH, V. H.: Nocturnal teeth-grinding: All night psychophysiology studies. *J. Dent. Res.,* 47:786–797, 1968.

69. SATOH, T. and HARADA, Y.: Electrophysiological study on tooth-grinding during sleep. *Electroencephalogr. Clin. Neurophysiol.,* 35:267–275, 1973.

70. SATOH, T. and HARADA, Y.: Tooth-grinding during sleep as an arousal reaction. *Experientia (Basel),* 27:785–786, 1971.

71. BALDY-MOULINIER, M., LEVY, M., and PASSOUANT, P.: A study of jactatio capitis during night sleep. *Electroencephalogr. Clin. Neurophysiol.,* 28:87, 1970 (abstract).

72. HISHIKAWA, Y.: Sleep paralysis. In: Guilleminault, C., Dement, W. C., and Passouant, P., *Narcolepsy, Advances in Sleep Research,* vol. 3. New York: Spectrum Publications, 1976, pp. 97–124.

73. KAYED, K., GODTLIBSEN, O. B., and SJAASTAD, O.: Chronic paroxysmal hemi-crania IV: "REM sleep locked" nocturnal headache attacks. *Sleep,* 1:91–95, 1978.

74. DEXTER, J. D. and WEITZMAN, E. D.: The relationship of nocturnal headaches to sleep stage patterns. *Neurology,* 20:513–518, 1970.

75. DEXTER, J. D.: The relationship between stages III + 4 + REM sleep and arousals with migraine. *Headache,* 19:364–369, 1979.

76. SAKAI, F., MEYER, J. S., KARACAN, I., DERMAN, S., and YAMAMOTO, M.: Nor-mal human sleep: Regional cerebral hemodynamics. *Ann. Neurol.,* 7:471–478, 1980.

77. GUILLEMINAULT, C., ELDRIDGE, F. L., PHILLIPS, J. R., and DEMENT, W. C.: Two occult causes of insomnia and their therapeutic problems. *Arch. Gen. Psychiatry,* 33:1241–1245, 1976.

78. RAVENSCROFT, K. and HARTMANN, E.: The temporal correlation of nocturnal asthmatic attacks and the D-state. *Psychophysiology,* 4:396–397, 1968 (abstract).

79. KALES, A., BEALL, G. N., BAJOR, G. F., JACOBSON, A., and KALES, J. D.: Sleep studies in asthmatic adults: Relationships of attacks to sleep stage and time of night. *J. Allergy,* 41:164–173, 1968.

80. KALES, A., KALES, J. D., and SLY, R. M.: Sleep patterns of asthmatic children: All-night electroencephalographic studies. *J. Allergy,* 46:300–308, 1970.

81. WYNNE, J. W., BLOCK, A. J., HEMENWAY, J., HUNT, L. A., and FLICK, M. R.: Disordered breathing and oxygen desaturation during sleep in patients with chronic obstructive lung disease (COPD). *Am. J. Med.,* 66:573–579, 1979.

82. COCCAGNA, G. and LUGARESI, E.: Arterial blood gases and pulmonary and

systemic arterial pressure during sleep in chronic obstructive pulmonary disease. *Sleep,* 1:117–124, 1979.

83. FLEETHAM, J. A., MEZON, B., WEST, P., BRADLEY, C. A., ANTHONISEN, N. R., and KRYGER, M. H.: Chemical control of ventilation and sleep arterial oxygen desaturation in patients with COPD. *Am. Rev. Respir. Dis.,* 122:583–589, 1980.

84. KEARLEY, R., WYNNE, J. W., BLOCK, A. J., BOYSEN, P. G., LINDSEY, S., and MARTIN, C.: The effect of low flow oxygen on sleep-disordered breathing and oxygen desaturation. *Chest,* 78:682–685, 1980.

85. BONE, R. C., PIERCE, A. K., and JOHNSON, R. L.: Controlled oxygen administration in acute respiratory failure in chronic obstructive pulmonary disease. *Am. J. Med.,* 65:896–902, 1978.

86. NOWLIN, J. B., TROYER, W. G., COLLINS, W. S., SILVERMAN, G., NICHOLS, C. R., McINTOSH, H. D., ESTES, E. H., and BOGDONOFF, M. D.: The association of nocturnal angina pectoris with dreaming. *Ann. Int. Med.* (Chicago), 63:1040–1046, 1965.

87. KARACAN, I., WILLIAMS, R. L., and TAYLOR, W. J.: Sleep characteristics of patients with angina pectoris. *Psychosomatics,* 10:280–284, 1969.

88. STERN, S. and TZIVONI, D.: Dynamic changes in the S-T segment during sleep in ischemic heart disease. *Am. J. Cardiol.,* 32:17–20, 1973.

89. KHATRI, J. M. and FREIS, E. D.: Hemodynamic changes during sleep in hypertensive patients. *Circulation,* 39:785–790, 1969.

90. ORR, W. C., MARTIN, R. J., IMES, N. K., ROGERS, R. M., and STAHL, M. L.: Hypersomnolent and nonhypersomnolent patients with upper airway obstruction during sleep. *Chest,* 75:418–422, 1979.

# 8

# Impaired, Sleep-related Penile Tumescence in the Diagnosis of Impotence

*Ismet Karacan, M.D., D.Sc.(Med.),*
*Robert L. Williams, M.D.,*
*Sabri Derman, M.D., M.Sc.D.,*
*and Cengiz Aslan, M.D.*

Because so much attention has been focused lately on the nosology, diagnosis, and treatment of various sleep disorders, and because general practitioners or psychiatrists so often hear their patients complain, "I can't sleep" or "I can't stay awake," it seems expedient to conclude that sleep is significant simply because it is so prone to being disturbed. Certainly, until efforts to sleep or to stay awake are consistently thwarted, nearly everyone takes for granted that at some fairly routine time in every 24-hour cycle, he or she will nod out for about seven or eight hours. Furthermore, physicians typically do not ask about the quality and quantity of sleep unless patients specifically complain about their sleep. This oversight persists despite:

1) Evidence that sleep and wakefulness are not mutually exclusive states of consciousness, but a continuum in which what happens in one state closely affects what happens in the other (1, 2, 3, 4); and
2) The discovery that the etiology of increasing numbers of medical disorders and diseases can be better understood when studied during sleep than during wakefulness (5, 6, 7, 8).

Sleep can be considered an ideal diagnostic state in which physiological capacity is minimally distorted by what the patient may choose to disclose or conceal or by his psychological status. The diagnosis of impotence is particularly susceptible to such distortions because it relies on the patient's perception that he is unable to get an erection, and about 90 percent of impotence is attributed, by default, to psychological factors (9, 10, 11, 12, 13). Therefore, sleep is more amenable than wakefulness to differentially diagnosing erectile impairment.

Just as, at first glance, daytime events appear to have little to do with the largely obscure functions of sleep, sleep and sex appear to be functionally far-removed, if not antagonistic, activities. However, our development over 18 years of an objective method during sleep of determining whether erection is physically possible — nocturnal penile tumescence (NPT) monitoring — suggests there is more to the relationship between sleep and sexual functioning than the bed in which both activities commonly take place.

Erectile impotence may be primary (lifelong), secondary (acquired after a period of satisfactory potency), generalized or situational (limited to certain situations or partners), total or partial. Impotence is differentially diagnosed as organogenic — the result of over 100 pathological conditions of the cardiovascular, endocrine, genitourinary, hematologic, neural, and respiratory systems, or pharmacological effects (8); psychogenic — resulting primarily from psychological and emotional problems ranging from anxiety to a major affective or schizophrenic disorder; or of mixed etiology involving both psychological and physiological factors. Major organic contributors to impotence include diabetes mellitus, arteriosclerosis, Peyronie's disease, alcohol, antihypertensive and psychoactive drugs, surgical procedures such as simple or radical prostatectomy, abdominal-perineal resection, three o'clock and nine o'clock sphincterotomy, trauma to the penis or spinal cord, priapism, and CNS lesions (8).

Psychogenic impotence that is not the result of a major mental disorder and not secondary to an organic disorder is classified in DSM-III (14) as "inhibited sexual excitement," a psychosexual disorder. In this manual of diagnostic criteria, the American Psychiatric Association (APA) describes inhibited sexual excitement as "recurrent and persistent inhibition of sexual excitement during sexual activity, manifested (in males) by partial or complete failure to attain or maintain erection until completion of the sexual act" (p. 279).

The Diagnostic Classification of Sleep and Arousal Disorders (15) refers to organogenic impotence as "impaired sleep-related penile tumescence," a condition in which the number and duration of penile erections polysomno-graphically recorded during sleep are significantly diminished relative to the expected values in normal potent men. Our research indicates that impaired NPT signifies an organic dysfunction in the complex mechanisms responsible for sustaining erection, while NPT within normal limits designates a lack of organic involvement and the probability of psychological etiology unless sensory deficits or penile pain are revealed in the physical examination. However, the discovery of organic pathology does not exclude its coexistence with psychological problems, which invariably evolve in long-standing impotence. Until the direct relationship between psychological factors and impotence is better understood, psychogenic impotence necessarily remains a default diagnosis. Nevertheless, while emphasizing the results of NPT monitoring, our evaluation procedure also includes psychiatric interviews and psychological tests to identify positive evidence of psychological involvement.

We recommend NPT monitoring as a mandatory step in the diagnostic evaluation of every man who seeks medical or psychiatric treatment for impotence. Referral to a sleep disorders center for a complete polysomnographic evaluation may seem inconvenient or superfluous to the physician familiar with the standard diagnostic procedure that has remained unchanged for over 30 years (16, 17). Certainly, the medical and developmental history, routine physical examination, and laboratory tests conducted in the standard procedure are important diagnostic tools, yet the patient's chief complaint—inadequate erection—is seldom assessed by directly observing the penis in an erect state, and objective psychological tests are rarely given to substantiate assumptions of psychological involvement (18). According to conventional procedure, impotence is considered psychogenic if a "known" organic cause of impotence is not discovered, impotence had a rapid onset, impotence occurs transiently and selectively, or spontaneous, masturbatory, or morning erections or nocturnal emissions are reported. These criteria are invalid because 1) not enough is known about the physiological mechanisms of erection to state clear cause-effect relationships between potential organic contributors and impotence; 2) routine examinations cannot uncover all relevant pathology; 3) variations in the degree of erection are disregarded; 4) the observation of morning erections depends on whether the patient awakens from REM sleep or another state in which erections are unlikely to occur; and 5) the absence of nocturnal emissions designates ejaculatory rather than erectile dysfunction. In general, the standard procedure's reliance on insensitive methods of locating physiological and psychological deficits presumed to be related to the patient's complaint makes its validity for differential diagnosis questionable.

Our development of NPT monitoring as an objective diagnostic tool for impotence is based on findings that all normal healthy males have nocturnal erections mainly during REM (19, 20, 21, 22, 23, 24, 25), the sleep phase characterized by autonomic activation and dreaming, and that NPT undergoes predictable quantitative and qualitative changes with age (26, 27). Further research confirmed that sleep-related NPT is stable and consistent when erectile capacity is physiologically intact: General or acute psychological factors do not significantly inhibit NPT (19, 20, 28); neither REM sleep irregularities (19, 26, 27, 28) nor level and recency of sexual activity (29, 30) affect NPT; and no healthy potent man recorded in our sleep disorders center has shown significantly impaired or absent NPT. Men with medical conditions likely to impair erectile dysfunction, e.g., diabetes (31, 32, 33, 34, 35), alcoholism (36), end-stage renal disease (37), spinal cord injury (38, 39), and Shy-Drager syndrome (40), have shown significant deficits in NPT. Such clinical findings have led to our assumption that:

1) NPT is a reliable index of physiological erectile capacity during the waking state;
2) Impotence is psychogenic if the patient has normal NPT for his age and no penile sensory deficits or penile pain are found;
3) Impotence is organogenic if NPT is abnormal for his age.

Routine follow-up evaluations of impotent patients to identify the specific pathology, as well as the success of cause-specific treatment, further support our assumptions.

Developed over the past 18 years, our recommended replacement for the outmoded standard diagnostic procedure emphasizes NPT monitoring as a direct test for organic involvement supplemented by developmental, sexual, marital, social, medical, psychiatric and drug histories; physical, neurological, and urological examinations; assays of testosterone and prolactin levels; a psychiatric interview, and a battery of psychological tests (18). The patient is instructed to avoid naps, excessive caffeine, alcohol, and nonessential drugs during the evaluation period; they can disturb sleep and NPT patterns.

A preliminary general physical examination focuses on the examination of the external genitalia for structural defects such as angulation due to Peyronie's plaque. Detection of penile sensory deficit and pelvic or penile pain is also important because these neurosensory problems are often not reflected as abnormal NPT, yet they may interfere with satisfactory intercourse. The length and base and tip circumferences of the flaccid penis are measured for selection of the appropriate size of the NPT transducer (41) used for NPT monitoring.

The objective of nocturnal penile tumescence monitoring is to determine whether NPT is normal, absent, or significantly diminished compared to normative data for the patient's age group. NPT is monitored on three consecutive nights at the sleep disorders center as each patient sleeps in a private, environmentally controlled bedroom. The first night serves as an adjustment period to laboratory and monitoring conditions; data typically reflect the well-documented "first-night effect" (42, 43, 44) in which sleep patterns tend to be atypical. The basic data on NPT patterns are compiled from the second night. The patient is forewarned that he will be awakened on the third night for a photograph of his fullest erection, evaluation of the degree and adequacy of erection, and assessment of penile rigidity.

In most normal men, increases in penile circumference represent the degree of erection. Therefore, two custom-fitted, mercury-filled strain gauges (41) monitor penile circumference changes continuously throughout each night; one encircles the base of the penis and the other is just caudal to the glans. Polygraph tracings from both locations are necessary because abnormal discrepancies in expansion between the tip and the base may contribute to impotence and vaginal penetration is generally difficult unless the base expands 0.5 to three times more than the tip. Impaired penile circulation or plaque deposits often result in inadequate tip expansion and rigidity while a structural abnormality may restrict base expansion.

Since abnormal NPT recordings may reflect abnormal sleep rather than impaired erectile capacity, the electroencephalographic (EEG) and electrooculographic (EOG) evaluations serve as a validity check on the NPT data (18). Bipolar, frontal, parietal, and occipital electrodes monitor EEG activity and electrodes at the outer canthi of the eyes monitor EOG activity. The EEG-EOG recordings detect abnormally reduced or fragmented sleep, especially REM sleep, and body-movement artifacts that cause artificial pen excursions on penile circumference change channels. In a patient with spinal cord injury who has muscle spasms in his lower trunk or legs, for example, the erection is probably not normal, but a segmental reflex. Our procedures for scoring NPT (8) and EEG-EOG activity are described elsewhere (45, 46).

Another validity check on penile circumference change, penile rigidity is assessed because penile expansion is not always a reliable index of penile rigidity due to great individual variations in this correlation. The finding that a man's penile tip circumference expansion is within the normal expected range does not necessarily ensure rigidity sufficient for vaginal penetration. Therefore, we (47) have developed a special device and procedure for directly measuring penile rigidity. When the patient is awakened during his fullest erection on the third night, a technician presses the cap of the force-application device on the glans until the penis visibly bends. A constantin-foil, precision strain gauge, positioned along the dorsal midline of the penis, automatically detects 10-degree bending. The gauge measures buckling pressures between 1 gm and 1000 gm; the average minimum buckling pressure enabling satisfactory intercourse is about 450 gm.

Also at this time, the patient and the technician estimate the degree of the patient's erection on a scale of zero to 100 percent. A large discrepancy between their estimates may suggest that the patient is unable to perceive accurately the size of his erection. According to preliminary analyses (18), impotent men with organically impaired NPT are more likely to overestimate degree of erection than are men with psychologically impaired and better NPT. Further research is needed to determine whether this overestimation reflects a true perceptual failure, a self-image problem, or a deliberate misestimation to obtain a penile prosthesis, a standard treatment for organogenic impotence. A photograph of the patient's erect penis taken during the awakening period not only provides visual evidence of maximum erectile capacity, disease processes, or any structural defects, but also serves as a guide for the surgeon if an implant is indicated.

The proximal organic causes of erectile failure are localized through several special procedures performed when the patient is awake and further verified by the monitoring of physiological processes during NPT. These procedures emphasize the detection of neural and vascular deficits.

In the physical examination, electrically induced, bulbocavernosus (BC)-reflex response latencies (49, 50) test the integrity of somatic segmental circuits for erection. Spontaneous bulbocavernosus-ischiocavernosus activity (BCA-ICA) (8) detected during nocturnal erections may reflect autonomic nervous system activities. Our finding (8) that spontaneous bursts of BC-IC muscle activity precede and accompany increases in penile circumference during NPT episodes suggests that the muscles pump blood into the penis during erection. That bursts of muscle activity are absent or abnormal in some impotent men suggests that functional defects in these muscles may reduce penile engorgement. Since the blood-pumping function is initiated in the higher CNS, and most episodes of NPT occur during REM sleep, dissociation between REM and NPT in an impotent patient suggests a CNS deficit.

Finger and penile electrodes monitor electrodermal activity (EDA) during NPT episodes. Our research (51) implies that an imbalance between sympathetic and parasympathetic activity possibly contributes to erectile dysfunction. The pattern of electrodermal activity, which measures sympathetic activity during sleep, is abnormal in some NPT-impaired men. In normal men, sympathetic activity (EDA storms) diminishes during REM-related tumescence; activity continues during REM sleep and the period in which tumescence would normally occur in some NPT-deficient patients.

Other compromises in autonomic function (52) are detected through EKG measurements of heart-rate variation and observation of pupillary responses to light. Failure of either the heart rate to correspondingly decelerate during one minute of deep, slow breathing or the pupils to contract in response to a sudden, bright light indicates disturbance in the autonomic nervous system.

Considering that vascular problems have been discovered in more than 60 percent of the patients presenting with impotence at our sleep disorders center, tests of vascular sufficiency are crucial diagnostic procedures. Comparing brachial and penile arterial pressures (35, 53, 54, 55) and measuring urethral temperature in the flaccid penis, as well as monitoring penile pulse volume during episodes of NPT (8), can disclose vascular insufficiency.

Penile blood pressure in the right and left central arteries that is much lower than brachial blood pressure generally indicates vascular pathology. However, well-developed accessory arteries that often compensate for occlusion in the major penile or epigastric arteries feeding the penis may yield a false-normal Doppler penile reading. The presence of these compensatory arteries, which alone cannot circulate enough blood to the penis to enable full erection, is detected during the Doppler examination by applying pressure to the femoral artery. Since this pressure cuts off the blood flow in the accessory arteries, a consequent absent or diminished Doppler sound in the penile artery indicates that the penile arteries proximal to the femoral-penile accessory arteries are not completely patent. Complaints of pain in the buttocks accompanied by erectile competence of short duration should alert the physician to the possible existence of this vascular condition (steal syndrome).

Whereas the Doppler (arterial pressure) tests performed during the physical examination identify general vascular pathology, the pulse volume test determines the extent to which such pathology contributes to erectile failure (18). A photoelectric transducer over the dorsal penile artery measures penile pulse volume. As nocturnal erection begins in normal men, pulse volume increases with penile circumference. There is little or no pulse volume response, however, in some impotent men.

We recently expanded our evaluation procedure to include penile temperature as a test of circulatory adequacy. If a thermometer is inserted through the urethra to the base of the penis, the penile temperature should be the same as the core body temperature measured deep under the back part of the tongue. A penile temperature at least $1^\circ C$ lower than the body temperature may designate circulatory problems.

Based on data from the other vascular tests, differential diagnosis of vascular pathology occasionally requires an arteriogram (56) or cavernosogram (57, 58); the former is more important than the latter because arterial insufficiency is more likely to impair erection than venous pathology in most patients.

Since optimal levels of testosterone (59, 60, 61), prolactin (62, 63), and luteinizing and follicle-stimulating hormones may be necessary for erectile adequacy, blood samples are assayed to evaluate endocrine status. Examination of the drug history and drug levels in the urine complete the physiological evaluation. If NPT is impaired in a patient who daily consumes antihypertensive, psychoactive, or other relevant drugs (64), he is scheduled for reevaluation under drug-free conditions.

The objective of the psychological/psychiatric evaluation is differential diagnosis independent of the NPT evaluation. Unfortunately, no objective, systematic equivalent to NPT monitoring currently exists for this part of the evaluation. Although the psychiatric interview and psychological testing are designed to uncover relevant psychopathology, there is no definitive method of determining the extent of its contribution to impotence. The identification of psychopathology does not necessarily signify psychological causation for erectile dysfunction. On the other hand, organic findings do not necessarily exclude psychological involvement. Indeed, most impotent men will show some reactionary emotional disturbance, especially when the impairment has been long-standing. Therefore, positive evidence of psychological etiology is sought although psychogenic impotence essentially remains a default diagnosis.

The psychiatrist obtains a complete history to corroborate findings in the patient's intake interview, identifies any psychological, marital, or social problems, and assesses the patient's general mental status. The interview focuses on the temporal development and exact nature of erectile dysfunction, the situations in which failure occurs, dynamic interaction with the partner, a comparison of current sexual functioning with previous typical levels, hospitalizations or treatments for psychiatric illness, and possible alcohol or drug abuse. The temporal relationship between any conditions revealed in the interview and the onset or intensification of impotence is carefully noted. The family and social histories are obtained from both the patient and his spouse interviewed alone and, when possible, together. Beutler et al. (65) provide a comprehensive explanation of psychonomic indicators for psychogenic impotence.

The psychological evaluation consists of a battery of written tests—the Shipley Institute of Living Scale (66), the Minnesota Multiphasic Personality Inventory (MMPI) (67), the Loevinger Sentence Completion Test for Men (68), the Derogatis Sexual Functioning Inventory (69), the Locke-Wallace Marital Adjustment Scale (70), the Profile of Mood States (71), the State-Trait Anxiety Inventory (72), and a special Reactions-to-Situations Scale (73) designed to assess performance anxiety. These tests also assess degree of psychopathology, current mood, cognitive efficiency, interpersonal expectancies and needs, sexual disturbances, and defensive style.

In DSM-III (14), the APA associates depression, anxiety, guilt, shame, frustration, somatic symptoms, compulsive traits, and any negative attitude toward sexuality to inhibited sexual excitement, the psychogenic form of impotence, but stresses the involvement of performance anxiety. The APA emphasizes that fear of failure and self-monitoring may further impair performance, lead to avoidance of sexual activity, and impede communication with the sexual partner. Masters and Johnson (11) offer a thorough explanation of performance anxiety. Although clinically nearly every psychological condition and personality characteristic has been associated with impotence, only functional psychoses and inverted sex drive have been clinically assigned definite etiological significance (74). Since most psychological factors in impotence are extrapolated from case studies and theoretical discussions, experimentally derived data are unavailable.

The patient's estimate of degree of erection is also considered in evaluating psychological etiology. Men with organogenic impotence appear to overestimate their degree of erection. Asking the patient to explain how he arrived at his estimation is often helpful for distinguishing among deliberate misestimations, self-image problems, or perceptual difficulties. In addition, patients' reactions to visual evidence of intact or impaired erectile capacity vary with their expectations. Certain patients have a vested interest in evidence of an organic deficit; they may want to obtain a penile implant or absolve themselves of "responsibility" for psychological impotence. The daytime sexual functioning of other patients improves when they are reassured that their impotence is not organogenic.

The final differential diagnosis represents the compiled, independent diagnoses of each team member—a urologist, an endocrinologist, a sleep researcher, a psychiatrist, and a psychologist, as well as any other specialists consulted such as a respiration and ENT team for a sleep apnea patient. The NPT findings are emphasized in determining whether impotence is primarily organogenic, psychogenic, or of mixed etiology. Absent or abnormally diminished NPT designates a high probability of organic involvement; absent NPT denotes more severe organic pathology than decreased NPT. Conclusions about the cause of organogenic pathology are drawn by collating the various test and examination results.

Unfortunately, our present series of physical, morphological, neural, vascular, endocrine, and psychological examinations are unable to specify the cause of impotence in about 10 percent of patients exhibiting impaired NPT and no gross psychopathology. This suggests that our current evaluation procedure may exclude a critical test for some obscure contributor to erectile dysfunction. A better understanding of erectile impairment in such patients awaits the more sophisticated study of the mechanisms of erectile failure, especially the role of neurotransmitters in erection, and the development of more sensitive means of 1) examining autonomic dysfunctions; 2) differentiating central from peripheral neural deficits; and 3) monitoring the interaction of psychological variables with physiological processes during sleep and sexual activity.

## REFERENCES

1. KLEITMAN, N.: Phylogenetic, ontogenetic and environmental determinants in the evolution of sleep-wakefulness cycles. *Proc. Assoc. Res. Nerv. Ment. Dis.,* 45:30–38, 1967.
2. TUNE, G. S.: Sleep and wakefulness in normal human adults. *Brit. Med. J.,* 2:269–271, 1968.
3. TAUB, J. M. and BERGER, R. J.: Acute shifts in the sleep-wakefulness cycle: Effects on performance and mood. *Psychosom. Med.,* 36:154–173, 1974.
4. WEBB, W. B.: Theories of sleep functions and some clinical implications. In: R. Drucker-Colin, M. Shkurovich, and M. B. Sterman (Eds.), *The Functions of Sleep.* New York: Academic Press, 1979, pp. 19–36.
5. KALES, A. and TAN, T. -L.: Sleep alterations associated with medical illnesses. In: A. Kales (Ed.), *Sleep: Physiology and Pathology.* Philadelphia: J. B. Lippincott, 1969, pp. 148–157.
6. FREEMON, F. R.: Sleep in patients with organic diseases of the nervous system. In: R. L. Williams and I. Karacan (Eds.), *Sleep Disorders: Diagnosis and Treatment.* New York: John Wiley & Sons, 1978, pp. 261–283.
7. WILLIAMS, R. L.: Sleep disturbances in various medical and surgical conditions. In: R. L. Williams and I. Karacan (Eds.), *Sleep Disorders: Diagnosis and Treatment.* New York: John Wiley & Sons, 1978, pp. 285–301.
8. KARACAN, I., SALIS, P. J., and WILLIAMS, R. L.: The role of the sleep laboratory in diagnosis and treatment of impotence. In: R. L. Williams and I. Karacan (Eds.),

*Sleep Disorders: Diagnosis and Treatment.* New York: John Wiley & Sons, 1978, pp. 353–382.

9. COOPER, A. J.: The causes and management of impotence. *Postgrad. Med. J.,* 48:548–552, 1972.

10. HASTINGS, D. W.: *Impotence and Frigidity.* Boston: Little, Brown and Co., 1963, p. 45.

11. MASTERS, W. H. and JOHNSON, V. E.: *Human Sexual Inadequacy.* Boston: Little, Brown and Co., 1970.

12. STRAUSS, E. B.: Impotence from the psychiatric standpoint. *Br. Med. J.,* 1:697–699, 1950.

13. WERSHUB, L. P.: *Sexual Impotence in the Male.* Springfield, IL: Charles C Thomas, 1959, pp. 27, 29.

14. *Diagnostic and Statistical Manual of Mental Disorders, Third Edition,* Washington, DC: 1980, pp. 275–279.

15. Association of Sleep Disorders Centers: *Diagnostic Classification of Sleep and Arousal Disorders,* Ed. 1, prepared by the Sleep Disorders Classification Committee, Roffwarg, H. P. (Chairman). *Sleep,* 2:111–112, 1979.

16. COMPERE, J. S.: Office recognition and management of erectile dysfunction. *Am. Fam. Phys.,* 17:186–190, 1978.

17. KESHIN, J. G. and PINCK, B. D.: Impotentia. *N.Y. State J. Med.,* 49:269–272, 1949.

18. KARACAN, I. and SALIS, P. J.: Diagnosis and treatment of erectile impotence. *Psychiatric Clinics of North America,* 3:97–111, 1980.

19. KARACAN, I.: The effect of exciting presleep events on dream reporting and penile erections during sleep. New York: State University of New York, Downstate Medical Center, Department of Psychiatry, 1965 (doctoral dissertation).

20. KARACAN, I., GOODENOUGH, D.R., SHAPIRO, A., and STARKER, S.: Erection cycle during sleep in relation to dream anxiety. *Arch. Gen. Psychiatry,* 15:183–189, 1966.

21. FISHER, C., GROSS, J., and ZUCH, J.: Cycle of penile erection synchronous with dreaming (REM) sleep. Preliminary report. *Arch. Gen. Psychiatry,* 12:29–45, 1965.

22. KARACAN, I., HURSCH, C. J., WILLIAMS, R. L., and LITTELL, R. C.: Some characteristics of nocturnal penile tumescence during puberty. *Pediatr. Res.,* 6:529–537, 1972.

23. KARACAN, I., HURSCH, C. J., WILLIAMS, R. L., and THORNBY, J. I.: Some characteristics of nocturnal penile tumescence in young adults. *Arch. Gen. Psychiatry,* 26:351–356, 1972.

24. HURSCH, C. J., KARACAN, I., and WILLIAMS, R. L.: Some characteristics of nocturnal penile tumescence in early middle-aged males. *Compr. Psychiatry,* 13:539–548, 1972.

25. KARACAN, I., HURSCH, C. J., and WILLIAMS, R. L.: Some characteristics of nocturnal penile tumescence in elderly males. *J. Gerontol.,* 27:39–45, 1972.

26. KARACAN, I., WILLIAMS, R. L., THORNBY, J. I., and SALIS, P. J.: Sleep-related penile tumescence as a function of age. *Am. J. Psychiatry,* 132:932–937, 1975.

27. KARACAN, I., SALIS, P. J., THORNBY, J. I., and WILLIAMS, R. L.: The ontogeny of nocturnal penile tumescence. *Waking Sleeping,* 1:27–44, 1976.

28. FISHER, C.: Dreaming and sexuality. In: R. M. Loewenstein, L. M. Newman, M.

Schur, and A. J. Solnit (Eds.), *Psychoanalysis — A General Psychology.* New York: International Universities Press, 1966, pp. 537–569.

29. KARACAN, I., WILLIAMS, R. L., and SALIS, P. J.: The effect of sexual intercourse on sleep patterns and nocturnal penile erections. *Psychophysiology,* 7:338–339, 1970 (abstract).

30. KARACAN, I., WARE, J. C., SALIS, P. J., and GOZE, N.: Sexual arousal and activity: Effect on subsequent nocturnal penile tumescence patterns. *Sleep Res.,* 8:61, 1979 (abstract).

31. KARACAN, I.: Clinical value of nocturnal erection in the prognosis and diagnosis of impotence. *Med. Aspects Hum. Sex.,* 4:27–34, 1970.

32. KARACAN, I.: Diagnosis of erectile impotence in diabetes mellitus. An objective and specific method. *Ann. Intern. Med.,* 92:334–337, 1980.

33. KARACAN, I., SCOTT, F. B., SALIS, P. J., ATTIA, S. L., WARE, J. C., ALTINEL, A., and WILLIAMS, R. L.: Nocturnal erections, differential diagnosis of impotence, and diabetes. *Biol. Psychiatry,* 12:373–380, 1977.

34. KARACAN, I., SALIS, P. J., WARE, J. C., DERVENT, B., WILLIAMS, R. L., SCOTT, F. B., ATTIA, S. L., and BEUTLER, L. F.: Nocturnal penile tumescence and diagnosis in diabetic impotence. *Am. J. Psychiatry,* 135:191–197, 1978.

35. KARACAN, I., WARE, J. C., DERVENT, B., ALTINEL, A., THORNBY, J., WILLIAMS, R. L., and KAYA, N.: Impotence and blood pressure in the flaccid penis: Relationship to nocturnal penile tumescence. *Sleep,* 1:125–132, 1978.

36. KARACAN, I., SNYDER, S., SALIS, P. J., WILLIAMS, R. L., and DERMAN, S.: Sexual dysfunction in male alcoholics and its objective evaluation. In: W. E. Fann, I. Karacan, A. D. Pokorny, and R. L. Williams, *Phenomenology and Treatment of Alcoholism.* New York: Spectrum Publications, 1980, pp. 259–268.

37. KARACAN, I., DERVENT, A., CUNNINGHAM, G., MOORE, C. A., WEINMAN, E. J., CLEVELAND, S. E., SALIS, P. J., WILLIAMS, R. L., and KOPEL, K.: Assessment of nocturnal penile tumescence as an objective method for evaluating sexual functioning in ESRD patients. *Dialysis Transplant,* 7:872–876, 890, 1978.

38. KARACAN, I., DIMITRIJEVIC, M., LAUBER, A., WARE, J. C., HALSTEAD, L., ATTIA, S., ALTINEL, A., and SALIS, P: Nocturnal penile tumescence (NPT) and sleep stages in patients with spinal cord injuries. *Sleep Res.,* 6:52, 1977 (abstract).

39. KARACAN, I., DERVENT, A., SALIS, P. J., WARE, J. C., SCOTT, F. B., DERVENT, B., and WILLIAMS, R. L.: Spinal cord injuries and NPT. *Sleep Res.,* 7:261, 1978 (abstract).

40. MOORE, C., KARACAN, I., and TAYLOR, A.: Erectile dysfunction in Shy-Drager Syndrome. *Sleep Res.,* 8:240, 1979 (abstract).

41. KARACAN, I.: A simple and inexpensive transducer for quantitative measurements of penile erection during sleep. *Behav. Res. Meth. Instr.,* 1:251–252, 1969.

42. RECHTSCHAFFEN, A. and VERDONE, P.: Amount of dreaming: Effect of incentive, adaptation to laboratory, and individual differences. *Percept. Mot. Skills,* 19: 947–958, 1964.

43. AGNEW, H. W., JR., WEBB, W. B., and WILLIAMS, R. L.: The first night effect: An EEG study of sleep. *Psychophysiology.* 2:263–266, 1966.

44. JOVANOVIC, U. J.: Der Effekt der ersten Untersuchungsnacht auf die Erektionen im Schlaf. *Psychother. Psychosom.,* 17:295–308, 1969.

45. RECHTSCHAFFEN, A. and KALES, A. (Eds.): *A Manual of Standardized Terminolo-*

gy, *Techniques and Scoring System for Sleep Stages of Human Subjects.* NIH Publication No. 204. Washington, D.C.: U.S. Government Printing Office, 1968.

46. WILLIAMS, R. L., KARACAN, I., and HURSCH, C. J.: *Electroencephalography (EEG) of Human Sleep: Clinical Applications.* New York: John Wiley & Sons, 1974.

47. KARACAN, I.: Evaluation of nocturnal penile tumescence and impotence, in press.

48. SCOTT, F. B.: The surgical treatment of erectile impotence. In: R. L. Williams and I. Karacan (Eds.), *Sleep Disorders: Diagnosis and Treatment.* New York: John Wiley & Sons, 1978, pp. 401–409.

49. ERTEKIN, C. and REEL, F.: Bulbocavernosus reflex in normal men and in patients with neurogenic bladder and/or impotence. *J. Neurol. Sci.,* 28:1–15, 1976.

50. VACEK, J. and LACHMAN, M.: Bulbokavernózni reflux u diabetiku s poruchou erektivity. Klinická e elektromyografická studie. *Cas. Lek. Ces,* 116:1014–1017, 1977.

51. WARE, J. D., KARACAN, I., SALIS, P. J., HIRSHKOWITZ, M., and THORNBY, J. I.: Patterning of electrodermal activity during sleep: Relation to impotence. *Sleep Res.,* in press.

52. CLARKE, B. F., EWING, D. J., and CAMPBELL, I. W.: Diabetic autonomic neuropathy. *Diabetologia,* 17:1–18, 1979.

53. GASKELL, P.: The importance of penile blood pressure in cases of impotence. *Can. Med. Assoc. J.,* 105:1047–1051, 1971.

54. ABELSON, D: Diagnostic value of the penile pulse and blood pressure. A Doppler study of impotence in diabetics. *J. Urol.,* 113:636–639, 1975.

55. BRITT, D. B., KEMMERER, W. T., and ROBISON, J. R.: Penile blood flow determination by mercury strain gauge plethysmography. *Invest. Urol.,* 8:673–678, 1971.

56. MICHAL, V., POSPICHAL, J., and BLAŽKOVA, J.: Ateriography of the internal pudendal arteries and passive erection. In: A. W. Zorgniotti and G. Rossi (Eds.), *Vasculogenic Impotence.* Springfield, IL: Charles C Thomas, 1980, pp. 169–179.

57. GINESTIE, J.-F.: Cavernosography. In: A. W. Zorgniotti and G. Rossi (Eds.), *Vasculogenic Impotence.* Springfield, IL: Charles C Thomas, 1980, pp. 185–190.

58. FITZPATRICK, T.: The venous drainage of the corpus cavernosum and spongiosum. In: A. W. Zorgniotti and G. Rossi (Eds.), *Vasculogenic Impotence.* Springfield, IL: Charles C Thomas, 1980, pp. 181–184.

59. RENNIE, T. A. C., VEST, S. A., JR., and HOWARD, J. E.: The use of testosterone proprionate in impotence: Clinical studies with male sex hormones (III). *South. Med. J.,* 32:1004–1007, 1939.

60. RABOCH, J. and STARKA, L.: Reported coital activity of men and levels of plasma testosterone. *Arch. Sex. Behav.,* 2:309–315, 1973.

61. LAWRENCE, D. M. and SWYER, G. I. M.: Plasma testosterone and testosterone binding affinities in men with impotence, oligospermia, azoospermia, and hypogonadism. *Br. Med. J.,* 1:349–351, 1974.

62. THORNER, M. O. and BESSER, G. M.: Hyperprolactinaemia and gonadal function: Results of bromocriptine treatment. In: P. G. Crosignani and C. Robyn (Eds.), *Prolactin and Human Reproduction.* New York: Academic Press, 1977, pp. 285–301.

63. CARTER, J. N., TYSON, J. E., TOLIS, G., VAN VLIET, S., FAIMAN, C., and FRIESEN,

H. G.: Prolactin-secreting tumors and hypogonadism in 22 men. *N. Engl. J. Med.,* 299:847–852, 1978.

64. STORY, N. L.: Sexual dysfunction resulting from drug side effects. *J. Sex. Res.,* 10:132–149, 1974.

65. BEUTLER, L. W., WARE, C., and KARACAN, I.: Psychological assessment of the sexually impotent male. In: R. L. Williams and I. Karacan (Eds.), *Sleep Disorders: Diagnosis and Treatment.* New York: John Wiley & Sons, 1978, pp. 383–394.

66. SHIPLEY, W. C.: A self-administering scale for measuring intellectual impairment and deterioration. *J. Psychol.,* 9:371–377, 1940.

67. DAHLSTROM, W. G., WELSH, G. S., and DAHLSTROM, L. E.: *An MMPI Handbook, Vol. 1: Clinical Interpretation.* Minneapolis: University of Minnesota, 1972.

68. LOEVINGER, J. and WESSLER, R.: *Measuring Ego Development, Vol. 1: Construction and Use of a Sentence Completion Test.* San Francisco: Jossey-Bass, 1978.

69. DEROGATIS, L. R.: Psychological assessment of sexual disorders. In: J. K. Meyer (Ed.), *Clinical Management of Sexual Disorders.* Baltimore: Williams and Wilkins, 1976, pp. 35–73.

70. LOCKE, H. J. and WALLACE, K. M.: Short marital-adjustment and prediction tests: Their reliability and validity. *Marr. Fam. Living,* 21:251–255, 1959.

71. MCNAIR, D. M., LORR, M., and DROPPLEMAN, L. F.: *Manual for the Profile of Mood States.* San Diego: Educational and Industrial Testing Service, 1971.

72. SPIELBERGER, C. D., GORSUCH, R. L., and LUSHENE, R. E.: *STAI Manual For the State-Trait Anxiety Inventory (Self-Evaluation Questionnaire).* Palo Alto: Consulting Psychologists, 1970.

73. SCHALLING, D.: The trait-situation interaction and the physiological correlates of behavior. In: D. Magnusson and N. S. Endler (Eds.), *Personality at the Crossroads: Current Issues in Interactional Psychology.* Hillsdale, NJ: Lawrence Erlbaum, 1977, pp. 129–141.

74. COOPER, A. J.: Factors in male sexual inadequacy: A review. *J. Nerv. Ment. Dis.,* 149:337–359, 1969.

# Part III
# SEXUALITY

# 9

# The Biology of Sex

## Seymour Levine, Ph.D.

There are probably few areas in the realm of biology which have received more attention at almost every level than that of the mechanisms regulating reproductive behaviors. Even if we narrow the definition of reproductive behaviors to include only sex behavior and eliminate those other aspects of reproduction which involve courtship and maternal behaviors, the literature is voluminous. There are, of course, many reasons for this overwhelming and pervasive interest in sex and sex-related behaviors. First is the critical role that reproduction plays in the maintenance of the species and in evolutionary theory. Within the context of modern versions of evolutionary theory (sociobiology) the central role of sex behavior is even further emphasized and given a predominant importance in the behavior of living organisms. Second is the overwhelming interest in sex and sex-related matters that somehow characterizes the human species. A third reason that the biology of sex behavior has received so much attention is that, in general, in most species sexual behavior is clearly definable and stereotypic, and a particular type of sex behavior almost defines each species. Given a behavioral pattern which has remarkably little variability from animal to animal and is remarkably consistent within species, it provides an extremely useful tool for understanding and studying in detail the underlying causal biological mechanisms which are related to the control of this particular behavior. Given the enormous literature in this field, it would be foolhardy to undertake any more than an attempt to high-

This research was supported by MH-23645 from NIMH, HD-02881 from NICH&HD, and Research Scientist Award MH-19936 from NIMH to Seymour Levine.

light the major biological determinants of sex behavior in what must be considered a relatively short review.

The major focus of this chapter will be an examination of the hormonal control of sexual behavior in both male and female mammals and, second, to illustrate how certain aspects of the behaviors themselves influence the regulation of the neuroendocrine systems controlling the pituitary-gonadal axis. It should be pointed out at the outset, however, that despite the extensive experimental information that is now available on the neural, as well as the endocrine factors involved in the regulation of sex behavior, very little is known of the physiological basis for sexual behavior in humans. A consequence of this problem is the existence of widely divergent views on the relative importance of physiological and psychological factors in the control of human sexual behavior. Normal reproductive function is dependent upon a complex set of interactions between the endocrine and nervous systems and the environment. Thus, for normal sexual function to occur, there must be an appropriate set of hormonal conditions, an intact central nervous system which must act as a receptor for these chemical substances (hormones), and, finally, an appropriate milieu which permits normal sexual behavior to be expressed as an absolute necessity for the full reproductive act to unfold.

## MALE SEXUAL BEHAVIOR

Male sexual behavior provides one of the few clear examples in which specific behaviors can be elicited by hormones given an appropriate environmental situation. To a large extent, the animal which has been most widely used for attempting to establish hormone-behavior relationships with regard to sex behavior has been the laboratory rat. When a male rat is placed with a receptive female, the male mounts the female repeatedly. On most occasions, the male achieves an intromission when mounting, then dismounts and grooms. After a relatively short interval, the male will mount and intromit again. After approximately 10 intromissions, the male will ejaculate. A post-ejaculatory period of approximately five minutes ensues during which the male sits quietly in the corner. It has been shown that during most of this post-ejaculatory period the male emits periodic supersonic vocalizations, exhibits a sleep-like EEG, and is normally not sexually aroused. A series of mounts and intromissions is then resumed and from four to 10 such series may occur before the male becomes sexually exhausted. This complex pattern of multiple intromissions before ejaculation is apparently an adaptation designed to enhance reproduction, since it has been demonstrated that multiple stimulation of the female genital tract is necessary to induce luteal activity in this short-cycled species (1).

The technique that has been used to modify the hormonal status of the male most directly has been removal of the testes (castration). In the rat, castration results in an immediate, progressive decline in the number of animals that show a complete pattern of sexual behavior. The diminution of sex behaviors follows an orderly sequence, in that initially ejaculation tends to drop out. The animal may continue to mount with successful intromissions, but ultimately intromissions no longer occur, and finally the animal ceases to show any mounting behavior. What is interesting, however, is that there is a considerable time lag between castration and the cessation of mating behavior in most subjects, and the duration of this time lag is highly variable and somewhat dependent upon the previous sexual history. It is important to note that if an animal is castrated prior to having any sexual experience, the sexual behavior will not occur. However, sexual behavior is elicited in these animals if testosterone is replaced, even after a considerable length of time following castration. After an animal has completely ceased showing any sexual behavior, testosterone treatment will reinstate it completely, although there is a relatively long time lag of one to two weeks before all animals of a group of castrated rats will exhibit complete mating behavior. The behavioral effects after treatment with testosterone appear to take a considerably longer time to be reinstated than some of the physiological consequences of testosterone treatment, such as regrowth of the atrophied prostate and seminal vesicles. Also, it appears to take a considerably larger dose of testosterone to reinstate sex behavior after it has been terminated than to reinstate other physiological effects which are a direct result of loss of testosterone.

Although it has been demonstrated that testosterone does play a major role in the regulation of sex behavior in the male rat, there is no clear-cut evidence that the amount of testosterone is in any way related to the degree of sexual behavior. It is a common occurrence that among normal healthy male rats there is a small percentage of these animals that are noncopulators. Although these noncopulators tend to have slightly lower circulating levels of testosterone, the levels are well above threshold necessary to maintain normal sexual behavior. The causes for these noncopulators is as yet not known. However, in a series of recent studies by Ward (2) it has been demonstrated that a higher percentage of noncopulators can be produced by subjecting the pregnant female to severe stress.

It is also interesting to note that there are other experimental manipulations which can quantitatively alter the sexual behavior of male rats without apparently changing testosterone levels. In an experiment done in collaboration with Drs. Merrill Mittler and William Dement (unpublished data), animals were tested for copulatory activity prior to being subjected to a period of REM deprivation. The animals were categorized according to their sexual activity obtained in the baseline as either low copulators, medium copulators, or high copulators. Low copulators were defined as animals who made one or fewer ejaculations in a standardized half-hour test, whereas medium and high copulators were categorized as making two or more complete ejaculatory series within the same half-hour period. It was found that following a period of sleep deprivation, the animals who were medium and high copulators showed no change in copulatory activity. In contrast, the low copulators significantly increased their amount of copulatory activity during sleep deprivation, and this increased sexual activity was maintained for a relatively long period even after recovery from the deprivation procedures (see Figure 1).

Although there is little question that male sexual behavior is predominantly regulated by circulating testosterone, the question remains: What is the androgen-sensitive tissue that modulates the behavioral response? Is the critical action of hormone on the genital region, spinal cord, or in the central nervous system (CNS)? There is evidence that testosterone acts at all levels. Testosterone regulates the growth of the penis, although no evidence exists that penis size in the adult can be increased by hormone treatment. Dr. Benjamin Hart (3) has demonstrated that reflexes operating at the level of the spinal cord are also facilitated by testosterone.

It does appear, however, that the primary site of action of testosterone in regulating sexual activity is the brain. Several investigators have implicated the anterior hypothalamic preoptic (AHPO) region as one of the major testosterone-sensitive areas. The basic experimental paradigm which is used to investigate the effects of hormone on the brain is to implant small amounts of testosterone in various parts of the brains of castrated rats after sexual behavior has disappeared. Davidson (4) demonstrated that with implants in the AHPO region, 75–80 percent of the animals exhibit full ejaculatory behavior on at least one to five of the biweekly tests. Testosterone implants in other areas of the brain either did not restore the behavior or did so less significantly. In addition, there was no evidence of significant increase in circulating testosterone as a result of the crystalline testosterone implants. Thus, the evidence seems to indicate that the primary action of testosterone is directly on the neural tissue. Even though the behavior of these implanted animals is significantly increased, the behavior is not quite as efficient as that observed in normal intact males. The brain does appear to be the direct site of the action. The action of testosterone on the genital region also plays an important part in maintaining the full ejaculatory behavior.

While examination of the role of testosterone in the maintenance of sexual behavior has been extensive with regard to the rodent, there is sufficient evidence both in primates and humans that testosterone may also be a vital

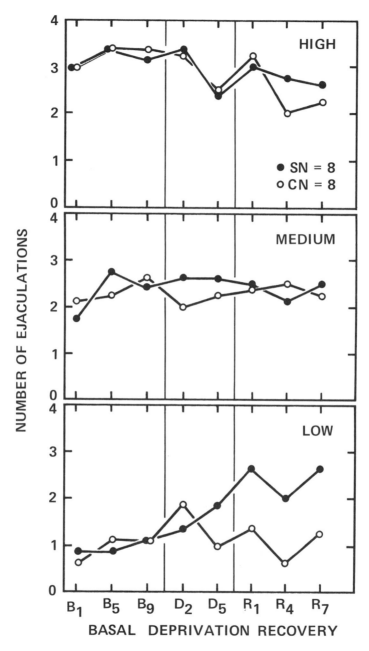

FIGURE 1. Alterations in sexual behavior of high, medium, and low copulators as a function of sleep deprivation. (S = sleep deprived; C = control).

factor in the maintenance of adequate sexual behavior. Unlike the rat, castrated rhesus macaques continue to show sexual behavior for a prolonged period of time, but sexual behavior does eventually disappear and can only be restored by replacement of testosterone. In human castrates, or in males with hypogonadism, treatment with testosterone restores sexual activity. Davidson and co-workers (5) demonstrated a short latency in the sexual activity response to administration and withdrawal of injected doses of long-acting testosterone in hypogonadal men. Plotting blood hormone levels against the frequency of erection, the results were similar to those observed in rodent experiments. Thus, the frequency of erections in males with hypogonadism appears to bear a dose-response relationship between testosterone and the number of erections. However, it is interesting that there are no studies which suggest that blood levels of testosterone within a normal range are correlated with sexual behavior. In a study of over 100 normal young men, Monti and associates (6) found no correlation between blood levels of testosterone and sexual activity. It does appear that in humans, as well as in other animals, there appears to be a threshold level of testosterone that is necessary for the maintenance of normal sexual activity, which is not markedly increased when the threshold levels are exceeded.

### Female Sexual Behavior

Beach (7) has proposed that female sexual behavior has three components: attractivity, proceptivity, and receptivity. Thus, the female must initially represent an appropriate stimulus which will elicit the male approach and behaviors in order for sexual activity to occur. There is a considerable amount of evidence indicating that attractivity may be based on certain olfactory characteristics of the female. The existence of substances that act as sex attractants in many insects has been well documented. Whether there exist specific pheromones in mammals has yet to be firmly established.

Proceptivity refers to the aspect of female sexual behavior which is used as a mechanism to solicit the behavior of the male. Female rats appear to be able to elicit sexual behavior by highly stereotyped rapid movements. In primates, proceptive behavior is often characterized by the female approaching males and going into a definitive presenting posture, exposing the genital region. Proceptive behavior is characteristic of most females in mammalian species. Although it is species-specific, such behavior has been shown, in general, to be an essential component of reproductive behavior.

Receptive behavior is almost self-defined—it is the willingness of the female to accept copulatory activity on the part of the male. Although females may indeed be highly receptive with regard to their ovulatory status, there are many social factors which contribute to receptivity. Preference for a particular partner has been shown to exist in dogs and in primates, so that some females will accept certain males and reject others. The lack of early social experience has been demonstrated to markedly affect receptive behavior to the extent that females reared in isolation, although capable of showing normal ovulatory patterns, are often unreceptive.

There is less known about the hormonal regulation of attractivity and proceptivity than about hormonal mechanisms that regulate receptive behavior. The latter is cyclic in most mammals. The cyclicity can be as short as four to five days in the case of the rat, can extend for a period of weeks, as in the case of dogs, or it can occur subject to two other aspects of cyclicity: 1) a circannual rhythm, or 2) an ovulatory rhythm occurring within the context of annual cyclicity. This pattern is clearly demonstrated in squirrel monkeys (8) and other primates who appear to have a specific seasonal period of reproduction, so that during the nonreproductive aspects of the year females are generally nonreceptive and noncycling. When cyclicity begins to occur, it occurs within the context of the annual season (see Figure 2).

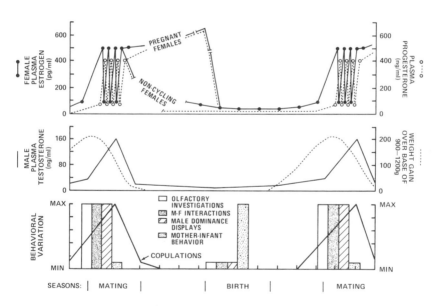

FIGURE 2. Idealized annual variation in reproductive behavior and physiology. Profile of ovarian steroids indicates that females are seasonally polyestrous (*upper*). Body weight and testosterone changes in males are also oriented to the annual mating cycle (*middle*). Heterosexual interactions, dominance, and copulatory behavior all increase during the delimited mating season (*lower*).

Female sexual receptivity, therefore, is a cyclic phenomenon. It is necessary, however, that there exist a coordination between cyclic behavior and cyclic reproductive ability. This is achieved generally in one of two ways. Either the female is sexually receptive only at a time which is close to ovulation (spontaneous ovulation), or the events associated with coitus induce ovulation (reflex ovulation). The extent to which hormones regulate female receptivity is probably best exemplified in the cyclic ovulator. The two critical hormones which appear to be associated with the regulation of receptive behavior are estrogen and progesterone. The ovulatory cycle normally consists of two phases: a follicular phase in which estrogen is the predominant ovarian hormone that is increasing in concentration, and the luteal phase during which the predominant hormone is progesterone. The period of maximum receptivity tends to occur at some time just prior to ovulation when there exists an appropriate balance of the hormones estrogen and progesterone.

The extent to which females are maximally receptive will, of course, depend on the length of the estrous cycle. Thus, in rodent females, the periods of maximal receptivity occur approximately every four days; in primates, which have longer ovulatory cycles, the duration of maximal receptivity will, of course, be greater. Ovariectomy leads to an immediate cessation of almost all aspects of female sexual behavior. Unlike the male, who will continue to show some aspects of sexual behavior following removal of testosterone, the female's dependence on estrogen and progesterone is almost complete. However, sexual receptivity can be completely reinstated if both estrogen and progesterone are given in the appropriate sequence that mimics what normally occurs during the ovulatory cycle. Therefore, the usual regime for hormonal replacement in the rat consists of a sequence of two injections of estrogen followed by a single injection of progesterone, which will normally bring 100 percent of ovariectomized females into maximal sexual receptivity. It should be noted, however, that if the doses of estrogen are sufficiently high, progesterone is not required for female sexual behavior to occur. Progesterone is an interesting hormone in the sense that it can have both facilitatory and inhibitory effects on sexual behavior. Thus, in the appropriate ratio with estrogen, progesterone appears necessary to facilitate sexual behavior. However, during the luteal phase (when progesterone levels are usually high) and during other reproductive conditions (such as pregnancy, when progesterone is also elevated), the female is normally sexually unreceptive.

The more evidence that is accumulated, the more it appears that the role of the female in regulating sexual behavior is extremely critical. While observing sexual behavior, it is common to assume that the initiator of most sexual encounters tends to be the male. However, in a recent experiment performed with squirrel monkeys (9), although the male does appear to initiate the various aspects of sexual behavior which include anogenital exploration, mounting, and intromission, the striking finding to emerge from this study was that the most significant correlation observed between hormones and sexual behaviors was not between male testosterone levels and male-initiated sexual approaches, but between estrogen levels of the females and male-initiated sexual approaches. Thus, as the female levels of estrogen increased, the sexual activity of the male in terms of the various components of squirrel monkey sexual activity, such as anogenital exploration, social exploration, approach, and mounts, all increased significantly and in an almost linear fashion with increases in the levels of estrogen.

Although in an animal such as the squirrel monkey testosterone and estrogen levels are seasonal and do peak at a particular time in the year, which facilitates sexual behavior and reproduction, an intriguing phenomenon has been observed in a number of laboratories which maintain squirrel monkeys, including our own (9, 10). It has been reported that, shortly after the formation of new groups of males and females, mating will occur and successful births will result from the induced breeding activity even when the group formations take place in the nonmating season. What is particularly interesting about this observation is that squirrel monkeys in stable groups will not normally show any sexual motivation during the nonmating season and, as indicated previously, the endocrine responses of both males and females are in a state of relative quiescence. Since mating is dependent upon the presence of appropriate levels of testosterone in males, and perhaps even more importantly upon cyclic fluctuations of circulating estrogens and progestins in females to induce ovulation, the assumption derived from these observations is that the formation of new groups causes endocrine changes which are independent of seasonal climatic changes in the ongoing annual reproductive cycle.

Several studies on other primate species, including macaques and talapoin monkeys, have indicated that males will show an increase in testosterone in the presence of females and, furthermore, that the hormonal response to females is partially dependent upon the dominance rank of the males. In order to systematically investigate the phenomena of endocrine changes induced by group formation, we initiated a study on squirrel monkeys (9) during the month of June, which is normally several months after the end of their mating season (which typically occurs between December and March in North America).

The study was conducted in three phases. In the first phase, nine male squirrel monkeys were initially held alone for four weeks. During that time, blood samples were taken and analyzed for testosterone and cortisol levels to determine whether either of these hormone levels could be used to predict which males would become dominant when the groups were formed. The males were then merged into groups, each containing three previously unfamiliar males. As usually occurs in small groups of squirrel monkeys, a linear hierarchy rapidly developed in each group. Dominant males directed more genital displays, engaged in more manual grabbing at subordinates, and were the recipients of these behaviors infrequently throughout the study. Blood samples were obtained from each male 24 hours after the formation of the groups and at weekly intervals thereafter. One month after the males were formed into groups, five females were added to each group. Blood samples were again taken 24 hours after the change in social conditions and at weekly intervals for three subsequent weeks. The results obtained from this study were striking. Within 24 hours after the all-male groups were formed, the dominant male in each group had significantly higher levels of both circulating testosterone and cortisol than did the second- and third-ranking males. These increases in testosterone levels persisted for the four weeks of the all-male groups. When the females were added, the relationship between the social environment and the hormone levels was even more accentuated. The dominant male underwent a further striking increase in plasma testosterone levels, while the subordinate male showed a decrease (see Figure 3).

Although this study demonstrated a strong relationship between dominance and testosterone, it is important to note that testosterone levels prior to

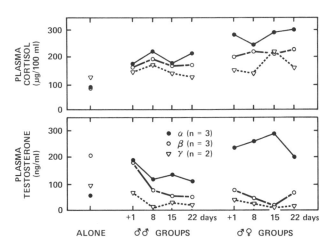

FIGURE 3. Cortisol and testosterone levels of adult males while living alone, and after the formation of unisexual and bisexual social groups.

group formation could not be used as a predictor of the subsequent status of males. The dominance hierarchy that emerged after the males were formed into groups bore no relationship to the previous hormone levels when the males were housed alone. It appears, therefore, that the social relationships between the males had determined each individual's output of testosterone, rather than the previously assumed relationship that testosterone is in some way related to the causes of dominance. Although it has not been possible thus far to determine all of the possible benefits that may occur by maintaining higher testosterone levels, in males higher levels facilitate the expression of certain behavior patterns. Testosterone has been associated with some olfactory behaviors in squirrel monkeys (11, 12) and castration of males alters the nature of the heterosexual relationships of the species.

The clearest effects of testosterone levels, however, have been demonstrated in a series of studies of reproductive function done in collaboration with Drs. Jeanette Chen and Julian Davidson (unpublished data). In these studies it was shown that in addition to seasonal variations in testosterone, there is a seasonal variation in the ejaculatory response. Ejaculation can be induced in animals via electrical stimulation; the particular measures of the ejaculatory response include latency to ejaculate following stimulation and the volume of ejaculatory fluid. When males have higher testosterone levels during the mating season, the latency to ejaculate is markedly decreased and the volume of ejaculatory fluid is significantly increased. Changes in these aspects of the ejaculatory response have also been examined during group formation in the nonmating season. Testosterone levels increased within 24 hours after group formation of the social groups. These hormonal changes were paralleled by a decrease in ejaculation latency and increases in ejaculation volume. These results could account for the capacity of group formations to induce sudden and fertile matings even during the nonmating season (see Figure 4).

The information concerning the dependence of sexual receptivity upon the appropriate levels of hormones during any particular cycle is fairly extensive and appears to indicate that sexual receptivity in all mammals with the possible exception of humans is strongly dependent upon the appropriate balance of estrogen and progesterone. Although under some captive conditions sexual behavior has been observed at times other than the mid-cycle, those conditions are extremely artifactual and usually involve maintaining animals in confined areas, permitting very few other behaviors to occur. However, in more natural conditions, it is apparent that monkeys, as well as apes (13, 14), appear to be most highly receptive at mid-cycle when other evidence of peak estrogen levels are apparent, such as swelling of the perineum in chimpanzees.

In women, unlike females of other species, the influence of hormones on

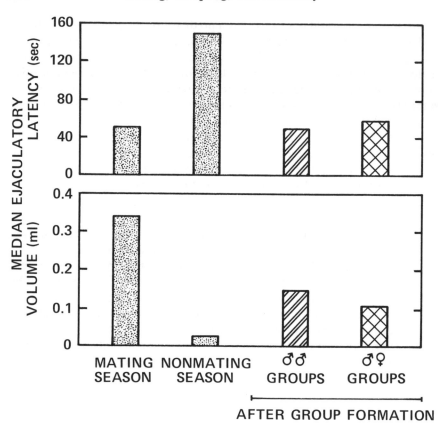

FIGURE 4. Ejaculatory responses of adult males at different times of the year, and after the formation of social groups in the nonmating season.

sexual behavior is not well established and does not appear to be of major importance. Although there is evidence that there may be some cyclicity in the extent of sexual behavior in human females so that the peak of sexual activity tends to occur around mid-cycle, it is apparent that this is mainly actuarial. In addition, ovariectomy in the human female does not lead to a cessation of sexual activity. There have been some suggestions that adrenal androgens may be in part responsible for the maintenance of sexual activity in ovariectomized human females. This area is somewhat controversial at the present time. The doses of androgen that have been used clinically to treat loss of libido in women are far in excess of those that occur physiologically. Michael and co-workers (15) studied the effects of physiological doses of estradiol, progesterone, and testosterone on the sexual behavior of ovariectomized female monkeys, giving daily injections of all three hormones in doses that duplicate plasma levels during the normal menstrual cycle. The behavioral response of the males to females given these hormones is identical to that of males interacting with intact females. When testosterone was omitted from the artificial cycle dose regimen, the males' ejaculatory behavior and the availability of the female are indistinguishable from those where all gonadal steroids were administered. Michael et al. thus concluded that although this study does not exclude a role for androgen in the female it does not suggest that the effects of androgen on female sexual receptivity are either basic or essential.

Evidence for the role of the central nervous system in regulating female sexual behavior comes predominantly from two sources: 1) a series of studies that have examined the uptake of estrogen into specific neurons of the central nervous system (16); and 2) studies using a technique similar to that used in males by implanting estrogen into specific areas of the brain in ovariectomized females to determine whether or not sexual receptivity can be induced (17). In the female rat brain, estrogen-concentrating neurons occur predominantly in the hypothalamus and in other limbic structures. The heaviest concentration of these estrogen-concentrating neurons extends from the medial preoptic area through the ventral premammillary nucleus. There are, however, areas in the lateral septum, hippocampus, and mesocephalic gray area that also contain estrogen-concentrating neurons.

I have previously discussed the technique of using implants of hormones placed directly into the brain to determine if there are specific neural sites which respond to gonadal hormones and, thus, are responsible for initiating sexual activity. This technique has been used successfully in males, but it should be noted that the first use of this technique was in a pioneering set of studies on females conducted by Harris and Michael (17). It was in their laboratory that the technique was developed for implanting minute fragments of solid hormone, in this case into the brains of ovariectomized cats. It was possible, using this procedure, to elicit sexual receptivity in the cat and to maintain continuous sexual receptivity for weeks without observing any change occurring in the genital tract, which remained in an atrophic anestrous state even though the females were showing sexual behavior. Using this technique it was possible, therefore, to map a neurological system that was estrogen-sensitive and was responsive by inducing behavioral changes without changing other aspects of physiological systems that are also estrogen-receptive. It was found that there did exist a region extending from the posterior mammillary area forward to the preoptic area and optic chiasm which with small implants of estrogen was capable of eliciting sexual behavior when placed throughout the system. The evidence indicates that there are also CNS neurons which appear to be particularly sensitive to other ovarian hormones such as progesterone. It appears relatively clear that there is a definitive CNS involvement in the regulation of sexual receptivity in the female mammal. In fact, it appears as though the regulation of sexual behavior in terms of hormone-central nervous system interaction is far more specific in the female than it is in the male when other areas, such as the genital region and the spinal cord, are also involved.

### Sexual Differentiation

Thus far I have concentrated on a discussion of the major influences that hormones exert upon the regulation and control of both male and female sexual activity. The action of these hormones on the adult animals has been designated as activational, since it is apparent that the presence of the hormones is necessary to activate and maintain a certain behavioral sequence, whereas the absence of the hormone tends to inhibit the expression of these behavioral patterns. There is another extremely important effect of hormones which has been designated organizational insofar as these hormones are exerting their action upon the brain during a period of development in which there are relatively few behaviors that are androgen-dependent. Yet the presence or absence of androgen during specific critical times in development will to a large extent determine whether or not the hormones in adulthood will have a specific action.

The brain appears to behave according to the same rules with regard to sexual differentiation as does the reproductive system (18). Inherently, the brain, like the reproductive system, is female and if not exposed to gonadal hormones at a critical period in its development, it remains so regardless of genetic sex. At least four major events are needed for the developing embryo to become male. If any of these is altered significantly, the tendency of the embryo is to continue in its development as a female or as a genetic male with many female characteristics. Initially, for maleness to occur at all, an X and a Y chromosome must be present in the genes, as compared to the development of the female in which there is a double X chromosome. In humans, 46 chromosomes are normally found. The major difference chromosomally between the male and the female is the presence of a Y chromosome in the male and its absence in the female. Human beings with only 45 chromosomes have only one X chromosome and no Y chromosome. Such XO persons are female. Other individuals have been found to have 47 chromosomes because they have two X chromosomes and a Y chromosome. Such XXY persons are male. The Y chromosome determines maleness — normally in XY individuals, abnormally in XXY individuals. The absence of the Y chromosome determines femaleness normally in XX individuals, abnormally in XO individuals. This, then, is the first step in what we have called an additive process: the addition of a Y chromosome is necessary to initiate the very process of maleness.

The next critical event in becoming a male is the formation of the male gonads, the testes. The mammalian sex organs initially appear in the fetus as two ridges of tissue — the genital ridges. Each ridge has an inner mass of tissue, the medulla, and an outer mass of tissue, the cortex. This undifferentiated gonad can go in the direction either of formation of an ovary, or in the case of males, of the more crucial sex organ, the testis. If the medulla begins to reorganize itself, the cortex atrophies and disappears and the resulting organ is a testis; conversely, if the cortex develops and the medulla retrogresses, the resulting gonad is an ovary. The formation of the testis in development precedes the formation of the ovary. There is little information as to the mechanism whereby the indifferent genital ridge becomes either testis or ovary but some active process does seem to be necessary for the medullary tissue to develop. If this process does not occur, the organism's indifferent genital ridge tends to develop as an ovary.

Once the testes are formed, however, further vital steps are needed for the organism to become totally male. The fetal testes must first secrete a duct-organizing substance and, second, male hormones (androgens) in order for the embryo to become male. The secretion of a substance from the fetal male testis is essential for both anatomical and functional differentiation of the male. During intrauterine life the fetus is equipped with the primordia of both male and female genital ducts. The Müllerian ducts serve as an analogue of the uterus and Fallopian tubes, whereas the Wolffian ducts have the potentiality for differentiating further into the epididymis, vas deferens, seminal vesicles and ejaculatory duct of the male. In the human, during the third fetal month, either the Müllerian or Wolffian ducts complete their own development while involution occurs simultaneously in the opposite structures. Secretions from the fetal testes play a decisive role in determining the direction of genital-duct development. In the presence of functional testes the Müllerian structures involute while the Wolffian ducts complete their development, whereas in the absence of the testes the Wolffian ducts are reabsorbed and the Müllerian structures mature.

Female development is not contingent on the presence of an ovary, since equally good development of the uterus and Fallopian tubes will take place even if no ovary is present. The influence of the fetal testes on duct development is unilateral since early removal of one testis leads to Müllerian development on that side while the male duct develops normally on the side on which the testis is intact. The systematic injection of androgen to a young embryo fails to duplicate the action of the fetal testes. When extremely high doses of androgen are applied locally, the Wolffian ducts exhibit signs of stimulation, but no inhibitory effect on Müllerian elements has been observed. These data have led to the belief that the fetal testes secrete a duct-organizing substance which is distinct from ordinary androgen.

The presence of normal male anatomical structure still does not ensure that the developing embryo will become functionally male. What do we mean by the concept "functionally male"? If we examine in detail some of the major differences between male and female sexuality, we note that there are sex dimorphisms in many aspects of reproductive physiology, stress physiology, metabolic processes and behavior. In particular, with regard to reproductive physiology and the behavioral aspects of maleness and femaleness, one of the principal acts of androgen during development seems to be the organization of the immature CNS into the male type. Once again we are talking about an active process: the presence of androgen during development acts upon the brain to program, in effect, patterns of maleness. The absence of androgen permits the ongoing process of femaleness to pursue its natural course. The evidence to support this theory is now abundant.

One of the principal distinctions between males and females with regard to reproductive physiology is the cyclic pattern of ovulation in the female of most mammalian species and its absence in the male. The human female ovulates about once every 28 days, the guinea pig about once every 15 days, and the rat once every four to five days. This process is regulated by hormones from the anterior pituitary gland. In cyclic fashion the anterior pituitary delivers to the ovary a follicle-stimulating hormone (FSH); this promotes the growth of the Graafian follicle which produces estrogen and also houses the ova, to be released at the times of ovulation. The anterior pituitary also releases luteinizing hormone (LH) which induces the formation of the corpora lutea and triggers ovulation. The formation of corpora lutea is clear evidence that ovulation has occurred. There is a continuing ongoing feedback system which is only interrupted in the normal "cycling" female by the onset of pregnancy. The male, in contrast, shows no such cyclicity. His testes continually receive LH from the anterior pituitary, but in the male LH causes the development of the interstitial cells of the testes, those cells which are predominantly responsible for testosterone production. The pattern of hormone production from the anterior pituitary of the female is cyclic in order to maintain the process of ovulation. The process of production of hormones in the male is for the most part noncyclic.

The pituitary gland is in itself not sexually differentiated. If a female pituitary is transplanted into a male, normal male functions will be maintained and, conversely, if the male pituitary is transplanted into a normal female, complete female function will also be maintained. The implications of these findings are that pituitary regulation does not come from the pituitary itself but from some other controlling mechanism. All the available evidence indicates that these controlling mechanisms are somewhere in the CNS. The clearest demonstration of the role of the testes in modulating CNS control of reproduction comes from studies in which newborn rats have been deprived of their testes. It has been dramatically demonstrated by the late Geoffrey Harris (19, 20) that, when these neonatally castrated males are allowed to grow, their pattern of anterior pituitary release of those hormones which regulate gonadal function (FSH and LH) is cyclic and indistinguishable from that of a normal female. If an ovary is transplanted into an adult male animal which has been castrated as a newborn, this ovary shows full cyclic ovulation. Thus, in such a case, a genetic male with XY chromosomes, a morphological male showing full sexual differentiation of anatomical structures, is still responding in terms of the CNS as a female. It should be noted that if, following castration, the male is given a single injection of testosterone, the ovulation that is seen in adulthood no longer occurs. Furthermore, if the newborn female is given a single injection of testosterone shortly after birth, she is also noncyclic and incapable of showing the normal patterns of ovulation. These studies provide one line of evidence which indicates that maleness is dependent on the presence of a male CNS and that, in order to have a male CNS, the fetal and neonatal testes must secrete androgen, which presumably acts upon the brain to differentiate it into the male type. There are definite critical periods in development for these events to occur. If the newborn male rat is castrated within 24 hours of birth, the CNS will continue to be female. But if this period exceeds approximately 72 hours, the male CNS has been permanently and irreversibly established.

The hypothesis of sexual differentiation of the brain is further substantiated when one examines the influence on adult sexual behavior of the presence or absence of testosterone in both the newborn male and female rat. As previously described, in most mammalian species the hormones emanating from the ovary and the testis exert profound control on sexual behavior. In normal circumstances the female rat becomes sexually receptive during a period in the estrous cycle when the appropriate hormonal balance exists between the ovarian hormones, estrogen and progesterone, that results in ovulation. If the female is deprived of the appropriate circulating hormones by ovariectomy, sexual receptivity is immediately abolished. However, when the appropriate hormones are replaced, either by sustained high doses of estrogen or by small doses of estrogen followed by progesterone, sexual behavior appears within a very short time after the progesterone administration.

In contrast to the cyclic pattern of receptivity shown by the female, the male rat is acyclic in its sexual behavior and will in normal circumstances copulate in response to an appropriate stimulus object. The biological adaptiveness of these two different patterns is readily apparent. For the female of most mammalian species, sexual receptivity is consistent with ovulation so that almost every sexual contact would result in pregnancy. But if the male also had a cyclic pattern of sexual activity, the conditions under which pregnancy would occur would, in the least, be infinitely more complex. When the male rat is castrated there ensues a period of time during which it is sexually active even in the absence of circulating hormones. Eventually the animal will cease normal sexual activity, but following replacement with testosterone will resume behavior that is indistinguishable from that of the normal intact male. However, no amount of estrogen and progesterone has yet proved capable of reliably eliciting in the adult castrate male patterns of sexual behavior typical of the normal female.

The evidence regarding normal patterns of sexual behavior and their dependency upon circulating hormones is consistent with the hypothesis that there are differences between the male and female brain with regard to patterns of hormone secretion and behavior. Thus, female sexual receptivity in the rat is easily elicited with the appropriate regime of estrogen and progesterone replacements following removal of the ovary. In the male these behaviors appear to be completely suppressed and cannot be elicited with doses of estrogen and progesterone that are a thousandfold higher than those required in the female (21). These findings show that one of the primary aspects of sexual differentiation in the rat appears to be suppression of the capacity in the normal male to respond to estrogen and progesterone.

The influence on sexual behavior patterns of androgen administered during development is demonstrated by two approaches to the problem: the administration of testosterone to an organism which normally would not have testosterone—that is, the female—or the removal of the testosterone-producing organs, the testes, during a critical period in the development of the male. In the case of the female, a single injection of testosterone can abolish female patterns of sexual receptivity. A female thus injected not only fails to show any signs of sexual receptivity in normal circumstances but also, when the ovary is removed, sexual behavior cannot be elicited by the appropriate replacement with estrogen and progesterone. This hormonal replacement would normally elicit complete sexual receptivity in non-testosterone-treated ovariectomized females. Further, if these females are treated neonatally with testosterone, they will show some increase in male patterns of sexual behavior following injections of androgen in adulthood (22). Conversely, although it is extremely difficult to elicit female receptivity in a male that has been castrated as an adult, if the testes are removed within 24 hours of birth sexual responses elicited by estrogen and progesterone administered in adulthood are completely indistinguishable from these responses in a normal female. Not only are they indistinguishable to the human observer but also normal adult males will respond to these estrogen- and progesterone-treated neonatally castrated males as if they were females in heat. Once again, a single injection of testosterone given shortly after castration to the newborn animal will completely reverse all these effects.

I have thus far assumed that the function of gonadal hormones in infancy is to organize the CNS with regard to neuroendocrine control of behavior. Although I have focused primarily on reproductive behavior, numerous reports in the literature have indicated that there are sex differences in nonsexual behavior. Indeed, if I am to make a convincing argument that the effects of androgen are to influence the CNS, then it seems reasonable to assume that other patterns of sex differences would also be influenced by these same hormones. There are now well reported differences (19) in activity patterns between males and females. Activity patterns of the female closely parallel estrous cycle activity and during the estrous phase of the cycle females show high peaks of activity. In contrast, the male shows no apparent activity cycle and overall activity levels are much lower. These female activity cycles can be mimicked in the neonatally castrated male by an ovarian transplant in adulthood. Thus, before the transplantation of the ovary, the male that has been castrated as a newborn shows a low level of random activity. However, the appearance of corpora lutea in the transplanted ovary marks the onset of female activity cycles which are again indistinguishable from those of normal females. During this period the neonatally castrated rat with the transplanted ovary also becomes sexually receptive on a cyclic basis. Sex dimorphisms have also been noted in other patterns of behavior, including emotional responses to novel situations and aggressive behavior.

During the course of the early studies on sexual differentiation, most of the inferences regarding CNS effects were based upon the results obtained from the various alterations in behavior which occurred as a consequence of the presence or absence of neonatal androgen. In recent years, however, there has been substantial evidence that certain anatomical aspects of the brain are sexually dimorphic and that these, too, are altered significantly by the presence of androgen during development. Raisman and Field (23), using electron microscopy, reported that there was a sexual dimorphism in the preoptic area of the hypothalamus of rats. Rats that were cyclic, including intact female rats, female rats given testosterone at a point beyond the critical period, and male rats that were castrated on Day 1 showed significantly higher spine synapses per unit area than noncyclic animals, including intact males, females given testosterone during the critical period, and males castrated beyond the critical period on Day 7. This is but one example of a series of observations which indicate that there may indeed be a multitude of differences in central nervous system function and structure between males and females, and that these functions can indeed be altered significantly by the presence or absence of androgen during critical periods of development (24).

For obvious reasons the research I have discussed thus far has been accomplished mainly in laboratory animals. In man the closest analogue to demonstrate the influence of testosterone during development on subsequent sexuality is the syndrome of testicular feminization (25). In this syndrome the internal ducts are predominantly male but the external genitalia resemble those of the female, although the vagina is shallow and ends blindly in a pouch. At adolescence, female secondary sex characteristics develop — notably, well-developed breasts and rounding of the body contours. The etiology of this disorder can be attributed to a peculiar process by which the target tissues become androgen-resistant. Thus, although the testes produce the appropriate hormones, the tissues apparently remain insensitive to androgen and consequently the syndrome of overt feminization is produced.

The clinical literature abounds with numerous instances of gender role reversals caused by pathological conditions, with resultant sexual ambiguities, in particular penile-like structures in female offspring. But it has been clearly demonstrated by Hampson and associates (26) that, to some extent, the gender role assigned to the individual born with distorted genitalia is dependent on the way in which he or she is reared. Thus, if the individual with such sexual ambiguity is treated as a male, it will generally assume a male gender role, although it may indeed have ovaries. Conversely, if the individual is brought up as a female, it will thus continue female, although again the internal genitalia and chromosomal patterns may be those of a male. Thus, at least as far as the human being is concerned, an additional process occurs in development which involves the establishment of gender role as a function of learning.

## CONCLUSION

For the most part I have discussed the importance of hormones on the regulation of sexual behavior. I have attempted to emphasize both the activational and organizational role of hormones. It is important to note that there are many aspects of these relationships that I have not dealt with, partly because of the restrictions in space and because of the enormous volume of data concerning many aspects of psychological and physiological regulation of sexual behavior. However, there is another set of relationships which should be further emphasized, which is the fact that not only do hormones participate actively in the regulation and maintenance of sexual behavior, but also sexual behavior is in fact an important dimension in regulating hormones. The influence of sexual behavior on endocrine state has been well established (1, 27). There is some recent evidence (28) that regular weekly heterosexual stimulation was associated with more regular menstrual cycles in women. Women engaging in regular sexual activity had menstrual cycles of approximately 29.5 days with a range of 26–33 days. Although the average menstrual cycle in women who had sporadic sexual activity or no sexual activity was essentially the same, the distribution had a much greater range. Further, sporadic coital activity does appear to be associated with a particular kind of infertility which is demonstrated by a short hyperthermic luteal phase (29).

The relationship between hormones and sexual activity and between sexual activity and endocrine function in humans is one of the remaining frontiers in the area of research related to the biological basis of sexual activity. The problems of studying human sexual activity are readily apparent. Most of the information obtained about sexual behavior is obtained from self-reports which are notoriously unreliable with reference to sexual activity. The appropriate manipulations which have been utilized so extensively in studying rodent and primate sexual behavior are also not available to workers attempting to examine human sexual activity and its biological basis. However, there have been enormous strides made in measurement techniques, and there is a growing body of information that indicates that within several decades a greater understanding of some of the biological factors involved in human sexual behavior will be achieved. However, sexual behavior, like most other behaviors, is indeed complex; not only are there important biological variables, but also these biological variables must be viewed at all times in the context of a psychosocial environment which also plays a major role in the control of sexual activity.

## REFERENCES

1. ADLER, N. T.: Effects of the male's copulatory behavior on successful pregnancy of the female rat. *J. Comp. Physiol. Psychol.,* 69:613–622, 1969.
2. WARD, I. L.: Prenatal stress feminizes and demasculinizes the behavior of males. *Science,* 175:82–84, 1972.

3. HART, B.: Sexual reflexes and mating behavior in the male rat. *J. Comp. Physiol. Psychol.,* 65:453–460, 1968.
4. DAVIDSON, J. M.: Activation of the male rat's sexual behavior by intracerebral implantation of androgen. *Endocrinology,* 79:783–794, 1966.
5. DAVIDSON, J. M., CAMARGO, C. A., and SMITH, E. R.: Effects of androgen on sexual behavior in hypogonadal men. *J. Clin. Endocrin. Metab.,* 48:955–958, 1979.
6. MONTI, P. M., BROWN, W. A., and CORRIVEAU, D. P.: Testosterone and components of aggressive and sexual behavior in man. *Am. J. Psychiat.,* 134:692–694, 1977.
7. BEACH, F.: Factors involved in the control of mounting behavior by female mammals. In: M. Diamond (Ed.), *Reproduction and Sexual Behavior.* Bloomington: University of Indiana Press, 1968, pp. 83–131.
8. MENDOZA, S. P., LOWE, E. L., DAVIDSON, J. M., and LEVINE, S.: Annual cyclicity in the squirrel monkey (*Saimiri sciureus*): The relationship between testosterone, fatting, and sexual behavior. *Horm. Behav.,* 11:295–303, 1978.
9. MENDOZA, S. P., COE, C. L., LOWE, E. L., and LEVINE, S.: The physiological response to group formation in adult male squirrel monkeys. *Psychoneuroendocrinology,* 3:221–229, 1979.
10. COE, C. L. and ROSENBLUM, L. A.: Sexual segregation and its ontogeny in squirrel monkey social structure. *J. Human Evol.,* 3:1–11, 1974.
11. HENNESSY, M. B., COE, C. L., MENDOZA, S. P., LOWE, E. L., and LEVINE, S.: Scent-marking and olfactory investigatory behavior in the squirrel monkey (*Saimiri sciureus*). *Behav. Biol.,* 24:57–67, 1978.
12. HENNESSY, M. B., MENDOZA, S. P., COE, C. L., LOWE, E. L., and LEVINE, S.: Androgen-related behavior in the squirrel monkey: An issue that is nothing to sneeze at. *Behav. Neur. Biol.,* 30:103–108, 1980.
13. COE, C. L., CONNOLLY, A. C., KRAEMER, H. C., and LEVINE, S.: Reproductive development and behavior of captive female chimpanzees. *Primates,* 20:571–582, 1979.
14. VAN LAWICK-GOODALL, J.: Some aspects of reproductive behaviour in a group of wild chimpanzees, *Pan troglodytes schweinfurthii,* at the Gombe Stream Reserve, Tanzania, East Africa. *J. Reprod. Fert. Suppl.,* 6:353–355, 1969.
15. MICHAEL, R. P., RICHTER, M. C., CAIN, J. A., ZUMPE, D., and BONSALL, R. W.: Artificial menstrual cycles, behaviour and the role of androgens in female rhesus monkeys. *Nature,* 275:439–440, 1978.
16. MCEWEN, B. S., DAVIS, P. G., PARSONS, B., and PFAFF, D. W.: The brain as a target for steroid hormone action. *Ann. Rev. Neurosci.,* 2:65, 1979.
17. HARRIS, G. W. and MICHAEL, R. P.: The activation of sexual behaviour by hypothalamic implants of oestrogen. *J. Physiol.,* 171:275–301, 1964.
18. LEVINE, S.: Sex differences in the brain. *Sci. Amer.,* 214:84–90, 1966.
19. HARRIS, G. W.: Sex hormones, brain development and brain function. *Endocrinology,* 75:627–648, 1964.
20. HARRIS, G. W. and LEVINE, S.: Sexual differentiation of the brain and its experimental control. *J. Physiol.,* 163:42–43, 1962.
21. JOST, A.: Embryonic sexual differentiation. In: H. W. Jones and W. W. Scott (Eds.), *Hermaphroditism, Genital Anomalies and Related Endocrine Disorders.* Baltimore: Williams & Wilkins Co., 1958, pp. 15–45.

22. HARRIS, G. W., and LEVINE, S.: Sexual differentiation of the brain and its experimental control. *J. Physiol.,* 163:379–400, 1965.

23. RAISMAN, G. and FIELD, P. M.: Sexual dimorphism in the neuropil of the preoptic area of the rat and its dependence on neonatal androgen. *Brain Res.,* 54:1–29, 1973.

24. GORSKI, R. A.: Sexual differentiation of the brain. In: D. T. Krieger and J. C. Hughes (Eds.), *Neuroendocrinology.* Sunderland, MA: Sinauer Associates, Inc., 1980, pp. 215–222.

25. SIMMER, H. H., PION, R. J., and DIGNAM, W. J.: *Testicular Feminization.* Springfield, IL: Charles C. Thomas, 1964.

26. HAMPSON, J. L.: Determinants of psychosexual orientation. In: F. A. Beach (Ed.), *Sex and Behavior.* New York: John Wiley & Sons, 1965, pp. 108–132.

27. MOSS, R. L. and COOPER, K. J.: Temporal relationship of spontaneous and coitus-induced release of luteinizing hormone in the normal cyclic rat. *Endocrinology,* 92:1748–1753, 1973.

28. CUTLER, W. B., GARCIA, C. R., and KRIEGER, A. M.: Sexual behavior frequency and menstrual cycle length in mature premenopausal women. *Psychoneuroendocrinology,* 4:297–309, 1979.

29. CUTLER, W. B., GARCIA, C. R., and KRIEGER, A. M.: Luteal phase defects: A possible relationship between short hyperthermic phase and sporadic sexual behavior in women. *Horm. Behav.,* 13:214–218, 1979.

# 10

# The Psychodynamic Approach
# to the Treatment
# of Sexual Problems

*Judd Marmor, M.D.*

In this chapter the terms "sexual dysfunction" or "sexual problem" will refer only to sexual problems of psychogenic origin. It should go without saying that good medical practice mandates that in every instance the clinician will take steps to rule out any causative or contributory factors of organic, physiologic, or pharmacologic origin.

Sexual dysfunctions have probably existed from the beginnings of human history. Although it is sometimes assumed that people in so-called primitive societies, free from sexual puritanism, have no problems in this area, this is not so. For example, Margaret Mead (1) has described anxiety among Balinese men that their marriages will fail because of impotence. Moreover, the age-old preoccupation with aphrodisiacs and magic potions to improve sexual performance gives further evidence that such anxieties have existed throughout the centuries. It is worth noting, however, that in earlier societies the concern about sexual dysfunction seems to have been entirely male-oriented.

Therapeutic techniques for these dysfunctions have always been linked to theories of causation. Thus, the ancient Greeks believed that semen came from the brain and spinal cord and that excessive masturbation (or copulation) would injure the senses and cause impotence. In the Middle Ages, when sexual dysfunctions were quite common due to widespread sexual guilt and anxiety, impotence was attributed to witchcraft or to evil magic. The treatment, therefore, consisted of denouncing, torturing, and burning the presumptive witch; exorcism was also employed to remove the magic spell. Indeed, the infamous *Malleus Maleficarum* (2) was heavily concerned with the problem of impotence and its emphasis on witchcraft was only secondary. It is noteworthy that there was no specific mention of female sexual dysfunction in the writings of the Middle Ages. Women were considered simply vessels for masculine satisfaction, and there was much hostility for them as being sources of sexual temptation.

In the 18th and early 19th century, physicians returned to the Greek theory that attributed sexual dysfunction to inordinate masturbation or other sexual excesses. The subsequent discovery of hormones lent a certain credibility to this theory on the assumption that semen was a hormonal product and that there was a finite supply of it that could never be replenished. Reading the medical tracts of that period is hair-raising! Not only impotence, but also insanity, feeblemindedness, epilepsy, and other physical disorders were all blamed on "excessive sexual activity" in youth. Even nocturnal emissions were considered a disease that was labeled "spermatorrhea." Much of this carried over into the early 20th century. Every Boy Scout Manual from 1911 to 1945 carried dire warnings of the serious consequences of masturbation. Some cases of impotence were attributed to too much horseback riding, on the assumption that such riding overstimulated the prostate. Freud himself laid heavy emphasis on excessive masturbation and coitus interruptus as explanations for some emotional difficulties in later life.

Medical treatments for sexual dysfunctions during this period were directed largely toward the control of masturbation and presumptive sexual excesses. One such measure involved spiked rings placed around the penis at night to prevent erections. A less sadistic device rang a bell whenever an erection occurred. Some authorities advocated tying the hands behind the back when the person was sleeping.

In the late 19th and early 20th century, the prevailing trend was to explain sexual dysfunctions as being due to genetic factors. Havelock Ellis considered them due to "an abnormally sensitive temperament," while Krafft-Ebing ascribed them to genetically based "degenerative" disorders. Later theories attributed the dysfunctions to a variety of vague organic conditions for which a wide spectrum of somatic therapies were prescribed. Thus, impotence was treated with techniques such as 1) *prostatic massage*, in the belief that inflammation or congestion of the prostate was the underlying problem; 2) *irrigation of the bladder*, on the assumption that bladder irritation or cystitis was etiologically involved; 3) *passage of cold metallic sounds*, on the theory that the lower urinary tract was inflamed, congested, or spastic; 4) *cauterization of the posterior urethra with silver nitrate*, on the hypothesis that the dysfunction was caused by a hypersensitive area in the posterior urethra; 5) with the introduction of various electrical techniques, *application of diathermy or electrical stimulation* to the testes, penis, or urethra on the assumption that these new magical agents would cure whatever was presumably wrong; 6) later still the *administration of testosterone* in the belief that male dysfunctions must be due to androgen deficiencies. This is a treatment that, unfortunately, is still widely employed despite conclusive evidence that androgenic deficiencies do not exist in the vast majority of male sexual dysfunctions; 7) *surgical techniques* such as tightening presumptively weak perineal muscles were also widely employed at one time; 8) both *internal and external prostheses* are still used, in cases of organic erectile dysfunction, but should have no place in the treatment of functional sexual problems.

Treatments for premature ejaculation during this period were directed toward either 1) diminishing psychic excitement by sedation, "thinking of other things," self-distraction by pinching or biting oneself, or contracting the anal sphincter; or 2) diminishing the presumptive physical hypersensitivity of the glans penis by the use of condoms, anesthetic ointments, or precoital masturbation.

It was not until the development of psychoanalytic theory that psychodynamic concepts of sexual dysfunction came to the fore. The major sexual dysfunctions with which psychoanalytic theory concerned itself were 1) impotence (erectile dysfunction in males); 2) premature or retarded ejaculation (ejaculatory dysfunction); and 3) "frigidity" (orgasmic dysfunction) in females. Functional vaginismus and dyspareunia were considered to be variant forms of frigidity. Disorders of sexual desire were not defined as a specific variety of sexual dysfunction even though diminution of libido was recognized as being present in individual cases.

In classic psychoanalytic theory the existence or development of impotence in men was believed to be derived from one or more of the following factors rooted in infantile or early childhood experiences: 1) a defense against incest-guilt with consequent castration anxiety; 2) a fear of women as expressed in the symbolism of the dentate vagina; 3) a defense against unconscious hostility and sadistic impulses toward women; 4) feelings of masculine inadequacy; and 5) an unconscious homosexual fixation. If current situational factors seemed to be involved in the symptom, the tendency of the classical analyst was to try, nevertheless, to demonstrate a link between the reactions to the current factors and the prior childhood factors mentioned above. In the same way, premature ejaculation and/or retarded ejaculation were attributed to similar early historical factors, with a particular emphasis on the issues of hostility to women (the premature ejaculation being interpreted as a kind of "enuretic soiling" of them), and/or of an unconscious wish to frustrate women or to withhold giving to them. Current situational factors, when present, were generally linked with historical antecedents.

Orgasmic dysfunction in women was usually attributed to a failure in the transfer of clitoral to vaginal erotogenicity that was believed to be a necessary event in normal feminine development. In addition, penis envy, incest guilt, hostility to men, generalized guilt about sex, poor feminine identification, and unconscious homosexuality, all rooted in early childhood relationships, were other factors to which relevance was ascribed in greater or lesser degree.

Based on these theoretical assumptions, whenever a patient was found suitable, classical long-term psychoanalytic treatment to remove the underlying unconscious conflicts, defenses, and fixations was considered the treatment of choice for all of these sexual dysfunctions. Although most patients experienced some benefit from working through these underlying guilts and anxieties, the results with regard to the removal of the sexual dysfunction itself were often less than satisfactory.

In the past two decades, however, largely as a result of newer researches into sexual physiology, notably by Masters and Johnson (3, 4), but also as a result of progress in psychoanalytic theory and technique, new approaches have evolved in the psychodynamic treatment of sexual dysfunctions which are substantially different from the traditional psychoanalytic approach even though they continue to lean heavily on certain basic psychoanalytic concepts. As the emergence of behavioral techniques in sex therapy is the focus of Chapter 11, suffice it for me to mention here that they have constituted a major contribution both to the understanding and treatment of these disorders.

A fact that is being increasingly recognized among workers in the field of sexual dysfunctions is that the simpler cases which respond to behavioral techniques alone are being seen less and less frequently, probably because they are being treated by a broad range of primary gatekeepers — family physicians, gynecologists, urologists, and marriage and family counselors, who have become conversant with the general outlines of the Masters and Johnson approach to the treatment of such disorders. As a result, psychiatrists are tending to see patients with more complicated problems in whom a limited behavioral approach has failed and in whom the psychodynamic and interpersonal factors must be worked through for the treatment to be effective.

What, then, are the major theoretical features of the newer psychodynamic approach to the treatment of sexual problems as compared to those of traditional psychoanalysis? They can be subsumed under three categories:

1) *A tri-phasic concept of sexual dysfunctions.** In contrast to traditional psychoanalytic classifications of sexual dysfunctions in terms of impotence and premature or retarded ejaculation in males, and frigidity, vaginismus or dyspareunia in females, most contemporary sexual therapists now differentiate three distinct phases of sexual function — desire, excitement, and orgasm — with separate dysfunctional manifestations in each.

The excitement disorders involve erectile difficulties in males, and failures of vaginal lubrication, genital and breast tumescence in females. The orgasmic disorders comprise premature or retarded ejaculation in men and orgasm difficulties in women. Disorders of these two phases have always been recognized.

Disorders of desire, however, constitute a new group that have become clearly differentiated only in the past decade. They appear in DSM-III under the designation of Inhibited Sexual Desire (ISD) (5). Harold Lief (6) has reported that as many as 40 percent of the patients applying to the Marriage Council of Philadelphia for help with sexual problems were suffering from ISD, and Helen Kaplan (7, 8) has also found it to be a relatively frequent occurrence.

These patients are often those who have failed to respond to short-term behavioral techniques and require more prolonged dynamic psychotherapy. They tend to be more repressed, to have deeper sexual anxieties and guilt, more disturbed relationships with their partners, and more tenacious defenses. Treatment results with this group are generally less satisfactory than for the excitement and orgasmic phase dysfunctions, although they vary with the duration and intensity of the disorder. Like the other dysfunctions, ISD may be either primary or secondary. It may be selectively present only with certain partners. The well-known Madonna-prostitute complex is an example in which men are able to experience sexual desire only with depreciated partners. In making the diagnosis of ISD the clinician should take into account factors that may normally affect the degree of sexual desire,

---

*These may occur in homosexual as well as heterosexual relationships.

such as age, physical health, constitutional differences in sexual appetite, frequency of sexual opportunity, interpersonal relationships with the partner, and other situational aspects of the patient's life.

2) *An increased recognition of the role of performance anxieties and situational factors.* There is increasing recognition among contemporary dynamic psychotherapists of the fact that not all sexual dysfunctions are reflections of unresolved infantile conflicts. Consequently, there has been an increasing sensitivity to the importance of performance anxieties and current situational factors in these disorders. Even in cases of primary dysfunctions in which early conflicts are most often relevant, one may encounter significant recent contributory factors. One such factor, for example, (that is possibly becoming less important as contemporary sexual mores become less restrictive) is the cultural ambience surrounding the early exercise of sexuality, particularly among middle-class youth. For many such young people the achievement of sexual intercourse is enveloped in societal restrictions that mandate secrecy and stimulate guilt. Thus initial sexual experiences often take place under circumstances or in settings where there is a high danger of being discovered or surprised. The associated anxiety and tension can result in erectile or orgastic failure. The memory of such an initial failure can haunt subsequent efforts and become the nidus for the development of severe performance anxiety and a vicious cycle of successive failures.

In secondary dysfunctions the relevance of situational factors is much greater, of course, and may indeed be predominant. Economic tensions, unemployment, depressive reactions, marital discord, a partner's loss of attractiveness, deficient tenderness, or lack of sexual competence, and a variety of emotionally traumatic experiences may be some of the factors involved. In males, a not infrequent cause of secondary dysfunction is excessive indulgence in alcohol, triggering a sexual failure which then becomes the basis for subsequent performance anxiety and a reinforcing pattern of repetitive failure.

One variety of secondary erectile dysfunction is related to the aging process with its diminution in the intensity and frequency of coital desire; this may occur particularly when pressure develops, usually from the woman, for coital contacts. In other instances the man himself may develop concern over the fact that it is taking him longer to achieve erection than was formerly the case. The result in such instances can be the development of performance anxiety in the man, and anxiety or hostility in the woman, with an ensuing dysfunctional sexual relationship. A clarification of the underlying physiological and psychological factors involved, with simple reassurance, is sometimes all that is psychodynamically necessary to resolve this problem.

3) *Seeing sexual function and personality structure as reciprocally related rather than dependent on infantile sexual vicissitudes.* In the contemporary approach, patterns of sexual behavior are seen not as outgrowths of specific infantile conflicts around sexuality, but more often as reflections of total personality organization. At the same time, it is recognized that disordered sexual development and function can, and often do, have a reciprocal effect upon behavior, self-image, and personality reactions.

## TREATMENT TECHNIQUES

Most contemporary dynamic psychotherapists have come to the recognition that it is not always necessary to work through the entire gamut of existing unconscious conflicts to achieve a satisfactory therapeutic outcome for the sexual dysfunction. Rather, it is possible to set more limited treatment objectives, along the line of focal psychotherapy, with the goal of improving just the sexual dysfunction. This involves limiting the therapeutic focus only to those interpersonal and intrapsychic conflicts that are specifically relevant to the sexual symptomatology. A major factor in such an approach usually involves improving the relationship with the sexually significant other, and improving the communication between the partners. Thus, in contrast to traditional psychoanalytic approaches which avoided even seeing, let alone working with, significant others, the contemporary approach usually mandates such conjoint interviews, at least for some of the time.

One of the major reasons that such focal psychotherapy was discouraged in traditional psychoanalytic theory was the assumption that removing a symptom without working through the total structure of unconscious conflicts and the defenses would inevitably prove unsatisfactory; that is to say, either the symptom would recur or it would appear in substitute form. This assumption, we now know, was based on a closed system concept of human personality organization. Open systems theory recognizes that the removal of a disabling symptom in and of itself can often result in such favorable internal feedback of an improved self-image, as well as gratifying external feedback from others, as to trigger a major reorganization of personality function without the necessity of a complete psychoanalytic restructuring.

Treatment techniques in the psychodynamic approach to the treatment of sexual problems are similar to those that are used in all contemporary dynamic psychotherapy and need no elaboration. Persons who are considered most suitable for this type of approach are, as in all dynamic psychotherapy, generally those who show evidences of ego-strength, who have a capacity to relate in a meaningful way to significant others as well as to the therapist in the transference situation, who have a capacity for insight, and who have an ability to be in touch with their own feelings.

Compared to traditional psychoanalytic treatment of the sexual dysfunctions, however, the newer psychodynamic approaches to sexual therapy present the following differences: 1) *The technique is flexible,* i.e., depending on the psychodynamic needs of the patient, therapy may be either on a one-to-one basis, or may involve conjoint therapy with the patient's sexual partner, group therapy, or any combination of the above, as indicated. 2) The contemporary psychodynamic sex therapist takes a *more active role* than in traditional psychoanalytic therapy, making interpretations and confrontations as well as offering specific recommendations for improving sexual function, where indicated. These recommendations *may include specific experiential tasks* similar to those prescribed by behavioral sex therapists. 3) *Greater emphasis is placed on current situational factors* such as the interpersonal relationship with the partner, traumatic factors, sources of performance anxiety, etc. This is not to imply that early life relationships and experiences are neglected or ignored. Rather, the historical past and the developmental sex history are utilized as important adjuncts to understanding the origin of the current problems, but the recovery of memories per se does not become the major focus of the therapeutic endeavor, nor is regression promoted or encouraged. However, the full range of relevant unconscious defenses, resistances, dreams, fantasies, and transference reactions is utilized and worked with.

I cannot emphasize sufficiently the importance of making an accurate psychodynamic diagnosis in working with these problems. This does not mean a phenomenological, descriptive DSM-III diagnosis, but rather a full exploration and understanding of both the inner and outer dynamic forces which have contributed to the development of the patient's symptoms. In order to achieve this, the psychotherapist must have a sound basic knowledge of personality development and psychodynamics. It is particularly important to carefully trace the circumstances under which the symptom first made its appearance. This often provides major clues to the understanding of the psychodynamic significance of the symptom and the reasons for its existence.

In conclusion, there are a few additional theoretical issues that I would like to address.

One of these is the myth that still persists in certain quarters about the presumptive difference between clitoral and vaginal orgasm. The usual argument made for this differentiation, sometimes by women themselves, is that they experience a much more intense and qualitatively gratifying orgasm from intravaginal intercourse than from clitoral manipulation. I do not question the authenticity or sincerity of such subjective responses. But what such proponents are confusing is the *intensity* of the total sexual response with the *locus* of the orgasmic discharge that is mediated by a specific center in the spinal cord. As long ago as 1954 (9), I pointed out that the difference between so-called clitoral and vaginal orgasms is explicable not in terms of the different origin or location of the orgastic response, but in the different intensity of it and in the degree to which cortical factors are contributory. In both males and females, the greater the degree of emotional excitement and involvement, the greater is the cortical reinforcement and enhancement of the total sexual experience; but the specific nature of the female orgastic response, i.e., the rhythmic contractions of the extravaginal musculature against the distended venous plexi and vestibular bulbs surrounding the lower third of the vagina, is the same whether it is produced by a sensual kiss, a highly erotic fantasy, or by clitoral *or* vaginal stimulation. Indeed, we should not forget that for many men and women the degree of sensual experience is *greater* during masturbation than during intercourse. It is an error to allow ourselves to make demands on our patients based on idealized moral or religious standards, rather than on scientific actualities.

In the same vein, it would be wise to abandon as a mandated therapeutic objective the myth of the need to have the sexual partners achieve their orgasms simultaneously. While one cannot deny the enormous gratification that is achieved by such an experience, to impose it on a couple is to set a perfectionistic goal which muddies up the broader and more important objectives of a sexual relationship. If contemporary sex therapy has taught us anything, it is that we have all tended in the past to place too much emphasis on the orgasm as the prime focus of the sexual experience. We are learning now to place greater importance on the total erotic experience, the mutual pleasuring, the communication of warmth, tenderness, and sensitivity. Certainly, orgasm is a much-to-be-desired climax to such a total experience, but how and when it is achieved should not be placed in a moral straightjacket, so long as mutual satisfaction is obtained.

One final comment concerns the incorporation of behavioral techniques into dynamic psychotherapy. It was Freud himself who first pointed out that there are situations, even in classical analysis, in whch interpretation alone is not enough, and in which a phobic patient, for example, must be urged to confront the phobic situation directly. This is a form of behavior therapy, and it is justified both by theoretical and therapeutic considerations. As Woods and I have pointed out in a recent publication (10), there are patterns of behavior that, although they have originated in early childhood experiences and relationships, may become so strongly reinforced over time that they acquire an autonomy which can result in their persistence even after the dynamic etiological factors have been resolved. This is particularly true of sexual dysfunctions, where early childhood anxieties and guilts become reinforced by later cultural and religious attitudes, interpersonal tensions, and performance fears. In the effort to root such patterns out later in life the psychodynamic and behavioral approaches to therapy are not contradictory or antithetical but, rather, are complementary. One of the unique contributions that modern psychodynamic sex therapy has made to psychiatry is in demonstrating the effective way in which these two approaches can be integrated to the enhancement of each.

## REFERENCES

1. MEAD, M.: *Male and Female.* New York: Wm. Morrow & Co., 1949.
2. SPRENGER, J. (1494): *Malleus Maleficarum.* London: Rodker, 1928.
3. MASTERS, W. and JOHNSON, V.: *The Human Sexual Response.* Boston: Little, Brown and Co., 1966.
4. MASTERS, W. and JOHNSON, V.: *Human Sexual Inadequacy.* Boston: Little, Brown and Co., 1970.
5. *Diagnostic and Statistical Manual of Mental Disorders, Third Edition.* Washington, DC: American Psychiatric Association, 1980.
6. LIEF, H.: What's new in sex research? Inhibited sexual desire. *Med. Aspects of Hum. Sexuality,* Vol. II, 7:94–95, July 1977.
7. KAPLAN, H. S.: *The New Sex Therapy.* New York: Brunner/Mazel, 1974.
8. KAPLAN, H. S.: *Disorders of Sexual Desire.* New York: Brunner/Mazel, 1979.
9. MARMOR, J.: *Some considerations concerning orgasm in the female. Psychosomatic Medicine,* XVI(3):240–245, May–June, 1954.
10. MARMOR, J. and WOODS, S. M.: *The Interface Between the Psychodynamic and the Behavioral Therapies.* New York: Plenum Press, 1980.

# 11

# Behavioral Approaches to the Treatment of Sexual Problems

## *Joshua Golden, M.D.*

### Introduction

Sex therapy as a specialized form of psychotherapy began to develop after the 1970 publication of Masters and Johnson's *Human Sexual Inadequacy* (1). As with all notable social events, the antecedents of a new approach to the treatment of sexual problems can be traced backward to a number of converging influences which made it possible. There was a history of concern with the psychological effects of sexual behavior which extends at least from St. Augustine (2), through the *Malleus Malleficarum* (3), and up to and beyond Sigmund Freud (4), whose theories of psychoanalysis were derived initially in a societal context where various forms of sexual repression were apparently common and thought to be important enough to warrant the blame for neurosis. Psychoanalytic theories popularized the belief that problems in sexual functioning were reflections of deeper, underlying intrapsychic conflicts. Reasonably, psychoanalytic treatment was given to resolve the underlying conflicts and relieve the sexual dysfunctions. Unfortunately, the impression left to posterity is that the results did not justify the efforts, at least in terms of improving sexual functioning in cost-effective ways.

Other social forces converged following World War II. Psychoanalysis flourished in the United States. There was the development of academic psychology, based on laboratory studies of learning which spawned "behav-

236

iorism." There was a climate of intermittent and sporadic rebelliousness against the established order of things which gave rise to the civil rights movement, the feminist movement, and most recently, the gay rights movement. There were social and commercial pressures to be more open and explicit about sexual issues and themes in our culture. A still rising incidence of premarital pregnancy and the media's pushing back the limits on sexual explicitness are examples. With some irony, psychoanalysis contributed to the lightening of sexual repression and made it possible for Havelock Ellis (5), Robert L. Dickinson (6), Alfred Kinsey (7, 8), and others (9) to make legitimate studies of human sexual functioning. The results suggested that sexual problems of human beings were extremely common; how common was hard to assess. Scientific surveys like that of Kinsey were expensive and difficult. The results, methodology, and even the undertaking of the study in the first place were vigorously criticized. It was clear that the subject of human sexual functioning was very important in our culture — so important that anything which implied the possibility of or a need for change met with a backlash reminiscent of the Church's reaction to Galileo.

The work of Masters and Johnson provided a description of a treatment for sexual problems which was relatively brief, presumed to be remarkably effective (10), and theoretically at least, available to almost anyone who might want it. In contrast to analytically derived psychodynamic approaches to the treatment of sexual problems, the early descriptions of sex therapy as popularized by Masters and Johnson appeared heretically superficial, ignoring deep, intrapsychic conflict. Treatment might take as little as two weeks or less; it concentrated on symptom removal; it was directive; therapists were active and to some extent judgmental, favoring a permissive attitude toward forms of human sexual expression. Not only was it effective, but it was a form of psychotherapy successfully developed and practiced by an obstetrician interested in infertility and a woman without formal training as a psychotherapist. The implied promise of a successful treatment to make one sexually better has continued to be a powerful lure to hordes of potential patients and therapists, eager as always to find a sure, simple, shortcut to psychotherapeutic results.

The psychiatric establishment, like many other institutions, has reacted defensively in the most part toward the change in ways of treating sexual problems. Rather than embracing the new technology, or even examining it carefully to learn what it may have to offer, psychiatry has ignored or uncomfortably tolerated the upstart. Formal attacks from the psychiatric strongholds of power have been rare. In the climate of benign neglect, other psychotherapists, counselors and lay persons have moved to fill the vacuum created by a growing demand for psychotherapy of sexual problems and a relative absence of psychiatrists trained to provide effective sex therapy.

At this point in time, it seems clear that the borders between psychodynamic psychotherapy and behavioral or other types of psychotherapy are blurring. A coalescence is forming in which whatever elements contributing effectively to the achievement of psychotherapeutic goals are being used. Accumulating evidence shows that behavioral and psychodynamic components are being melded into effective therapy for depression, eating disorders, chronic schizophrenia, phobias, and presumably other ills that flesh is heir to. Sex therapy is now but one other example of the developing trend. Psychiatric training programs are belatedly conforming to the change in psychotherapeutic theory and practice. For sexual problems a psychiatric background, founded on a familiarity with clinical medicine, is particularly useful for practicing the specialized form of psychotherapy that sex therapy represents. The reasons supporting that viewpoint are defined in the following paper.

### PREVALENCE OF SEXUAL DISORDERS

It is axiomatic in our culture that sexual competence is highly prized. While it is important to be sexually adequate, it is more important not to be sexually inadequate. Sexual inadequacy is humiliating, and people identified as sexually "abnormal" are objects of ridicule. While it is considered unseemly to brag about one's sexual competency, at least beyond adolescence, it is clear to almost everyone that being sexually desirable and sexually functional is admirable. An advertising industry blooms with profits based on the value of sexiness to consumers who pay, amazingly, for products which suggest that they may gain allure from buying and using them. With a few important exceptions, all people are expected, in contemporary culture, to take part in sex, to enjoy it, and to make sure their partner enjoys it. Anything less is pitiable. While not too long ago people were supposed to feel guilty over enjoying lusty feelings and sexual activity, especially if they were women, now they feel guilty for not feeling sexual interest or enjoying sexual pleasure. As a consequence, people who feel sexually inadequate are reluctant to admit to it. Feelings of adequacy and competency as a person may be equated, at least in one's own mind, with sexual adequacy. No one is comfortable feeling sexually inadequate, not when the concept of "normality" is that everyone else is adequate.

Determining the prevalence of sexual dysfunction in a population is difficult because people are reluctant to incriminate themselves. They want to be helped, but it is more important that they not be abnormal. The stigma may be worse than the stigma of being mentally ill. Recent surveys (11, 12) have estimated the prevalence of sexual dysfunction, variously defined, as between 15 and 50 percent. In a recent study (12) of 100 selected "happily married" couples, it was found that there was significant sexual dissatisfaction in 40–50 percent of the men and 50–60 percent of the women. The implication of such findings is that otherwise psychiatrically healthy, happily married people have a surprisingly high prevalence of sexual dissatisfaction. What must be the prevalence for the rest of the population, a sizable percentage of whom are not so happily married nor so psychiatrically sound? Presently, surveys of sexual dysfunction do not have a methodology which "normalizes" people with sexual problems. If people can be made to feel that it is safe, "normal," and probably remediable to have a sexual dysfunction, then they will be inclined to acknowledge it. Then, we may establish a prevalence approaching 100 percent for reasons to be discussed.

One of the myths that our culture purveys is that sexual functioning is natural, and does not need to be learned or taught. Clinical experience belies this notion, and a large body of experimental data on primates (13) supports the observation that sexual functioning must be organized by experience — that is, learned. The potentiality for sexual expression is part of our natural endowment. Without the opportunity to observe sexual activities or to learn from experience, humans do not know how to function. The courting rituals and social skills in finding a partner and deciding to be sexual are obvious examples of behavior which needs to be learned. How to interact sexually, where to touch, how to move, and what to do with our organs also needs to be learned.

### ETIOLOGY OF SEXUAL DYSFUNCTION

The conflicts between reality and our unrealistic expectations explain the high prevalence of sexual dysfunction in otherwise normal and healthy people. Our culture values sexual competence and denigrates sexual inadequacy. Sexual functioning must be learned. Yet our culture mistakenly informs us that sexual functioning is natural, and that learning is not necessary. Furthermore, opportunities for learning are discouraged. Masturbation is discouraged. Guilt is induced in those who explore sexuality, in themselves or others. Sexual expression is sanctioned only for those whom our culture defines as properly sexual. That means that one is either married or old enough. The expectation is that we are supposed to be sexually proficient when we first attempt sex. This is particularly true for men. Women may be naive when they begin sexual activity because their partners can teach them. While there is an implication that learning is necessary or useful for women, no such implication exists for men. The result of high expectations for performance and limited opportunities to learn how to perform, together with no sense that it is even necessary to learn, all contribute to performance anxiety. Anxiety, however, interferes with sexual performance. The more anxious one is, the worse the performance. The worse the performance, the more anxious one becomes.

The vicious cycle is made worse by the belief that each of us is largely responsible for our partner's sexual pleasure and responsiveness. Because most people tend to feel sexually insecure and somewhat inadequate, one partner's failure to perform because of anxiety may trigger concerns that the failure is somehow the fault of the other partner. We get defensive and seek reassurance from our partner that their problem is not our fault. They are at least as embarrassed and humiliated by sexual failure as we are. They tire of apologizing, and commonly avoid discussing the sexual difficulties. They may try to place some of the blame on their partner, who probably feels somewhat responsible anyway. The partners both feel anxious about their performance, and embarrassed about feeling at fault. They commonly get angry and upset with one another, and find themselves fighting. Anger is not usually conducive to feeling sexual. The partners avoid the pain of sexual failure by withdrawing from one another and avoiding attempts at sexual intimacy. If they do try, out of a feeling that they ought to prove themselves rather than because they are seeking pleasure, they are preoccupied by thoughts of failure. In Masters and Johnson's terms, they are spectators and not full participants in the sexual encounter because they are observing themselves and their partner's responses. The sexual response seems to work better if one is "mindless," focused on the feelings being experienced, or thinking erotic thoughts. When one is distracted, by whatever cause, the sexual response is diminished. The distraction may be anxiety about sexual failure, anger at a partner, pain, a telephone call, guilt, or anything else that displaces conscious attention from erotic thoughts or feelings.

Because of the importance of being sexually "normal," and because of the almost inevitable anger, withdrawal and lack of open communication between dysfunctional partners, sexual dysfunction in one person contagiously involves the other partner. The ambient level of sexual insecurity is so high that we all tend to feel vulnerable. If one person is troubled in a relationship, both people are likely to be troubled. Sexual dysfunctions always produce nonsexual relationship difficulties. Nonsexual conflicts in a relationship usually, but not always, produce problems in the sexual relationship as well. In the predictable effort to avoid the pain of failing sexual encounters, couples often go weeks, months or years without attempting sexual relations. Commonly, one or both will seek other sexual partners, perhaps to experience the pleasure of sex, but more likely because they are trying to prove themselves. They want to feel attractive and sexually competent. If their anxiety about performing is great enough, they may not perform adequately with a new partner, thereby furthering their growing conviction that they are sexually impaired. If they do manage to function well with a new partner, they may conclude, inappropriately, that the problem is the fault of the old partner with whom they have been failing in the past. It is much more comfortable to blame our partner than it is to accept ourselves as being part of the problem, and needing to change. The additional stresses of keeping an affair clandestine contribute to the level of conflict a sexually dysfunctional couple experiences. And if they didn't have trouble enough, the fact that they may have a sexual outlet with someone else lessens their motivation to try to work out the problems with the partner who shares their dysfunction.

### THE ROLE OF ILLNESS AND DISABILITY IN SEXUAL DYSFUNCTION

Sexual problems are highly prevalent in a population of normal, psychiatrically healthy people. Obviously, many people are not so normal, nor psychiatrically healthy. What must be the effect of physical or psychiatric illness or disability on sexual functioning? For a relatively small segment of the ill or disabled population, the effect is positive. Some people feel relieved because the development of illness or disability puts them into a category of people who ordinarily are not thought of as being sexual. If sexual activity has been unpleasant, and if they have been avoiding it because of failing to meet their expectations, illness or "the sick role" allows them to withdraw, honorably, from the sexual struggle. Still others benefit sexually because the onset of illness or disability motivates a profound reassessment of their lives and their priorities. Many couples take more time to be with one another, improve their communication, enhance their pleasure in intimacy of all sorts, and consequently improve their sexual relationship. For all the other ill or disabled people, the sexual adjustment suffers. Not only does the person with the illness or disability suffer, but the partner, presumably healthy and able-bodied, suffers as well. Because of fear, ignorance, and impaired communication, couples worry about harming themselves, or spreading an illness by sexual contact. They feel unattractive and unworthy of sexual attention. Just when the onset of illness or disability makes them more needy, vulnerable, and dependent on others, the probable abandonment of an active sexual life makes them less likely to be able to attract or hold a partner who may want or expect to be sexual in their relationship.

### A BEHAVIORAL APPROACH TO TREATMENT

Assessment of the factors which contribute to a psychiatric disorder is a part of any psychotherapeutic system. Psychodynamic as well as behavioral therapies are based on an understanding of what the causes of any disorder may be. In the realm of sexual dysfunctions, the implications for treatment are particularly interesting because the assumptions about causation are so different and the treatment approaches, theoretically, at least, are so divergent. A psychodynamic hypothesis might be that intrapsychic conflict, specifically, repressed sexual feelings deriving from unresolved Oedipal or pregenital problems, causes the sexual symptom. Treatment would take the traditional form of a relatively long-term, intensive talking between the identified patient and the therapist. Confrontation, interpretation, free association, dream analysis, investigation of past history and working through the transference distortions would all lead, hopefully and ultimately, to insight — that is, rational and emotional understanding of the causes of the disorder. Then, it should improve. Cure might follow because the patient would think differently, feel differently, and act differently. Therapy would be conducted with a patient identified as the primary cause and major sufferer from the problem. If other people, such as the identified patient's sexual partner, were to be affected by the problem, they would not be treated at all, or they would be referred in all likelihood to another therapist for prolonged exploration of their intrapsychic conflicts over repressed sexual feelings.

A behavioral approach would also assess the causes of the disorder. Proceeding from the assumptions already stated, the problem would be examined in both partners, as a sexual unit, if at all possible. The assessment would explore the patient's current and past sexual behavior, specifically concentrating on the circumstances coincident with the development of symptoms. If there have been periods of good sexual functioning in the past, it would be useful to identify what behavior occurred and what circumstances affected the partners to foster the success. Sexual expectations, such as how one should behave or what is normal, are defined since they have great influence on whether one sees oneself as normal. The level of knowledge about sexual anatomy, physiological response, partners' sexual preferences, contraceptive practices, and related activities are important because sexual ignorance is thought to be so common in causing symptoms of dysfunction. Since impaired communication between the partners is found either as a contributing original cause of the symptom, or as a secondary effect of a troubled sexual relationship, the communication between partners about sexual specifics is directly observed.

Since anxiety about sexual performance is so common, it tends to be a problem in couples who are dysfunctional. It is usually possible to identify performance anxiety and to demonstrate its role in causing impaired responsiveness in the partners. Certain myths about sexual behavior and conduct are explored because of their effects on the couple. People commonly believe that they are responsible for their partner's pleasure, and their partner is responsible for them. Sexual activities are supposed to occur spontaneously, without planning or deliberation, as a "natural" event. All sexual encounters are supposed to proceed smoothly and uninterruptedly from initiation to termination with thrusting of an erect penis into a receptive vagina leading ideally to orgasm for both partners, but at least for the male in all cases.

For a small, uncertain percentage of sexually dysfunctional people, physical factors contribute to the problem. The knowledge in this area is growing rapidly as research expands into the hormonal and neurovascular causes of sexual dysfunction. The effects of drugs, prescribed and not prescribed, are better understood to cause impairment of sexual functioning in many instances. A review of the relevant medical factors is an important part of the initial assessement. Careful history is taken and appropriate physical examination and specialized testing, such as nocturnal penile tumescence monitoring, may be done.

### Treatment

Behavioral treatment is directed at changing behavior. There is not an assumption that attending to underlying intrapsychic causes will be curative. Whenever possible, treatment is directed simultaneously toward both sexual partners by the therapist who may be an individual of either sex. Male-female co-therapy teams have value, but it has not yet been established that the benefits from having two therapists of either sex treating a heterosexual couple provide enough value to compensate for the additional costs. As with most psychotherapy, the important variables determining outcome are the severity of the patients' problems and the skill and experience of the therapist.

The usual structure of the treatment is that the sexually dysfunctional partners meet on a regular basis with the therapist. After an assessment period which varies in length depending on the nature of the problem and the preferences of the therapist, treatment begins. Meetings with the therapist may be daily, weekly, or at other intervals. Between meetings, the sexual partners are directed to engage in prescribed activities, individually and with their partner, which include sexual intimacies. The directed activities usually occur in the privacy of surroundings selected by the partners. Sexual contact between therapists and patients is unethical, potentially harmful to patients, and is never condoned. Treatment generally lasts from 10 to 20 sessions.

Patients are asked to keep careful written records of their prescribed activities. What was to be done, what they did, how they evaluated it, how they thought their partner evaluated it, and whatever else they observed are recorded. Each partner keeps an individual record. In order to encourage candor, the partners are usually asked not to discuss their records with one another. They each bring the records to the therapist who reviews them as part of the process of evaluating the experience of the previous assignment. Then another assignment of more sexually intimate behavior is given to the couple, depending on how they did in the previously directed activities and what the goals of treatment are. Usually, the goals are fairly precise. They are to change a specific symptom or behavior — for example, to achieve erections reliably in sexual situations, or to be able to experience orgasm in response to the partner's stimulation.

From the brief foregoing description, it is obvious that the sexual partners have to be willing and able to meet together with the therapist and with one another to engage in the prescribed behaviors between meetings. Treatment programs have been devised for patients without partners but these are generally less effective. Such programs, which often take the form of individual therapy, or group therapy of several patients without partners, are directed toward providing the patient with the knowledge and skills necessary to encourage a sexual partner to eventually participate with them.

### Contraindications for Sex Therapy

Where a couple has so much antagonism and conflict that it is impossible and inconceivable for them to engage in intimate sexual activities, a behavioral sex therapy approach is contraindicated. Therapeutic efforts should be directed toward improving the nonsexual relationship problems if possible. Then, perhaps, there may be enough goodwill and less blame and recrimination, so that the usual sex therapy approach is feasible. A possible exception to this approach is the situation where the couple has related well toward one another prior to the development of sexual problems. If their conflict and acrimony is the result of the usual blaming and withdrawal that follows failure to live up to sexual expectations, it may be that a sex therapy approach could work to rapidly resolve the relationship problems.

Another contraindication to the behavioral approach to sex therapy is the presence of severe psychiatric illness in a partner. If that illness, severe depression or paranoid psychosis, for example, prevents or seriously impairs one's ability to follow specific behavioral directions to engage in sexual intimacy with another person, sex therapy will be lengthy, difficult, and probably unsuccessful. Therapy should first be aimed at relieving the underlying illness and creating or restoring the conditions that might make sexual intimacy possible.

*Definition of a Sexual Problem*

Sexual behavior, particularly those aspects of it that are troublesome or cause anguish, usually occurs with at least one other person. How that other person evaluates the sexual relationship is of equal importance with one's own evaluation in defining a sexual dysfunction. Our expectations about sexuality, determined by past experience, familial and religious values, and the influence of media and other carriers of the culture lead us to define ourselves as sexually normal or abnormal. For example, a couple may have enjoyed a sexual relationship for years in which the male partner ejaculated very shortly after intromission in coitus and the female partner never experienced orgasm. Without knowledge of other possibilities, they may have been satisfied, even delighted with their relationship. If they were to learn that they could expect more than they were getting, such as more prolonged coital thrusting by the male, and various stimuli leading to orgasm for the female, they might define themselves as sexually dysfunctional. Many other examples are available to support the concept that patients define themselves as having a problem. Frequently, ignorance, inhibition, and unrealistic expectations for sexual performance are the basis for patients' defining themselves as sexual failures.

Another consideration relevant to sexual functioning is the special relationship sexual behavior has to morality. There are many "shoulds" and "should nots" attached to sex. "Sex should be spontaneous" is one example. "Women should not tell men how to caress them" is another example. Not infrequently, a sexual problem exists because one or both partners are not doing something which would improve or correct the problem, although they may know perfectly well what to do. "I should not have to tell him. He should know" is a typical comment from a dissatisfied woman about her lover. "I get aroused if I fantasize about . . ." is a typical beginning, ". . . but I don't do that because it is wrong to fantasize when you are involved with your lover" is the typical ending of the statement. People may know what to do, but they don't do it because they believe it is wrong, improper, or abnormal. Their attitudes may be the cause of their sexual difficulties in the same way that ignorance or unrealistic expectations of performance may lead to dysfunctions.

*Therapeutic Principles*

A behavioral approach to sexual problems is specifically designed to correct the etiologic factors identified in the assessment phase. If patients have attitudes that sexual activities should not be planned or discussed, it would be appropriate to try to change those attitudes. The therapist might use the authority vested in him by the patient who views the therapist as a "sex expert." The patients might be referred to other authorities, in the form of books or films, selected consciously by the therapist to aid the patients in modifying their attitudes in the direction the therapist thinks would be help-ful in correcting their problems.

There is no neutrality here; neither is the therapist imposing his values on the patients. While the therapist's judgments are to some extent inevitably in-fluenced by his own values, he should be guiding the patient in the direction which leads to cure. Just as sexual behavior is learned, so is sexual dysfunc-tion learned. One must learn to be functional also, and that involves changing as many of the causal factors of the dysfunction as possible, including modify-ing attitudes, gaining information, and acquiring skills. It would be unethical and unproductive for a therapist to expect or require a couple or an individual patient to attempt behavior which is unacceptable to them. Frequently at the onset of treatment the therapist will outline for the patients what the treat-ment is going to be. If some of the possible behavioral assignments, such as masturbatory activities, for example, would be against the patient's sexual values, it is important that the therapist know that. Other activities accept-able to the patients must be devised or the patients will need to be persuaded on the basis of a rationale morally acceptable to them that they should change their attitudes and do what is prescribed.

Because a behavioral approach to sex therapy is specifically designed to modify a variety of factors thought to contribute to the causation of the prob-lem, it is possible and generally useful to explain the therapy fully to patients before beginning treatment. There is little need or advantage to having the patient ignorant and wondering about what will be done to him. Neither is it necessary nor helpful for the therapist to maintain distance, anonymity, or an aura of mystery in order to enhance the development of transference feelings. Strong feelings do develop in a relationship between patients who are suffer-ing and needy and the therapists from whom they expect and seek help. In the behavioral sex therapy model, the treatment is ordinarily relatively brief. Therapists and patients are more likely to assume the role of colleagues than a traditional therapist-up, patient-down relationship characteristic of psycho-dynamic therapies. At the beginning of behavioral sex therapy, the responsi-bility for what happens and what behavioral assignments are prescribed is largely that of the therapist. By the end of therapy, the patients are develop-ing their own assignments. When the responsibility is gradually switched from the therapist to patient during the course of treatment, the patient has a more solid feeling of competence and control over his sexual life at termina-tion. Therapy is not something mysterious which is done to him. Rather, it becomes something reasonable and understandable which he has been able to do to himself and which he and his partner can do again in the future, should it be necessary or useful.

### Attitude Change

One of the common sexual attitudes which causes people to become dysfunctional is that sexual behavior is natural and does not need to be learned. People also believe that sexual activity should be spontaneous, unplanned, not mechanical, and successful at all times. Contrary to these common beliefs, it is probably true, and certainly more useful to think, that sexual behavior is not all "natural." The potential to function sexually is part of nature's endowment, but the ability to function effectively needs to be learned and organized by experience. If people have an initial expectation that they must be competent, even expert, when they begin sexual activity, they are almost certan to be disappointed at the results. It is also harder to learn if it is too hard to fail. If the consequences of sexual activity are that people feel embarrassed and inadequate, and unreasonably conclude they are failures, they become anxious and avoid sexual activities.

The behavioral approach tries to change sexual attitudes to conform with what is reasonable and heuristic. Treatment is designed so that patients cannot fail. The goals and objects of the behavioral assignments are set so that patients are asked to do only those things that they can achieve by will and effort. Goals such as experiencing sexual arousal, getting an erection, or having an orgasm, which are not under conscious control, are not asked of a patient until after he or she has begun spontaneously to have those experiences while doing other assignments.

Many people subscribe to the belief that hard work will succeed, and the harder one tries, the more likely one is to succeed. In some sexual activities, the harder one tries to get an erection, for example, or to will an orgasm, the worse the results and the greater the likelihood of failure. A common feature of behavioral sex therapies is asking the patients to agree voluntarily to a ban on the activities in which they have been failing. If their presenting problem is the male's inability to get an erection or inability to maintain it in coitus, the couple would be asked to avoid attempts at coitus, to avoid attempts to produce an erection, and if an erection occurred during other prescribed activities, to agree not to use it. If the problem were the female's inability to achieve orgasm during the sexual activity, the couple would be asked to avoid orgasm. If, during sexual stimulation, she felt orgasm were imminent, they should stop the stimulation until the sensations subside. These voluntary proscriptions relieve performance pressure which contributes to failure. If the couple breaks a ban and fails, the therapist can then explain it as an example of what may happen if the treatment steps are not followed. There is an implied message that success will come if the treatment steps are followed. If they break the ban and are successful, often for the first time in months or years, a gentle chiding from the therapist will serve to note their success, diminish the significance of the performance, and remind them of the risks of further discouragement that would follow from yet another experience of failure.

In addition to a temporary ban on activities that could reinforce the cycle of failure, the therapist institutes activities that the patient will experience as successes. Sexual roles are redefined by the therapist. For example, instead of the expectation that the sexual partners are competent and experienced, they take the role of novices, or naive learners. Partners are considered to be responsible primarily for their own sexuality and pleasure rather than assuming expertise about their own self as well as their partner. Partners are asked to learn as much about their own bodies, sensations, and sexual preferences as possible. Assigned activities may include examining their own body, visually and tactilely, and experimenting with touch and caress in areas of the body not ordinarily used for erotic stimulation.

As patients gain knowledge of themselves sexually, they are encouraged and trained in communicating that knowledge to their partner. Eventually, the partners may attain, through practice in talking and touching, a situation in which each partner has taught the other what their sexual likes and dislikes are. Then, assuming that partners have a wish to please one another, they have the tools to accomplish that goal. The responsibility for the success of the sexual encounter rests with each person's taking the obligation to let their partner know, whenever necessary, whether what is happening is what is desired, and whether it is being done effectively.

### Communication Training

Communication between partners is extremely important. Most people are quite inhibited in sexual communication under the best of circumstances. Sexually dysfunctional couples never have clear or constructive communication about their sexual problems. It may be that some couples who experience sexual problems do communicate effectively, but they never find their way to sex therapists. Perhaps they cure themselves by utilizing the same procedures therapists use when trying to correct communication deficits. Training in effective communication is a common feature of behavioral therapies. Patients are taught to express themselves clearly but constructively. It is important to convey information without conveying blame. Most couples, reacting to the humiliation of their past sexual failures, tend to blame each other. That leads only to a greater sense of failure, anger, and withdrawal. The therapist may model verbal ways of communicating sexually, then rehearse the patients and give them constructive feedback before sending them home to practice the techniques. Patients may be asked to demonstrate to a partner how they caress themselves, and then the partner is asked to try it, while the receivers of the caress guide their hand, for instance, to refine their attempts to do it successfully. Most people are initially more competent in identifying and expressing what they don't like about a partner's lovemaking technique. They usually need training in finding some positive or successful aspect in what the partner does, so that the person responding to the constructively intended criticism may feel some competence and adequacy. That may lessen the likelihood of their becoming defensive and resistant to the therapy.

### Expanding the Sexual Repertoire

Because sexual competence is so highly regarded in Western culture, many people struggle to develop a successful way of functioning sexually and then tenaciously and monotonously do it the same way each time. They are reluctant to try anything new or different because they are concerned more with performance than pleasure, and they are afraid to fail. Often a couple, who will have developed an extensive repertoire of activities that they employ as part of their sexual encounters, will abandon all enjoyable behaviors if they lose the ability to do what they feel they should be able to do. For example, some couples engage in manual and oral-genital stimulation to orgasm for the female as part of a routine sexual scenario, which concludes with coitus with the male and perhaps the female having orgasm with the erect penis in the vagina. Some men who lose the ability to get an erection abandon all of the sexual activities they formerly employed, including those forms of stimulation which brought their partner to orgasm via noncoital techniques. Because they think of sex as placing an erect penis in a receptive vagina, when they can no longer perform in that way, they stop being "sexual." A common feature of a behavioral approach to sex therapy is the development of an extensive repertoire of enjoyable sexual activities. Sex is broadly defined to include a wide variety of pleasurable activities, including touching, talking, and holding, as well as coitus and orgasm. Since people are so eager to be good lovers and please their partners, it is useful to remind them that their partners will view them more favorably if they continue to give pleasure in whatever ways they may be able to do so.

An interesting paradox about sexual behavior is that some responses, such as getting an erection or experiencing an orgasm, are more likely to occur if one is not trying to produce them. In other words, one is more likely to be able to get an erection if it is not necessary to have one. By developing a repertoire of varied and enjoyable sexual activities, compatible with a couple's values, and within their capabilities, the therapist relieves the performance anxiety which interferes with those responses like erection or orgasm that are not consciously controllable by the patients.

An additional benefit of expanding the sexual repertoire is the heightened interest and enjoyment that follows from efforts to be innovative and sexually creative. Monotony is less likely to stultify the relationship. Patients are often asked, when caressing a partner, to "make it interesting for yourself as the giver of the caress." In situations where patients are instructed to do the same type of assignment more than once, such as caressing a partner's body, they are asked to ". . . do something differently than you have ever done it before." It is helpful to advise patients to plan their activities in advance of the encounter with a partner. An effort is often made to get the partners to think not about what they like and enjoy, but about what their partner might enjoy. Most people assume that what they like is what their partner will like. This is as true of nonsexual activities as it is of sexual relationships. Unfortunately, such a basic misconception breeds an enormous amount of disappointment and unhappiness.

One of the common early behavioral assignments given to many sex therapy patients is the so-called "romantic evening." Patients are instructed to plan and carry into action an evening or encounter that their partners will find romantic or arousing. The patients are warned to be wary of the pitfall of assuming that their partner will find romantic what they themselves experience as romantic. The task is one of trying to understand what appeals to one's partner and then devising ways of creating the circumstances that evoke the desired feelings. There is often an instruction precluding any physical or overtly sexual activity. The "romantic evening" is restricted to the mental sphere. With the safety of knowing that no sexual failure can occur, patients are usually willing to try it. When they are successful in creating the setting their partner finds romantic, they are reinforced by the partner and the therapist. If they do not create the circumstances their partner finds romantic, it may be that they have not put enough thought or planning into the effort. Sometimes they do not know what their partner finds romantic, and it is appropriate that the couple learn to communicate their preferences to each other. No matter what the outcome of the assignment, it is stressed to the patient that something useful and positive is learned. Thus, the assignment is defined as successful.

Implicit in such an assignment is the pattern of devoting thought and effort to keeping the sexual relationship interesting and appealing to both partners. Spontaneity and naturalness may be desirable but they are particularly hard to attain for couples who are lacking in experience, confidence, and skill. Once they have practiced enough, they may be able to be "natural" and spontaneous. A good sexual relationship requires continuing effort. It cannot thrive if it is relegated to a low priority. Many couples consider their sexual relationship to rank behind making the children's lunch, washing the dinner dishes, reading business reports, or watching the late news. Apart from their reluctance to engage in sexual activities because of fear of failure, many couples find their lives so full of other activities that they have little or no time for sex. The behavioral approach stresses the need for time, effort, and creativity to make the sexual relationship successful. Many of the assignments are designed to lead the couple to accept those principles.

*Systematic Desensitization*

One of the standard behavioral techniques is systematic desensitization. It may involve attempts at reduction of anxiety in response to specific stimuli. People learn techniques of relaxation and then pair the relaxed state with a graduated amount of the anxiety-provoking stimulus. Since anxiety about anything can interfere with sexual arousal, and since anxiety about performance is so common in sexually dysfunctional patients, systematic desensitization is used in many ways. One common approach is to create a hierarchy of situations which occupy a continuum from most to least anxiety-provoking. Patients are then asked to determine the point on the continuum at which they can tolerate the anxiety. By repeated, graduated exposure and possibly pairing the exposure with relaxation, anxiolytic drugs, or other techniques, the patient grows accustomed to each progressive step.

The technique of sensate focus exercises illustrates the use of systematic desensitization in a sex therapy context. Patients begin where anxiety is low. They may give and receive caresses of such neutral areas of the body as the hand, the foot or the face. They progress to nongenital body caressing, then caressing of the body including genitalia, but without the goal of producing arousal or orgasm. Next might be attempts to produce arousal (after it is already established that the patients are experiencing arousal), and ultimately attempts to achieve orgasm with a partner in a variety of ways.

Vaginismus is an involuntary spasm of the levator ani muscles which makes vaginal penetration by a penis painful or impossible. Treatment of vaginismus also is structured as an in vivo, systematic desensitization. Women are first taught to contract and then relax the perivaginal muscles. Then, depending on the woman's level of comfort, she or her partner may place a small object, such as the tip of her little finger, at the vaginal introitus. She then contracts the muscles to close the introitus as long as necessary until the muscle is fatigued. Meanwhile, she exerts gentle pressure of the finger on the introitus. When she is ready to relax the muscle, the finger will gently fall partly into the vagina. The procedure is repeated, always under the woman's control, with objects of increasing size, until she can admit and comfortably tolerate objects in her vagina larger than an erect penis. The next step might be for her to do the same procedures with her partner's penis, and finally for him to control intromission. If the woman was not comfortable using her own fingers or touching her own genitalia, the procedure might be modified by using another object such as a dilator, or by having her partner carefully insert objects of graduated size.

It is important to realize that these treatment approaches must be modified and adapted sensitively to the individual patient's needs. Indiscriminate application of standardized procedures to all patients usually fails. A recent example is a 42-year-old man who presented with an initial complaint of lack of sexual desire for his wife though he was sexually aroused by women he met in casual encounters on his travels. He had been raised by a domineering, overpowering father who was very moralistic and traditional in his sexual values. The patient experienced great anxiety in any sexual contact with his wife, and he could not bear to look at her naked in the light. The couple's rare sexual encounters occurred in the dark under the bedclothes. Oedipal conflicts were obvious. When the therapy had progressed to the point when the couple were ready for mutual caressing, the man's anxiety at the sight of her nude body overwhelmed him. The couple were then given the assignment of having the wife hold a sheet in front of her nude body with the top of the sheet at the level of her eyes. He sat in front of her, comfortably, in a well lit room and she gradually lowered the sheet. If he became too uncomfortable to tolerate the anxiety she would stop at his request until he became comfortable enough to allow her to proceed. After two or three trials of this assignment, he became comfortable with her nudity. The case was treated successfully by novice therapists in nine weekly visits.

### Thought-blocking and Thought Substitution

Since the etiology of sexual dysfunctions is considered to be multi-determined, therapy is directed via various modalities to correct as many of the etiologic factors as possible. Where ignorance of sexual anatomy and physiology is relevant, patients are educated about anatomy and physiologic response. If unrealistic expectations and inhibiting attitudes contribute to a sense of failure or anxiety about performance, therapy is aimed at changing the expectations and attitudes. Patients who have defined themselves as failures and who are experiencing failure are directed to engage in activities that lead to success in a sexual context. Successful experiences build confidence and people are eager to do what they do well and successfully. The converse is also true. Notwithstanding the various factors which contribute to sexual dysfunction, including organic factors and drug effects, the final common pathway leading to impairment is anxiety. The anxiety may stem from many sources but it is significant primarily as anxiety about performance. Patients who are not able to do what they want, and who have experienced failure sexually, are preoccupied by thoughts of failure. Instead of approaching a sexual encounter with eager anticipation of pleasure, they dread it as another opportunity for humiliation.

There are two basic behavioral approaches used to combat the distracting effects of performance anxiety on sexual arousal. One is the technique of sensate focus exercises. These caressing assignments are given to patients with the specific instruction that they attend or focus only on the sensations they are giving or receiving. Operationally, sexual responsiveness seems to be maximal when the person is unself-conscious, essentially "mindless," and absorbed in the sensations they are experiencing. The sensate focus exercises train patients to attend to what they are feeling rather than what they are thinking. A logical consequence of each partner's accepting responsibility for their own sexual pleasure is that they may then be freer from distracting thoughts about whether the partner is satisfied or pleased. For example, a man suffering from inability to get an erection with a partner probably thinks more about whether he will get and maintain an erection, and what his partner will think or say about him, than he does about how it feels to have his genitals caressed. The more his consciousness is on his thoughts, the less it is on his feelings and the less likely it is that he will respond naturally.

Another technique used commonly to address the same problem is thought substitution. Patients are asked to identify erotic thoughts and to develop or use sexual fantasies. If thinking non-erotic thoughts can diminish arousal, it is also true that thinking erotic thoughts can enhance arousal. There are a variety of ways to assist people in redeveloping their ability to fantasize, if they have difficulty doing it. Most of the problems with using fantasy have to do with the patients' sense that it is wrong or bad to do so. As with many other aspects of sexual conduct, they are anxious to feel normal and they may fear that it is abnormal to fantasize, especially about someone or something that seems improper when they are with their partner. The therapist's taking the responsibility for the patient and indicating that it is useful, proper, and normal to fantasize, particularly in the service of improving the sexual relationship, are often all that are needed to reassure the patient.

### Record-keeping and Maintenance Programs

Another common feature of behavioral approaches to sex therapy is systematic record-keeping. Throughout treatment patients are asked to record their activities, their reactions, their thoughts, their impressions of their partner's reactions and thoughts, and anything else they feel may be relevant. Many therapists write out the behavioral assignments after getting both partners' agreement to comply with what has been prescribed. The patients are instructed to keep the written accounts from their partners. This may permit them to record their reactions more candidly than they would if their partner reviewed them as well as the therapist. The written accounts supplement the discussions of the assignments which take place in the therapist's office. The written assignments are effective in confronting resistances, because patients who might otherwise say, "I didn't do it because I misunderstood or I forgot," have the specific information available for reference. Frequently, written records provide a richer and freer account of problems and differing viewpoints than are obvious from a conjoint discussion.

When therapy is concluding successfully, with resolution of symptoms or the consensual attainment of specified goals, a maintenance program is prepared. Patients and therapists review the course of therapy, identify the techniques used to solve past problems, anticipate future problems, and plan the treatment steps that would be useful in solving the possible problems. Written records of past assignments are useful for this task. Hopefully, the patients leave with a sense of being competent to deal with their own problems if necessary, although they may return for more expert help if they want or need to do so.

### Therapist Self-disclosure

Psychodynamic therapies, founded on psychoanalytic theory and practice, rely importantly on the development and resolution of transference issues. Behavioral therapies have tended historically to place less emphasis on the relationship between therapist and patient. At least the behavioral theorists have minimized the mediating effect of the therapeutic relationship on causing therapeutic change. Some behaviorally oriented sex therapists cautiously and consciously employ self-disclosure to patients as a way of enhancing progress. Because of their embarrassment over feeling sexually abnormal, people do not ordinarily discuss their sexual problems with others. They assume that everyone else is sexually functional, because that is the message the culture conveys. In sex therapy, some therapists will tell patients about sexual problems they may have had, and presumably have overcome. The intention is to help the patient feel more normal and less stigmatized. If the therapist, who is a "sexual expert" and generally thought by patients to be competent, has sexual problems, it may be less disturbing for the patient to have problems. Also the therapist's ability to overcome problems in learning to be sexually functional is a positive example for patients who may question whether they can benefit from therapy. However, the potential for mischief is abundant when therapists disclose aspects of their personal sexual experience to patients, and the use of self-disclosure is inconsistent among behavioral therapists.

### Resistance

In behavioral sex therapy many subtle factors combine to influence therapeutic outcome. Patient motivation, the severity of the patients' problems, the therapist's skill, and the efficacy of the therapy are obvious components. In determining outcome, the most important variable is whether patients are willing to do their behavioral assignments. Patient resistance and the therapist's ability to deal with resistance are the basic element of any psychotherapy, including behavioral sex therapy. While there are many areas of overlap between psychodynamic and behavioral sex therapists, there are some interesting differences. Interpretation and attempts to produce insight are not stressed by behavioral therapists. They assume that most resistance is motivated by fear of failure, but they know from experience that if patients will do the sensitively designed behavioral assignments they may experience success. Assignments are written out so patients have a harder time "forgetting" what they agreed to do. Common excuses, such as "there was not enough time" or "something important happened," are discussed with patients when the assignments are given, so that patients are conscious of the possibility of resisting. The therapist may anticipate problems with limited time, for example, by asking patients to plan their activities for a specific day and time, early in the week between visits, so they do not find themselves having procrastinated until no time is available.

Some behavioral sex therapists use systems of rewards and punishments to combat resistances. Patients may be asked to deposit a meaningful sum of money into the therapist's care. If the patients do all the assignments they have agreed to in the therapist's office when the tasks are assigned, they get all the money returned to them. If they fail to do what they have agreed to do, a portion of the deposited money will go to the patient's favorite charity or perhaps to a destination very aversive to the patient, such as the American Nazi Party.

Therapists very consciously and deliberately encourage patients. They restructure and redefine the patients' self-concept as a sexual failure, emphasizing the patient's strengths, their efforts to change, and their successes. By conscious use of the therapist's approval as a reward and reinforcement, patient behavior is shaped in the direction desired by patients and therapists.

In related fashion behavioral sex therapists use an exploration of the patient's past history to identify past sexual successes. It is easier to work from the patients' strengths than to try to build upon their weaknesses. If patients can be assigned tasks that they accomplished successfully in the past, but neglected since, they are more likely to be successful with them in the future. Historical information which enlightens patients about the past influences which may have led to their dysfunction can also be useful. It is not emphasized when one is working in a brief therapy format, primarily because it does not seem to be helpful enough to justify the expenditure of valuable therapy time.

### CONCLUSION

While behavioral sex therapy has many features that have become systematized like all other psychotherapies, it must be tailored to the unique needs of individual patients. There is no standard approach, although many patients with similar problems respond to the same techniques. There is a definite need for sex therapists to be solidly grounded in psychotherapy. Problems of marital or relationship conflict are ubiquitous. Other psychiatric problems related to mental or physical illnesses and their treatments can complicate sex therapy. Ultimately, it is the skill of the therapist in modifying and adapting the tools of behavioral sex therapy to his patients' needs that is the distinctive feature of good sex therapy.

### REFERENCES

1. MASTERS, W. H. and JOHNSON, V. E.: *Human Sexual Inadequacy.* Boston: Little, Brown and Co., 1970.
2. AUGUSTINE OF HIPPO, SAINT.: *Confessions.* c. 400 A.D.
3. SPRENGER, J. (1494): *Malleus Malleficarum.* London: Rodker, 1928.
4. FREUD, S.: *Collected Papers.* London: Hogarth Press, 1953–56.
5. ELLIS, H.: *Studies in the Psychology of Sex.* Philadelphia: Davis, 1921.
6. DICKINSON, R. L.: *A Thousand Marriages.* Baltimore: Williams and Wilkins, 1931.
7. KINSEY, A. C.: *Sexual Behavior in the Human Male.* Philadelphia: W. B. Saunders, Co., 1948.
8. KINSEY, A. C.: *Sexual Behavior in the Human Female.* Philadelphia: W. B. Saunders, Co., 1953.
9. BRECHER, E. H.: *The Sex Researchers.* Boston: Little, Brown and Co., 1969.

10. ZILBERGELD, B. and EVANS, M.: "The Inadequacy of Masters and Johnson." *Psychology Today,* August 1980, pp. 29–43.
11. BURNAP, D., GOLDEN, J. S.: "Sexual problems in medical practice." *J. Med. Educ.* 42:7, July 1967, pp. 673–680.
12. FRANK, E., ANDERSON, C., and RUBENSTEIN, D.: Frequency of sexual dysfunction in "normal" couples. *N. Engl. J. Med.* 229:111–115, 1978.
13. HARLOW, H. F., and HARLOW, M. K.: Psychopathology in monkeys. In: H. D. Kimmel (Ed.), *Experimental Psychopathology: Recent Research and Theory.* Academic Press: New York, 1971.

# 12

# Near Miss: "Sex Change" Treatment and Its Evaluation

## *Robert J. Stoller, M. D.*

### INTRODUCTION

Since 1953 (1; see also 2), a fantasy held by people for millennia—that one could change sex—has seemed to become reality. This solution to an unacceptable sense of bisexuality has pressed the light and dark sides of people's imagination, as we know from the comedies and dramas, stories, myths, and visual portrayals of artists back almost to the beginning of preserved records. And in the dreams of ordinary people, in the agonies of paranoid psychotics, in the erotic behavior of all sorts of folks (diagnosable or not), and in the structure of identity, we find this ubiquitous effort to come to terms with impulses toward or fear of turning into someone of the opposite sex. (The most powerful investigation of the subject is that of Freud [e.g., 3, 4], who found bisexuality and its permutations to be a bedrock of human behavior. A recent extended and lively review is that of Kubie [5], who, oddly, writes as if Freud had not covered the same ground four decades before.) The issue for our discussion now is the latest version of this struggle: "sex change."*

I shall not, in this commentary, present data from a properly constructed

---

*I shall use "sex change" rather than "sex transformation," "sex reassignment," "sex conversion," "sex surgery," or "gender transmutation" because "sex change" is the shortest, most direct, and least euphemistic expression of what the patients desire, and therefore most clearly measures the failure of the effort to change sex. When quote marks are used, I am referring to the effort; without quotes, I indicate the wish. At present it is not possible to change sex; the punctuation is used to indicate the falsity of the claim that such an option exists.

piece of scientific work; my experience is too meager for that. Instead, I speak from a knowledge of the literature and from working with a scattered sample of patients selected in an unplanned manner, as part of a study on masculinity and femininity (not on "transsexualism").

More than with most objects of endocrinologic and surgical interest, the desire to change sex reaches deep into most of us. But the elemental passions that result have invaded the medical procedures and also the research that surround the treatment. We should all wonder—and out loud, not secretly in the corridors—to what extent scientific exploration and medical decisions are adulterated by the personal biases of the experts. When, for instance, does high morality corrupt one's research?

These introductory remarks serve, then, not only to justify my lack of good enough data but to suggest that those with more data may not really be more objective, or, in certain important ways, more informed.

### SUMMARY OF HORMONAL AND SURGICAL PROCEDURES

There can be few physicians not at least sketchily familiar with the procedures that lead to "sex change"; this review serves only to remind you of these practices in order to establish my perspective that all aspects of this subject are controversial. There are three main medical contributions to the treatment:

1) Secondary sex characteristics are to be reversed, primarily by hormones (and in the case of males, electrolysis for hair removal).
2) Surgically, in the male, the testes and penis are removed, scrotum and penile skin preserved, perhaps a stump of the penis is kept to function as a clitoris, and a fascial plane dissected to produce the space that, when lined with penile skin and skin graft (some surgeons use gut) will be a vagina. Labia are built from the scrotum. Surgically, in females, breasts are removed, panhysterectomy performed, and—though with little success, I think—a phallus produced by grafts (but one that is nonfunctional erotically and often incapable of transporting urine).
3) The psychiatrist serves as the gatekeeper who decides which patients should receive these treatments. My impression is that most psychiatrists (in some regards, perhaps all of us) are incompetent for this task because the indications are unclear.

### A LIST OF CONTROVERSIES

All aspects of "sex change" treatment are controversial. Most people think there is just one controversy and that it is a new one: There should/should not be "sex change" surgery because the results are/are not good. But actually, many controversies are intertwined with that one, and they add up to a situation that, to me, smells to Heaven. Let us put our noses to it.

All the items below deserve some discussion and some a whole paper; but I shall, with most of them, settle for only listing them or for giving them a few words. Even so, you will at least be aware that a controversy is present. Although each of the following controversies has both its practical and theoretic aspects, let me arbitrarily divide this discussion into two categories.

A. Practical Issues in the Decision-making Process
1) Morality*
    (a) The libertarian position: The patients, most of the public, most physicians not involved in these treatments, and most physicians (including psychiatrists) who participate in the treatment respond to "sex change" as if it were an over-the-counter nostrum: Those who want it and can afford it can have it; let people have the treatments they choose; they will live with the consequences, good or bad.
    (b) The anti-libertarian position: "Sex change" should be forbidden. Almost all of the few psychoanalysts who have spoken on the matter believe "sex change" procedures are wrong in principle, for the treatments ignore the psychodynamic pathology at the bottom of transsexualism (6, 7, 8). (Transsexualism in these discussions is not precisely defined.) Transsexuals, from this perspective, create their transsexualism out of conflicts and defenses that hormones and surgery bypass. The patients deserve the best possible treatment, and that is not "sex change," which not only does no good, but also can lead to disastrous consequences. These writings often describe transsexualism as, at best, a facade that masks psychosis.

    A different anti-libertarianism is that of — surprisingly — the ultimate medical libertarian, Szasz. Although he feels that people must have the right to determine their own treatments and that dangerous, even mortally dangerous actions such as addiction and suicide are beyond our rights of interference, he takes the opposite position about the choice of having genitals removed. He finds that the term "transsexualism" is not just confusing or misapplied, but rather is "like much of the modern psychiatric mendacity characteristic of our day"; "sex change" is a fake, is abusive, and is antifeminist (9).
    (c) The religious position (e.g., the Bible, Canon Law): "Sex change"

---

*Note my putting morality and ethics on the practical, not theoretic, side.

destroys reproductive capacity and encourages homosexuality. It opposes Natural Law and therefore is a sin, since those who receive it do so responsibly, of their own choice, with free will.

2) Ethics: (If your positions are already set, you may not believe there are people on the opposite side of these positions; or if you know there are such people, you cannot believe their positions are ethical.) Which of the following are ethical? Says who?

(a) Surgeons who say that psychotherapy (including psychoanalysis) is not indicated, is not necessary, is useless, or is harmful.

(b) Psychotherapists (including analysts) who believe that surgery is not indicated, is not necessary, is useless, or is harmful.

(c) Physicians and hospitals who say the high financial costs are necessary and worth it.

(d) Psychiatrists who say that those who request "sex change" are either frank or disguised psychotics and that to change the body's outer form is collusion with delusion.

(e) Those who say that although the surgery is "psychosurgery" in that no physical illness is present, the results are worth the risks.

(f) Those who say that the procedures, hormonal and surgical, are still experimental and should be restricted to research institutions.

(g) Those who say that the procedures are not experimental but are established, accepted treatment within the community's standards.

(h) Those who say the surgeons and endocrinologists are only technicians, are not the primary decision-makers, are not—except for their technical skills—responsible agents throughout all stages of the treatment, whether at the stage when actively involved or not.

(i) Those who say that physicians who, in the media, promote themselves and their treatments, help patients by instructing them and the public.

3) Preoperative evaluations—to do or not to do? (You will not understand that controversy attends each of the following items unless you are informed that, for each, there actually are practicing physicians who, without feeling their work is incomplete, omit any or all of these next items.)

(a) History-taking back to childhood, with efforts at corroboration from families, friends, schools, etc.

(b) Extensive physical workup to determine if there are somatic contributions to the disturbed gender identity.

(c) Complete routine physical examination before administering hormones, surgery.

(d) Mental status examination to rule out psychosis (active or latent), severe depression, true psychopathy (vs. antisocial behavior secondary to the gender disorder), organic brain disorder, suicide risk.

(e) Extended psychologic examination (by interview, psychologic tests) to determine the gender identity diagnosis.

4) Among those physicians willing to offer treatment, what criteria should be used for deciding:

(a) Which patients shall be treated: primary transsexuals, secondary transsexuals, non-transsexuals, psychotics, children, family members; society.

(b) Which treatments: which preoperative management, which kind of psychotherapy, which behavior modification technique, which established or experimental hormonal/surgical procedures; exorcism.

(c) If the indications for treatment are legitimately different for private practitioners than for university research centers.

(d) If the indications for treatment are different for pragmatic treatment than for research (and its added costs).

5) Follow-up data collection — immediate and long-term — to do or not to do on the following issues:

(a) Results effected by hormones, surgery.

(b) Psychologic function.

(c) Social adjustment, including work.

(d) Effects on interpersonal relations.

(e)  Complications, physical and psychiatric.

6) Follow-up data collection — how to do (i.e., methodology).

7) Follow-up in order to offer continuing management and treatment:

(a) Psychologic management, including psychotherapies, to improve and extend results.

(b) Treatment of complications, physical and psychiatric.

8) Legal Issues — the following subjects are still controversial in the law:

(a) Documentation by means of one's sex — birth certificate, name, driver's license, marriage license, passport.

(b) Marriage, divorce, annulment.

(c) Contracts.

(d) Estate planning (e.g., if the will leaves a bequest to a son but the latter is now legally changed to a female).

(e) Community property.

(f) Medical (governmental or private insurance) and welfare payments; eligibility for rehabilitative services.

(g) Adoption of children.

(h) A spouse's claim that "sex change" interfered with the marriage contract.

(i) Cross-dressing as evidence of intent to defraud.

(j) Cohabitation with people of one's original sex is homosexuality.

(k) Surgery as negligence, mayhem.

(l) Informed consent.

B. Theoretic Issues

1) Criteria for diagnosis.

2) Differential diagnosis.

3) Research techniques for discovering and measuring strength of attitudes about masculinity, femininity, social adjustment, happiness and unhappiness, goodness and badness.

  (a) Statistically adequate samples vs. *n* of 1 in depth.

  (b) Whose opinion do we use—patients', families', researchers', neutral judges', the treating physicians'?

  (c) Influence of researchers' moral and scientific scruples on their conclusions.

4) Hypotheses about etiology:

  (a) Somatic (e.g., prenatal hormones, X-Y antigen, diencephalic centers for same-sex erotism).

  (b) Psychologic: psychodynamics, conditioning.

  (c) Social.

  (d) Reincarnation.

5) Origins of gender identity.

Let us now look more closely at a few of these items.

### The Recent, Visible Controversy

In 1979, Meyer and Reter published a paper (10) that, coming from the most noted of all programs for "sex change," that at Johns Hopkins, had great impact. They followed up 50 of a sample of 100 patients who applied for surgery; of the 50 followed up, 15 had had surgery. Of the 35 unoperated, 14 eventually had surgery and 21 were still interested in having it (making up, therefore, an oddly formed sample from which conclusions should be drawn with caution). To save myself a rewrite summary, I quote Hunt and Hampson (11):

> The outcome criteria were based on residential change, psychiatric contact, legal involvement, Hollingshead job level, and gender appropriate sexual cohabitation choices. . . . The report did not separate male and

female subjects or assess changes in interpersonal relationships, family acceptance, or psychopathology other than psychiatric contacts as outcome variables. The subjects who had had surgery showed a trend toward improvement, but the improvement was not significantly different from that in the subjects who did not submit to a gender-trial period and receive surgery (p. 433).

To quote Meyer and Reter:

> Socioeconomically, operated and unoperated patients changed little, if at all, with operated patients demonstrating no superiority in job or education . . . five-year follow-up is certainly ample to demonstrate socioeconomic improvement and stability. The failure of the operated group to demonstrate [in that time] clear objective superiority over the unoperated is all the more striking (p. 1014) . . . Sex reassignment surgery confers no objective advantage in terms of social rehabilitation, although it remains subjectively satisfying to those who have rigorously pursued a trial period and who have undergone it (p. 1015).

Therefore, "sex change" was discontinued at Johns Hopkins, where, years before, enthusiasm for the treatment had been brought to public attention.

Rebuttals appear as fast as the laborious process of publication permits. They will continue (11, 12, 13, 14). They focus on the methodology of data-collecting in the Johns Hopkins study. Hunt and Hampson, after reviewing earlier published follow-up studies and pointing to the problems in them, examined the methodology of the Meyer and Reter work. They disagreed that the unoperated patients were really a control on the operated group, for some of the unoperated group eventually were operated, and there is reason to think that in time more still will try for "sex change." In addition, they stated:

> Although it is certainly useful to know what happens to individuals who do not have surgery, it is not valid to use them as a control. An approximation of a control group might be those who are willing and able to go through the trial period but are not offered surgery because of overly masculine features. Those who are unable or unwilling to go through the trial period would appear to be so dissimilar from those who had surgery as to even raise questions about the diagnosis (p. 433).

They then reported on their own series of 17 operated cases:

> The subjects as a whole improved in the areas of economic adjustment, interpersonal relationships, sexual adjustment, and acceptance by the

family, which had the highest rate of improvement. There were no changes in level of psychopathology, as judged by their criminal activities, drug abuse, and degree of psychopathology, that interfered with work or interpersonal relationships (p. 434). . . . None of the 17 transsexuals regretted the decision to have surgery. . . . In spite of the considerable pain, expense, and delay, they would all choose the same course (p. 435). . . .In our study the strongest positive gains were in the areas of sexual adjustment and family acceptance, which were either not recorded or not evaluated in earlier studies (p. 436). (See also [15].)

Still more recently appeared an editorial by Fleming, Steinman, and Bocknek (14). They say, in regard to the Meyer and Reter study:

> The major variables used to assess adjustment before and after the surgery were arrest records, cohabitation with members of the "appropriate" or "inappropriate" sex, psychiatric records, and employment history. Perhaps the most serious failing of the study has to do with Meyer's selection and definition of these as his only major outcome variables (p. 452).

They disagreed with the method used to rate adjustment.

> For example, it assigns the same score ($-1$) to someone who is arrested and someone who cohabits with a non-gender-appropriate person. From this same set of cryptic values comes the assertion that being arrested and jailed ($-2$) is not as bad as being admitted to a psychiatric hospital ($-3$) or that having a job as a plumber (Hollingshead level 4) is as good ($+2$) as is being married to a member of the gender-appropriate sex ($+2$).
> On what basis are these values assigned? Should we infer from a score assignment of ($-1$) that anyone who has any psychiatric contact is in trouble? Psychiatry has for too long proselytized that all of us can gain from seeking psychiatric guidance for Meyer to reassign a stigma to seeking such help (pp. 452–3).

Next they attack the variable of cohabitation, finding that Meyer and Reter do not say what they mean by this term and that the positive or negative ratings are arbitrary; and, is "living in isolation . . . more adaptive than living with someone whatever his/her sex?" (p. 453). They proceed through other categories, raising questions whether Meyer and Reter's conclusions can be legitimately drawn from the uncertain methods used for collecting information, that Meyer and Reter's "objective factors are filled with great ambiguities and [we] wonder if reporting emotional data could have been any worse. Meyer and Reter seem to forget the value judgments that underlie their study almost as if assignment of a numerical value rids one of the findings' subjective and qualitative elements and thus raises one's findings to a level of 'pure science' " (p. 455).

Satterfield (13) has reported on 22 patients operated on at the University of Minnesota. Follow-up revealed "a significant improvement in psychological functioning."

By far the most complete review of follow-up studies I know is that of Lothstein (12). His opinion is the same as mine:

> Those who believe sex reassignment surgery is beneficial for certain patients must acknowledge the lack of hard empirical evidence supporting their views and the lack of even acceptable diagnostic criteria for selecting good SRS [sex reassignment surgery] candidates. Those who argue against SRS must account for the reported widespread patient satisfaction with the procedures and evidence of resulting positive life changes. . . . In spite of the many clinical research studies on transsexualism, very little is actually known about the medical-surgical, social-psychological effects of SRS. Many questions are left unanswered. For example, which, if any, patients derive the most benefit from SRS? What data support the continued use of SRS as a treatment regimen? What is the crucial test for determining the prescription of SRS?
>
> . . . In order to apply the results of . . . follow-up studies to the wider group of postsurgical transsexuals, we must determine whether those who have been studied represent an adequate cross section of all SRS patients. If not, this sampling bias is a primary methodological problem inherent in all of the published SRS studies. A review of those studies reveals other serious methodological problems including: a lack of universally accepted criteria for diagnosing gender dysphoria and determining suitable SRS candidates; lack of an adequate control group; considerable variability among gender identity clinic programs, as well as the quality, training, and experience of clinical staff; failure to include basic data on patients' race and age; frequent use of non-operationalized criteria for improvement — such as patients' subjective feelings of happiness; use of college grade level systems for evaluating outcome; failure to provide data on the length of time between evaluation, surgery, and follow-up; failure to employ uniform diagnostic labels; failure to use standardized clinical instruments to assess patients, even within a single study; limitation of clinical investigation to gross, social-psychological variables, ignoring indepth psychological analysis; use of hypothetical post hoc analyses to provide missing presurgical data; and use of biased evaluators interpreting outcome data. This list is by no means exhaustive.

In brief, the question is whether the Johns Hopkins study is methodologically too flawed to permit one to draw conclusions.

This controversy leads to broader questions—much more important, I think, than those about "sex change." How do we find what a person is thinking? How do we assign quantities to beliefs? Out of what immeasurable components are the algebraic sum responses "Yes" and "No" composed? When attitudes are as complex, as multilayered, as ambiguous, as ambivalent, as undefined as "happiness" and "unhappiness" and "goodness" and "badness" (because those are what Meyer and Reter, Hunt and Hampson, Fleming, Steinman and Bocknek, and all the rest are really trying to track down), how are we to judge a 4 rating on a scale of 1 to 10? And may not the researchers' morality be even more important in these controversies than this fuzzy business of measuring "happiness" (a.k.a. "adjustment")?*

How useful are questionnaires and standardized interviews for issues close to the heart? Which is better, and when: data collected by a stranger or near-stranger, one's therapist, a family member? Would an answer be different at a different time of day, or a different day, a different year? In a different setting? Told to a questioner who has a different style of relating to the person questioned?

These rating methods, with their sophisticated (sophistical?) sampling techniques, their controls, their statistical constraints, work as well for fools, hacks, liars, propagandists, cultists, and innocents as they do for hard-core geniuses or even honest workers. When does a larger *n* not flatten all obstacles?

We are better off remembering that questionnaires and statistics in some circumstances are risky, that there is a price paid when we try to get guarded people to give fast answers to sensitive questions. Anyone who comes to know others, by treating them or by living with them, gets a different sense of their attitudes as the relationship deepens. But researchers usually do not have the time, interest, or—sometimes—ability to allow intimacy and trust to grow. The challenge is to get good data faster and yet not contaminate the results.

You need not worry I might forget that the case studied in depth also generates dubious data. When being my analyst, I can see good reasons, in some circumstances, for not trusting my first response—or sometimes the fifth—to my own questions. Should we not, then, for the sake of science, check the motives—not just the tables—of all researchers (from analysts to statisticians) studying values-laden attitudes? Can we suspect our colleagues sometimes start out already with the answers? Is not "sex change" a treatment easily contaminated by personal and professional beliefs, commitments, anx-

---

*Let us not fool ourselves: Research on "transsexualism" or "sex change" is as soggy with morality and righteousness as a rum cake is with booze.

ieties, defenses? We should not pretend these issues cannot infiltrate each step in our work.

### CONTROVERSY: VOCABULARY, DEFINITIONS, CONCEPTS

Although this is not a paper on origins of the desire for sex change, most discussions of the treatment issues struggle, for good reason, with problems about etiology and its relation to diagnosis. For instance, if we think the urge results primarily from a shift in diencephalic function caused by opposite-sex prenatal hormones (16) or reversal of H-Y antigen (17, 18), the patient talking to us stirs us differently than if we think the same patient's condition is heavily influenced by intrapsychic conflict or by aberrant family dynamics (19, 20).

A concept that can carry the data related to these sorts of etiologic explanations is "core gender identity," the sense — the conviction — of being a male or of being a female (not just of being masculine or feminine). It begins to develop from birth on, is established in the first two or three years of life, and is pretty much fixed by age three and a half to five. It is the product of biologic factors (such as effects of prenatal hormones on the CNS), sex assignment, and parental influences in infancy and early childhood.

By no means is core gender identity synonymous with "gender identity" — the totality of one's masculinity and femininity. Gender identity results from development of which core gender identity is only the first stage and to which later experiences — oedipal conflicts and their resolutions, latency, puberty, adolescence, and all the rest of one's life — contribute heavily.

In the vast majority of people, core gender identity is clear-cut and easily determined. However, those with sorely disordered gender identity, especially those who want "sex change," complicate, with their facades, disguises, confusions, and complex mixes of masculine and feminine elements, our task of finding that core. And if that fundament has in it a sense of being both male and female — as is found in some hermaphrodites and, in a different way, in primary transsexuals (see below) — then our evaluation requires unusual experience and skill.

But hermaphrodites and primary transsexuals make up only a handful of those who want "sex change." The rest (I shall be referring to them as secondary transsexuals), though they have severe disturbances in masculinity and femininity, strike me as having a pretty intact sense of maleness or femaleness. Their psychopathology is in good part the result of defenses raised to protect that sense of identity (21). For some of these people, then, destroying their anatomic definition of self assaults their core gender identity and leads to such unhappy sequelae as psychosis, depression, or the need to be once more reassigned, this time to their original sex.

Let us move on to the term "transsexualism." By now most physicians are familiar with the fact that "transsexualism," used as a diagnosis, is a problem. Still, a review and a more detailed discussion will help me with our main task: to think on the controversy regarding the ethics and efficacy of physicians' efforts to change people's sex. There are—though not everyone knows this—multiple meanings for "transsexualism" and no generally accepted definition. Although "ism" implies a state, a condition, a dynamically organized complex of behaviors and thoughts, the label is most frequently used, by both laymen and physicians, to refer to anyone who wants or anyone who has a reassignment of sex. As a result, a term with a scientific, diagnostic ring to it—transsexualism—in fact bears no such weight. At best, one might consider this usage to refer to a syndrome, but even that is not accurate, since within the request for "sex change" or the accomplishing of it are myriad behaviors and attitudes. Certainly, when one is familiar with a number of such people, one recognizes that transsexualism, as the term is commonly used, does not refer even to a syndrome but rather to a mix of different syndromes, symptoms, signs, desires, proclamations. And if a diagnosis is a label for a set of interdependent signs and symptoms (syndrome), underlying dynamics (physiologic and/or psychologic), with common etiology, then "transsexualism" falls as far short as would descriptions such as "cough," "abdominal pain," "greed," "stamp collecting," or "desire to be a psychiatrist." The individuals who experience any one of these states share in less than they differ.

This play with words is not a pedantic indulgence. Instead, it points us in that direction so necessary for sensible decisions in medical treatment: the differential diagnosis. Having written too often on this subject, I hate to do so again but must in order to make certain clinical problems clear.

I divide those who wish for or have already received "sex change" into the following categories (which, as with most psychiatric diagnoses, are more clearly defined in print than in the clinic). In the following, because only males fit several of the categories, I shall mostly present a differential for males.

### Primary Transsexuals

These are anatomically and physiologically normal males who are, at the time you examine them, the most natural-appearing feminine males you have ever seen. In their ordinary daily behavior, they are indistinguishable from girls and women considered feminine by their society. This description is true at whatever age you see them: early childhood, later childhood, adolescence, young adulthood, middle age, or senescence. They give a history that they have been this feminine all their lives, from the beginning of any behavior that can be called masculine or feminine (which may be as early as a year) and with no episodes of masculinity or of even transient commitments to typically masculine roles (such as marriage, masculine professions, service in the military, heterosexual erotic behavior). They know they are biologically male, but, since early in life, they have openly said that they want their bodies changed to female. From early childhood, they have wished to dress and live exclusively as do females. They get no erotic pleasure from putting on females' clothes. They do not consider themselves homosexual, except in the anatomic sense that they are turned on exclusively to males, and they reject sexual advances made by overtly homosexual men; a prime measure to them that a man is homosexual is that the latter is interested in the transsexual's male genitals.

(Note: For years, this was the group I called transsexuals [or true transsexuals], relegating the rest of those requesting "sex change" to some vaguer category, such as "pseudo-transsexual" or "non-transsexual seeking sex reassignment" [19, 20]. However, this confused colleagues, since for them "transsexual" had always had the broader meanings of a person who wants sex change or who claims to be trapped in the wrong body. I feel that it is better, therefore, to accept the common usage. We can then add clinical strength to our labeling if the subcategories of primary and secondary are used.)

### Secondary Transsexuals

This is a wastebasket category made up of men requesting "sex change" whose life history is different from the primary transsexual in that the cross-gender behavior does not begin in earliest childhood, is punctuated with episodes of unremarkably masculine behavior, and (with rare exceptions) is laced with experiences of pleasure from the male genitals.

I can make out four life patterns that precede the announcement by these people that they are transsexuals and therefore have a right to "sex change." The most common, I think (there are no adequate statistics, so one cannot be sure) is via a progression over years, during which the patient feels himself to be a homosexual, with a slant toward the feminine or effeminate side, with, in time, a sense that one would do better if female. The second group proceeds via transvestism (fetishistic cross-dressing); after a longer or shorter period of putting on women's garments to get excited, these men notice they enjoy dressing less for erotic pleasure than to feel like (their version of) a woman. The third group arrives at the desire for sex change via a more or less exclusively overtly heterosexual commitment, including marriage, fatherhood, and a work history in typically masculine pursuits. In the fourth, there has been no strong commitment to any erotic style—heterosexual, homosexual, or perverse — but instead only a weak or absent erotic need in a man who had not been manifestly aberrant in gender behavior. (I have not studied such a patient, though I worked for years with one who made such a claim.)

## Intersexuals

These are genotypic and/or phenotypic males with a clear-cut somatic disorder of sex (e.g., chromosomal defects, certain forms of hermaphroditism) accompanied by a strong sense of belonging to the sex opposite to that to which one was assigned and committed at birth.

## Psychotics

Many men with paranoid psychoses suffer delusions and hallucinations related to being insufficiently manly (e.g., that they are homosexual, that they are womanly, or that their bodies are being changed in a female direction). In addition, and far rarer, there are reports of men with transient psychoses for whom the transsexual impulses are consciously desirable, not threatening; when these men are given "sex change" treatment, the psychoses remit.

In order to resolve uncertainties of diagnosis and the resulting controversies regarding who would benefit from which treatment, the fulsome phrase "gender dysphoria syndrome" was introduced (22, 23). It represents the awareness that although "transsexualism" sounds like a well-secured diagnosis, it is not. The clinical reality is that the desire to change sex is found in many types of gender-disordered people. Those who prefer "gender dysphoria syndrome" do so because they feel the desire for "sex change" can only be judged a *syndrome*, a collection of signs and symptoms, not the larger degree of understanding implied by *diagnosis.**

Despite this advantage, I do not use "gender dysphoria syndrome." First, we are *not* dealing with a syndrome, that is, a complex of signs and symptoms, but rather with a desire (wish, demand) that is embedded in all sorts of different people who suffer all sorts of signs and symptoms. To talk of a gender dysphoria syndrome, then, is like talking of a suicide syndrome, or an incest syndrome, or a wanderlust syndrome.

Second, "gender dysphoria syndrome" is meant as a reaction against the effort at differential diagnosis. The label serves as a statement that people with disorders of masculinity and femininity make up a continuum, not a series of discrete entities, as implied by a differential diagnosis. That is true, as it is in so much of psychiatric diagnosing,** (especially with neuroses and

---

*However, the author of the term, when introducing it, said the syndrome is a disease (22).
**"In DSM-III there is no assumption that each mental disorder is a discrete entity with sharp boundaries (discontinuity) between it and other mental disorders" (24, p. 6).

character disorders), but it is also slippery. The concepts "clinical entity" and "continuum" are no more incompatible in gender disorders than in the spectrum of visible light: One cannot say where red ends and orange begins, but red is not yellow. It is not even orange.* For me, the advantage of trying to separate out clinical entities from the morass of gender disorders lies especially in our being able to search for etiologies if we do not dissolve the differences in one mix called "gender dysphoria syndrome." By separating out, say, primary from secondary transsexualism and the transvestite route to secondary transsexualism from the homosexual route, we *can* find clusters that differ from each other clinically and in certain etiologic factors. (These exercises have been published elsewhere [25].)

In brief, then, "gender dysphoria syndrome" ends up with most of the disadvantages that "transsexualism" has when the latter is used by the general public and the medical profession at large. Both terms say too little because they cover too much. Nonetheless, I find "gender dysphoria syndrome" better than the pseudo-diagnosis "transsexualism" in that the wording of the former indicates that it is not masquerading as a diagnosis and therefore cannot aid in the abuses promoted by the pseudo-diagnosis.**

When, for different purposes, I look at the gender disorders as if they form continua rather than discrete entities, I work with the following hypotheses: In anatomically normal males, there will be more femininity the more intimately and the longer the boys are in an extremely loving and intimate symbiosis with their mothers and the less their fathers are present as models for masculinity and as shields to stand between the boy and his mother's needs to maintain that excessively close symbiosis. The first prediction, then, is that the more we see these family dynamics, the more we shall expect to find femininity in the boy. The prediction works as well from the opposite direction: If we have an anatomically normal, feminine male of any age, the amount of the femininity and the amount (if any) of masculinity also present will be determined when we examine how many of the above family dynamics are present and in what proportions. In other words, we can make our predictions either by knowing the dynamics and estimating the result or by knowing the result and then estimating what the dynamics had been in the boy's infancy. I predict, then, on studying a secondary transsexual that both the exces-

---

*The clinical situation, I know, is not quite as simple as the metaphor suggests, but I let the metaphor stand rather than inflict on the reader the lengthy description of dozens of cases with which I could support the argument.

**The most glaring of these abuses is the patient who, wanting to change sex, gives his desire the diagnostic label and, thereby legitimized, expects the treatment to follow. By awarding himself a diagnosis, he converts an impulse into a disease.

sively close mother-infant symbiosis and withdrawn and passive father of primary transsexualism will be less and less likely as one finds more and more masculine elements. The data confirm the prediction (19, 20).

Here are findings on female transsexuals that complete this review of the differential diagnosis (See also 20, Chapter 18.) First, the differentiation between primary and secondary transsexualism is less clear in females in that almost all who request "sex change" do so after a longer or shorter period of overt homosexuality. Second, fetishistic cross-dressing being almost unknown in women, it is not one of the routes to the request for sex change. Third, I recall no cases of genotypic or phenotypic females nor any of psychotic females who requested sex change to males.

So much for this vocabulary exercise on the word "transsexualism." Let us now take up a few more terms that, without discussion, might leave us confused: "sex change," "sex transformation," "sex reassignment."

Although there can be sex reassignment, there cannot yet be — I believe — sex change or sex transformation. Sex reassignment is a social phenomenon to be accomplished by legal means and by convincing others to accept one's changed role (new name, new clothes, new job, new voice, etc.). In brief, the term does not imply that one has changed sex, for that would require chromosomal and anatomic reversal, but only that an assignment — and therefore a role — has changed. Guppies can change sex; humans cannot. Cosmetic surgery and manipulating secondary sex characteristics with hormones or electrolysis create biologic facsimiles only (26).

These meanings are not arbitrary rulings but, rather, touch on fundamental treatment issues. For instance, those who state that sex is truly changed do so in order to legitimize the treatment and thereby make it more available. On the other hand, those primary transsexuals I have followed for years all know it is impossible to change sex by ingesting hormones and by altering the appearance of genitals; in saying this, they are communicating the despair that came from their knowledge. You must understand that they believe that "sex change," as helpful as it was, could not give them what they most wanted: a true change of their sex (20, Chapter 20).

## WHO DECIDES WHEN "SEX CHANGE" IS INDICATED

As with any medical treatment, "sex change" should have reliably established indications so that patients are not harmed and are also helped. That would seem an absurd statement for this day and age, it being so obvious. And yet, although the treatment has been visible, desired, and increasingly accepted since 1953, the arguments about its suitability persist, intensified. Here is a treatment situation in which powerful hormones are used without restriction; they not only change body form and destroy reproductive capacity but have unknown effects in each sex with prolonged use. Surgical procedures are also easily dispensed (not freely — they are very expensive), though they destroy reproduction and, being of significant technical difficulty, inherently have operative and anesthetic morbidity, if not mortality.

And all this is for unclear indications. You must understand, if you do not already know it, that the criteria for suitability have never been established. In the 1950s, when I first made contact with such patients, there seemed no great problem in this regard; if the surgeons felt someone was suitable, they operated, as often as not independent of psychiatric evaluation. In the 1960s I became increasingly upset about this medical free-wheeling and that no one heavily involved in working with these patients expressed concern. (There were, of course, those with little direct experience who lectured us on the origins, dynamics, and clinical picture, and on the indications for and morality of treatment [e.g., 6, 7, 8, 26].) By the 1970s, no follow-ups had appeared other than a few sketchy and anecdotal reviews or meager, uncontrolled series, reports that would be unacceptable elsewhere in medicine. Most of all, there was still no controversy, among those treating the patients, about the wisdom of the procedures. (I tried to get these experts' attention [19, 20, 27, 28, 29] but have seen no published response. Even Kubie and Mackie's tongue-lashing [26], filled with good sense, passion, and prejudice, created no stir, perhaps because they were not working with transsexuals.) Had I not observed this disreputable business, it would surely seem bizarre now.

What was going on? Let me, in answering, turn to (on) the groups responsible. In order of increasing blame, they are the public, the patients, the uninvolved medical community, the non-psychiatric physicians who are applying their treatments, the media, and finally the mental health professionals, with psychologists and psychiatrists in first place.

*The public.* The public — in this case meaning just about everyone — has always been intrigued by this primally disquieting subject. Here sits an enthusiastic audience for the drama of sex change.

*The patients.* Once upon a time, there were, of course, no transsexuals. We had not invented the disorder or the solution, and so there was no problem. I know of only a handful of reports, before our present era, on males or females with so powerful a transsexul wish that they reassigned themselves to the opposite sex (30); undoubtedly there were plenty more, silent, hopeless. Less implacably driven people — homosexual, transvestic, or whatever — lived more or less humbly with whatever compromises they could manage. But now there seems a cure for this unhappiness, and with the propaganda published in and out of medical circles, anyone with a troubled gender identity hopes to be made whole quickly and efficiently. Encouraged by the lack of criteria for diagnosis or indications for treatment, and not told otherwise by the experts, these people diagnose themselves as transsexuals and, encouraged by what they have read and heard, recommend themselves for hormones and surgery. Their only task, they believe, is to force wide the gates to the treatment to which they feel entitled.

*The uninvolved medical profession.* The two major medical aspects of "sex-change"—hormones and surgery—are powerful manipulations of anatomy and physiology, with short-term consequences that have never been studied by the standards accepted elsewhere in medicine and with unknown long-term consequences. Yet the physicians not personally involved in the treatment have raised no questions, shown no concern in their professional organizations, literature, or schools. There must be few other circumstances in the history of modern medicine comparable to this.

*Non-psychiatric physicians involved in treatment.* Endocrinologists, surgeons, and others—specialists or not—who would create change of sex divest themselves of responsibility for their treatments (beyond the immediate responsibilities that always come with, say, giving injections, anesthesia, or surgery). They note that they are only the technical arm—the machinery, as it were—and that the decision for them to act is made by the psychiatrist. (Let us ignore here the individuals or jurisdictions where no demand is made for psychiatric approval or the situation we know sometimes occurs: psychiatrists who rubberstamp their approvals.) The contribution of this group to the present mess—controversy is too nice a word—is their abdication of good sense when they are beyond the reach of their prescription pads or operating rooms. Uncharacteristically content to be blind servants, admitting lack of interest in the psychiatric aspects of this issue, and uninterested in reporting on immediate and long-term complications, they have failed our profession and society at large. But the blame is not mainly theirs.

*The media.* Certain journalists, TV gossipists, movie-makers, and publishers have linked the patients' and the doctors' exhibitionism to the public's pleasure in freak shows in a venture profitable to all the participants. In this trade where everyone is satisfied for a price, the media are the pushers.

*Mental health professionals.* Here are found those most responsible for this shameful episode in the history of medical practice. These people, not really surprisingly, have been as susceptible to the primeval desires and anxieties at the bottom of the interest in "sex-change" as everyone else. And they have been happy to feed the curiosity of the less-informed. Poor research, poor practice, poor data, and poor ideas have gone hand in hand with high visibility, in pandering, along with the media, to feeding the misperceptions of public and patients.

It need not have been this way had the medical profession acted with integrity. It is obvious that "sex-change" is an exciting subject, and no one is surprised that it has been popular. But our profession could have short-circuited the reactions that led to today's obvious controversies. The controversies were there from the start. It is medicine's fault that they were ignored all these years. Instead, we have done poorly by the public, our patients, and ourselves. We failed in two ways. First, we should have insisted the treatment be kept experimental, in that way restricting its use and development to responsible investigators. Better quality work could have been done; we know from the good examples set by several university clinics. Second, had this cautious approach been valued, the public and patients could have been educated to know that these treatments were not freely available, were uncertain in their effects, had their physical and emotional dangers — in other words were controversial from the start.

Who can blame the patients for their high hopes before "sex change"? They are deeply troubled people. When social disgrace is added to intrapsychically induced conflict, it takes no great intuition to sense these patients' suffering and how happy they are on learning that there is supposedly a cure for their suffering. If they can wrap all their troubles into one bundle called transsexualism, then happiness forevermore awaits them after a morning in the OR.

From public, to patients, to medicine at large, to the endocrinologists and surgeons, to the media, everyone acted mostly from self-interest, with minimal ethical friction. But what about the mental health professionals — psychologists, social workers and especially psychiatrists?

On the other hand, there are those — physicians and others — who feel hormones and surgery should never be used. How well have these advisors performed? From where came their convictions?

Their argument is based on the sensible position that the surest treatment is that which aims to modify causes of disorder. The desire to change sex originates, they feel, in profound conflicts and is the manifestation of defensive maneuvers invented to ease the pain of these conflicts. Therefore, treatment should consist first in discovering the conflicts and their dynamics and, those insights captured, in freeing the patient to find better solutions. From this point of view, to condone the use of hormones and surgery and to encourage the patient to live as if a member of the opposite sex is to allow the patient to remain maximally and permanently ill. Just as you would not, as a matter of treatment, agree with a grandiose paranoid that he really was Napoleon, so you should not agree with the patient who insists he or she is in the wrong body. (That a patient even makes such a claim is, in this argument, prima facie evidence of delusion; and delusion is psychosis; and psychosis is to be rooted out.)

Even if we grant that this reasoning is correct (and I do not believe it always is), we are left with an empirical question: Why are there no reports of the successful psychoanalysis of a patient who wanted "sex change"? Why are there not even any reports that reveal, with data gathered from an analysis, the dynamics — not to say, the causes — of this desire to sex change? What is the purpose of demanding that analysis — a treatment unproven for profound gender disorder, terribly complex, and expensive — be the only one allowed?

We should not, however, confuse this position with the one saying that many of those seeking sex change could, with a careful psychiatric evaluation and psychotherapy, discover that what they want is not provided by hormones and surgery (31–41). Lothstein and Levine (41) have given us the best review there is of the literature on the problems and uses of psychotherapy in helping patients with strong transsexual urges. Beyond that, Lothstein, in a series of papers (34–41), has written more and with more thought than anyone else on the indications for and types of psychotherapy most suited for particular clinical issues. His work confirms the impression a few of us had expressed: Many patients who insist they need "sex change" are really far from sure, even including some who have passed successfully. Although gender disorder rarely remits with psychotherapy, patients find themselves and in doing so become aware that "sex change" will not suit their gender identity.

I still do not know to what extent hormones and surgery are worth using in those patients who, shortly after or years after treatment, say they are glad to have undergone "sex change" even though they know they could not truly change their sex. For me, none of the reports, before or since that of Meyer and Reter, settles the issue. Stubbornly, I am still more impressed by the few patients I have followed for years than by the larger numbers of patients that colleagues report on by means of standardized ratings.* None of those I have followed feel that they have used their lives well, though all are happy that they had a "sex change" and all say they would not change their present problems and miseries for what existed before treatment (20). But we physicians cannot forget that the cost of this equivocal happiness may be high: in dollars, complications, professionals' time, and low yield to society at large. And because we have done such a terrible job of follow-up, we cannot measure the size of that cost or the counter-balancing value of patients' relief in living in their new sex. We can only give our private, morality-laden, ethics-laden opinions.

Are these controversies due to investigators having different data? Yes.

---

*This is not to say that I do not respect a more scientific methodology. I mean only that, so far, the data being fed into the computer are far less reliable than the machine's capacity to calculate.

Different methods of collecting data? Yes. Different interpretations of the same or comparable data? Yes. When data depend on follow-ups, are positions weakened because patients are flagrantly unreliable? Yes. But these factors do not fully explain the controversies. The reasons are more human, more awful. Although, as you have seen, I have not presented a compelling argument—that would require clean and adequate amounts of data—I believe that almost all of those involved in research on "sex change," no matter which sides of which controversies they take, have reported data that are suspect and conclusions that are not yet supported by facts: Methodology and a rhetoric of objectivity are molded to fit conclusions sought. (Is that not true for most hot controversies?)

This happened, I think, because, beneath the visible controversies on research and treatment are deep old moral issues. Hook us up to a plethysmograph and watch the dials spin when we hear: "homosexual," "bisexual," "heterosexual," "fetishist," "promiscuity," "masturbation," "sexual intercourse," "penis," "vagina," "breasts," "hair." Until we acknowledge the moral issues researchers on sex carry to their laboratories and clinics, it will be mighty hard to trust the data. But is that not the case in so much of the psychiatrist's body of knowledge, far beyond these problems of sexuality? Are we not all aware of the unending risk that private morality corrupts public objectivity? Here are items from our working vocabulary, a language shot through with moral judgments: "ego strength," "psychopathy," "perversion," "latent psychosis," "narcissism," "masochism," "compulsion," "alcoholism," "reaction formation," "identification with the aggressor," "primitive," "schizoid," "poor judgment," "infantile," "anal erotic," "counterphobic," "resistance," "denial," "negative transference," "low frustration tolerance," "therapeutic alliance," "hysterical," "passive," "aggressive," "neurotic," How about even "doctor" or "patient"? Ours is a "scientific" lexicon that is easily misused in order to hide a therapist's private and shamefaced evaluation of a patient. (We hardly dare say—even to ourselves—"brave" or "cowardly," "selfish" or "generous," "cooperative" or "manipulative," "warm" or "cold," "secretive" or "open," "worthwhile" or "a scoundrel," "dirty" or "clean," "moral" or "immoral," "cruel" or "kind," "good" or "bad.") Everyone knows all this.

We like and dislike patients (often at the same time) and translate those convictions, sometimes with good cause, into "treatable" or "untreatable," "good prognosis" or "guarded." Patients who display some aspect of our ego ideal, such as courage, honesty, capacity to love, will be forgiven a lot of pathology; those whose behavior incites us must bear our wrath, though we may be too well-mannered, insensitive, or unconscious to express it openly. Morality may be the stiffest countertransference of all.

### COMPLICATIONS

What goes wrong in "sex change" treatments? No more sickening remark could be made in this age of modern medicine than that, for the mishaps on the following list, there are no statistics about frequency, severity, or mortality: the usual morbidities and mortalities associated with anesthesia and extensive surgery (e.g., hemorrhage, anuria, cardiac arrest, embolus), perforation of viscera, failure of the grafted phallus to take in females, scarring of the artificial vagina in males with loss of some or all patency, chronic cystitis, strange-looking genitals, abnormal urethra with resulting abnormal urinary stream, sloughing of skin grafts, chronic infections (of vaginas or postmastectomy); paranoid psychosis, psychotic depression, chronic though nonpsychotic depression, suicide, hopelessness, regret at the "sex change"; lawsuits.

What are the long-term effects, if any, of chronic opposite-sex hormone intake? Does cancer ever result? How many female patients now have normally functioning male genitals? How many males have received a normal-looking vulva or a vagina that retained its full size without scarring down? How many patients need further surgery to correct the effects of complications? I know of no acceptable report on complications, as if they were beneath the dignity of the treating physicians to study, even in order to report — if it were true — that they are insignificant.

### CONCLUSIONS

After scattering about in this paper my opinions and biases, implications and pronouncements, I should now draw them together.

1) Little good has come from the social experiment of "sex change." We do not know how many patients have severe gender problems; how many have been treated; how many were helped and in what ways they were helped; how many are less well off and in what ways; what are the complications and how many patients suffer them; what are the names and forms of the disorders that bring patients for treatment; what are the etiologies, dynamics, and clinical manifestations of these conditions; which treatments are the best suited for which patients; what research should be done and how it should be carried out; what criteria we can use to judge reports written on the subject.

I wonder, as I write: Can the situation really be this bad? Without question, colleagues who have been more enthusiastic are as aware of the ethical issues and feel themselves to be as committed to ethical practice as those of us who are worried. There seem to have been no disastrous consequences for most patients. Most of the participants — patients and doctors — were responsible, informed, and willing partners, and most are more comfortable than less with the results. Perhaps we have been witness to nothing worse than a freak phenomenon, a lunatic fad that may now be burning itself out. It is possible that gender identity clinics — what a euphemism — will be closing down soon, the Pygmalions drifting off, the patients giving up their hope of the miraculous cure. If so, we shall probably be left with nothing in our armamentarium more glamorous than those difficult, uncertain, and all too modest techniques known as "management" and "psychotherapy," fortified, perhaps, by new developments in diagnosing and treating children and by effective and human behavior modification techniques.

2) I was, I believe, the first of those who had worked in depth with "sex change" patients not to share the enthusiasm that, by the late 1960s, had developed in regard to using hormones and surgery for treatment. My position now is what it was then: Most people requesting the change will not benefit much from it. They are better served by careful evaluation, psychotherapy, and/or behavior therapy. On the other hand, the years have not yet revealed treatments that, for a small number of patients, do as well as does "sex change." My impression is still that the most feminine of males and most masculine of females do better with "sex change" than without. Were surgery no longer available, primary transsexuals would be trapped, but most secondary transsexuals — by far the largest group seeking "sex change" — would be at least no worse off, free to find their identities and not literally cut off from themselves.

3) But impressions are not worth much if not augmented by strong data. In these years, I have also complained (and — let me add in bleak righteousness — with few others joining in) that we did not have enough data to judge competently which patients would do better with which treatment. Time has shown that we not only still do not have these data but that reliable methods for collecting the information have not yet been applied. No wonder we are not convinced when colleagues, even on the basis of their formal research, conclude pro or con about any aspect of "sex change."

4) Partly because of these problems of doing follow-up, but for other reasons still unclear, new treatment techniques are introduced, enthusiastically reported, but then do not take hold, e.g., behavior modification for adults (42), for children (43), psychotherapy for children (44).

5) My suggestion, starting years ago, that hormones and surgery be considered experimental and provided only in university research settings has since been endorsed by one or two colleagues but never implemented. Everyone has paid a price for that.

6) There has been some interest (e.g., 22) in my idea (19, 45) that a differential diagnosis of severe gender disorders be developed to improve both our

clinical work and our attempts to understand better the nature of gender identity. That effort, however, is blurred when we go for the wastebasket terms "transsexualism" or "gender dysphoria syndrome."

7) For all the scientific frosting in publications on "sex change" (e.g., updating of techniques of hormonal and surgical treatments, collecting of information on social variables, concern about sampling methods, statistical examination of pre- and post-treatment results), I do not find our colleagues' data more reliable than my impressionistic ones. In fact, the failure to study patients in depth, by means of years-long contact (as probably can only be done in an extended piece of psychotherapy), often leaves me quite uncertain about the real nature of the clinical statements compacted into the tables of numbers that reinforce most studies.

8) Years ago I felt that, regarding "sex change," whatever we did was wrong but that we might, with care, be able to do less wrong. I fear that the same is still true today; we have not moved the subject very far. After almost 30 years, the case for "sex change" is still unproven: both the treatments and the patients (of both sexes) have been, at most, near misses.

## REFERENCES

Note: There is a large literature — hundreds of papers — on many of these controversies, e.g., single case follow-ups, small series follow-ups, psychosis and transsexualism, varieties of surgical techniques, psychotherapy in transsexualism, behavior modification techniques in children and adults, differential diagnosis, etiology, methodology for follow-up research, animal studies, genetics, hormonal states, ethics, criteria for diagnosis, pre- and post-operative management, transsexualism and borderline states, psychodynamics of transsexualism. transsexual variants, psychoanalysis and transsexualism, cross-cultural studies, historical surveys, prevalence surveys, legal aspects, transsexualism and psychopathology. Only the following references, however, are chosen and these because they discuss aspects of controversies taken up at length in this paper.

1. HAMBURGER, C., STURUP, G. K., DAHL-IVERSON, E.: Transvestism: Hormonal psychiatric, and surgical treatment. *JAMA,* 152:319–396, 1953.
2. ABRAHAM, F.: Genitalumwandlung an zwei Maennlichen Transvestiten. *Z. Sexualwissenschaft,* 18:223–226, 1931.
3. FREUD, S. (1905): *Three Essays on the Theory of Sexuality. S. E. VII.* London: The Hogarth Press, 1953.
4. _____ (1937): Analysis Terminable and Interminable. *S. E. XXIII.* London: The Hogarth Press, 1964.
5. KUBIE, L. S.: The desire to become both sexes. *Psychoanal. Quart.,* 43:349–426, 1974.
6. OSTOW, M.: Letter to the editor. *JAMA,* 152:1553, 1953.
7. SOCARIDES, C. W.: A psychoanalytic study of the desire for sexual transformation ("transsexualism"): The plaster-of-paris man. *Int. J. Psychoanal.,* 51:341–349, 1970.

8. Volkan, V. D.: Transsexualism: As examined from the viewpoint of internalized object relations. In: T. B. Karasu and C. W. Socarides (Eds.), *On Sexuality*. New York: International Universities Press, 1979.

9. Szasz, T.: Book review of *The Transsexual Empire*, by Janice G. Raymond. New York Times Book Review, June 10, 1979.

10. Meyer, J. K. and Reter, D. J.: Sex reassignment. *Arch. Gen. Psychiat.*, 36: 1010–1015, 1979. Copyright 1979, American Medical Association.

11. Hunt, D. D. and Hampson, J. L.: Follow-up of 17 biologic male transsexuals after sex-reassignment surgery. *Am. J. Psychiat.*, 137:432–438, 1980.

12. Lothstein, L. M.: Sex reassignment surgery: Historical, bioethical and theoretical issues. Manuscript, 1980.

13. Satterfield, S.: Outcome of transsexual surgery. Paper read at American Psychiatric Association Annual Meeting, San Francisco, 1980.

14. Fleming, M., Steinman, C., and Bocknek, G.: Methodological problems in assessing sex-reassignment surgery: A reply to Meyer and Reter. *Arch. Sex. Behav.*, 9:451–456, 1980.

15. Hunt, D. D. and Hampson, J. L.: Transsexuals: A standardized psychosocial rating format for the evaluation of results of sex reassignment surgery. *Arch. Sex. Behav.*, 9:255–263, 1980.

16. Dörner, G., Rohde, W., Stahl, F., Krell, L., and Masius, W-G.: A neuroendocrine predisposition for homosexuality in men. *Arch. Sex. Behav.*, 4:1–8, 1975.

17. Eicher, W., Spoljar, M., Cleve, H., Murken, J-D., Richter, K., Stengel-Rutkowski, S.: H-Y antigen in trans-sexuality. *Lancet*, II:1137–1138, 1979.

18. Engel, W., Pfäfflin, F., and Wiedeking, C.: H-Y antigen in transsexuality, and how to explain testis differentiation in H-Y antigen-negative males and ovary differentiation in H-Y antigen-positive females. *Hum. Genet.*, 55:315–319, 1980.

19. Stoller, R. J.: *Sex and Gender, Vol. I*. New York: Science House, 1968.

20. _____: *Sex and Gender, Vol. II*. London: Hogarth Press, 1975.

21. _____: *Perversion*. New York: Pantheon, 1975.

22. Fisk, N.: Gender Dysphoria Syndrome (The How, What, and Why of a Disease). In: D. R. Laub and P. Gandy (Eds.), *Proceedings of the Second Interdisciplinary Symposium on Gender Dysphoria Syndrome*. Stanford, CA: Stanford University Medical Center, 1973.

23. Meyer, J. K.: Clinical variants among applicants for sex reassignment. *Arch. Sex. Behav.*, 3:527–558, 1974.

24. *Diagnostic and Statistical Manual of Mental Disorders*, Third Edition. Washington, DC: American Psychiatric Association, 1980.

25. Stoller, R. J.: Gender identity disorders. In: H. I. Kaplan, A. M. Freedman, and B. J. Sadock (Eds.), *Comprehensive Textbook of Psychiatry III*. Baltimore: Williams and Wilkins, 1980.

26. Kubie, L. S. and Mackie, J. B.: Critical issues raised by operations for gender transmutation. *JNMD*, 147:431–443, 1968.

27. Stoller, R. J.: Editorial — A biased view of "sex transformation" operations. *JNMD*, 149:312–317, 1969.

28. _____: Male Transsexualism: Uneasiness. *Am. J. Psychiat.*, 130:536–539, 1973.

29. STOLLER, R. J.: The indications are unclear. In: J. P. Brady and H. Keith H. Brodie (Eds.), *Controversy in Psychiatry*. Philadelphia: W. B. Saunders Co., 1978, pp. 846-855.

30. BULLOUGH, V. L.: Transsexualism in history. *Arch. Sex. Behav.,* 4:561-571, 1975.

31. NEWMAN, L. E. and STOLLER, R. J.: Nontranssexual men who seek sex reassignment. *Am. J. Psychiat.,* 131:437-441, 1974.

32. KIRKPATRICK, M. and FRIEDMANN, C. T. H.: Treatment of requests for sex-change surgery with psychotherapy. Am. J. Psychiat., 133:1194-1196, 1976.

33. MORGAN, A. J.: Psychotherapy for transsexual candidates screened out of surgery. *Arch. Sex. Behav.,* 7:273-283, 1978.

34. LOTHSTEIN, L. M.: Countertransference reactions to gender dysphoric patients: Implications for psychotherapy. *Psychotherapy: Theory, Research and Practice,* 14:21-31, 1977.

35. _____: Psychotherapy with patients with gender dysphoria syndromes. *Bull. Menn. Clin.,* 41:563-582, 1977.

36. _____: The psychological management and treatment of hospitalized transsexuals. *JNMD,* 166:255-262, 1978.

37. _____: The aging gender dysphoric (transsexual) patient. *Arch. Sex. Behav.,* 8:431-444, 1979.

38. _____: Psychodynamics and sociodynamics of gender-dysphoric states. *Am. J. Psychother.,* 33:214-238, 1979.

39. _____: Group therapy with gender-dysphoric patients. *Am. J. Psychother.,* 33:67-81, 1979.

40. _____: The adolescent gender dysphoric patient: An approach to treatment and management. *J. Ped. Psychol.,* 5:93-109, 1980.

41. LOTHSTEIN, L. M. and LEVINE, S. B.: Expressive psychotherapy with gender dysphoric patients. *Arch. Gen. Psychiat.:* In Press.

42. BARLOW, D. H., REYNOLDS, E. J., and AGRAS, W. S.: Gender identity change in a transsexual. *Arch. Gen. Psychiat.,* 28:569-579, 1973.

43. REKERS, G. A.: Assessment and Treatment of Childhood Gender Problems. In: B. B. Lahey and A. E. Kazdin (Eds), *Advances in Child Clinical Psychology,* Vol. I. New York: Plenum Press, 1977.

44. GREENSON, R. R.: A transvestite boy and a hypothesis. *Int. J. Psychoanal.,* 47: 396-403, 1966.

45. STOLLER, R. J.: The term "transvestism." *Arch. Gen. Psychiat.,* 24:230-237, 1971.

# Part IV
# THE STANLEY R. DEAN
# AWARD LECTURE

# 13

# The Fate of Catecholamines and Its Impact in Psychopharmacology

## *Julius Axelrod, Ph.D.*

The past 25 years have seen remarkable changes in the growth of the neurosciences. These developments have had far-reaching influences in psychiatry, pharmacology, endocrinology, and cell biology. Central to this growth has been the increase in our knowledge of neurotransmitters, the chemical messengers of nerves. The concept of chemical neurotransmission was first conceived by a graduate student at Cambridge University, T. R. Elliot, about 75 years ago. He made the astute observation that a newly discovered constituent of the adrenal medulla, the catecholamine adrenaline, has the same effect on a number of organs as that produced by stimulation of the sympathetic nerves. Elliot then proposed that sympathetic nerves produce their effects by releasing a chemical substance similar to adrenaline. It took many years to provide experimental proof for chemical neurotransmission. In 1921, Otto Loewi, an Austrian pharmacologist, provided the proof of chemical neurotransmission by a beautiful and compelling experiment. Loewi placed two frog hearts in a vessel with a physiological solution bathing both hearts. Upon stimulation of the vagus nerve of the first heart, the rate of the second was reduced. This indicated that stimulation of a nerve in the heart released a chemical substance which slowed the beat of the second heart. The vagus nerve transmitter was soon identified as acetylcholine by Henry Dale. At about the same time Walter Cannon showed that sympathetic nerves could release an adrenaline-like substance which he called sympathin. Cannon also found that sympathin is released in stress, fear, and anxiety. In 1946, Ulf von

Euler isolated the sympathetic nerve transmitter and identified it as noradrenaline.

I was intrigued by a paper by Barger and Dale published in 1910 in which they showed that compounds related in structure to the catecholamine adrenaline can mimic the action of the sympathetic nervous systems. These compounds were named "sympathomimetic amines." Many sympathomimetic amines such as amphetamine, ephedrine and mescaline affect behavior. To get some insight into the action of these amines, I began studies on the fate of amphetamine and ephedrine in the body. I found that amphetamine and ephedrine were metabolized by a variety of chemical changes involving hydroxylation and demethylation. This work also led to the discovery of enzymes that transform these drugs that were later to be shown to metabolize most drugs.

The introduction of antidepressants and antipsychotic drugs in the 1950s had a profound effect in psychiatry as well as pharmacology. At about the same time the neurotransmitters, noradrenaline and serotonin, were found to be present in the brain, it was observed that reserpine, a drug used to treat mental illenss, depleted these amines in the brain. Pharmacological studies showed that LSD antagonized the pharmacological action of serotonin. It was also apparent that the hallucinogens, mescaline and LSD, resembled the neurotransmitters noradrenaline and serotonin in chemical structure. Monoamine oxidase inhibitors, compounds that blocked the metabolism of noradrenaline and serotonin, were introduced as antidepressant agents. All of these events set the stage for an intense research effort to show the relationship between neurotransmitters and mental illness.

## Fate of Noradrenaline in Sympathetic Nerves

In 1957, at a seminar of the Laboratory of Clinical Science, Seymour Kety described an intriguing observation by Hoffer and Osmond that adrenochrome, an oxidation product of adrenaline, produced hallucinations. They proposed that schizophrenia might be due to an abnormal metabolism of adrenaline. At that time little was known about the metabolism of adrenaline in the body. Because of my research in the metabolism of compounds related to adrenaline, such as ephedrine and amphetamine, I initiated studies on the fate of catecholamines in the body. I spent three frustrating months searching for an enzyme that converted adrenaline to adrenochrome. Just at that time I read an abstract that reported that patients with an adrenaline-forming tumor, pheochromocytoma, excreted large amounts of 3-methoxy-4-hydroxymandelic acid (VMA). This immediately gave me an important clue to a possible route for catecholamine metabolism. Since VMA is closely related in structure to adrenaline, a likely route for the metabolism could be via methylation of the 3-hydroxy group. If this were so, then an intermediate product should be 3-methoxyadrenaline. In a series of experiments I found that 3-methoxyadrenaline which we later named metanephrine was a normal constituent in nerves and tissues. After the administration of adrenaline (epinephrine) or noradrenaline (norepinephrine), there were large increases in the excretion of O-methylated metabolites of these catecholamines. Using the methyl donor S-adenosylmethionine, the enzyme that O-methylates catecholamines, catechol-O-methyltransferase (COMT) was discovered. As a result of these experiments the metabolic route of catecholamines was elucidated (Figure 1). Catecholamines were found to be metabolized by two enzymes, one involving

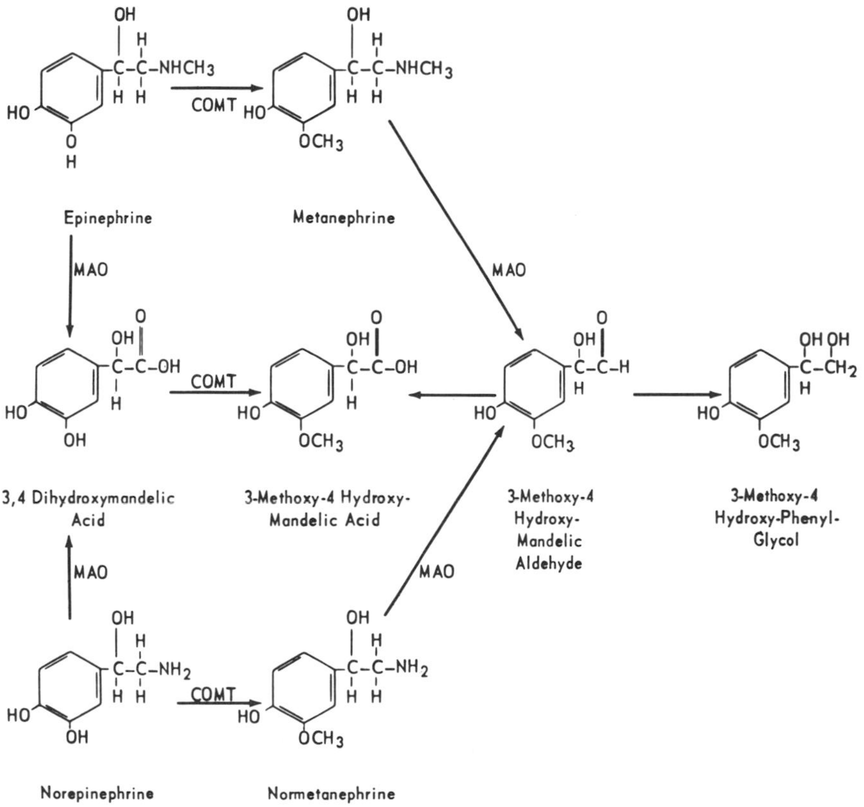

FIGURE 1. Route of metabolism of adrenaline (epinephrine) and noradrenaline (norephinephrine).

COMT and the other MAO. In the course of this work several new metabolites of catecholamines were identified, normetanephrine, metanephrine, 3-hydroxyphenylglychol (MHPG) and methoxytyramine. MPHG was reported to be a major metabolite of noradrenaline in the brain and was subsequently found to be decreased in certain affective disorders. When the metabolic fate of adrenaline was elucidated, a study comparing its metabolism in normal and schizophrenic subjects was made possible. No difference in the metabolism of adrenaline in normal or schizophrenic subjects was found.

As a consequence of the discovery of COMT, we synthesized radioactive [³H]methyl-S-adenosylmethionine. This led to the discovery of several other methyltransferase reactions which metabolized many biologically active biogenic amines: phenylethanolamine N-methyltransferase, the enzyme that forms adrenaline; histamine N-methyltransferase, an enzyme that inactivates histamine; indoleamine N-methyltransferase, an enzyme that can make endogenous hallucinogens; and protein carboxylmethylase, an enzyme that methylates the carboxy group of proteins. Recently, we described an enzyme that methylates phospholipids in membranes. This enzyme was found to be critical in the transduction of receptor-mediated biological signals through membranes. This discovery has led to a change in the direction of my research in the past three years.

A necessary property of neurotransmitter action is the capacity of tissues to terminate its action rapidly. About 20 years ago it was believed that the physiological effects of catecholamine neurotransmitters were ended by the action of the enzyme MAO. However, after complete inhibition of the enzyme, the physiological effects of catecholamines still persisted. Inhibition of COMT also failed to terminate the effects of catecholamine administration, indicating that there were other mechanisms for rapidly ending the actions of catecholamines. A clue for a rapid inactivating mechanism for catecholamines came with the use of radioactive noradrenaline. When [³H]noradrenaline was injected into cats, it persisted in tissues rich in sympathetic nerves long after its physiological effects disappeared. This suggested that the catecholamine was taken up in sympathetic nerves and held there. To prove this, we denervated the superior cervical ganglia of a cat on one side only and injected [³H]noradrenaline. The injected radioactive catecholamine was taken up on the innervated but not the denervated side. These experiments indicated that noradrenaline is inactivated by rapid uptake into sympathetic nerves and stored there in a physiologically inactive form. This finding provided a stimulus for further work on the mechanism of action of adrenergic and psychoactive drugs. In subsequent work using [³H]noradrenaline radioautography and electron microscopy, we showed that the catecholamine neurotransmitters were taken up by sympathetic nerves and stored in dense core vesicles. When sympathetic nerves that had previously taken up [³H]noradrenaline were stimulated the radioactive transmitter was released.

Studies using electron microscopy and histology clarified the cell structure of the sympathetic neurons. It consists of a cell body where the enzymes that make catecholamines are localized, a long axon, and highly branched nerve terminals. The nerve terminals contain thousands of swellings or varicosities. The enzymes that synthesize the neurotransmitters are translocated from the cell body to the varicosities in the nerve terminals by a process of axoplasmic transport. It is at the varicosities that the neurotransmitter is liberated. Catecholamine neurotransmitters are released by exocytosis, a process in which the storage vesicle fuses with the outer membrane of the varicosity and forms an opening through which not only the neurotransmitter is discharged into the synaptic cleft, but also other contents of the vesicle, including the enzyme dopamine-$\beta$-hydroxylase, are released. The neurotransmitter then binds to a specific recognition site on the surface of the effector cells in close juxtaposition to the nerve terminal. When the neurotransmitter interacts with the receptor, it sets off a series of complex chemical and physical changes in the membrane, permitting the cell to carry out its specific function. Most of the neurotransmitter is then rapidly inactivated by reuptake into the sympathetic neurons. Some of the catecholamines are metabolized by COMT and by MAO in the effector cell, and some are discharged into the circulation where they are physically removed and ultimately metabolized in the liver. A model for the fate of catecholamine neurotransmitters is depicted in Figure 2.

The initial work on the fate of catecholamines was obtained using peripheral tissues. The brain contains dopaminergic, noradrenergic and adrenergic neurons and it was of interest to study the metabolism and physiological disposition of catecholamines in the brain. Because catecholamines do not cross the blood brain barrier, information regarding the storage, release, and metabolism of these amines was obtained by intraventricular or intracisternal injections of [³H]noradrenaline into the rat brain. After such injections of [³H]noradrenaline, it was selectively taken up into nerve terminals and stored in dense core vesicles. Upon release, the noradrenaline was metabolized by O-methylation and deamination. Like the peripheral nerve, the catecholamines in the brain can be inactivated through reuptake by the nerve terminals.

### EFFECT OF PSYCHOACTIVE DRUGS

Once the mechanism whereby catecholamines are released and inactivated was described, it was possible to understand the action of many drugs. Using

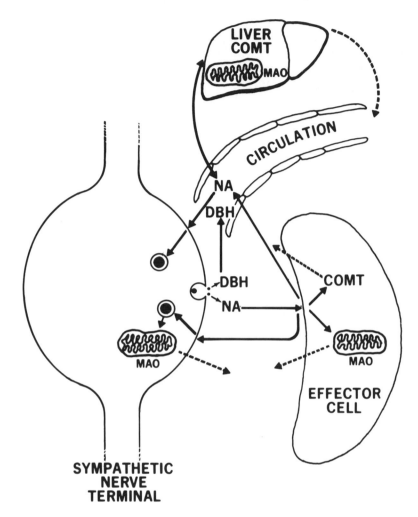

FIGURE 2. Fate of noradrenaline at the sympathetic nerve terminal.

radioactive noradrenaline we were able to show the effect of amphetamine and other sympathomimetic amines. Amphetamine was found to have two actions: it released catecholamines from their storage sites and blocked the reuptake of these amines (Table 1). This then produces an excessive amount of catecholamines to interact with their respective receptors. The psychotic action of amphetamine is considered to be due, to a great extent, to its ability to release catecholamines and to activation of postsynaptic receptors, mainly dopaminergic. Blocking the dopamine receptor by antipsychotic drugs such as chlorpromazine overcomes the behavioral effects of amphetamine. Cocaine, another psychoactive drug, acts by blocking the inactivation of noradrenaline by reuptake and causes an excessive release of this amine in the brain (Table 1). We have already observed that antidepressant drugs block the inactivation of catecholamines by reuptake in peripheral nerves. A relationship between the clinical effectiveness of antidepressant drugs and their ability to block reuptake in brain noradrenergic nerves has been discovered.

Reserpine depletes catecholamines from brain aminergic neurons and sometimes causes clinical depression in patients who receive excessive amounts of the drug (Table 1). This observation, plus the fact that monoamine oxidase inhibitors could also be used to relieve affective disorders, led to the proposal of the catecholamine hypothesis of depression. This hypothesis states that mental depression is caused by a decreased availability of catecholamines in the brain. Affective disorders can be relieved by drugs that increase the amount of catecholamines available to these postsynaptic receptors. Although this hypothesis has been subjected to critical comments, it stimulated a considerable amount of productive research in biological psychiatry.

BIOSYNTHESIS OF CATECHOLAMINES AND THEIR REGULATION

Catecholamines are synthesized in the nerve tissue and adrenal medulla by four enzymes: tyrosine hydroxylase (TH), dopa decarboxylase (DDC), dopamine-$\beta$-hydroxylase (DBH) and phenylethanolamine N-methyltransferase

TABLE 1
Effect of Psychoactive Drugs on Catecholamines

| Drug | Effect on catecholamines | Behavioral effect |
|---|---|---|
| Reserpine | Depletes | Causes depression |
| Amphetamine | Releases and blocks reuptake in nerves | Paranoid psychosis |
| Cocaine | Blocks reuptake, causes release in brain | Psychosis |
| Tricyclic antidepressants | Blocks reuptake | Relieves depression |
| Monoamine oxidase inhibitors | Blocks metabolism | Relieves depression |
| Antipsychotics | Blocks dopamine receptors | Relieves psychosis |

(PNMT) as follows: tyrosine $\xrightarrow{\text{TH}}$ dopa $\xrightarrow{\text{DDC}}$ dopamine $\xrightarrow{\text{DBH}}$ noradrenaline $\xrightarrow{\text{PNMT}}$ adrenaline. Although catecholamines are in a state of flux, continuously being synthesized, released and metabolized, they maintain a constant level in nerves. This is due to a variety of adaptive mechanisms that mainly control the biosynthetic enzymes. There are rapid and slow regulating mechanisms for the control of catecholamine synthesis. Rapid regulation involves the rate-limiting enzyme in the biosynthesis, tyrosine hydroxylase, through a negative feedback mechanism. Low levels of catecholamines in the neurons, resulting from increased nerve activity, changes the kinetic properties of TH so that it more rapidly converts tyrosine to dopa. High levels of catecholamine inhibit this enzyme. The molecular mechanism for this regulation is due to phosphorylation and dephosphorylation of TH which changes the affinity of the enzyme for the substrate tyrosine and the cofactor tetrahydrobiopterin.

A slower adaptive process for catecholamine biosynthesis is caused by prolonged activity of sympathetic nerves and the adrenal medulla. Increasing activity of the adrenosympathetic system by drugs, stress or nerve stimulation causes a slow but steady increase in the amount of TH, DBH, PNMT in sympathetic ganglion, cell bodies in brain, and adrenal gland. The release of these biosynthetic enzymes can be interrupted by preganglionic denervation indicating that the induction of these enzymes is a transsynaptic event.

There is a relationship between catecholamine biosynthesis and the endocrine system. The synthesis of adrenaline from noradrenaline by PNMT in the adrenal medulla is regulated by ACTH and glucocorticoids (Figure 3). We have shown that the removal of the pituitary results in a profound reduction of PNMT activity in the adrenal gland of the rat. This activity is restored by injecting ACTH or glucocorticoids. Thus, high levels of glucocorticoids arising from the adrenal cortex are necessary to maintain the adrenaline-forming enzyme, PNMT.

### Stress and Catecholamines

The role of the adrenosympathetic system in stress was recognized by Walter Cannon many years ago. Experimental stress in animals caused by immobilization, cold, electroshock, insulin, etc. causes a steady increase in tyrosine hydroxylase, dopamine hydroxylase and PNMT in the adrenal gland and nerves. This increase is due to a transsynaptic induction of these enzymes. Psychosocial stress in mice also elevates the activity of the catecholamine biosynthetic enzyme.

During the past few years extremely sensitive radioenzymatic methods for the accurate measurement of noradrenaline and adrenaline in plasma of ani-

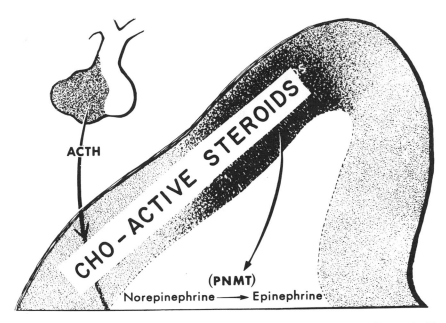

FIGURE 3. Regulation of the adrenaline-forming enzyme PNMT by ACTH and glucocorticoids.

mals and humans were developed. This was made possible by the use of the enzymes COMT and PMNT which transfer a highly radioactive [³H] methyl group from S-adenosyl-methionine to catecholamines. Recently there have been many studies examining the effect of mild and severe stress on the adrenal medulla and/or sympathetic nerves by measuring the plasma adrenaline and noradrenaline levels. Mild stress such as mental arithmetic, public speaking, and smoking causes an elevation of adrenaline and noradrenaline. Severe stress such as cold, hyperglycemic hemorrhage, and surgery results in large increases in plasma catecholamine levels.

## CLINICAL IMPLICATIONS OF CATECHOLAMINES

The discoveries concerning catecholamines in the past decade have had a marked influence on our understanding and treatment of cardiovascular, neurological, and mental diseases. One of the more important developments in medicine was the introduction of effective drugs for the treatment of cardiovascular diseases such as hypertension. Many of the drugs used for the treatment of hypertension (reserpine, guanethidine, $\alpha$-methyl dopa) affect the storage, release, or metabolism of catecholamines. The involvement of the sympathetic nervous system in cardiovascular diseases was suspected for many years. In a study using rats in which hypertension was induced experimentally by deoxycorticosterone and NaCl, we found that the turnover of catecholamines was markedly increased in the sympathetic nerves of the heart. A direct relationship between the degree of increase in catecholamine turnover and the extent of elevation of blood pressure was found. Removal of salt from the diet and the administration of natruretic drugs reduced blood pressure in hypertensive rats and brought the catecholamine turnover in the heart back to normal values. After further work it became apparent that hypertension was caused by disturbances of adrenergic nerves in the central nervous system. Using immunological and microdissection techniques, it was found that there was an increased activity of these adrenaline-containing nerves in the brainstem in experimental hypertension. The administration of drugs that block PNMT, the adrenaline-forming enzyme, reduced the blood pressure in rats with experimental hypertension.

The introduction of dopa for the treatment of Parkinsonian disease by Hornykeiwicz and Cotzias was a direct outgrowth of basic catecholamine research. It was observed that the depletion of the catecholamines dopamine and noradrenaline in the brain, by reserpine, causes Parkinson-like symptoms in rats. To increase the catecholamine levels in the brain, dopa was administered. Catecholamines do not cross the blood brain barrier but dopa does. Dopa is converted to dopamine in the brain and also overcomes the Parkinson-like symptoms in reserpine-treated rats. This prompted an examination of the dopamine concentration in brains of patients who died of Parkinson's disease. A marked deficiency in this amine was found in the corpus striatum of these subjects. Dopa was then administered to patients with the disease with remarkable clinical effectiveness.

The possible role of catecholamines in affective disorders was noted above. For many years, dopamine was suspected to be involved in schizophrenia. Dopamine receptors were found to be present in the brain. It was soon found that antipsychotic drugs blocked these receptors (Table 1). Further work then showed that antipsychotic drugs bind to dopamine receptors in the brain with an affinity related to their potency as therapeutic agents for schizophrenia. Disturbances in catecholaminergic nerves were also found in neurological diseases such as dystonia and dysautonomia.

## Sympathetic Nerves, the Pineal Gland and Circadian Rhythms

My interest in the pineal gland stemmed from the discovery of melatonin (5-methoxy-N-acetylserotonin) in the gland by A. Lerner some 20 years ago. Melatonin is related in structure to the neurotransmitter serotonin and it has an O-methyl group. Because of the chemical structure of melatonin and the observation that the pineal, an organ of unknown function, is innervated by noradrenaline-containing nerves, we were prompted to study how this compound was synthesized and regulated. We soon found the enzyme that makes melatonin and elucidated the biosynthetic pathway from tryptophan as follows: tryptophan → serotonin → N-acetylserotonin → melatonin. The melatonin-forming enzyme hydroxyindole-O-methyltransferase (HIOMT) was found to be almost exclusively localized in the pineal gland.

Circadian rhythms of serotonin, N-acetylserotonin and melatonin were found in the pineal gland. Serotonin levels were highest during the daytime and N-acetylserotonin and melatonin were highest at night. This prompted a series of experiments in our laboratories and elsewhere to find out how these 24-hour cycles were generated. Denervating the sympathetic nerves leading to the pineal abolished these rhythms. Preganglionic denervation and lesions in the suprachiasmatic nucleus in the hypothalamus also abolished the serotonin, N-acetylserotonin and melatonin rhythms. All of these observations indicated that the 24-hour rhythm of indoleamine in the pineal arises from the suprachiasmatic nucleus. This nucleus sends its diurnal message via the sympathetic nerves to the pineal gland. Sympathetic nerves appeared to release more noradrenaline at night than during the daytime.

The rhythmic release of noradrenaline at night results in an increase of N-acetylserotonin in the pineal. This provided an opportunity to study adrenergic receptor response and its regulation. The pineal cell was found to have $\beta$-adrenergic receptors, which upon stimulation with noradrenaline released from nerves generated cyclic AMP from adenylate cyclase, which then caused a marked increase of N-acetylserotonin, the precursor to melatonin (Figure 4). When rats were left in constant light there was a diminished release of noradrenaline. This resulted in an increase in the responsiveness of the $\beta$-adrenergic receptors. With the increased nerve-firing of the pineal at night, $\beta$-adrenergic receptors became desensitized. Changes in sensitivity of $\beta$-adrenergic receptors, as well as release of noradrenaline produced by daylight and darkness, provided an amplification and dampening system whereby small changes in the release of catecholamines produced large increases and decreases in the melatonin levels in the pineal.

Recently, accurate methods for the measurement of melatonin in human plasma have been devised. Humans, like animals, appear to have circadian rhythms of melatonin which are regulated by changes in sensitivity of $\beta$-adrenergic receptors. Plasma melatonin levels in man should provide insight regarding the responsiveness of $\beta$-adrenergic receptors in normal and disease states.

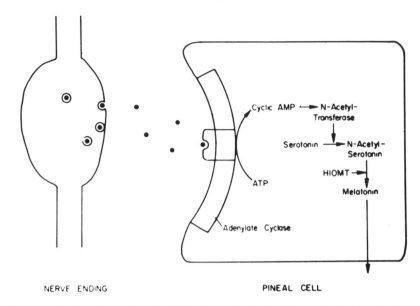

FIGURE 4. Action of noradrenaline (0) in the synthesis of melatonin in the pineal cells.

## LIPIDS AND THE TRANSMISSION OF
## CATECHOLAMINE NEUROTRANSMITTER SIGNALS

In the past three years the research of my laboratroy has been directed towards the biochemical mechanisms whereby catecholamines and other neurotransmitters transfer their messages through membranes. The transduction of neurotransmitter signals through the cell membranes permits cells to carry out their specific function. Cell membranes consist of a lipid bilayer in which neurotransmitter receptor molecules are imbedded. Receptor molecules face the outside of the membrane while adenylate cyclase, an enzyme that generates the second messenger, cyclic AMP, faces the inside of the membrane. Cyclic AMP is a key compound which, through the transfer of the phosphate group, turns cells on or off. We have found two enzymes in cell membranes that methylate phosphatidylethanolamine to form phosphatidylcholine. In the process of methylation these lipids are translocated from the inside to the outside of the membrane and also increase the fluidity of the membrane.

The interaction of catecholamines with $\beta$-adrenergic receptors stimulates phospholipid methylation and increases membrane fluidity. This then enhances the lateral mobility of the receptor on the cell surface and offers a greater chance to couple with adenylate cyclase facing the inside of the membrane. This then generates more cyclic AMP which then activates the cell to carry out its function. Our work on phospholipid methylation has expanded and led to other exciting areas of research.

## BIBLIOGRAPHY

AXELROD, J.: Noradrenaline: Fate and control of its biosynthesis. In: *Les Prix Nobel.* Imprimerieal Royal P. A. Norstedt & Soner, Stockholm, 1971, pp. 189–208; *Science* 173:598–606, 1971.

AXELROD, J.: Neurotransmitters. *Scientific American,* 230:59–71, 1974.

AXELROD, J.: The pineal gland: A neurochemical transducer. *Science,* 184:1341–1348, 1974.

AXELROD, J.: Biochemical and pharmacological approaches in the study of sympathetic nerves. In: F. G. Worden, J. P. Swazey, and G. Adelman (Eds.), *The Neurosciences: Paths of Discovery.* Cambridge, MA: The MIT Press, pp. 191–208, 1975.

GLOWINSKI, J. and AXELROD, J.: Effects of drugs on the disposition of H[3]-norepinephrine in the rat brain. *Pharmacol. Rev.,* 18:775–785, 1966.

HIRATA, F. and AXELROD, J.: Phospholipid methylation and biological signal transmission. *Science,* 209:1082–1090, 1980.

# Index

301